INTO THE DARKEST PLACES

INTO THE DARKEST PLACES
Early Relational Trauma and Borderline States of Mind

Marcus West

KARNAC

First published in 2016 by
Karnac Books Ltd
118 Finchley Road
London NW3 5HT

British Library Cataloguing in Publication Data

A C.I.P. for this book is available from the British Library

ISBN-13: 978-1-78220-122-9

Typeset by V Publishing Solutions Pvt Ltd., Chennai, India

Printed in Great Britain

www.karnacbooks.com

To Liz
who has borne with me through the darkest times

CONTENTS

ACKNOWLEDGEMENTS

I am extremely indebted to my patients for their generosity in allowing me to write about our work together. Every person I asked for permission agreed, which I have found both moving and humbling, particularly due to the sensitivity of our work. I am very much aware that what I have written does not do justice to the subtlety, depth, and breadth of our journeys and I apologise for that.

I would like to thank Anne Tyndale, Ann Hopwood, Mary Barnett, Bob Withers, Mary Addenbrooke, Jean Knox, Linda Carter, Pramila Bennett, Warren Colman, Anne Ashley, William Meredith-Owen, and Susanna Wright for their personal support through difficult times. There were many others as well and I hope they will forgive not being named.

I would like to thank Fiona Chandler, William Meredith-Owen, Pramila Bennett, and Paul Goldreich for their invaluable comments on drafts of this book, or chapters herein, as well as members of the Society of Analytical Psychology's Analytic Group for feedback from an early presentation of this work. Any and all errors, omissions, and shortcomings are my responsibility.

I would also like to thank David Sagar and Carol Jones for their particular thoughtfulness and generosity in the preparation of the book.

I am very grateful to my son-in-law, Joshua Tutt, for painting the fine picture for the cover.

And finally, thank you to Karnac Books, particularly Oliver Rathbone, Constance Govindin, Rod Tweedy, Cecily Blench, Kate Pearce, and Alex Massey, for their helpfulness and forbearance throughout the process of publishing, as always.

ABOUT THE AUTHOR

Marcus West is a training analyst of the Society of Analytical Psychology working in private practice in Sussex, England. He is a member of the editorial board of the *Journal of Analytical Psychology* and is currently chair of Psychotherapy Sussex. He has published papers and book chapters, taught, and given lectures in this country and abroad on a range of subjects, including identity, narcissism, borderline phenomena, attachment, spiritual experience, envy, trauma, and dreams. He was joint winner of the Michael Fordham Prize in 2004. He is author of two previous books, both published by Karnac: *Feeling, Being and the Sense of Self—A New Perspective on Identity, Affect and Narcissistic Disorders* (2007) and *Understanding Dreams in Clinical Practice* (2011).

INTRODUCTION

This book reinstates trauma, and early relational trauma in particular, to what I suggest is its rightful place at the heart of our understanding of psychological distress and analytic thinking. Although it was not my intention when I started writing the book, the book offers an integration of analytic theory, trauma theory, and relational theory, yet represents a critique of each. First, it critically revisions analytic understanding, attitudes, and techniques in the light of a trauma perspective, offering, in particular, a different view of borderline states of mind. Second, it argues that working with the extreme states of mind consequent upon traumatic experience requires an analytic attitude in order to safely and fully address the individual's early traumatic experience as it has come to be embodied and elaborated in their personality and ways of being with others. Third, it provides an understanding of the pressures and dynamics in the analytic relationship which challenges some relational models of analysis, suggesting that the analytic task may precisely require the working through of what feel like inhuman experiences, thereby properly accompanying the patient "into the darkest of places". I have come to realise just how radical and contentious the book is— there is something here to challenge, or offend, most practitioners, depending on their turn of mind.

The central organising concept of the book is a developed and elaborated view of Jung's complex, which is understood to embody both trauma-related internal working models and primitive responses to the trauma (which constitute narcissistic defences). This conceptualisation of the complex thus draws on the insights from trauma theory regarding the primitive, somatic-affective reactions to trauma (and early relational trauma), although the book focuses on the relational outworkings of these experiences as they have come to be embodied and embedded in the individual's personality and as they are met with in the consulting room.

* * *

A recognition of the significance of early traumatic experience has been at the heart of both psychoanalysis and Jungian analysis since their inception. Freud's earliest theory, his seduction theory, was essentially centred on trauma. As well as many other things he also bequeathed us an understanding of fixation points, enactment, and repetition compulsion (much of which was drawn from the work of Pierre Janet, whose work has been largely overlooked until recently). However, in relation to trauma, Freud came to emphasise inner-world fantasy, relating to infantile sexuality and the Oedipus complex, over real-world trauma; later Kleinian thinkers have come to enhance this split further.

Jung's work also began with trauma with his word association experiments, and he developed the concept of the complex, drawing on Janet's conceptualisation of "fixed ideas". Yet his interest also moved away from the trauma itself, shifting instead towards the archetypal, collective layer of the psyche, the collective unconscious as he called it, which is particularly accessible when ego-functioning has been disrupted by trauma, as I shall be explaining (Jung, 1911–1912, para. 631). Whilst Jung stressed the need for integration of the disparate, dissociated elements of the psyche, which is also key to this book, and went on to develop a detailed picture of the intersubjective, mutually influencing relationship between patient and analyst (presaging the insights on the intersubjective field and relational psychoanalysis by many decades), he was not able to follow through his insights into offering a safe and effective way of working with patients with a borderline psychology. Many later Jungian analysts have turned to psychoanalysis for guidance in this area. Michael Fordham, integrating psychoanalytic influences, took Jung's work forward with his conceptualisation of "defences of the self" (Fordham, 1974), an area which I develop further in this book.

Despite these beginnings rooted in trauma, in reading analytic papers there is almost always a disjunction between the appreciation that "behind this particular syndrome" (whatever that may be) there lies traumatic early relational experience, and a full understanding of how that has affected, and continues to directly influence, the individual. This book aims to address that disjunction.

In the last three decades there have been many ground-breaking contributions from trauma therapists, attachment theorists, intersubjectivists, and relational psychoanalysts, as well as from infant researchers and neuroscientists. Specifically relevant to this book is a growing appreciation of the foundational role of early relational trauma in borderline states of mind, with Herman, Perry, and van der Kolk (1989) proposing that borderline personality disorder significantly overlaps with what Herman has termed complex post-traumatic stress disorder (complex PTSD). Fonagy and colleagues have come to a similar recognition from a psychoanalytic and attachment theory perspective (Fonagy, Steele, H., Moran, Steele, M., & Higgit, 1991; Fonagy, Gergely, Jurist, & Target, 2002; Fonagy, Gergely, & Target, 2008).

I will be outlining and summarising many of these contributions, which give us radical new insights into the traditional difficulties and challenges of analytic work. However, the accommodation between psychoanalysis and trauma work has been at best uneasy and at worst conflicting, with sometimes radically different attitudes and methods being adopted. I believe these conflicts follow from the realities and difficulties of working with states of mind that sometimes feel impossible to bear, for both patient and analyst.

Trauma therapists have been critical of analytic techniques, suggesting that they are too cognitively based, ignore the somatic and affective elements, expose the patient to unbearable and unworkable levels of distress, and are thus inhuman and anti-relational, as well as being unrealistic, ineffective, unhelpful, critical, punitive, and retraumatising. As a consequence they have frequently adopted alternate ways of working, trying to manage the therapy in a certain way, and frequently promoting positively toned ways of relating.

Whilst understandable, I believe these ways of working have limited the recognition and integration of the blackest and most destructive elements of the patient's experience, and their primitive responses to their traumatic experience. It is precisely the all-too-human "inhuman" aspects of relationship that are traumatic and need addressing. These theorists have not fully recognised the way in which traumatic experience has become embodied and embedded in the individual's character structure and, in particular, the ways in which it becomes manifest in the analytic relationship.

Thus, whilst the re-enactment of early trauma and abuse is always a feature of the analytic relationship, these non-analytic practices can unwittingly fuel re-enactments particularly strongly (or at least an analytic attitude is important in being able to recognise the enactments), sometimes leading to the breakdown of the analysis (Davies & Frawley, 1992a; this book Chapter Eleven). I have found that only when the analyst is prepared to accompany the patient "into the darkest places" whilst maintaining an analytic stance, can the most disturbing, disruptive, and unbearable aspects of the trauma be worked through and integrated, as I will describe below. The attitude of facing the trauma directly is itself a divisive practice and instinctively many practitioners of all denominations balk at it.

Similarly, many analytic practitioners have selectively focused on certain, limited, aspects of the individual's reactions to trauma, frequently their internal reactions, with the link to the original trauma being lost completely. I believe that this has occurred partly due to the patient's clinical presentation, where the powerful affects associated with the trauma disrupt the individual's thinking, containing, and memory-storage functions, so that there is no coherent, autobiographical narrative. At the same time the affective-somatic reactions related to the original trauma become free-floating (dissociated) and attach themselves powerfully to current experience (van der Kolk, 1996a). It is these limited reactions that psychoanalysts have then privileged, divorcing them from the larger picture.

Thus, as I have touched on already, whilst apparently recognising the ongoing significance of real-world trauma, Freud focused primarily on the individual's fantasy life and conflicts relating to infantile sexuality, Klein focused on the individual's innate destructiveness and envy, and Jung focused on experiences of the collective unconscious which follow upon the disruption of ego-functioning (I will give a more detailed account of each theorist's relationship with trauma in the relevant chapters below). Whilst all of these phenomena are related to trauma, each theorist's particular explanations and focus are largely divorced from it.

When Freud met with resistance from patients to moving on from their trauma, he understood it in terms of the negative therapeutic reaction (Freud, 1923b) and, ultimately, the death instinct (1937c), a field of exploration much elaborated on by Klein. I would suggest instead that the patient's stuckness follows from the disruption of ego-functioning implicit in trauma, as well as from the conflicting reactions to the trauma that become embedded and elaborated within the personality, powerfully influencing the nature of the individual's relationships and making it difficult to construct a coherent and effective identity. I will argue that until this conflict is understood and worked through, the individual is trapped by the traumatic complex or, to put it slightly differently, the individual is staying true to their most powerful and foundational (traumatic) experiences—even though they have little choice but to do so.

When analysts such as Ferenczi and Bowlby have persisted in focusing on the real-world trauma they have frequently been marginalised within the psychoanalytic community, although this real-world focus has been key in the development of relational psychoanalysis (Seligman, 2003). Rosenfeld's (1987) more recent recognition of the significance of trauma has been under-appreciated and sometimes criticised in psychoanalytic spheres (viz. Steiner, 1989); although this is not wholly the case—see Bohleber (2007, 2010), Garland (1998a), Peláez (2009), and others.

In a previous book (West, 2007) I explored how the psyche protects itself against narcissistic wounding—wounds to the core of the self— by throwing up narcissistic, borderline, hysteric, and schizoid defences which become incorporated and rigidified into personality organisations. However, I did not then fully recognise the primitive, affective-somatic roots of those reactions, nor did I document the individual's intricate, ongoing relationship with the trauma. This was a major omission. In this book I hope not only to rectify this, but also to present a framework that integrates the isolated elements on which Freud, Klein, and Jung, as well as Ferenczi and Bowlby, have focused, under the auspices of a larger picture which gives traumatic experience its proper place.

Having said that this book offers an integration of analytic theory, trauma theory, and relational theory, it is probably more correct to say that it offers a different perspective on each, showing how the core values of each theory address the limitations and difficulties associated with the others. I believe that psychoanalysis, Jungian analysis, and trauma therapy need each other.

Outline and contents

Having recognised that in psychoanalysis, and Kleinian psychoanalysis in particular, any appreciation of traumatic experience is largely divorced from the individual's particular reactions to the trauma, this book puts forward a developed understanding of Jung's concept of the complex which supplies the missing link between traumatic experience and the individual's reactions to that experience.

The complex is understood to embody both the trauma-related patterns of behaviour—the internal working models (Bowlby, 1969)—as described by Knox (1999), as well as the primitive defences of the core self (common to all mammals) that are thrown up in response to trauma. These become embedded and elaborated in ways that are conflictual and make it difficult to develop a coherent identity and an effective, agentive self (Liotti, 2004a). Under the influence of the traumatic complex the individual acts imperatively to avoid the trauma and retraumatisation (as evidenced by Jung's earliest word association experiments), often calling on idealised "solutions" and ways of relating.

The book explores the way that the traumatic complex affects and dominates the personality to a greater or lesser extent. This offers a way of understanding borderline functioning and borderline states of mind in terms of the nature and degree of disruption of ego-functioning following trauma, and offers a way of delineating borderline from neurotic forms of functioning. Although both are influenced by traumatic complexes, in borderline states of mind ego-functioning (the ego complex) is disrupted to a greater extent. Whilst this book is primarily focused on working with borderline states of mind, these insights are equally applicable to working with neurotic forms of functioning.

The individual with a borderline personality organisation functions in ill-adapted ways due to this disruption of ego-functioning. These are not understood as being inherently destructive or self-destructive but rather as the individual staying true to, and recapitulating, their early traumas. This can hopefully allow the foundational traumatic experience to be recognised, understood, and worked through.

Crucially, the original traumas and traumatic patterns of relating are reflected and reconstructed in the analytic relationship in a detailed way (Davies & Frawley, 1992a; Gabbard, 1997). This recognition offers an invaluable framework in which analyst and patient can access and know about that experience, understand what is happening in the analytic relationship, bear and understand the frequently unbearable affective experiences that are called up, and resist forms of behaviour that avoid the real difficulties (the traumas) being addressed; this avoidance can otherwise lead to an impasse or breakdown of the analytic relationship. This provides an account of the analytic relationship that sets phenomena that have usually been understood in terms of projective identification, destructive narcissism, the negative therapeutic reaction, and the death instinct, in a broader narrative frame, where projective identification is seen as one element of a wider dynamic rooted in early traumatic experience.

This framework also facilitates the analyst maintaining an analytic attitude, which enables them to stay with what the patient brings and for the patient's experience to emerge clearly into the analytic relationship.

The picture that develops through this way of exploring the patient's states of mind and ways of relating are usually readily comprehensible to both patient and analyst, and are inherently non-critical and non-pathologising. Most importantly this picture responds to the heartfelt, plaintive calls from the patient that have frequently been unheard, unseen, or misunderstood. This perspective thus offers a way of safely and effectively working with the most distressing and disturbing states of mind. It offers a way of accompanying the patient into the darkest of places and returning into the light of day—a process I liken to Orpheus' journey through the underworld in order to try to free his wife, Eurydice (Chapter Twelve).

The chapters in detail

Chapter One offers an outline of the characteristic clinical picture and some of the issues with which the analyst meets, as well as describing the limitations of existing theory. Chapter Two outlines some of the main understandings of borderline phenomena, differentiating the different ways the term has been used, and gives more detail of the clinical picture and the clinical challenges. Chapters Three and Four give outlines and summaries of trauma theory, and relational and attachment theory.

Chapter Five begins to unfold and explore the developed understanding of Jung's concept of the complex and describes how primitive defensive reactions become elaborated into narcissistic, schizoid, borderline, hysteric, and obsessional personality organisations—the upper levels of the personality familiar to psychoanalysis. Chapter Six describes the way in which trauma-related internal working models, "contained" by the complex, are embodied and expressed in the personality and, crucially, how this occurs on different levels and in conflicting forms—in direct form, as "subject" to the trauma, and in reversed form, in identification with the aggressor (please note that this term is used in two different senses in this book, as will be discussed later on). One side of this opposition is usually, initially projected onto/into others (typically, but not always, the aggressor role), thus binding the individual to the object. This reversal of the original experience is one of the elements that causes the conflict characteristic of borderline functioning, both alienating the individual from themselves and preventing the development of a coherent identity. These "ways of being with others" (Stern) or forms of "implicit relational knowing" (Lyons-Ruth) are manifested on different levels—objective (real world and historical), subjective (internal), transference (in relationship, particularly to the analyst), and archetypal (the impersonal/transpersonal, powerful, generalised patterns deriving from early experience). My experience has been that only when the trauma-related internal working models have been recognised and accepted on *all* these levels and in both direct *and* reversed forms, does the traumatic complex's domination of the personality become significantly reduced.

Chapter Seven gives a microanalysis of the analytic relationship (the transference level, mentioned above), demonstrating how these trauma-related patterns of behaviour manifest themselves and can be worked through. Chapter Eight looks at the disruption of ego-functioning and the relationship between the ego and the core self, outlining what I call broad and flexible ego-functioning—a conceptualization that challenges the classical Jungian view of the ego and offers an alternate way of looking at paranoid-schizoid and depressive phenomena. Chapter Nine looks at idealisation and sees it as intrinsic to the defences against trauma and as an attempt to avoid retraumatisation. Chapter Ten offers an extended clinical example and relates it to the theory put forward in the preceding chapters.

The following three chapters all discuss different issues related to the analyst and to analytic technique. Chapter Eleven describes the particular dynamics and pressures on the analyst to protect the patient from retraumatisation in ways that can lead to enactments, potentially resulting in the breakdown of the analysis. This is explored in relation to the mutually influencing, intersubjective nature of the relationship, and, in particular, the difficulty working with "inhuman" elements of the patient's experience. It offers an alternate account of phenomena that have been discussed in terms of defences of the self (Fordham, 1974), the x-phenomenon (Symington, 1983), or have been responded to by some relational analysts, such as Benjamin (2004), through disclosure and positively toned ways of being (see Meredith-Owen, 2013b). Chapter Twelve describes the particular "journey" that the analyst may need to go through within the analysis in order to meet the challenges that the patient with a borderline personality organisation brings; in particular, the way the analyst has to be able to deal with the defeat of their own ego-functioning, and to temporarily put to one side their ego perspective in line with the defeat of the patient's ego due to the original trauma. The chapter ends by exploring the impasse reached in Michael Fordham's analysis of his patient K, as documented in the pages of the *Journal of Analytical Psychology*. Chapter Thirteen describes how an analytic attitude is necessary in order to fully respect what the patient is bringing and safely work through the trauma, as well as presenting a reconceptualisation of the analytic attitude where traumatic experience is considered as central.

The following four chapters look at different facets of the most primitive response to trauma—the freeze/submit/collapse response. Chapter Fourteen explores the issues of shame and how the collapse response can keep the individual stuck in regression. Chapter Fifteen explores the experience of individuals who are "in thrall to the spectre of death", concentrating on experiences of annihilation and suicidal ideation which entrap the individual, relating it back to a collapse/submit response. This is contrasted with what Joseph (1982) called an "addiction to near death" and what Meltzer (1990) thought of in terms of the claustrum. Chapter Sixteen explores the fragmentation and dissociation associated with the collapse response in relation to dissociative identity disorder. Chapter Seventeen focuses on working with the primitive, dissociated, somatic elements of trauma.

Chapter Eighteen explores the way in which Jung's own early relational trauma throws light on his subsequent life experience and theorising; this contrasts with Winnicott's pathologising picture. In passing, it looks at the nature of spiritual experience in relation to what Jung described as the self.

Chapter Nineteen briefly outlines the working through of the traumatic complex and the development of the individual's ego-functioning and sense of agency; it then rounds up and concludes.

* * *

The amount of theory that this book covers is voluminous, and I do not claim that my presentation of it is in any way exhaustive, in fact just the opposite, as I have deliberately tried to make the narrative more accessible and readable, not trying to pre-empt every possible objection or charge of omission (in contrast to my practice in my first book (West, 2007), which, I felt, suffered as a result). I hope that this might leave more space for the reader to engage and debate with what I have written.

I am also aware that there is some repetition of the main themes in various chapters. This is because I recognise that it is unlikely that someone will read the book through at one sitting, but rather that readers may dip into various chapters on different occasions.

I would like to say at the outset that I have little or no interest in mindlessly categorising individuals, and certainly not of "reducing" them to mere labels. If I attempt to group together certain individuals' experiences, it is to better understand them, their distress and motivations, and what underlies their difficulties. As will become clear, in one sense the term borderline becomes redundant, as the individual's particular early relational experiences are understood to play the central role in their development and life experience. Yet even these do not ultimately "define" the individual, but rather, through understanding and working through their traumatic experience, the individual can be freed to fully develop, use, and manifest themselves in satisfying and fulfilling ways. The term borderline is, for me, left as a signifier of the particular kinds of reasons that the individual's struggle to reach this position may have been so difficult.

My abiding principle of analytic practice has been one of journeying with the patient, discovering and rediscovering the theory along the way, and I very much appreciate Thomas Ogden's (2009) viewpoint of "rediscovering psychoanalysis". I recognise that anyone reading this book will, hopefully, challenge, confirm or disconfirm, and rediscover what I have described for themselves, in their own idiom and in their own time. I see this book as something like a map, and if I sometimes signal "Here be dragons", I hope I have sufficiently demystified those dragons, for both patient and analyst, making them more comprehensible, accessible, human, bearable, and manageable.

CHAPTER ONE

Early relational trauma and borderline states of mind

For some patients, their experience of trauma is clear and they consciously flag it up from the beginning of the analysis; however, for many others the trauma manifests in a more disguised form, in anxieties, somatic reactions or borderline states of mind, and has become embedded in their personality and ways of relating. In this chapter I will outline some of the ways that early relational trauma can manifest in these situations. In the following chapters I will address the way that borderline organisations are traditionally understood in psychoanalytic frames of reference (Chapter Two), the history and innovations of trauma theory (Chapter Three), and early relational trauma in relation to attachment and intersubjective ways of understanding human interactions (Chapter Four).

Outline

The individual in whom borderline states of mind predominate has typically experienced a profound, early relational trauma that cannot be simply "got over". Such traumatic experience sets the person at odds with themselves and the world. The experience occurring early in life, for example, of being unloved or unwanted, of being disliked or hated,

1

or of being deprived, ignored, or abused, powerfully disrupts and comes to dominate the individual's personality. This experience, which they cannot bear, is set at the heart of their identity and is installed in implicit/procedural memory as one of the individual's key internal working models (Bowlby, 1969).

Whilst the individual cannot bear this sense of themselves, yet if they do acknowledge it, it feels as if it is who they really are. Mostly, however, they cannot bear to accept themselves and so are alienated from their core selves, feel self-critical and self-attacking, and readily fall into envy of others. Furthermore, being foundational to their identity, they feel that they cannot possibly change, so that they feel, over time, trapped, condemned, despairing, and hopeless.

In addition, the individual will usually experience powerful counter-responses to the trauma, often mirroring, in a talion-like manner, the original traumatising ways of relating themselves, which also feel unacceptable and causes further self-hatred. There is, therefore, an intense conflict which makes constructing a coherent identity very difficult, as Liotti (2004a) describes.

Trauma is, by definition, an experience which the individual's psyche cannot bear, contain, or integrate at that time (van der Kolk, 1996b). This could be what Winnicott describes as the baby being left for too long, so that they experience, "unthinkable anxiety" or "the acute confusional state that belongs to disintegration of the emerging ego structure" (Winnicott, 1967, p. 369). The experiences that I am describing have usually occurred on many occasions over a long period. Bessel van der Kolk describes what happens when the experience is "too much":

> intense arousal ("vehement emotion" [Janet's term]) seems to interfere with proper information processing and the storage of information in narrative (explicit) memory … [so that] memories of trauma may have no verbal (explicit) component whatsoever. Instead, the memories may have been organized on an implicit or perceptual level, without any accompanying narrative about what happened. (van der Kolk, 1996b, pp. 286–287)

The free-floating, affective-somatic elements form what Jung, borrowing from Janet, called "feeling-toned complexes". These complexes incorporate both the primary, primitive defences against the trauma, and the patterns of relating associated with the trauma (the trauma-related internal working models (Knox, 1999)). These elements, not being integrated with the rest of the personality ("having no verbal (explicit) component"), are experienced as very real, powerful, and current (often more real, powerful, and true than "ordinary experience", namely, that which has been integrated with the ego). These elements are readily triggered and associate themselves with any hook in the present, thus locating the traumatic experience very much in the here and now.

If, for example, the analyst asks the patient to wait in the waiting room before the start of the session time, or does not answer personal questions, or leaves too much or too many silences, they may be experienced as cold, uncaring, withholding, cruel, or sadistic if this experience happens to be associated with the person's early experience of the caregivers' unavailability in some way (rather than being seen "simply" as professional and clear-boundaried, as it might be experienced by someone who has not had that early experience and whose ego-functioning has not been disrupted). Such views will be held with utter conviction as the patient deeply experiences the analyst in this way.

Thus a negative transference is readily set up where the analyst is seen as cold, distant, and untrustworthy, despite whatever good or caring intentions they may hold privately towards the patient. These events—being kept waiting in the waiting room, silences, or not answering personal questions—can become the continual salt in the patient's wounds, with the patient insisting that the analyst recognise the agony and distress to which they are subjecting them. This can run to the analyst being persuaded or cajoled into making allowances in terms of waiting or silences, or trying to "prove" that they do care, that they *are* a feeling human being, and that they are not simply "following the rules" (discussed in full in Chapter Eleven).

I will be describing how it is an important part of the microanalysis of the interaction between patient and analyst, to identify what is being triggered by which particular aspect of the analyst's behaviour (Chapter Seven). This can help make sense of the experience so that it is not seen (by the analyst or by the patient) as simply an "over-reaction", as (meaninglessly) "paranoid", or as the analyst actually being cruel and sadistic. However, simply identifying what has triggered this experience will not, in itself, alter the patient's sense of the analyst (and more on what the analyst "actually" feels below). I will explore this more in the second half of the book.

These feeling-toned complexes are of such an intensity and complexity that they disrupt the individual's ego-complex. The ego-complex is that part of the psyche which orients us towards the world, holds our personal history and view of ourselves, and attempts to anticipate what will happen (although this latter part goes on unconsciously (West, 2007)). This is the feature which delineates borderline from neurotic functioning, as in neurotic functioning the individual's ego-functioning is not dominated by the trauma-related complex and is able to function in a relatively well-adapted manner—the individual can carry on to a significant extent "as normal", apparently getting over, or at least getting round, their traumas/complexes. For all individuals there will inevitably be complexes of varying power and complexity that may be triggered at certain times and under certain conditions. (For individuals with a neurotic character structure, a mid-life crisis is frequently initiated by the breakdown of the existing coping strategies which ran over the top of the underlying conflicts).

For the individual with a borderline psychology, however, their ego has incorporated these experiences into their sense of themselves, partly in order to allow them to anticipate what will happen and accommodate themselves to their traumatic circumstances. Often, these early experiences come to form core beliefs, such as, "I am too much for other people", "People do not like me" (Ogden, Minton, & Pain, 2006, p. 3) and even, "There is nothing to like, I am not a person". As time unfolds a second order of beliefs develop: "No one would like someone as negative and hopeless as me", or "It is my fate to be like this".

This "negative" experience, at the heart of the person's identity and in conflict with their imperative attachment needs, makes it almost impossible to develop a coherent identity, suited to functioning in the everyday world. Of course, whilst these defensive organisations may have assisted the individual at some point in their life, making their emotional life more manageable, perhaps through lowering their expectations of being responded to, and perhaps even saving their life in "submitting" to a violent bully, these reactions cannot just be changed through rational introspection as they have become part of who the individual is.

The person cannot bear to be who they deeply experience themselves to be, yet they cannot manage successfully, in the long-term, to be anything else. As a result they feel flawed, wrong, cursed (Balint describes this as the "basic fault"). The individual will often feel that there is a void at the core of their identity as they cannot let themselves "be" who they fear themselves to be, for example, someone who is not liked, or is hated. Whilst they may proclaim these self-beliefs, pre-empting someone else from stating them, or in "identification with the aggressor"[1] (Ferenczi, 1932a), they cannot in practice really accept them as this would be truly unbearable. Liotti (2004a) and Meares (2012) both also understand conflicts in identity as representing the fundamental core of borderline functioning.

The person whose ego-functioning has been disrupted in this way will inevitably feel ill-adapted to the world. They can see that in order to "get on" you need to have confidence in yourself and be able to reach out positively towards others, but they just cannot congruently do so. In addition therefore, they feel a failure, bad and "no good". These experiences are confirmed with each new interaction. As I have said already, they may very likely experience a deep, agonising envy of others who (appear to) thrive, which further confirms their sense that they are bad. There may be more primary responses to the trauma/deprivation itself, such as rage, outrage, violence, or murderousness, that also leave the individual feeling that they are bad or that they have been singled out for punishment or torture. Kleinian perspectives take these inner reactions and responses to be the primary ones, as I will explore.

A therapist who does not have a deep appreciation of trauma may unwittingly confirm and strengthen these self-views in a similarly well-meaning way to their friends or family. They will point out that the world is "not really like that", that the person has no need to fear others, that they are essentially "good", and that they do have good, worthwhile capacities and qualities.

Whilst such attempts are usually welcomed at first, they are not truly believed and, frustratingly for all concerned, they do not really go in. The person comes to feel bad that the kindly reassurance (if it comes at all) does not really help, and they feel like a colander who cannot retain a good sense of themselves. Alternatively they may require the reassuring view to be continually restated, which each time is less and less effective, and leaves the person feeling increasingly dependent on the other's views. These factors give another turn to the vicious circle and are a further element in the person feeling bad about themselves.

In the long run, these well-meaning messages from friends or the analyst disconfirm the person's deepest experience of themselves and confirm that they are wrong to feel as they do. It may make them feel that the analyst cannot really accept them as they actually experience themselves to be. Sometimes such "positive" re-framings are met with hostility, and the analyst is told that they are talking from their own enviably comfortable position and that they do not understand the patient or have the faintest idea what their life is really like.

A different response from the analyst is to point out that they may be working from a "pathogenic belief" (Weiss, 1993), that these self-beliefs are destructive, and that the person is bringing about (or at least playing a large part in) their own bad experiences. The patient almost certainly knows this already. A further step is to suggest that the patient is in some way "doing this on purpose", whether this is because they want to defeat the analyst (this might be seen as a projective identification of their own sense of failure), or whether they are manifesting a "negative therapeutic reaction" (Freud, 1923b) and "prefer suffering to getting better" as a manifestation of their masochistic tendencies (Freud, 1924c), or as an example of the death instinct in operation (Freud, 1937c). These interpretations are usually experienced as critical and punitive, even though the patient might readily join in with the self-criticism or, according to Joseph (1982), may even be unconsciously intending to induce such responses in the analyst.

I have made variations of such interpretations on many occasions and, whilst it is sometimes important to challenge the patient's corrosive, negative self-view, reframe their experiences, and help them see things in a wider context, I have found that these comments have only a limited, and frequently a negative, effect (van der Kolk describes something similar (2014, p. 128)). This is not only because the interpretation feels like a criticism and is alienating, but because it is not the kind of interaction that is helpful, and does not reflect a full understanding of the situation.

I have come to understand that in their apparently self-destructive and ill-adapted behaviour, the individual is staying true to their original, most powerful, experiences of trauma, which desperately need to be recognised, accepted, and understood. In order to really draw the poison out of the patient's early experiences the analyst has to also profoundly accept and appreciate the reality of those experiences and "locate" the original experience to which it belongs (as far as that is possible) (Chapter Ten).

This requires that the analyst learns the language of non-ego experience—the language of the defeated ego (see below), and appreciate the manner in which the exposed core self operates according to primary process functioning. This is not "pathological" in the sense that this is a normal, necessary form of functioning; however, it usually goes on unconsciously as part of processing the individual's experience. Due to the disruption of ego-functioning, it has been brought to the surface and come to dominate, so that the individual is on continual red-alert, with ill-consequences for adapted functioning.[2]

As the trauma-related patterns of interaction have become installed in implicit memory they will inevitably be reconstructed and relived in the analytic relationship. This is a co-construction, involving both patient and analyst, and I will be exploring the mysterious processes by which this happens in later chapters. Sometimes the progress of the analysis depends upon the analyst and the patient allowing themselves to participate, sometimes more, sometimes less consciously in this reconstruction, and the analysis is necessarily delayed until it becomes possible for them to safely do so. This is what I mean by accompanying the patient into the darkest places, and I hope this book will make clear the process by which this can happen.

It can lead to the individual being able to accept themselves, and to feel accepted, as they are rather than as they feel they should be, or even as they may want to be. This process may therefore entail much mourning for what they had hoped to be and what they had hoped to receive and experience—idealisation is understood as an intrinsic element of trauma (Chapter Nine)—as well as a difficult struggle to accept what happened and how they are as a result. This is not necessarily a quiet, passive acceptance, but may well include a murderous, raging, longing for revenge, as well as a wishing for the person who let them down or abused them to suffer—and at some point this will likely include the analyst.

Significantly there may be great resistance for the patient to allow themselves to behave this way towards others, similar to the way they were treated, and yet this reaction will have been constellated in them on a primitive level. It is a response that they may well find abhorrent and defend against, reacting against it when they experience it in others. Whilst Kleinians may see this in terms of the individual projecting this part of themselves into the other in the process of projective identification, I see it, instead, in terms of the individual reacting to the retraumatising other and having to do some considerable work on themselves to recognise their talion reaction to the other—their identification with the aggressor (Chapter Six).

As I will explore further, I have found that the "witnessing" of the original trauma by both analyst and patient is highly significant. On some occasions this "simple" exchange has been almost miraculous in lifting the spell of the original trauma and allowing the events to find a natural place in the person's sense of themselves in the context of a life that is now moving forward. Freud and Breuer discovered this long ago (Breuer & Freud, 1893). It is as if the psyche has been simply "waiting for this moment to arrive", as John Lennon and Paul McCartney put it in their song "Blackbird"—a song that seems to me to sum up the experience of trauma to the core self so beautifully (with the "blackbird" being a fitting symbol for the traumatised soul). Before this point nothing has been able to shift the person's distress and prevent their anguished reliving of the original trauma.

As I have just described, most significantly, this acceptance and exploration is not limited to what the person actually experienced directly, but also to how they reacted to/against it and incorporated it within them—their primitive reactions and their identification with the aggressor. Thus a vital aspect of working the complex through is to recognise the ways the patient may enact a form of the same trauma both upon themselves and others. As I will explore in Chapters Five and Six, this recognition of the traumatic pattern of behaviour, in both direct and reversed forms and on different "levels", is often the key aspect of resolving the conflict and helping the individual develop a realistic identity out of their opposing, contradictory, and conflicting reactions.

The analyst's empathic acceptance is not, therefore, simply the analyst's identification with the patient, and a "sympathetic" recognition of the traumatic experience. Many practitioners have found that a simple identificatory attitude does not resolve the trauma but may instead reinforce the individual in a "victim" position. Such experiences have no doubt played a part in analysts concentrating instead on the patient's internal reactions, whether that is infantile sexual or oedipal phantasies in the case of Freud, or destructiveness and envy in the case of Klein. Rather, the approach I will be outlining entails an in-depth exploration of the impact and consequence of the trauma in all its forms.

As I have mentioned, a significant aspect of working with such traumas is the individual's wish for an idealised, conflict-free world where there is no possibility of further traumatisation. This is often expressed as the patient's wish for the analyst to be warm, "human", and to idealistically protect the patient, and certainly not to be bad and retraumatising. The patient's idealisation, indeed the whole dynamic, needs to be sensitively addressed as it is central to whether the analyst clearly confronts the person's traumatic experience or colludes with avoiding it (Chapter Nine); this dynamic is active from the outset of the analysis.

A defining characteristic of trauma is that is represents a defeat for the patient's ego—it was overwhelmed by powerful affect. One result of this is that the analyst has to primarily recognise and help the patient to process the patient's affective-somatic responses; the analyst's rational-based interpretations in themselves have minimal effect. This, in turn, represents a defeat for the analyst's ego and it is at this point that the analyst tends to engage in overtly encouraging or covertly blaming interpretations that are unhelpful and, ultimately, miss the point (Chapter Twelve).

Until the analyst can bear this defeat and understand why the patient cannot do what they cannot do, or must do what they must do, an impasse will remain. This is not merely about understanding but also about bearing. It raises the question of what experiences the analyst can personally bear, and the extent to which they have worked through their own traumatic complexes as, until they have done so, it is unlikely that they will feel able to "expose" the patient to something that feels, to both patient and analyst, unbearable and unresolvable. It also raises the question of the analyst's ability to trust themselves, the patient, and the analytic process sufficiently, and relinquish their own ego-functioning and "think" in the plane of primary process function and non-verbal affective-somatic modes of communication (Chapter Twelve).

Whilst the patient's thinking about their traumatic experience and their understanding and cognitive functioning in general might be impaired, this is not simply or necessarily a matter of resistance, as Freud understood it at first, or −K, as Bion would have put it, but rather an inevitable aspect of the effect of trauma on the psyche itself (see the quote above from van der Kolk). And whilst Fonagy understandably emphasises the development of the ability to think about and understand the other in the resolution of traumatic experience—what he calls the capacity to mentalize—this can overemphasise the cognitive aspects rather than recognising the way the individual must inevitably enact their experience in the absence of a proper cognitive understanding of it.

In one sense, working through the traumatic complex amounts to nothing more nor less than expanding the individual's awareness and ability to encompass and bear these primitive, primarily somatic-affective reactions to trauma which normally occur below the level of consciousness and which induce intense shame due to the exposure of the core self and the disruption of the person's everyday functioning. This also entails recognising the upper-level, emotional and cognitive elaborations of these primitive "roots" of the personality.

Notes

1. I use the term "identification with the aggressor" in two different senses in this book; first, whereby the child identifies with the aggressor and takes themselves to be bad/wrong—the sense in which Ferenczi uses the phrase, and second, whereby the individual identifies with the aggressor and enacts the aggressive/abusive role. I hope the sense in which I am using the terms is made clear by the context.
2. I will discuss this red-alert in terms of hypervigilance (Chapter Three), and understand that the need for sameness and aversion to difference, characteristic of primary process functioning, derives from the primitive appraisal (Bowlby, 1969) of experience, which goes on from the beginning of life, in order to recognise whether this new experience is the same as previously good experience or previously bad experience (Matte Blanco, 1975, 1988; West, 2004, 2007).

CHAPTER TWO

The clinical picture and the traditional psychoanalytic understandings of borderline phenomena

In the previous chapter I outlined the most salient features of the clinical picture, partly laying out the future direction of this book. In this chapter I will look in greater detail at how the individual with a borderline psychology might present in analysis, the particular interpersonal/analytic issues that may arise, and the traditional ways these issues have been thought about and addressed.

A brief outline of the term "borderline"

The term borderline is used in two different, but overlapping, ways. One use, as it was originally outlined, designates a particular kind of personality organisation; I will call this the "narrow definition", and it harks back to the original formulation by Adolf Stern in 1938. The second, a more recent, "broader definition", refers to a general set of phenomena, including a disturbed form of thinking and object relationship, and a preponderance of primary process functioning—impaired reflective function and mentalization in Peter Fonagy's (1991) terms.

The concept is further complicated by having been, in the 1970s, 80s, and 90s, the term most frequently used to theorise about patients, thus spawning many similar-but-different conceptualisations, and, furthermore, supplanting the previously most frequently used term, narcissism. There is, of course, considerable overlap between the concept of narcissism and both the narrower and broader uses of the term borderline.

I understand "trauma" as co-extensive with "narcissistic wounding", meaning a traumatic wounding to the core of the self (another term that will need defining). This narcissistic wounding calls up primitive defensive reactions which become incorporated into narcissistic, borderline, schizoid, hysteric, or obsessional personality organisations, which are all forms of narcissistic defence. I will argue that psychoanalytic theorists have insufficiently understood or addressed the traumatic roots and outworkings of these phenomena—and until recently neither had I (viz. West, 2004, 2007).

* * *

Adolf Stern's (1938) original conceptualisation has stood the test of time and I will outline it here as it gives a good sense of the term. He identified ten main features:

- "narcissism", which he saw as due to a "deficiency of spontaneous maternal affection" which thus led to "affective narcissistic malnutrition";
- "psychic bleeding", where there is complete psychic collapse when the individual encounters pain and trauma;
- "inordinate hypersensitivity";
- a "rigid personality"—he described both psychic and bodily rigidity;
- "negative therapeutic reactions" where, as Freud described, instead of the patient making improvements when an appropriate interpretation is made the patient appears to get worse;
- "constitutionally rooted feelings of inferiority deeply embedded in the personality";
- "masochism and self-pity";
- "a deep, organic insecurity and anxiety" which leads to "extreme and clinging dependency";
- the use of projection, for example, a paranoid experience of a hostile environment;
- and "difficulties in reality testing", particularly in personal relationships.

Gunderson and Singer (1975), in a classic paper giving an overview of the term, describe the individual with a borderline psychology as typically forming an intense relationship with the therapist, and having a strong tendency to regress. They recognise a prominence of anger and depression, with varying degrees of anxiety and anhedonia (lack of pleasure). Impulsive acts are also characteristic they say, although these tend to co-exist, perhaps curiously, with good social functioning. Schmideberg (1959) describes this as a "stably unstable" organisation, although there can be transient, reversible, limited psychotic symptoms that are usually triggered by particular stresses.

Otto Kernberg is probably the psychoanalytic theoretician most associated with this concept. He describes a characteristic "ego pathology" where there are manifestations of "ego weakness", which he sees as including a lack of tolerance of anxiety, impulse control, and capacity for enjoyment and creative achievement. He states that there is a shift towards primary process thinking, and the presence of specific defensive mechanisms, in particular splitting, as well as idealisation, projection, projective identification, denial, and omnipotence (Kernberg, 1975).

Peter Fonagy has, over the years, with many different colleagues, developed a broader conceptualisation and definition of the borderline concept and borderline phenomena, particularly linking them to early relational trauma. At first, he saw borderline phenomena, and specifically the difficulty in thinking about oneself or others, as due to the fact that the person cannot bear to think about what is in the mind of the other, as that is, for example, too painfully negative, critical, hateful, uncaring, or murderous (Fonagy, 1991). Over time he has come to develop his understanding to recognise the role of early attachment patterns and, in particular, the parents' inability to think about their child as an individual in their own right—their ability to mentalize— and he relates this specifically to disturbances of borderline psychology (Fonagy, Gergely, Jurist, & Target, 2002; Fonagy, Target, Gergely, Allen, & Bateman, 2003; Fonagy, Gergely, & Target, 2008). The model presented here overlaps with Fonagy and his colleagues' work in some ways, and has drawn a good deal from it, although there are a number of differences, as will become clear.

Similarly Liotti (2004a, 2007) has very much recognised the conflict in constructing a coherent identity, stressing that early attachment disorganisation is "essentially a dissociative process" characterised by "severe dissociation, splitting among ego states, and fragmentation of the self" which he links specifically with borderline functioning (Liotti, 2007, p. 130). Meares (2012) also hypothesises that the conflict over identity is central to borderline phenomena, as well as recognising the reversal of the abusive role, as I will be exploring further in detail. I will return to Fonagy's, Liotti's, and Meares' work in subsequent chapters.

I will therefore be discussing borderline personality organisation in a narrow sense, akin to Stern's outline, although understood to be rooted in a primitive freeze response (Chapter Five), and also, I hope not too confusingly, will be discussing borderline states of mind in a broad sense, by which I mean states of mind where ego-functioning has been disrupted and trauma-related conflicts predominate. This may also occur for individuals with a neurotic psychology, although these tend to occur less frequently under normal circumstances.[1]

Particular features of the clinical picture

The following quote from Christopher Bollas begins to bring us closer to the clinical experience. He writes:

> The borderline person ... has experienced the primary object as causing so much turbulence to the self that inner states of mental turmoil have become equivalent to it. ... [Due to an uneven experience of the mother, the person] construct[s] an ideal object—stitched together out of bits of the good mother—as a fragile alternative to the other mother. Unfortunately, this solution is always a temporary one, because the borderline feels that his or her core object is to be found only through turbulent states of mind. Unconsciously, therefore, the borderline character seeks out turbulence, turning molehills into mountains, and escalating irritations into global states of rage. ... In the transference they will split the analyst, between a fragile idealised object and a denigrated object that feels more true, more primary. (Bollas, 2000, p. 9)

The individual with a borderline personality organisation struggles with life and often feels tortured by it, as they are not able to progress or to feel good about any progressions they do make. They are all the while being disturbed and upset by new or anticipated events which they experience as intensely distressing, anxiety-provoking, and sometimes life-threatening. These are events that trigger a re-experiencing of the affects associated with the original traumas—a retraumatisation—and, as I will describe, a terrifying state of psychic collapse. Such experiences feel extremely real and immediate to the patient, and the analyst can very easily come to take them at face value.

The individual with a borderline personality organisation is thus often disinterested in the "niceties" of analysis as they want and need help and relief from their exposed, agonising, and unbearable-feeling situation, whether that is an immediate crisis or an intolerable long-term state of affairs. If splitting starts off as a normal process of division between good and bad experience it develops, for the individual with a borderline personality, into a split between those who retraumatise the individual and those who protect them from trauma. As traumatic experience is (by definition) unbearable to the individual the split is extremely highly charged.

Ron Britton describes the individual's sensitivity and splitting as the individual being a "thin-skinned narcissist" (using Rosenfeld's term). Furthermore, the person often struggles with traditional analytic inter-pretations and reacts against the analyst's separateness, thinking, ana-lysing, and self-containment. As one of Britton's patients once put it, "stop that fucking thinking!" (Britton, 1989, p. 88).

Michael Fordham, in the most read paper in the post-Jungian litera-ture, describes the way such individuals react against the parts of the analyst which they see as "technical and mechanistic", and attempt to "unmask and obtain" a "good, hidden part" of the analyst for them-selves. Thus they may treat the analyst's comments and interpretations as cold, unfeeling, and theoretical, or even as attempts by the analyst to defend themselves against their own "infantile parts" which the patient holds they are projecting into the patient; they may react "with denigra-tion ending up in loud groans, screams or tears whenever the analyst speaks" (Fordham, 1974, p. 193).

He describes how the patient becomes extremely distressed and can come to feel that their pain, terror, dread, and confusion is directly caused by what they see as the analyst's "sadism, cruelty and destruc-tiveness". The analysis can sometimes run into considerable difficulty and impasse under these circumstances, with the patient becoming des-perate and flooded with affect, so that the analyst might be led into relaxing boundaries, making disclosures, giving tokens and so on.

Fordham counsels that the analyst should not "try 'being himself' any more than he is already so doing by making confessions or giving information about himself etc."; he recommends that "the analytic attitude needs to be maintained" and that it is not desirable for the analyst to become "excessively passive or guilty at the amount of pain, terror and dread that the patient asserts the analyst causes" (ibid., p. 196). Fordham describes these phenomena as part of a "transference psychosis" where the patient is defending against what they experience as "not-self" parts of the analyst, that is to say, parts of the analyst that are different from the patient. He holds that it is due to an attempt by the patient to maintain an infantile perverted state of mind, although I will argue that this is precisely a re-enactment that gives analyst and patient access to the early and originally irreconcilable infantile situation (according to James Astor, Fordham did recognise that the patient was attempting to "bring [these states of mind] into relation with another person" (Astor, 2004, p. 492)).

These issues of boundaries, enactment, disclosure, and self-containment are vital ones that I will address later. Relational psychoanalysis offers a different perspective on this and many contemporary trauma therapists are critical of traditional psychoanalytic attitudes and methods of interpretation as I will discuss further.

Resistance and repetition

As I described in Chapter One, if the therapist offers an understanding of what is going on, and even if they "correctly" name the original trauma, the patient will not necessarily "get better". Freud was well aware of this phenomenon and at first understood it in terms of resistance. He then recognised that there were certain patients—I suggest that they are exactly those with a borderline personality organisation—of whom he wrote:

> There are certain people who behave in quite a peculiar fashion during the work of analysis. When one speaks hopefully to them or expresses satisfaction with the progress of treatment, they show signs of discontent and their condition invariably becomes worse. (1923b, p. 49)

Freud called this a "negative therapeutic reaction" and suggested that these individuals "prefer suffering to being cured". Over time, he linked this to a number of factors: unconscious guilt, and the individual's wish to prove their superiority over the analyst (1923b), masochism (1924c), superego resistance (1926d), and, ultimately, in his descriptively named paper "Analysis terminable and interminable", the "irreducible nature of the death instinct" (1937c). Freud also, importantly, introduced the concept of repetition compulsion (1914g), a concept much influenced by Janet's work—where someone unconsciously returns to and repeats traumatic experiences in order, Freud held, to try to master them—as I will explore in detail in the next chapter.

I will be suggesting that the reason the individual becomes dissatisfied when "progress" is spoken of, is that they "know" that the trauma has not been sufficiently recognised, addressed, or worked through. There is a profound way in which the individual who experienced significant early relational trauma remains true to this trauma, despite its current destructive consequences, and they cannot bear for certain elements to remain unknown; it is as if they cannot bear to abandon their infant self which originally experienced the trauma. There may be further motivations, as described throughout the book, for example it becomes a familiar way of engaging others and relating (Chapters Five and Six); however I understand these as secondary.

Freud said, following Janet, that the compulsion to repeat was an attempt at mastery—a notion that has come in for some criticism (see Courtois (2010, pp. 233ff.) and the feminist approach). I will suggest that the conflicting reactions to the trauma, as embodied in the traumatic complex, need to be recognised and worked through in order for this "mastery" to occur—a similar point is made by Liotti (2004a, 2007), although in a slightly different frame. Certainly the individual attempts to bring the traumatic experience into their "sphere of omnipotence", as Winnicott (1974) put it, seeking out and taking control of forms of humiliation, risk, death, or whatever the original form the trauma took.

Regression

As Gunderson and Singer note, these individuals have a strong tendency to regress. Michael Balint (1968) made an extensive exploration of this area, and proposed that patients regress to the level of "the basic fault", which was his term for what was then known as the pre-verbal, pre-genital or pre-oedipal level. He says that at this level, relationship operates at a level of primary love. Similar to Fordham's descriptions, quoted above, Balint writes:

> interpretations given by the analyst are not experienced … as interpretations … [but rather as] … an attack, a demand, a base insinuation, an uncalled-for rudeness or insult, unfair treatment, injustice, or at least as a complete lack of consideration, and so on; on the other hand, it is equally possible that the analyst's interpretations may be experienced as something highly pleasing and gratifying, exciting or soothing, or as a seduction; in general as an irrefutable sign of consideration, affection, and love …. [T]he analyst's every casual remark, every gesture or movement, may matter enormously and may assume an importance far beyond anything that could be realistically intended. (Balint, 1968, p. 18)

He continues:

> A further important quality of this relationship is the immense difference of intensity between the phenomenon of satisfaction and frustration. Whereas satisfaction—the "fitting in" of the object with the subject—brings about a feeling of quiet tranquil well-being which can be observed only with difficulty as it is so natural and soft, frustration—the lack of "fitting in" of the object—evokes highly vehement and loud symptoms. (ibid., p. 17)

Overall Balint characterises the form of relationship that follows as

> a two-person relationship in which, however, only one of the partners matters; his wishes and needs are the only ones that count and must be attended to; the other partner, though felt to be immensely powerful, matters only in so far as he is willing to gratify the first partner's needs and desires or decides to frustrate them; beyond this his personal interests, needs, desires, wishes, etc., simply do not exist. (ibid., p. 23)

The individual is thus experienced as extremely self-centred and narcissistic. Balint distinguished what he calls benign from malignant regression, writing that in some treatments only one, or at most a few, periods of regression or new beginning occurred, after which the patient spontaneously emerged from his primitive world and felt better, or was even cured—as predicted by Ferenczi; while with some others it seemed that they could never have enough; as soon as one of their primitive wishes or needs was satisfied, it was replaced by a new wish or craving, equally demanding and urgent. This in some cases led to the development of addiction-like states which were very difficult to handle, and in some cases proved—as Freud predicted—intractable. (ibid., p. 138)

The difference between benign and malignant regression can be explained precisely by whether the individual's ego-functioning is fundamentally disrupted and compromised, as for the individual with a borderline psychology, or whether the individual's ego-complex can operate fairly effectively despite their traumatic complexes. In the latter case, the periods of regression correspond to when the individual is, for a time, drawn into a traumatic complex and loses touch with their more usual ego-functioning.

The Kleinian contribution

Winnicott says patients need to regress: Melanie Klein says they must not: I say they are regressed. (Bion, 1992, p. 166)

This quote indicates one of the contrasts between the Freudian Middle School analysts, such as Balint and Winnicott, and Melanie Klein's position. She focused on these kinds of clinical issues in a different way, seeing regression in terms of what she called the paranoid-schizoid position, a concept that was the outgrowth of her concept of projective identification.

Klein documented the early relationship between mother and infant and in particular the mother's breast, which she observed the infant "splitting" into "a good (gratifying) and bad (frustrating) breast". She stated that this process is normal but that it can also be observed in adults in certain (problematic/pathological) circumstances.

She felt that not only did the individual try to "suck dry" and possess the good breast (good experiences) and expel the bad breast (bad experiences) but that also good and bad parts of the individual themselves—parts of their ego—were projected, so that "the mother is not felt to be a separate individual but is felt to be the bad self" (or the good self) (Klein, 1946, p. 8). She saw this as an oral- and anal-sadistic attack on the object, "meant not only to injure but also to control and take possession of the object" (ibid., p. 8). She felt that the individual is "weakened and impoverished" by the projection of these parts of themselves into the other, leading to "an over-strong dependence on these external representatives of one's own good parts" (ibid., p. 9), which are then experienced as persecutory. She called this process projective identification and thought that it was characteristic of what she called the paranoid-schizoid position.[2]

Klein is clearly trying to address similar phenomena here, as well as trying to account for the situation where the individual's ego does not function well (it is regressed), where the individual sees their objects as intensely good or bad (splitting), is aggressively dependent on and controlling towards their object, and is persecuted by anxieties. Whereas Balint was (later) to suggest that there could be positive potential in the regression, Klein felt the process was necessarily pathological, other than for the infant.

Furthermore, whilst Klein did recognise the contribution of external circumstances,[3] she understands these phenomena primarily in terms of internal conflicts writing, for example:

> I hold that anxiety arises from the operation of the death instinct within the organism, is felt as fear of annihilation (death) and takes the form of persecution. The fear of the destructive impulse seems to attach itself at once to an object—or rather it is experienced as the fear of an uncontrollable overpowering object. (Klein, 1946, p. 4)

Bion

Wilfred Bion developed Klein's view, seeing projective identification as a natural form of communication. In his "theory of thinking" (1962a), he understood that the parent or analyst uses their developed thinking (which he called alpha-function) to contain the more primitive affective and somatic elements (which he called beta elements). Related to this he had a theory of containment, where the parent's ego-functioning (their thinking, alpha-functioning) acts as a necessary container for the infant (the contained) (1962b). He thought that projective identification only became "excessive" when the individual had had early difficulty with their affects/beta elements being received and contained by the parent and that they therefore had to force them into the object/the analyst (Bion, 1959).

Whilst many people adopt Bion's reframing of Klein's concept of projective identification, the picture I will outline does address and account for the aggression that Klein described in terms of anal- and oral-sadistic attacks on the object. And whilst Bion's view accords more with the contemporary understanding of parent–infant relations, these are now understood in a much more nuanced way—see Beebe and Lachmann (2002, 2013).

I will address further Kleinian contributions, such as Herbert Rosenfeld's understanding of omnipotent narcissistic object relations, Ron Britton's view of the patient's objection to the analyst thinking, Donald Meltzer's concept of the claustrum, Betty Joseph's understanding of an addiction to near death experience, and John Steiner's conceptualisation of psychic retreats, later in this book.

The limitations of the traditional understandings

Whilst these theorists recognise the role of trauma to a greater or lesser extent, none, I would argue, have sufficiently recognised its primary, ongoing significance in the clinical situation, nor found a way to effectively address it. Without this, first, interpretations tend to be experienced as unbearable, punitive, critical, and alienating (Steiner (1993) tried to address this by introducing analyst-centred interpretations where the analyst does not highlight their separateness from the patient but rather interprets how the patient may see them).

Second, the analyst imputing intention (even if unconscious intention) to the patient tends not only to be experienced as blaming and shaming, but also does not address the subjective reality that these aspects of the self function implicitly, far below the level of conscious intention. They are also frequently alien and dissociated from the core identity. Similarly, interpreting the patient's fear of attack as a projection of their own aggression is only one aspect of the phenomenon (see below).

Third, the essence of the trauma and the primitive reactions to the trauma are missed, leading to the patient feeling misunderstood and reinforcing their feelings of wrongness; Britton (1998, p. 57) describes the feeling of being misunderstood as one of the prime characteristics of borderline functioning. When trauma is properly taken into account the person's behaviour, previously seen as perplexing or self-destructive, can be understood, and its purposive nature revealed. Whilst it is frequently recognised that the person's behaviour was formerly adaptive (but is no longer necessary or appropriate), it is vital to fully explore the extent to which it may be continuing to fulfil an important function in relation to a traumatic complex that is still readily retraumatised.

Fourth, without an understanding that the early relational trauma is being recreated in the analytic relationship in a detailed manner the analyst can easily be led into enactments, as they will likely not understand what the patient is urging upon them so passionately. Therapies that, implicitly or explicitly, foster regression as a means of working through, as described by Ferenczi and Winnicott, for example, are problematical, as documented by Balint, as great pressure can be put on the analyst to enact certain roles, which can lead to the breakdown of the analysis and/or the abuse of the patient (I will explore this further in Chapter Eleven).

Finally, recognising the trauma as central has frequently been seen as unhelpfully over-identifying with the patient, becoming ineffective and "merely sympathetic", confirming the person in their "victim" role. The understanding outlined here is more complex, looking at the way that trauma-related modes of behaviour (primitive defences and internal working models) are played out on various levels, intra- and inter-personally, both directly, as victim, and in reversed mode, in identification with the aggressor. In addition, the need to be able to relinquish and mourn the wish for an ideal rescuer/saviour figure is understood to be central to the process of working through the trauma (rather than simply as one amongst other primitive defences, e.g., Kernberg, 1975), as well as the need to address the shame associated with the trauma, and the consequent difficulty in functioning in a reality-oriented manner.

Notes

1. Whilst there is clearly some overlap between the Kleinian conceptualisation of the paranoid-schizoid position and borderline states of mind, I do not believe Kleinian analysts would see the paranoid-schizoid

position in terms of disruption of ego-functioning; I will discuss this further in Chapter Eight.

2. She contrasted this with the depressive position, where "the loved and hated aspects of the mother are no longer felt to be so widely separated, and the result is an increased fear of loss, states akin to mourning and a strong feeling of guilt, because the aggressive impulses are felt to be directed against the loved object" (Klein, 1946, p. 14).

3. She wrote, for example, "I hold that the introjected good breast forms a vital part of the ego, exerts from the beginning a fundamental influence on the process of ego-development and affects both ego-structure and object-relations" (Klein, 1946, pp. 3–4).

CHAPTER THREE

A brief outline of trauma theory

Definitions

Bessel van der Kolk defines trauma as "an inescapably stressful event that overwhelms [the individual's] existing coping mechanism" (van der Kolk, 1996b, p. 279); Freud (1894a) described trauma as the ego being overwhelmed and helpless. Van der Kolk describes further how

> Janet proposed that intense arousal ("vehement emotion") seems to interfere with proper information processing and the storage of information in narrative (explicit) memory … [so that] memories of trauma may have no verbal (explicit) component whatsoever. Instead, the memories may have been organized on an implicit or perceptual level, without any accompanying narrative about what happened. (van der Kolk, 1996b, pp. 286–287)

The individual cannot therefore integrate the traumatic experience with their existing personality (ego) and certain aspects of it are dissociated (the term dissociation is rife with difficulty as I will explore later). Whilst there may be vivid recollections of certain elements of the events—powerful affects or physical sensations, sometimes called flashbacks—these can co-exist with substantial amnesia (van der Kolk & McFarlane, 1996, p. 10). It is worth noting that the term flashback can be misleading as it is often thought to mean the unexpected emergence of an image or memory, whereas frequently it is feelings and somatic reactions that are regularly triggered by something almost subliminal in the person's experience. These often constitute the core of transference experience.

Whether a particular event is traumatic or not is therefore a subjective matter, as something that one individual might experience as traumatic at a particular time another might not. This can cause misunderstanding and recrimination, and frequently self-recrimination, with the traumatised individual experiencing much shame for not being able to cope with the experience that others have tolerated, and for continuing to be affected by what appear to be "relatively minor" events.

Of course, the person's age and "the developmental stage at which an individual is traumatised has a major impact on the degree to which mind and brain are affected" (van der Kolk, McFarlane, & Weisaeth, 1996, p. x). The early relational traumas that I will be concentrating on often come at an age where the ego has not developed sufficiently to provide a coherent coping mechanism to deal with potential traumas; this led van der Kolk (2005) to delineate the term "developmental trauma disorder". Furthermore, some individuals appear to have powerful coping capacities that turn out to be developed from primitive fight, flight, or vigilant responses, so that whilst the individual may appear to be assertive, powerful, and in control, or robust and stoical, they may well be all the time desperately defending their precarious sense of self.

Post-traumatic stress disorder

If an individual copes, it is because their ego has been able to absorb, adapt to, and accommodate the experience. When this has not been able to happen, their ego-functioning can be substantially disrupted to the extent that they might be considered to have post-traumatic stress disorder (PTSD). As van der Kolk, McFarlane, and Weisaeth write,

> PTSD is a condition that severely disrupts individuals' capacity to perceive, represent, integrate, and act on internal and external stimuli because of major disruptions in the neural systems associated

with attention, working memory, and the processing of affective stimuli. (1996, p. x)

The simplest example of PTSD is of single incident trauma that occurs in adulthood where the individual has had little previous experience of trauma. This may be a car accident, a mugging, a sexual assault, a terrorist attack, or an event related to war. These events are sometimes called "big T traumas" and distinguished from "little t traumas", such as ongoing early experience of a depressed, unavailable mother, or an angry, violent father. As I will have little to say about big T traumas, wishing to concentrate instead on early relational trauma, I will not follow this usage. The distinction might also be taken to imply that, just because the events were far away in time or were of a relational nature, they were less "traumatic", which is not the case; on the contrary, early relational trauma is frequently a lot more pernicious as it can affect and dominate the individual's whole personality and life experience.

Cognitive behavioural therapy and EMDR (eye movement desensitisation and reprocessing) are effective forms of treatment for individuals who have experienced single incident trauma as an adult. These treatments make the intense affects more manageable, either directly (EMDR) or through a structured process of understanding, adjustment, and management by the conscious ego in relation to the affects (CBT). This allows the individual to return to their normal sense of self, and gain a manageable perspective on the events, in other words, to return to ordinary ego-functioning (Richman, 2013; van der Kolk, 2014).

Trauma in childhood, however, is often of a different nature. Whilst experience of physical, sexual, or verbal abuse may be clearly traumatic, equally a parent's prolonged unavailability, inconsistency, emotional bullying or neglect of the child will lead to substantial relational trauma (see for instance, Lanius, Vermetten, and Pain (2010), who describe this as a "hidden epidemic"). This gives rise to powerful defensive responses to the trauma, as well as the child's accommodation to living in a traumatic environment, and the development and incorporation of internal working models which allow the child to attempt to predict, and therefore have some degree of control over, their environment.

These internal working models are deeply embedded in the individual's personality, as will be explored in the following chapters. Treatment methods such as EMDR[1] and CBT are thus less effective in these situations, as the therapist needs to be able to work with the elaborations of the trauma within the personality itself, and intricately trace its roots to the early traumatic experience. There is frequently, therefore, no stable ego-functioning or "secure base" for the individual to be able to establish effective cognitive responses to the maelstrom of affective and somatic experience.

Judith Herman, one of the early pioneers of trauma work, described the trauma when the child's early attachment needs, which are imperative and can bear little frustration, are disrupted. She delineated "Complex PTSD" (Herman, 1992, pp. 119ff.) to describe the personality changes which follow from chronic abuse and repeated trauma (often due to subjection to totalitarian control over a prolonged period). She outlined the consequences in relation to affect regulation (including dysphoria, suicidal preoccupation, self-injury, labile rage, and sexuality), consciousness (including amnesia, depersonalisation, and dissociation), self-perception (including shame, guilt, and helplessness), relations with others (including withdrawal and mistrust), systems of meaning (hopelessness and despair), and the perception of the perpetrator (including preoccupation and idealisation). I will be employing the term early relational trauma to include all of the above phenomena.

A number of theorists have suggested that the term trauma has become overused so that an individual might refer to anything that they find difficult to deal with as "traumatic". Krystal, for example, proposed limiting the term to what he called "catastrophic trauma", where the individual's ego is overwhelmed and they collapse in a state of helplessness and hopelessness, often progressing to what he called a catatonoid state (Krystal, 1978, p. 111). I do not follow this limitation of the use of the word as individuals almost always have a number of significant responses to a traumatic event other than complete collapse, as I will explore in detail below.

I understand early relational traumas, and the responses and defences thrown up in response to them, to be foundational elements in the psyche which can be seen to underpin and determine both the development and form of the individual's personality. Trauma-related complexes can be discerned in everyday analytic work, throwing new light on well-known analytic impasses.

* * *

The history and development of our understanding of trauma

Jean-Martin Charcot (1825–1893) and Pierre Janet (1859–1947)

Jean-Martin Charcot, working at the Salpêtrière Hospital in Paris, was the leading physician of his day working on nervous disorders and, in particular, hysteria (he has also been called the founder of modern neurology). He was the first to make the link between hysteria and underlying trauma. He described his patients' suggestibility follow-ing a *"choc nerveux"*, which could put them into a mental state similar to that induced by hypnosis. At that time hysteria was considered to encompass a broad range of disorders that might now be categorised as dissociative, somatisation, conversion, borderline personality, and post-traumatic stress disorders (van der Hart & Friedman, 1989).

Charcot's work on hysteria was taken up and much developed by his pupil, Pierre Janet, who laid down the foundation stones of trauma theory which are still sound today. Through extensive study, observa-tion, and the use of hypnosis, Janet concluded that dissociation was the characteristic underlying mechanism behind hysteria. He proposed that a traumatic event gives rise to "vehement emotions" in the individ-ual which cannot be integrated with their existing cognitive schemes and are thus split off—dissociated. The memory traces of the trauma remain in the form of what Janet called "fixed ideas"—*idées fixes*—in the mind of the individual. These are thoughts or mental images that take on exaggerated proportions and have a high emotional charge (Janet, 1894). They are not integrated with the normal personality and they disrupt normal consciousness.

Janet gave one example of a woman who made a curious, involun-tary jump whilst walking, which turned out to correspond exactly with the little jump that she had made when trying to commit suicide by throwing herself into the Seine (Janet, 1893a, 1893b, 1893c). He sug-gested that these individuals become "attached" to the trauma (Freud later called this "fixation"), their personalities cannot enlarge any more, and the effort to keep the fragmented traumatic memories out of con-scious awareness erodes their psychic energy.

Janet was the first to introduce the concept of the subconscious (Ellenberger, 1970, p. 406) to describe the "collection of memories that form the mental schemes that guide a person's interaction with the environment" (Janet, 1904, quoted in van der Kolk, Weisaeth, & van der Hart, 1996, p. 52). He distinguished two different ways in which the mind functions—activities that "preserve and reproduce the past", and activities which are directed towards synthesis and creation, that is to say, integration (which I would understand as functions of the core self and the ego, respectively). He described the narrowing of the field of consciousness, as well as the patient's deep involvement with the therapist (then called *rapport magnétique*), and he outlined many therapeutic techniques, including a three-stage model of treatment which is the basis of techniques recommended by many practitioners working with trauma and dissociation today[2] (e.g., van der Hart, Nijenhuis, & Steele, 2006).

Whilst Janet followed Charcot's lead in investigating the nature of traumatic memory and dissociation, two of Charcot's other pupils, de la Tourette and Babinsky, focused their research on the phenomenon of suggestibility that Charcot had noted. Following Charcot's sudden death in 1893, and with Babinsky taking over as head of the Salpêtrière Hospital, Charcot's notions of the traumatic origins of hysteria were rejected, with the emphasis being put instead on suggestibility and the individual's "willpower". This led to First World War trauma victims being put through treatment programmes aimed at "boosting" the patient's "desire for health" that we would now consider ineffective and questionable, if not inhuman (see van der Kolk, Weisaeth, & van der Hart, 1996, pp. 49–50).

The challenge to, frustration, and threatened defeat of, the doctor's or analyst's own ego-functioning, inevitable in this work with patients who don't simply "get better", is frequently unbearable for the doctor and I would suggest that it is one of the reasons that trauma has repeatedly fallen out of fashion—you cannot simply appeal to the patient's reason. I will discuss this further in Chapter Twelve.

Janet became a lone voice in the field, and his focus on the trauma itself eventually fell out of fashion, whilst Freud's psychoanalysis and the emphasis on the individual's fantasies and inner conflicts held sway for most of the twentieth century.

Sigmund Freud

Freud had attended some of Charcot's lectures and had been much impressed by them and by the link between hysteria and trauma.[3] Between 1895 and 1897, following his patients' accounts of early sexual experiences, Freud maintained that in neuroses, and in hysteria in particular, the original trauma is always linked to real sexual encounters with an adult close to the patient. These experiences could be anything from sexual advances to actual sexual activity and "are to be described as sexual abuses in the narrowest sense" (Freud, 1897b, p. 253). This was known as the seduction theory.

However, as he accumulated more clinical material and undertook his own self-analysis, he began to question his theory, doubting that sexual abuse was as widespread as he had thought, and coming to believe that the *fantasy* of seduction, rather than the actual event, played a decisive role (Freud, 1895c, p. 264). Related to this, Freud developed his theory of infantile sexuality. It is important to note, of course, that by no means all early relational trauma is sexual in nature, so that the seduction theory was intrinsically flawed in concentrating on sexual abuse, reflecting, as it did, Freud's primary focus on sexuality.

However, in concentrating on what Freud describes as the hysterical subject's "fantasy", it could be that his patients were elaborating on an affective-somatic fragment of their experience, or even a counter-response to a trauma, which will be improperly remembered; for example, individuals who have been sexually abused frequently have hyper-sexualised somatic or ideational responses to the abuse. To describe this as wholly "fantasy" is manifestly incorrect as will become clear throughout this book.

In exploring the absence of acknowledgement of actual trauma in psychoanalysis, Person and Klar (1994), in addition to recognising the issue of the absence of coherent memory in trauma, point out that psychoanalysis has confused and conflated unconscious memories with unconscious fantasies. They quote Anna Ornstein who writes: "When Freud introduced the concept of 'psychic reality' … he replaced the factual reality of unconscious memories with the psychic reality of unconscious fantasies" (Ornstein, 1983, p. 383).

Despite his abandonment of the seduction theory, Freud emphasised, throughout his life, that sexual seductions of children occur more often than we may like to think, that any sexual abuse had a pathogenic effect, and that any resultant neurosis could not be attributed to fantasy alone (Hanly, 1986; Quinodoz, 2005, pp. 15–23). He wrote, for instance: "Phantasies of being seduced are of particular interest, because so often they are not phantasies but real memories" (Freud, 1916–1917, p. 370).

Despite this recognition, the shift of emphasis towards fantasy and inner conflict, and away from the primary concentration on the actual trauma, has had a painful history in psychoanalytic theory, with patients' experiences frequently being disbelieved, disregarded, and/or interpreted as "merely" fantasy. It is tragic that the absence of a coherent memory and narrative about the trauma, and the related confusion and lack of coherence, which is a definitive characteristic of trauma, has played a significant part in the patient's experiences being labelled simply as "unacceptable impulses".

Krystal (1978) suggests that Freud concurrently held two separate models of trauma. One was the "unbearable situation" model, where the ego is overwhelmed by affective states (the model he derived from Charcot & Janet); the other was the "unacceptable impulse" model, where the sexual and aggressive wishes of the child threaten the ego and motivate defences against the conscious awareness of these wishes (see also, van der Kolk, Weisaeth, & van der Hart, 1996, p. 54).

Of course, the actual trauma does instigate many powerful reactions and responses from the individual which are conflicting and difficult to integrate into a coherent ego identity (the particular nature and form of these reactions is very important and will be explored in Chapters Five and Six of this book). However, these reactions are a direct response to the trauma itself and are thus a secondary rather than a primary phenomenon. In the process of analysis it is important for these reactions to be related back to the originating trauma, for reasons I will discuss below, as Person and Klar (1994) and van der Kolk, McFarlane, and Weisaeth (1996) point out.

Jung and the complex

Early in Jung's career he began working on a series of word association experiments with colleagues which related directly back to Charcot's and Janet's work on neurosis and hysteria, and the "nervous shocks" which underlie them. Through the subject's delayed, emotion-laden, or peculiar responses to 100 stimulus words[4] Jung was able to demonstrate the presence of "feeling-toned complexes", which he directly linked to Janet's fixed ideas (Jung, 1934).[5] Jung recognised that these complexes were split-off, splinter elements of the psyche which were unacceptable and disturbing to the conscious mind (the ego) and which conflicted with the individual's conscious attitudes. He writes, strongly echoing Janet:

a "feeling-toned complex" ... is the *image* of a certain psychic situation which is strongly accentuated emotionally and is, moreover, incompatible with the habitual attitude of consciousness. ... [I]t has ... a relatively high degree of autonomy, so that it is subject to the control of the conscious mind to only a limited extent, and therefore behaves like an animated foreign body in the sphere of consciousness. (Jung, 1934, para. 201, original italics)

He called the collection of impulses and parts of the psyche unacceptable to the ego, "the shadow" and, differently to Freud, did not see them simply as unacceptable sexual impulses that needed to be kept in check, but rather as parts of the psyche which need to be integrated (see Astor, 2002). He thought that "the opposites" were always in play with these parts of the psyche, and that if a person's conscious attitude was, for example, proper and respectable there would be another part of the personality in opposition to this that was primitive, earthy, and unsocialised (Jung, 1917/1926/1943, pp. 53ff.). He thought that one aspect of the task of development—individuation as he called it—was the recognition, acceptance, and accommodation of these opposites within the personality (the ego). For example, regarding Freud's recommendation of abreaction (the expression and release of affect) as the prime means of treating trauma, he writes, "the essential factor is the dissociation of the psyche and not the existence of a highly charged affect and, consequently, the main therapeutic problem is not abreaction, but how to integrate the dissociation" (Jung, 1921/1928, para. 266).

This emphasis on acceptance and integration is a key element in the position outlined in this book. Regarding integration, Jung thought that "the symptom ... helps to give expression to the unrecognized side of the psyche" (Jung, 1917/1926/1943, para. 27).

Jung cites one example of an attractive young woman who was admitted to hospital with melancholia, although this diagnosis was later changed to schizophrenia (Jung, 1963, pp. 135ff.). She had some years previously been romantically interested in the son of a wealthy industrialist, but believing he did not return her affections, she had married someone else and had had two children. Five years later an old friend who was visiting her told her that her marriage had been a great shock to this young man who had, it now emerged, had feelings for her. At that moment her depression set in. Worse was to follow, however, as, when bathing her children a few weeks later, being preoccupied with her dark and unhappy thoughts, she had allowed her daughter to suck on a sponge laden with bathwater—the water used for bathing in that area was not safe to drink. The young girl fell ill with typhoid and died; she had been her mother's favourite. At this point her depression became acute and she was admitted to hospital.

From the word association tests Jung ascertained that the young woman felt she was a murderer and felt extremely guilty about what she had done, as well as grieving the loss of the industrialist's son. When Jung told her what he had found he reports that "the result was that in two weeks it proved possible to discharge her, and she was never again institutionalized" (Jung, 1963, p. 137).

However, like Freud, Jung's focus and interest in the originating traumas themselves waned and he came to explain the experiences of being overwhelmed and taken over by powerful parts of the personality in terms of the archetypal layer of the psyche. Writing specifically about regression and the recreation of the "infantile milieu" he says:

> A person sinks into his childhood memories and vanishes from the existing world. He finds himself apparently in deepest darkness, but then has unexpected visions of a world beyond. The "mystery" he beholds represents the stock of primordial images which everybody brings with him as his human birthright, the sum total of inborn forms peculiar to the instincts. I have called this "potential" psyche the collective unconscious. (Jung, 1911–12, para 631)[6]

I will be exploring the powerful/overwhelming characteristics of what Jung calls the pre-infantile period that he describes as archetypal, but will suggest this has more to do with the disruption of ego-functioning and the characteristic operation of the core self. I believe that the visions from the collective unconscious that he describes have a more personal nature that he supposes, as I will be describing in Chapter Eighteen which explores Jung's own early relational trauma. I will also be proposing a developed view of Jung's concept of the complex in Chapters Five and Six, which I will suggest offers us a very good framework within which to explore the individual's reaction to trauma.

Ferenczi and the object relations school

An early casualty of this theoretical split concerning reality *vs.* phantasy within the psychoanalytic profession itself was Freud's relationship with his close colleague Sándor Ferenczi. Ferenczi effectively became ostracised from the psychoanalytic community over his pioneering work focusing on his patients' actual experiences of trauma and, in particular, sexual abuse.

Ferenczi described eloquently how the main defence available to a child who is helpless and vulnerable in the face of an overpowering adult is an "identification with the aggressor", whereby the child identifies with the abuser's perspective, keeping the abuser "good". He described how the child cannot bear too much "shock", how too many shocks lead to fragmentation and dissociation (Ferenczi, 1932a, 1932b), how trauma disrupts memory so that it may be necessary to repeat the trauma in the benign, more favourable circumstances of the analysis so that it can be "perceived by the subject for the first time" (Ferenczi, 1985). Ferenczi held that whether or not another adult, for example, the mother, supports the child's view that an abuse has occurred will be crucial to whether the child is able to metabolise the experience (Ferenczi, 1932a; Peláez, 2009).

Peláez (2009) suggests the disagreement between Freud and Ferenczi may have been due to a fundamental disagreement about trauma, with Ferenczi resuscitating a view of trauma that emphasised real-world experience, akin to Freud's seduction theory, which Freud had abandoned, as well as challenging Freud's view of the death instinct which Ferenczi felt was a reaction triggered by the object rather than being intrinsic to the subject.

On the other hand, Michael Balint (who was Ferenczi's patient), suggests that the rift between Ferenczi and Freud might have been due not only to the differing emphasis and understanding between the men, but also to Ferenczi's techniques and attitudes in response to the patients' traumas and the regressions associated with them. Balint describes how Ferenczi "respond[ed] positively to the patient's expectations, demands, or needs, now that he had learned to understand them in their true significance" (Balint, 1968, p. 151).

Balint suggests that Ferenczi might have misinterpreted Freud's concerns over the relaxation of "classical" attitudes and techniques regarding abstinence, as opposition, and have felt that he was not being understood (Balint, 1968, ch. 23). Instead, Balint suggests that it might well have been that Freud was cautious due to both his own experience with malignant regressions and that of his colleagues, such as Jung, who did not maintain their analytic boundaries on occasion, for example, with his patient Sabina Spielrein, as was well known to Freud.

Balint claims that Ferenczi was aware of the problems associated with his methods, in particular, that the improvements in his patients only lasted "as long as he was able to satisfy their cravings" (ibid., p. 151). Ferenczi's alteration of his methods is very significant and I will be exploring the pressures put on the analyst by the patient's distress, and what may be enacted as a result, in Chapter Eleven. I will suggest that the impasse can be resolved if the analyst can appreciate their role in embodying "inhuman" aspects of the patient's early relational trauma.

Klein

Melanie Klein is perhaps the person most associated with emphasising the internal object and downgrading the significance of the real-world, external object. She followed on from Freud's emphasis on the drives and took up his understanding of the death instinct as a primary way of understanding the patient's apparently self-destructive behaviour as expressed, for example, in their "resistance" to getting better, which Freud described in terms of the negative therapeutic reaction. As Jean Knox puts it, for Klein, "[e]xternal events are perceived and reorganised within the framework of the relevant pre-existing unconscious phantasy and frequently distorted by it (Perlow, 1995: 157)" (Knox, 2003b, p. 210). Klein specifically disagreed with Fairbairn's view that "to begin with only the bad object is internalized" (Klein, 1946, p. 3), holding instead that "anxiety arises from the operation of the death instinct within the organism" (p. 4).

The British object relations school

In contrast to Klein and the Kleinian school, the British object relations school, including Fairbairn, Guntrip, Balint, Winnicott, and others did maintain the significance of real world trauma and in particular early relational trauma. Winnicott writes, for example:

> The feeling of the mother's existence lasts x minutes. If the mother is away more than x minutes, then the imago fades, and along with this the baby's capacity to use the symbol of the union ceases to be a fact. The baby is distressed, but this distress is soon *mended* because

the mother returns in x + y minutes. But in x + y + z minutes the baby has become *traumatized*. In x + y + z minutes the mother's return does not mend the baby's altered state. Trauma implies that the baby has experienced a break in life's continuity, so that primitive defences now become organized to defend against a repetition of "unthinkable anxiety" or of the acute confusional state that belongs to disintegration of the emerging ego structure. (Winnicott, 1967, p. 369, original italics)

Jean Knox (1999) suggests that contemporary psychoanalysis has returned to an appreciation of trauma in recognising the role of anxiety aroused by traumatic events, and extending the understanding of trauma to include attachment and separation issues. Knox suggests that the work of Joseph Sandler on the significance of representations offers an alternate way of understanding the psyche to that of the drive model. Knox writes:

Sandler suggested that internalization is the core process; it is an organizing activity whereby mental models are gradually built up in the mind of the infant. This organizing activity eventually creates a "representational world", which provides a mental map both of the external world and of the child's own sensory responses; it depends on the child's perceptions whereby information is taken in via the senses and then organized into meaningful patterns in the mind, mental representations. (1999, p. 518)

Knox goes on to suggest that Sandler's understanding of how representations are internalised and developed is coherent with Bowlby's understanding of internal working models and Stern's conceptualisation of RIGs (representations of interactions that are generalised), or what he would later call "ways of being with others" (Stern, 1985/1998), and that these can all be understood to be very close to Jung's understanding of the complex. I would suggest that, in addition, the complex embodies the individual's primitive defensive reactions to the trauma (see Chapter Five).

The wilderness years for trauma

The acknowledgement of the significance of trauma has had a curious, troubled, and sometimes tragic history, with the same phenomena having to be rediscovered by subsequent generations; as van der Kolk, Weisaeth, and van der Hart (1996) put it,

> the importance of psychic trauma has taken the strange form of a "repetition compulsion". Because of periodic denials about the reality of trauma's effects on the human soma and psyche, hard-earned knowledge has been repeatedly lost and subsequently rediscovered *de novo*. (p. 67)

Within psychoanalysis the main emphasis has remained on the individual's conflicted drives and phantasies. In the psychiatric field, particularly concerning war trauma and "shell shock", the issue of trauma frequently became politicised; for example, in Germany, Bonhoeffer and his colleagues believed that the real cause of traumatic neuroses among their patients was the availability of compensation to the victims—a secondary gain (ibid., p. 51).

Post-traumatic stress disorder

Particularly following the Vietnam war there was a pressing need for war veterans' experiences to be recognised, and following the work of Chaim Shatan and Robert Lifton, as well as Sarah Haley, the clinical description of PTSD was finally recognised in the American Psychiatric Association's *Diagnostic and Statistical Manual of Mental Disorders, Volume III* in 1980 (APA, 1980).

One of the main threads in the rediscovery and rehabilitation of the significance of trauma and the gradual development of the diagnosis of PTSD, was the work of Abram Kardiner, who

> built on Freud's observations concerning the alternating repetitions and defensive processes so characteristic of traumatic neurosis. He added the idea that the traumatic event has a direct physiological impact on the individual; he also emphasised that the traumatic event initiates a neurotic reaction that is not accounted for by pre-morbid factors. (Brett, 1996, p. 120)

Kardiner (1941) noted that "pathological traumatic syndrome" consists of an altered conception of the self in relation to the world, based on being fixated on the trauma and having an atypical dream life, with chronic irritability, startle reactions, and explosive aggressive reactions. He believed this was due to the fact that "the ego dedicates itself to the specific job of ensuring the security of the organism, and of trying to protect itself against recollection of the trauma" (ibid., p. 184, quoted in van der Kolk, Weisaeth, & van der Hart, 1996, p. 57). He thought of the trauma as a "*physio*neurosis" where the biological system remains "ever present and unchanged" in the state in which it was at the time of the original trauma.

Post-traumatic stress disorder (PTSD) is diagnosed when an individual experiences disturbing recurrent flashbacks, avoidance or numbing of memories of the event, and hyperarousal, which persist for more than a month after the traumatic event, resulting in "significant distress or impairment of major domains of life activity". Van der Kolk, Weisaeth, and van der Hart state that "[d]issociation at the moment of the trauma appears to be the single most important predictor for the establishment of chronic PTSD" (ibid., p. 66).

Although the work had initially been focused on war veterans, from the 1980s there was a slow recognition and in fact a growing demand, that women's traumatic experience be recognised as well, particularly in relation to sexual abuse. Judith Herman (1981), Herman and Schatzow (1987), Alice Miller (1981, 1984), Leonard Shengold (1975, 1979, 1989, 1992), and others, as well as, polemically, Jeffrey Masson (1984) insisted that the significance of the actual abuse was being deplorably overlooked. A powerful feminist critique/perspective developed to address this, which powerfully critiqued psychoanalysis for ignoring the actual plight of women and children (Courtois, 2010, pp. 233ff.).

In parallel, and outside of psychoanalysis, people who had been working with individuals who had been raped or sexually abused were acutely aware of the pressing need for these individuals' experiences to be recognised. These therapists developed their own treatment protocols and methods, often deeply informed by the feminist perspective (see Courtois, 2010; Herman, 1992). As already described, Judith Herman, recognising the deeply problematic effects of chronic early trauma, went on to delineate Complex PTSD (1992) and van der Kolk has detailed what he called developmental trauma disorder[7] (2005).

Later editions of the American Psychiatric Association's DSM have further refined and developed the classification of PTSD and trauma. For example, whilst in 1980, in DSM III, PTSD was diagnosed as a form of anxiety disorder, by 2013, in DSM V, it was recognised in its own right as a trauma and stress-related disorder. In fact, DSM V represents a marked shift in the acknowledgement of the significance of trauma underlying many psychiatric syndromes.

In 1992 Davies and Frawley (1992a) published their landmark paper on working psychoanalytically with people who have been sexually abused. Their paper and subsequent book (1994) are required reading for anyone working in the field, and I will refer to them frequently in what follows.

Kalsched (1996, 2013), Knox (1999, 2003a, 2003b), Wilkinson (2006, 2010), and Wirtz (2014) have also done much to introduce the perspective of trauma into Jungian analysis, as I will be exploring later.

"The body remembers"

A fundamental recognition by those working with people who have experienced trauma is the powerful somatic and affective reactions, the "*physio*neurosis" as Kardiner called it. Rothschild (2000), from whom I have taken the quote "the body remembers" for this section, was one of the first to try to integrate the findings that had emerged through work on trauma with mainstream psychotherapy. In a clear and succinct manner she described how the effects of trauma are remembered by the body, and the way that they emerge and can be worked with in therapy. This book aims to extend her work to include early relational trauma that has been more thoroughly and conflictually embodied and elaborated within the personality.

Pat Ogden, Kekuni Minton, and Clare Pain (2006) have developed a thoroughgoing sensorimotor approach to trauma, which draws together much of what has been learnt about trauma and is an important resource for anyone interested in the field. They recognise that the reactions to trauma are held in the primitive parts of the brain, and they call on Paul MacLean's (1990)[8] concept of the "triune brain" (three brains in one) to help understand the complex interrelation of somatic, affective, and cognitive functioning in the brain.

MacLean's triune brain theory holds that the most primitive part of the brain—the "reptilian brain" (the basal ganglia)—is a basic motor system responsible for innate behavioural knowledge and responses related to exploration, fear, anger, and sexuality (this is shared with many animals). In addition there is the old "mammalian brain" (the limbic system), which holds affective knowledge and reactions, including social emotions such as maternal acceptance and care, social bonding, separation distress, and rough and tumble play (shared with many mammals). "On top of" this there is the "neomammalian brain" (the neocortex), which provides the higher cognitive functions and declarative/propositional knowledge (mostly human functions which may be shared to a limited extent with certain other mammals) (Panksepp, 1998, pp. 42 ff. & ch. 4). As Ogden, Minton, and Pain put it, "the three levels of information processing—sensorimotor, emotional, and cognitive—can be thought of as roughly correlating with the three levels of brain architecture [reptilian, mammalian, neomammalian]" (2006, p. 5).

A striking example of the sensorimotor effects of trauma was described by Peter Levine (2005, p. 26) in mammals.[9] He describes a video of a polar bear that is chased down by an airplane, shot with a tranquilliser dart, and then tagged. As the animal comes out of its state of shock it begins to tremble; this trembling intensifies into a near-convulsive shaking and, when that stops, the bear takes some deep breaths and appears to recover. Reviewing the convulsive shaking in slow-motion, Levine notes that the movements are actually co-ordinated running, biting, and fighting movements, and he suggests that this corresponds with the bear completing the escape that was interrupted when it was tranquillised.

Levine has described how in humans, "incompleted action tendencies" of fight, flight, freeze, or collapse can also become frozen and locked into the body. Reconnecting with the body and completing these action tendencies on the physical level allows the person to heal from the trauma. His work aims to allow discharge of this reaction and to connect the individual to other action tendencies that might be more empowering, for example, the fight response. In later chapters I will be describing working through experiences of collapse, submission, and defeat and corresponding experiences of death and annihilation.

Janet described how incompleted actions lead people to live in the past, whilst Freud described the phenomenon in terms of repetition compulsion. As Ogden, Minton, and Pain put it: "[l]ong after the original traumatic events are over, many individuals find themselves compelled to anticipate, orient to, and react to stimuli that directly or indirectly resemble the original traumatic experience or its context" (2006, p. 65). Or as Herman (1992) writes:

> When neither resistance nor escape is possible, the human system of self-defense becomes overwhelmed and disorganized. Each component of the ordinary response to danger, having lost its utility, tends to persist in an altered and exaggerated state long after the actual danger is over. (p. 34)

When there has been traumatic experience, powerful sensorimotor and affective responses (embodied in the traumatic complex) disrupt cognitive functioning; as van der Kolk, McFarlane, and Weisaeth put it:

> In many regards, PTSD should be considered as an information-processing disorder that interferes with the processing and integration of current life experience. Individuals with this condition become overwhelmed by both the extraordinary overload of information associated with the traumatic memory, which they are then unable to integrate, as well as the lower demand characteristics of the day-to-day environment. The disruption of memory and concentration and the emotional numbing in PTSD are indicative of broader problems in managing and processing day-to-day stimuli. (van der Kolk, McFarlane, & Weisaeth, 1996, p. x)

As a result, there is a difficulty in addressing traumatic experience exclusively by means of "top-down" cognitive processing. As Ogden, Minton, and Pain describe, "[f]or the traumatized individual … the intensity of trauma-related emotions and sensorimotor reactions hinders the ability of top-down processing to dominate subcortical activity" (2006, p. 9). Or as van der Kolk puts it:

> Describing traumatic experiences in conventional verbal therapy is likely to activate implicit memories in the form of trauma-related physical sensations, physiological dysregulation, involuntary movements, and the accompanying emotions of helplessness, fear, shame, and rage, without providing the resources to process these nonverbal remnants of the past. When this sequence occurs, trauma victims are likely to feel that it still is not safe to deal with the trauma; instead they will tend to seek a supportive relationship in the present. The therapist thereby becomes a refuge from a

life marked by ineffectiveness and futility. (Ogden, Minton, & Pain, 2006, p. xxiv)

Ogden, Minton, and Pain therefore recommend working directly with the sensorimotor sequelae of the trauma, for example, by asking a client

> to mindfully track (a top-down, cognitive process) the sequence of physical sensations and impulses (sensorimotor process) as they progress through the body, and to temporarily disregard emotions and thoughts that arise, until the bodily sensations and impulses resolve to a point of rest and stabilization. (Ogden, Minton, & Pain, 2006, p. 24)

In regard to their way of working overall they write:

> Top-down approaches that attempt to regulate overwhelming sensorimotor and affective processes are a necessary part of trauma therapy, but if such interventions overmanage, ignore, suppress, or fail to support adaptive body processes, these traumatic responses may not be resolved. Similarly, bottom-up interventions that result in bottom-up hijacking, or fail to include cognitive and emotional processing, can sabotage integration and may lead to endless repetitive flashbacks, secondary retraumatization, or chronic trauma kindling (Post, Weiss, Smith, Li, & McCann, 1997). In order to treat the effects of trauma on all three levels of processing, somatically informed top-down management of symptoms, insight and understanding, and bottom-up processing of sensations, arousal, movement, and emotions must be thoughtfully balanced. (ibid., p. 25)

In regard to the triggering and potentially retraumatising effect of working with trauma, Ogden, Minton, and Pain describe the hyper- and hypo-arousal that is a central feature of trauma, as is described in relation to PTSD above, and describe how individuals frequently oscillate between these two extremes.

Hyperarousal is the experiencing of "too much" activation to be able to process information effectively, and the individual is tormented by hypervigilance, intrusive images, powerful affects, and body sensations. Hypoarousal is the experiencing of "too little" activation—a numbing sense of deadness or emptiness, passivity and possibly paralysis, being too distanced from the experience to process it effectively. Both poles interfere with cognitive functioning (ibid., p. 26).

Hyperarousal mobilises energy in anticipation of vigorous activity enabling us to carry out fight and flight responses (Levine, 1997; Rothschild, 2000). Because of the accelerated pace of emotions, sensations, and sensory stimuli, however, the capacity for reflection is disrupted and the individual's behaviour is often reactive and impulsive (Ogden, Minton, & Pain, 2006, p. 34)—a characteristic often noted in the functioning of individuals with a borderline personality organisation. Hypoarousal enables survival-related immobilisation responses such as freeze, submission, and collapse, as well as loss of memory, motor weakness, passivity, fugue, and confusional states. Whilst all of these reactions may be life-saving at the time of the trauma, they can be extremely problematic and maladaptive if they persist in the long term.

Bremner (1999) proposed there are two types of PTSD (Lanius et al., 2010), one characterised by hyperarousal, with a re-experiencing of intrusive flashbacks, the other characterised by hypoarousal, primarily involving dissociative symptoms (see also Schmahl, Lanius, Pain, & Vermetten, 2010).

Siegel (1999) has recognised how these more primitive reactions interfere with cognitive functioning and the individual's ability to effectively work on the trauma, and he described the traumatised individual's "window of tolerance" between hyperarousal and hypoarousal in which the individual can "think and talk about their experience in therapy and simultaneously feel a congruent emotional tone and sense of self". Ogden, Minton, and Pain recommend that "[t]herapists must consistently employ techniques facilitating interactive repair to keep clients' arousal within a window of tolerance" (2006, p. 61). They write: "We suggest that these potential changes in orienting are more easily developed in the client by helping them *practice* changing their orientation process on a sensorimotor level rather than through discussion" (p. 69, original italics). And Jean Knox writes: "A patient whose attempts to work through past trauma triggers acute primary dissociation, or the frozen numbness of secondary dissociation, is not free to imaginatively explore fantasies and dreams" (2013, p. 496).

Stephen Porges (1995, 2004, 2005, 2011) has explored the interaction between the parasympathetic and sympathetic nervous systems and developed his "polyvagal theory", which describes different forms of response to threat, relating it to the activation of different branches of the vagal nerve. He argues that the most developed response to threat is through activation of the ventral parasympathetic branch of the vagal nerve, which governs social engagement (alertness, control of facial muscles, head tilting and turning, muscles governing prosody, eye and ear regulation) allowing the individual to engage optimally with others and, under threat, to reason with a potential attacker.

His theory holds that if this system does not work, the more primitive, mammalian, sympathetic system is engaged, with the amygdala "sounding the alarm", readying the individual to meet the threat with heightened alertness and ultimately ready for fight or flight.

If this system is also unsuccessful in assuring safety, the most primitive response in the vagal hierarchy, the other branch of the parasympathetic nervous system—the unmyelinated dorsal branch of the vagus nerve—triggers the primitive, reptilian, freeze or collapse responses (he uses the term freeze to cover both freeze and collapse). This enables survival-related immobilisation such as feigning death, behavioural shutdown, fainting, and collapse.

It is worth noting that the neuroscientist Jaak Panksepp understands the mammalian defence systems not to be discrete systems in their own right, although he acknowledges these patterns of behaviour do occur (1998, p. 203 & p. 391 fn. 95) but to emerge from more basic systems, namely the "highly overlapping and interactive emotional systems" of RAGE and FEAR.[10] He describes seven such systems in all (although he acknowledges there may be others). The first four "primal emotional circuits" mature soon after birth, they are the SEEKING, RAGE, FEAR, and PANIC systems, and these are supplemented by the "more sophisticated" LUST, CARE, and PLAY systems.

He understands the fight response to be an activation of the RAGE system, the flight response to be the FEAR system activated intensely, the freeze response as the FEAR system activated mildly, and the collapse response as the activation of the PANIC system (1998, p. 54).[11] He says the PANIC system, named after a panic attack, "generates loneliness and separation" and "is important in the elaboration of social emotional processes related to attachment" (p. 52).

Before leaving this chapter it is important to note that trauma theorists such as van der Kolk, Ogden, Minton, and Pain (2006) and many others are critical of psychoanalytic theory and psychoanalytic approaches to trauma. This is not only because of psychoanalysis' attitude to trauma in the past, but also because of what is seen as a concentration on and overemphasis of the cognitive elements, whilst (relatively) ignoring the affective and somatic elements, as well as the retraumatising effects of its methods: primarily addressing the cognitive rather than the affective-somatic level, not assisting the individual to manage hyper- and hypo-activation, nor assisting the patient to remain within the window of tolerance. The overall criticism is that its methods are anti-relational, inhuman, and retraumatising and do not recognise or address the trauma as primary.

Somewhat oversimplifying you could say that trauma therapy concentrates on the effects of the trauma on the individual, whilst psychoanalysis concentrates on the individual's inner, elaborated response to trauma and that frequently the link to the trauma has been lost. I would suggest that these form the two sides of the same coin, and that both are not only necessary but the links between the two need to be clearly delineated.

In the following chapter I will look at early relational trauma from relational and attachment perspectives, particularly bringing in the work of John Bowlby and of Beatrice Beebe and Frank Lachmann. In that context I will be exploring the foundational behavioural patterns from a neuroscientific, attachment, and psychoanalytic perspective. I will be exploring the conflict between analytic and trauma-centred attitudes and techniques in later chapters, especially Eleven, Thirteen, and Seventeen.

Notes

1. van der Kolk (2013—conference in Boston, USA) states that EMDR is successful in less than twenty per cent of such situations.
2. First, stabilisation, symptom-oriented treatment, and preparation for addressing of traumatic memories; second, identification, exploration, and modification of traumatic memories; third, relapse prevention, relief of residual symptomatology, personality reintegration, and rehabilitation.
3. He named his eldest son Jean-Martin in Charcot's honour (van der Kolk, 2014, p. 181).
4. Words such as bread, table, war, ink, love, dog, head, faithful, water, stroke, and lamp.
5. Mary Main "noted that the various forms of insecure attachment are directly discernible in the dysfluencies and incoherence in narrative process, markers of which include changes of voice, contradictions,

lapses, irrelevancies, and breakdowns in meaning during discussions of familial relationships" (Slade, 2008, p. 773).

6. He also writes: "The personal layer ends at the earliest memories of infancy, but the collective layer comprises the pre-infantile period, that is, the residues of ancestral life" (Jung, 1917/1926/1943, para. 118).

7. Which is understood to follow from multiple exposures to interpersonal trauma such as abandonment, betrayal, physical or sexual assaults, or witnessing domestic violence (van der Kolk, 2014, pp. 359–362).

8. MacLean originally developed his concept in the 1960s and presented it further in his book *The Triune Brain in Evolution* (1990). The neuroscientist Jaak Panksepp (1998, p. 43) says that the concept of the triune brain is a simplification from a neuroanatomical point of view, yet it is a useful tool in helping us understand these complex processes.

9. van der Kolk, Greenberg, Boyd, and Krystal (1985) point out that the vast literature on how animals respond to extreme stress has proved to be extremely helpful.

10. Panksepp (1998, p. 51) uses upper case letters to refer to the "genetically ingrained brain emotional operating systems" and to distinguish these systems from specific feelings or functions. For example, he used to call the SEEKING system the curiosity/interest/foraging/anticipation/craving/expectancy system—it is clear why he wanted a snappier name! Essentially the SEEKING system functions "to coax animals to move from where they are to where they can consume the fruits of the world" (ibid., p. 54).

11. This appears to conflict with Porges' understanding, which links the freeze response to the more primitive, reptilian system through a different branch of the vagus nerve.

CHAPTER FOUR

The relational and attachment perspective

Attachment and intersubjectivity

A paper that is central to this book, and one that is surely required reading for all psychotherapists, is the Boston Change Process Study Group's[1] (2007) paper, "The foundational level of psychodynamic meaning: implicit process in relation to conflict, defense, and the dynamic unconscious". In that paper the authors write:

> Relational transactions involving action and interaction have been considered the "surface" level of meaning in previous analytic theorizing. However, the level of implicit relational knowing encodes the most profound aspects of human experience, including their elements of conflict, defense and affective resistance, and this level can no longer be considered "surface" or superficial. … The "deep" level, as depicted in our interpretations, is in fact derived from the "surface" level of moment-to-moment exchange. In this framework we assert that the local level, where implicit relational knowing is enacted, is the foundational level of psychic life. It is where psychodynamic happenings, including affect, conflict, and defense, originate. (p. 144)

As an example, the Boston Change Group describe an extract from a videotaped home observation of a young depressed mother and her eighteen-month-old toddler. They write as follows:

> the mother is sitting on the couch and her son is also on the couch sitting a foot or two away from her drinking from his bottle. She is sitting stiffly in the far corner of the sofa staring into space, smoking a cigarette with one hand and resting her other arm along the back of the couch in the direction of her son. Her toddler finishes his bottle and stands up on the couch, bouncing up and down for a minute or two. Then he pauses before flopping over on to his mother's lap. At this point, without moving her stiff and remote arms, she jerks her head towards him and barks, "I *told* you not to jump on the couch!" … Given the timing of her attack, her distaste did not have to do with his standing on or bouncing on the couch but with his making playful physical contact with her. In other sequences on the same videotape we see her son walk up to her and reach out his hand towards her knee, only to pull it away suddenly before actually touching her. (p. 146)

They continue:

> His mother's aversion to affectionate touch appears to have led him to inhibit his own initiatives around seeking physical contact with his mother. As this pattern is repeated over time, it is being preserved as part of his implicit relational knowing and is likely to color later interactions with others. (p. 146)

The "implicit relational knowing" that the Boston Change Group describe is a developed version of John Bowlby's concept of internal working models based in his attachment theory, on which so many of the workers in this field call. I will briefly outline his theory here.

Attachment theory

John Bowlby observed a pattern of angry protest followed by despair when young children were separated from their mothers (Robertson & Bowlby, 1952). He was not convinced by the explanation given by psychoanalytic theory that suggested this was because the mother feeds the infant and that the pleasure experienced upon having hunger drives satisfied becomes associated with the mother's presence (Cassidy, 2008). Bowlby recognised that infants become attached to their caregivers even if they do not feed them and he hypothesised that this attachment has a biological basis which he linked to Darwin's evolutionary theory. Thus, "genetic selection favoured attachment behaviours because they increased the likelihood of child–mother proximity, which in turn increased the likelihood of protection and provided survival advantage" (Cassidy, 2008, p. 4).

There was therefore no need for attachment to be viewed as the by-product of a more fundamental process or "drive". This theorising in terms of an "attachment behavioural system" brought Bowlby into conflict with the psychoanalytic community by which he was, for many decades, ostracised.[2] Bowlby also challenged psychoanalysis' privileging of fantasy over reality in psychological functioning (Slade, 2008), presaging the line trauma theorists were to take some years later.

Bowlby had a fruitful collaboration with Mary Ainsworth who studied infants' attachment in the light of Bowlby's proposals, and later developed an assessment tool called the "Strange Situation", which allowed a classification of different attachment styles—anxious–avoidant and anxious–resistant—as is described in some depth below. In addition to the attachment system, Bowlby described other behavioural systems: the exploratory, defence, sociability, caregiving, play, energy regulation, and sexuality systems.

Bowlby's and Ainsworth's work was taken forward by Mary Main who developed a third category of attachment, "disorganised" (Main & Solomon, 1990) and this has further been supplemented by the category of "unable to classify" (Hesse, 1996). Main also, importantly, demonstrated the link between early forms of attachment and adult psychopathology. She developed the Adult Attachment Interview (AAI) (George, Kaplan, & Main, 1985) and postulated that early forms of attachment had their counterparts in adult attachment patterns (Main, Kaplan, & Cassidy, 1985), as follows:

- Anxious/avoidant infant classification—"dismissing" adult attachment classification.
- Anxious/resistant infant classification—"preoccupied" adult attachment classification.

- Disorganised/disoriented infant classification—unresolved adult attachment classification.

Hesse (1996) later described a "cannot classify" category of adult attachment. These are all forms of insecure attachment.

Researchers into adult attachment tend to describe attachment in relation to two vertices—avoidance and anxiety. Behaviours associated with the dismissive attachment style are "avoidant", "deactivating", and "dismissing", whilst behaviours associated with the preoccupied attachment style are "anxious", "hyperactivating", and "preoccupied" (Slade, 2008, p. 766). Slade suggests that the dismissive modes downplay and minimise affect—she describes these as obsessional defences, while the preoccupied modes maximise and intensify affect in order to establish closeness—she describes these as hysterical defences (p. 771). Another dimension that is recognised is that of organised *vs.* disorganised, which relates to the degree of psychological structure available for containing and regulating emotional experience (p. 771)—this is another way of describing the level of ego-functioning that Jung, following Janet, described as an *abaissement du niveau mental.*

Main's work provided an invaluable bridge to psychoanalytic theory, and in particular object relations theory, as her and her colleagues' work was providing evidence that "the quality of early experience, and particularly early relationship, influences adult ways of thinking, knowing, and feeling … and [that] the effect of such influences is routinely transmitted from one generation to the next at the level of *structure*, rather than *content*" (ibid., p. 771, original italics).

These propositions are central to both attachment theory and object relations theory. As Fonagy, Gergely, and Target (2008) also add in their review of the commonality between psychoanalysis and attachment theory, "intense relationship experiences are internalized and aggregated over time, thereby forming schematic mental structures that shape both later interpersonal expectations and self-representations" (p. 784).

Bowlby called these internal working models, Stern incorporated this into his concept of "representations of interactions that are generalized" or, as he later called them, "ways of being with others" (Stern, 1985/1998), Lichtenberg (1989) developed the concept of "model scenes", Bretherton (1991) called them "scripts", Bucci (1993, 2011) called them "emotional schemas", and Lyons-Ruth (1998) developed the concept of "implicit interpersonal knowledge". Understanding interactions in terms of the attachment behavioural system is a very broad brushstroke approach, whereas calling on internal working models allows a great deal more individual detail (Fonagy, 2001, p. 12).

One of the difficulties in integrating the insights from attachment theory is that, at first, the findings from research in relation to the classification of attachment patterns for infants was difficult to apply to work with adults. Whilst Main's work in relation to adults has taken this forward a great deal (see, for example Slade, 2008 or Liotti, 2004a, 2007, described below), the approach outlined in this book, integrating a trauma and an analytic approach, deconstructs the attachment patterns still further by looking at the conflicts and dynamics involved, for example, in being drawn towards and at the same time pushing away someone upon whom you rely (a disorganised attachment pattern—see below).

Mentalization

Peter Fonagy and his colleagues have further developed one aspect of attachment theory, focusing on the finding that the

> security of infant attachment proved to be strongly predicted not only by that parent's security of attachment during pregnancy (Fonagy, Steele, & Steele, 1991), but even more by the parents' capacity to understand their own childhood relationships with their own parents in terms of states of mind (Fonagy, Steele, Moran, Steele, & Higgit, 1991). (Fonagy, Gergely, & Target, 2008, pp. 792–793)

They refer to this ability to understand interpersonal behaviour in terms of mental states as "mentalization" and "reflective function". This involves both a self-reflective and an interpersonal component, is both implicit and explicit, and concerns both feelings and cognition.

It is, perhaps, important to note that the notion of the impairment or lack of development of mentalization overlaps with the recognition that trauma/early relational trauma disrupts cognition and ego-functioning, as recognised by trauma theorists, although Fonagy and his colleagues' explanation tends to suggest more cognitive and intentional processes at work. Fonagy, Gergely, and Target (2008, pp. 796–797) sum up the effects of early experience on mentalization as follows:

> Considered in relation to attachment, mentalization deficits associated with childhood maltreatment may be a form of decoupling, inhibition, or even a phobic reaction to mentalizing. First, adversity may undermine cognitive development in general (Cicchetti, Rogosch, & Toth, 2000; Crandell & Hobson, 1999). Mentalization problems may also reflect arousal problems associated with exposure to chronic stress (see Cicchetti & Walker, 2001). Finally, a child may avoid mentalization to avoid perceiving an abuser's frankly hostile and malevolent thoughts and feelings about him or her. (e.g., Fonagy, 1991)

Fonagy, Gergely, Jurist, and Target (2002) explicitly describe the impact of early experience on mentalization in respect to borderline personality disorder, where they detail how

> failing to find *himself* in his mother's mind, [he] finds the mother instead. The infant is forced to internalize the representation of the object's state of mind as a core part of himself. But in such cases the internalized other remains *alien* and unconnected to the structures of the constitutional self. (p. 11, original italics)

They go on to described how the child dissociates from pain by using the alien self to identify with the aggressor and that this involves:

> (a) a further repudiation of mentalization, at least in attachment contexts, (b) disruption of the psychological self by the emergence of a torturing other within the self, and (c) vital dependence on the physical presence of the other as a vehicle for externalisation. These features, in combination, account for many aspects of disordered functioning in borderline patients. (pp. 12–13)

This is another way of describing the conflict inherent at the core of the individual's identity (point (b) above), although I would suggest that the relationship with the traumatising other becomes embodied and elaborated in the individual's own personality through (trauma-related) internal working models. The earlier and more centrally related to key caregivers this experience is, the more it is inherent, albeit conflictually, in the individual's core identity.

I will discuss the challenge of helping a client come to terms with such hostile relationships, as well as conflicting beliefs and attitudes— which they call the alien self—particularly as they are constellated in the analytic relationship in Chapters Five, Six, Seven, and Ten.

Liotti's attachment and relational theory perspective

Giovanni Liotti (2004a, 2007) is one of many who links adult psycho- pathology to disorganised attachment patterns. Liotti cites Schuengel, Van Ijzendoorn and Bakermans-Kranenburg (1999), as having gathered "[e]mpirical evidence that not only aggressive attitudes, but also fright- ened and dissociative behaviour of the caregiver towards the infant can cause disorganization in the infant's attachment behaviour" (Liotti, 2007, p. 128). He explains the origins of disorganised attachment in terms of a conflict between two different inborn control systems—the attachment system and the fight/flight (i.e., defence) system. He writes:

> The attachment and defence systems normally operate in harmony as exemplified in flight from the source of fear to find refuge in proximity to the attachment figure. However, where the caregiver is at the same time the source and the solution of the infant's fear, there is a clash (Liotti, 2004a, b). Being exposed to frequent interac- tions with a helplessly frightened, hostile, frightening, or confused caregiver, infants are caught in a relational trap: their defence sys- tem motivates them to flee from the frightened and/or frightening caregivers, while at the same time their attachment system moti- vates them, under the commanding influence of separation fear, to strive to achieve comforting proximity to them. Thus, the disorgan- ized infant is bound to the experience of "fright without solution" (Cassidy & Mohr, 2001; Main & Hesse, 1990, p. 163). (Liotti, 2007, p. 129)

He describes this as a "type of early relational trauma that exerts an adverse influence on the development of the system in the infant's brain that copes with stress (Schore, 2003)". He links the trauma back to the "innate contingency detection module whose function is to explore the environment in search of mirroring experiences (Koos & Gergely,

2001)", resulting in the system functioning in a seriously dysfunctional manner (see also West, 2004, 2007, & below). Specifically, it leads to a rapid "switching" between attention to the self and the other, which represents a "dissociative style of attention and information processing that researchers and theoreticians regard as typical of attachment disorganization (Liotti, 1992, 1999; Lyons-Ruth, 2003; Main & Morgan, 1996)" (Liotti, 2007, pp. 129–130). Liotti specifically relates disorganised attachment, with its concomitant dissociative processes characterised by "severe dissociation, splitting among ego states, and fragmentation of the self", with borderline functioning (ibid., p. 130).

This is the pattern of the child who at the same time clings to the caregiver and turns away from them that is described so vividly and in such detail by Beebe and Lachmann (2013—and see Chapter Seven in this book). I will give an example of this clinging for comfort whilst unable to be comforted or, put slightly differently, desperately wanting to connect whilst feeling unconnected and unable to connect, at the end of this chapter.

Liotti (2007) further describes how the caregivers' subtle or explicit reactions to their own traumas and losses might well activate the child's "caregiving system" such that "the disorganized child is likely to have an experience of the self during attachment interactions of at least three types of contradictory and reciprocally incompatible ways of responding: care-seeking, caregiving, and defensive fight/flight" (p. 135).

He describes how such individuals "typically show multiple, non-integrated dramatic representations of self and attachment figures, shifting between hostility, helplessness, and compulsive caregiving (Lyons-Ruth, Yellin, Melnick, & Atwood, 2003, 2005)". He has previously suggested (1995, 1999, 2004a, 2004b) that these representations and patterns are manifested in the "drama triangle" (Karpman, 1968) of three reciprocally incompatible roles: the helpless victim, the powerful-benevolent rescuer, and the powerful but malevolent persecutor.

These patterns are reflected in caregiving or domineering-punitive strategies that allow the child to exert some active control over the parents' attention and behaviour. These strategies give the child some relief from the unbearably chaotic experience of disorganisation by inhibiting the attachment system and activating the caregiving system, thus offering the child some degree of organisation.

Liotti also hypothesises that "some disorganized children resort to a general inhibition of relational needs and tend to withdraw from all types of close affective interaction", which he links to "schizoid personality disorder". He further hypothesises that some disorganised children resort, at times, to activation of the sexual system in order to deal defensively with attachment motivations and the activation of a disorganised internal working model. The activation of these alternate systems—aggressive, caregiving, or sexualised—offer only temporary relief and do not resolve the underlying disorganised attachment pattern (2007, p. 140). He gives the example of the collapse of the caregiving system instituted by a thirty-two year old physician on learning that her younger sister had, after all, been abused by their father, as she had (pp. 140ff.).

Like a number of relational theorists, Liotti (2007) does not work through the darker side of the trauma—how it has been incorporated into the individual—but rather attempts to bypass the individual's negative ideation, self-image, and splitting, by recommending using two different therapists who will each challenge the inevitable negative view of the other when the trauma is triggered in the transference–countertransference.

Attachment and intersubjectivity

Beatrice Beebe and Frank Lachmann (2013) describe a comprehensive study of infant–mother interactions at four months and twelve months old and attempt to trace "the origins of attachment" (the title of their book) in the four-month-old infants' interactions with their mothers.

Through microanalysis of videotaped interactions Beebe and Lachmann have developed a "dyadic systems approach" (2002, 2013), which describes how the mother and infant co-create their face-to-face communications. This occurs as "each person monitors and coordinates with the partner, and at the same time regulates his or her own inner state" (p. 5). Over time each partner develops expectancies of "how I affect you" and "how you affect me", as well as how each one's own self-regulation processes unfold. These expectancies have been variously known as implicit relational knowing (Lyons-Ruth, 1999), emotional schemas (Bucci, 1993, 2011) and internal working models (Bowlby, 1969), as described earlier.

It is important to note that this kind of implicit relational knowing is stored in what is called implicit or procedural memory, where the procedural knowledge for tasks such as walking, riding a bicycle, or driving a car are stored. This kind of memory is different from explicit, autobiographical, declarative memory as it is primarily concerned with activity that is carried out unconsciously and it is not immediately accessible through introspection (see Lyons-Ruth, 1998).[3]

Study of the video interactions showed that any particular interaction is not generated in a linear fashion, wholly in response to what the other has just done, but rather that the individual's expectancies lead them to pre-empt and prejudge what will occur and, like some subtle unconscious dance for which the steps are already half-known, the interaction is uniquely co-created by both, in line with semi-familiar patterns.

In detail, Beebe and Lachmann noted how mother and infant engage in mirroring of the other's facial expressions. They write that "the key mechanism is the perception and production of similarity" (2013, p. 26) and discuss this in terms of contingency (Ch. 3), a phenomenon I explored in earlier work linking it to adult psychopathology and the work of Matte Blanco (West, 2004, 2007). When there is a "mismatch" in the mirroring, which is entirely normal in any interaction (Tronick & Gianino, 1986), this causes distress and the mother and/or the infant may act to try to repair the mismatch. The infant attempts to do this through cooing, gesturing, crying out, or registering their distress in other ways, thus trying to re-engage the (m)other and re-establish a harmonious link.

Tronick and Gianino describe how, if the infant is successful in repairing the mismatches, they can "experience positive emotions and establish a positive affective core" (p. 156). Their effectiveness at "getting through" to the other increases their sense of agency (see Knox, 2010), and allows them to internalise a pattern of interaction that they bring to interactions with others (Tronick & Gianino, 1986, p. 156). However, if the infant is repeatedly unsuccessful in repairing mismatches they come to feel helpless, focus their behaviour on self-regulation, limit their engagement with their social environment, and "establish a negative affective core" (ibid., p. 156).

In the video material described by Beebe and Lachmann, the infants' distress at the continuing mismatch can be observed in their crying, agitation, and turning away from the mother and, in one case, of the infant being sick. This negative affective core that Tronick and Gianino describe is characteristic of individuals with a borderline psychology (Kernberg, 1975; West, 2007).

This kind of functioning, characterised by distress at mismatching, is significant as it characterises not only the early form of relationship between infant and caregiver, but also persists as a continuous form of primitive functioning that goes on unconsciously in and between adults. It is this sensitivity that, for example, makes us embarrassed by our social gaffes, bridle at criticism, feel foolish when we make a mistake, and wary of expressing what we really think in so far as it might be in conflict with the views of whatever group we are in.

Philip Bromberg, rooted in the perspective of relational psychoanalysis, defines trauma as occurring when, in relationship with another, self-invalidation or self-annihilation is inescapable, and the mind is flooded by powerful affects that disrupt the individual's capacity to think. His emphasis is on how these "precipitous psychological events … disrupt the patterns of meaning that constitute the person's overarching experience of self" or, in other words, how the normal multiplicity of self-states are unlinked so that the person's normal sense of self is disrupted. They thenceforward live their lives "in the shadow of the [emotional] tsunami" that has already occurred. The process of psychoanalysis, for Bromberg, is about helping patients reclaim their dissociated self-states (Bromberg, 2011).

In my terms, Bromberg is describing how facing, rather than avoiding, their traumatic experiences allows the individual to integrate them and develop or regain a coherent sense of self, rather than being continually alienated from themselves by the traumatic complex. It is exactly this kind of conflict in the experience of self that lies at the heart of the borderline individual's psychology.

This distress at mismatches is very significant when working with individuals whose ego-functioning has been disrupted or compromised through trauma and has developed into borderline functioning. This more primitive form of functioning (when ego-functioning is disrupted) is also known, with different emphases and extensions, as primary process functioning (Freud), beta functioning (Bion), the functioning at the basic fault (Balint), and the functioning of the paranoid-schizoid position. I will go on to describe how these early experiences become incorporated in the individual's negative, core, self-beliefs which are central to the individual and central to the work in adult psychotherapy.

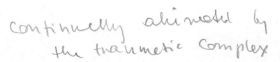
continually alienated by the traumatic complex

Disorganised patterns of attachment

Beebe and Lachmann's work demonstrates in detail how the failure to repair relational mismatches appears to link directly to particular attachment patterns. For example, using the separation-reunion test developed by Ainsworth, Blehar, Waters, and Wall (1978), known as the "Strange Situation", mother and infant participate in three-minute periods of play, separation, and reunion, whereupon the sequence is repeated a second time. In the first separation the infant remains with a "stranger", in the second the infant is alone.

In the reunion episodes, an infant is classified as having a secure attachment pattern if they can be easily comforted, using the mother as a secure base, and then return to play. Infants who show little distress at separation, avoid the mother at reunion, and continue to play on their own are classified as having an insecure–avoidant attachment pattern. Infants who are distressed at separation but cannot be comforted by the mother's return and do not easily return to play are classified as having an insecure–resistant attachment pattern.

If, in the reunion episodes, the infant simultaneously approaches and avoids the mother, for example, holding the door open for her but then ignoring her, the infant is classified as having a disorganised attachment pattern. These infants appear apprehensive and confused, and show simultaneous conflicting responses, for example, reaching their hands out to mother but at the same time backing off, or clinging to mother but with their face averted (Beebe & Lachmann, 2013, pp. 6–7). Liotti, quoted above, described a similar conflict of trying to flee from the frightened/frightening caregivers whilst at the same time being bound to them by attachment needs.

Beebe and Lachmann propose that infants who will go on to be classified as having a disorganised attachment pattern cannot develop an expectation of feeling "sensed" or "known", particularly when distressed, and that

> [d]isturbances of recognition were identified in all communication
> domains … In attention, the infant may feel not seen; in emotion
> the infant may feel not joined, and stonewalled when distressed; in
> orientation the infant experiences looming impingements; and in
> touch the infant is not touched more tenderly when he shows more

aroused touch patterns. At times these infants may feel alarmed or threatened. (ibid., p. 62)

Working with adult patients one can readily observe how they continue to experience the same kinds of distress, as if it has been locked in, waiting for recognition. If the analyst fails to recognise or respond appropriately to this distress, the same mismatches can be continually re-enacted in the analysis. Before I give an example of these kinds of interactions in the analytic setting, I will briefly discuss whether the kinds of experiences I have just described should be understood in terms of trauma.

Trauma, early relational trauma, and trauma-related internal working models

Beebe and Lachmann write:

> The intense distress experience of future disorganized infants is often agitated and frantic, and at moments alarmed or threatened. When threatened we change from a state which is open to social engagement to states of fight–flight, freeze, or collapse (Porges, Doussard-Roosevelt, & Maiti, 1994). Clinically we observed such behaviours in future disorganized infants at 4 months. For example, after one mother greeted her intensely distressed infant with a big smile, we observed highly active, forceful infant movements of jerking the body while turning away from mother in the chair, which could be considered a precursor of "fight–flight". We observed moments of "freezing" when one mother poked and pushed her infant's face and head, but other than a blink, nothing in the infant's face or body moved. We also observed moments of infant "collapse" … [they go on to describe an infant falling limp like a ragdoll]. (2013, p. 63)

Bureau, Martin, and Lyons-Ruth (2010) describe how

> the experience of threat is very different during infancy … [and that] during early life, a *hidden trauma* can occur, resulting not from physical assault but from the unavailability of a responsive attachment figure to comfort and regulate the stress of the fear-evoking

events that are a daily part of the infant's experience. (p. 48, original italics)

In their paper, which is in an excellent collection of papers about the "hidden epidemic" of these "hidden traumas" of early neglect (Lanius, Vermetten, & Pain, 2010), they go on to discuss the long-term consequences associated with "early unresponsive care, including increased dissociation, depression and the self-damaging behaviours characteristic of borderline personality disorder". The collection of papers as a whole, citing literally thousands of studies (see van der Kolk & d'Andrea, 2010), offers compelling evidence of the long-term consequences of early relational disturbances. Lyons-Ruth, Dutra, Schuder, and Bianchi (2006) suggest that mother–infant interactive dysregulations are "hidden traumas" in which the child becomes shut out of the process of dialogue itself (Beebe & Lachmann, 2013, p. 67).

It is clear that these aversive experiences in infancy and childhood lead to both the primary trauma responses of fight, flight, freeze, and collapse, and to trauma-related internal working models related to these disturbing relational patterns. I understand both threads to be significant aspects of the traumatic complex and will demonstrate how both are woven into the psychology of, and work with, adult patients.

Clinical example—Dorothy

I have written about Dorothy twice before (West, 2007, 2010). Whilst in previous work together we made good progress, we have needed to explore the detail of our interactions and thus to elucidate her early relational dynamics in order to fully address her difficulties. I will describe a session which demonstrates some of the patterns of relating that have been described above.

In the session, Dorothy told me that she had been feeling terrible, that she woke feeling very anxious and bleak, that she felt very bad that she was feeling like this at this stage of the analysis, that she shouldn't be feeling this now, that she was convinced that she had done all she could, that she couldn't change any more, that "this is it", and that she should set a date to end the analysis.

Here, she is moving towards me desperate for help whilst, at the same time, moving away and cutting off from the relationship in a similar pattern to the child who eagerly opens the door for mother whilst turning away from her[4] (Dorothy actually used to turn away when I opened the door to her when we first began meeting). Whilst, as Bowlby said (see Chapter Six), the turning away is only "apparent" and the person does still want to maintain the attachment, the turning away is a significant factor that must be addressed, not least because the individual is perplexed as to why it is that they can't get what they want.

In the session I begin to try to explore whether there is anything particular making her feel this way today, to which she responds "no", and goes on to detail a number of experiences over the previous days where friends have been unavailable or uninterested. She does not pause between examples to give me a chance to respond so that I feel, again, at the same time flooded-wanted and kept out, as if she were turning to me for help and turning away. I know that she finds exploring her difficulties painful, as if we are uncovering "something wrong with her" and that "she can't do it right"—this makes me the dangerous other who is a threat, as well as a place of refuge ("fright without solution")—this touches on her relationship with her father.

Over time I have got beneath my "secure", ego position and got in touch with my primitive interpersonal reaction to this, so that I can at times find this exclusion by her, and being seen as a threat, painful. I thus recognise that I am in a similar position to her as a child, wanting to make contact with her extremely anxious mother who could not bear her child's distress or approach, and who then retreated into her "own little world". At the same time I know that Dorothy can experience me as not responding enough, or in the way she would like—warmly and appreciatively—so that she experiences me as the mother who doesn't like her, and who is unavailable and unresponsive to her needs and distress.

There is therefore a detailed reconstruction here of her early dynamic with her mother in both direct and reversed form, with Dorothy sometimes reliving the trauma in direct form and sometimes, in identification with the aggressor, excluding me.

My experience of distress allows me to talk of the distressed, excluded child's experience in a heartfelt way, as well as describing her rejecting response to me as someone she perceives as both depriving and a threat. This is a down-to-earth explanation that makes sense to her and is inherently non-blaming. I can then point out that she is not wrong or bad, as she feels, and explore her wish to get rid of this distressed part of herself (an identification with her mother expressed on the subjective level) and thus "just get better", "get on with it", and end the analysis. I suggest that her "feeling worse" is in fact her bringing this early dynamic into painful high-relief, where we can better appreciate her extremely difficult and traumatic early experience of not being able to get through to her mother who could, in some very real way, not bear her.

Dorothy feeling bad about herself also represents a form of Fairbairn's moral defence (see Chapter Eleven), which allowed her to feel that she was wrong but that her mother was good, and thus Dorothy was able to maintain the link to her. Feeling that she is bad or wrong also gives her an illusory sense of control over such relationships and keeps alive the phantasy-wish that if only she could do better herself she could get what she wants from her mother and others.

When I first met Dorothy she was in dire crisis, was broken down, distressed, tearful, and terrified much of the time. Her hyperactivation and distress meant that she drew others to her out of concern in the role of having to "pick up the pieces" (West, 2007, pp. 211ff.), and this included me. Through our work together she now functions very well socially and at work, she is much more together and does not rely on her friends in the way she used to. This has meant that she has lost one aspect of her source of intimacy with others, with her difficulties now being, as Meltzer (1968) put it, "gathered into the transference". We are thus left to recognise her frozen hypoactivation, where people are experienced as toxic and dangerous (which characterised many of her family interactions). This helps us understand her underlying withdrawal and isolation, and the conflict between making contact and withdrawing, which has been the *leitmotif* of her experience.

We have also needed to further explore her very distressing "collapse" response, which lay behind her experience of breakdown and disintegration, as well as her terror, insecurity, neediness, shame, and humiliation, and her conviction that there was something wrong with her.

In this clinical example I have particularly outlined her disorganised attachment pattern (see Carter (2011) for another clinical example of working with a disorganised attachment pattern) as well as addressing, in passing, other elements of the dynamic that I will go on to explore in more detail in the following chapters. These are the primitive responses to trauma (Chapter Five), the trauma-related internal working models on different levels and in direct and reversed forms (Chapter Six), a microanalysis of the analytic relationship (Chapter Seven), the pressures on the analyst and the moral defence (Chapter Eleven), the defeat of the analyst's ego (Chapter Twelve), the analytic attitude (Chapter Thirteen), and the collapse response and continued regression (Chapter Fourteen).

Notes

1. I will refer to them as the Boston Change Group in line with others e.g., Beebe and Lachmann 2013.
2. Fonagy (2001, pp. 1–4) states that all parties became rigid in their opposition, caricaturing the other position in an unhelpful manner.
3. The Boston Change Group write: "While we are describing here the earliest manifestation of conflict in the domain of the implicit, it is crucial not to equate the implicit with the nonverbal or preverbal (Lyons-Ruth, 1999). The implicit can be revealed through verbal as well as nonverbal forms of interaction. However, the implicit aspects of meaning are not in the content of the words themselves. The implicit meaning exists, so to speak, between the lines …" (BCPSG, 2007, p. 153).
4. This mirrors the behaviour described by Kreisman and Straus in their book entitled *I Hate You—Don't Leave Me* (1989/2011).

CHAPTER FIVE

Trauma, complex, and narcissistic defences of the core self—from fight and flight to personality organisation

Ogden, Minton and Pain write:

> A defensive action, such as freezing or fighting, becomes a generalized response to perceived threat, causing traumatized clients to feel that they cannot cope with everyday challenges. (2006, p. 87)

It has been my experience that these "defensive actions" are elaborated further and integrated into the personality. These primitive reactions to the trauma are one of the core elements of the traumatic complex, the other being the internal working model developed in relation to the trauma, which I will explore in more detail in the next chapter. In this chapter I will explore how these primitive mammalian defences of fight, flight, freeze, and collapse, as well as the ongoing hypervigilance that is a result of the trauma, underlie, and form the essential core of, narcissistic, schizoid, borderline, hysteric, and obsessional personality organisations. There is significant overlap between these personality organisations and the attachment patterns that attachment theory outlines, as I will explore below.[1]

State vs disorder

In so far as these primitive defensive reactions all represent defences of the core of the self they are all narcissistic defences (for a discussion of these organisations in relation to narcissism see West, 2007, although the current book deepens that understanding in relation to trauma and the primitive defence systems). Thus I will argue that traumatic experience, which calls up these primitive defences, lies at the heart of psychoanalytic ways of thinking in ways that are not traditionally recognised.

Whilst all of these primitive defensive reactions—defensive fight, avoidant flight, incapacitated freeze, hopeless collapse and submission, and anxious vigilance—occur in all of us at times, certain reactions can become predominant for the individual, largely due to the particular nature of their early experience, and they form their predominant personality organisation. Christopher Bollas (2000, p. 4) distinguishes character states from character disorders (I call the latter personality organisations), and suggests that we each contain various states of mind—narcissistic, borderline, hysteric, and schizoid—but that a "normal" person shifts between such states fairly freely. It is only when a particular state predominates and the individual becomes fixed in that state that Bollas talks of character disorder. In Chapter Sixteen I will also describe different forms of dissociative identity disorder.

Part of the elaboration that goes on in the personality is the way that these primitive defensive reactions are overlaid by and interact with other experiences, and other more particular and varied internal working models. Thus an individual whose initial impulse is to "fight" will do so in ways that relate to their particular, sensitive, trigger points (complexes), and in the form related to their early experience, whether that might be aiming for intellectual superiority or physical bullying.

I will now explore some of the ways that the primitive mammalian defensive reactions manifest and are elaborated into different personality organisations and attachment patterns.

The fight response and the narcissistic personality organisation

The fight response can be seen to be the primitive response that underlies, and becomes elaborated into, a narcissistic personality organisation. Here, the individual holds the other person responsible for what they feel, and angrily blames and seeks to control the other in an attempt to make them vouchsafe the individual's good (idealised) experience, feeling the other has a moral duty to do so. As I have caricatured it,

"I am right, *you* must change" (West, 2007, pp. 203ff.). The individual has characteristically had such a substantial experience of early trauma that they can bear no more bad experience and they eject any difficult, negative, or painful feelings into the other. This can readily represent a reversal of their own traumatisation—an identification with the aggressor. In terms of attachment this would correspond with an insecure–resistant attachment pattern or a dismissive adult pattern.

The flight response and the schizoid personality organisation

Similarly a flight response can be seen to be the essence of a schizoid personality organisation. Here, the individual avoids and denies difficult experience, limiting their own experience and view of themselves and remaining closed off from painful core experience and the effect of others. Characteristically they feel that the other will not be interested and won't want to listen to them, so they feel they have to do something to make the other appreciate them. Thus the individual wishes for an idealised, conflict-free relationship, tries to provide this for others, and is disappointed and critical of others when they do not reflect these high standards, perhaps leading the individual to withdraw further, disgruntled, resentful, and disillusioned. This corresponds with an insecure–avoidant attachment pattern, which Liotti (2007) also links with a schizoid personality organisation. I have caricatured this as, "I am good, *that's* not me".

The freeze response and the borderline personality organisation

A freeze response is the core of a borderline personality organisation (in the narrow sense of the term), where the individual is held in thrall to, and is repeatedly triggered by, negative, disconfirming, annihilating, frustrating, and rejecting experiences from which they cannot seem to escape (they are rendered powerless and "frozen"). Negative experiences are at the core of their being, as I have described in Chapter Four, and the individual has little hope that things could be otherwise. Because negative experiences resonate so powerfully, and are felt to characterise "who the individual is", good experience has significantly less effect, and sadly little lasting effect, on the individual with a borderline personality organisation, who feels unable to hang on to it. I have described, quoting Tronick and Gianino (1986), how this negative experience and core negative sense of self is built up from repeated mismatches in relationships that are insufficiently repaired.

The individual with a borderline personality organisation characteristically feels that the other won't love them or care about them and is hurt, angry, and despairing about it. They present their distress angrily and hopelessly, wanting the other to "pick up the pieces" of their broken life (West, 2007, pp. 211ff.), continually testing the world and challenging the other to prove that they do care, or confirm that they don't. At the heart of this personality organisation, as it is presented in reversed form, the individual is themselves essentially rejecting of relationship as it is experienced as too toxic (Rosenfeld sees this in terms of destructive narcissism). The wish for an ideal, reparatory object to "make good" past experience, and the fear of the toxic elements of the real object, leads the individual to both approach and reject the object at the same time in a disorganised attachment pattern.

The collapse/submit response and the hysterical personality organisation

At the heart of the hysterical personality organisation are experiences of collapse and submission in response to the threatening object, often to the point of the experience of dying. Thus suicide—the taking of the experience of dying and being killed off into the person's sphere of omnipotence—is integral to the hysterical personality organisation.[2] The collapse might be because the individual is overwhelmed by the threat or power of the other, or because it is not safe to respond in any other way, for example, to fight. Porges describes this as the most primitive response to threat, whilst Krystal (1978) proposed that trauma should be defined only in these terms. The individual with a hysterical personality organisation has thus learnt from very early on, as Bollas puts it, to "suspend their own idiom", to dissociate from/ vacate themselves and put themselves in the hands of the other, for better and for worse. The hysteric, who has submitted to the other (in one respect at least) and abandoned themselves on the other's "doorstep", demands, desperately, and plaintively: "You won't abandon me, will you?", "How could you not love me?", "How could you let me down?", "Why do you hate me?". Slade suggests that this way of being maximises and intensifies affects in order to establish closeness (Slade, 2008, p. 771).

Hypervigilance and the obsessional personality organisation

At the heart of anxious and obsessional personality organisations lies the hypervigilance with which the individual is always scanning for threat.[3] The individual is thus constantly anxious, is trying to remain all the time in control and to know "what to do" in order to limit the range of their emotional experiences and, ideally, to eliminate anxiety completely. They are preoccupied by, and ruminate over, potential catastrophes, and nothing can be said to adequately reassure them that these will not occur. When the reassurance fails, the individual may resort to obsessional physical or mental activity, such as hand-washing, checking, or negative thinking, which takes on a life of its own.

The individual with an obsessional personality organisation is characteristically, continually checking: "Do you love me?", "Do you care?", "Will you abandon me?", "Perhaps you'll abandon me now as you must be getting tired of reassuring me?", "Perhaps you have stopped caring (as I am too much for you)?" This constant activity frequently leaves the individual exhausted, burnt out, and inevitably feeling a failure for not being able to ward off all possible threat and control their feelings. It often leads to depression.

Multiplicity and the underlying collapse response

Many of the individuals whom I will be describing demonstrate more than one of these defensive reactions and personality traits and, whilst one will often dominate, there will frequently be a shift from one to another over time; for example, moving from a helpless, despairing borderline position, to an angry, fighting, narcissistic position. I will describe the positive function of each of these reactions at the end of this chapter.

I have described these as different ways of defending the core self from narcissistic wounding (a wound to the core self is by definition a narcissistic wound) and these represent the narcissistic defences described by psychoanalysis (Bollas, 2000; West, 2007). Annihilation and disintegration represent the most profound forms of wounding to the core self. Recognising the primitive, traumatic roots of these personality organisations is one way in which trauma can be reinstated to what is, I suggest, its proper place within analytic theory, and serves to help bridge the unhelpful gulf that has emerged between analytic theory and trauma theory.

The more I have worked with people in the frame I am describing here however, the more I have found that experiences of powerlessness, collapse, annihilation, and disintegration underlie each of the personality organisations described above. To some extent each of these personality organisations and defensive reactions represent a way of defending against these most primitive and appalling terrors of annihilation and disintegration—the individual's back is against the wall (or rather the precipice) and they will fight, comply, preempt, submit, or be continually vigilant in order to prevent re-experiencing those terrors. I will give clinical examples of these below.

The narcissistic personality organisation and the fight response (and an example of intergenerational trauma)

Adam was brought up by his extremely strict, controlling, distant, and often punitive father following his mother's tragic early death after prolonged illness. He came for analysis, recognising that he needed help as things were not going well for him either in the workplace or in relationships. His academic excellence had meant that he had initially risen well in work situations, although when he achieved some measure of power himself he would turn on his superiors, upbraiding them for their lack of people-centred values and the way they treated those below him, whom he sought to protect. When his bosses sacked him he was outraged, and this outrage was the prime focus for him coming to analysis; his attempt to be an idealised father figure had backfired.

We could readily recognise his hostile attitude towards those in positions of power, and how this mirrored his attitude towards his father, and this was reflected in the analysis by his wary attitude towards me—whether I would be any good, whether I would exploit him, whether he would get his money's-worth from me, whether he would be free to "escape" from analysis. Furthermore, there was a touchiness about him as he frequently took offence, related slights to himself, reacted to them, and didn't let things pass. Thus when someone had wounded him he found it difficult to let it go (I will discuss self-preoccupation below). Again and again we could see his primitive "fight" response in action.

Relationships were particularly challenging for him as he wanted to have access to satisfaction and closeness without having to risk being vulnerable himself. Potential partners had to "get it right", and be prepared to be told where they had got it wrong. This was only if he could trust that they might want him in the first place, a view rooted in his early loss and sense of rejection by his mother. Frequently he would therefore turn to phantasy and pornography in order to attempt get his needs met. Here he reversed the positions of power and vulnerability that he had experienced as a child, and phantasised being the one to exploit the vulnerable, needy woman for his sexual pleasure, finally being able to be the one in control whilst his needs were satisfied.

In the process of exploring his early life we recognised that he had come to reject his mother following many experiences of her unavailability, rejection, and tantalising disappearance (both emotional or actual) due partly to her illness; in other words, he had come to identify with the aggressor. He had thereafter remained primarily in the rejecting role, in what might be classified as an insecure–resistant attachment pattern, or a dismissive adult attachment pattern, or as an example of destructive narcissism (Rosenfeld, 1987).

An intergenerational trauma

Yet simply recognising the reversal of the pattern—see the next chapter—did not much alter his fascination with and addiction to this kind of pornography; we needed to go deeper into the roots of the experience. I noted that in the particular way he used the internet there was some danger of him being exposed in his responsible work position. I also noted how he was very quick to see whether I would be horrified, disgusted, or judgemental about his use of porn. I found myself wondering a number of times about the quality of his relationship with his mother and whether he had in some way been subjected to the primitive agony of humiliation, rejection, and disgust to which he was wanting to subject others and that he was courting re-experiencing himself in his risky behaviour.

We then stumbled across some information that led us to suspect that his mother had been sexually abused, which might have led to her disgust with this baby boy and her unconscious ambivalence about having to attend to his needs and bodily demands. We did know for certain that he had been left unattended for inordinately long periods of time, and had continued rocking well into his pre-adolescent period, and on one early occasion had rocked his cot across the room so that it barricaded the door. Understanding this intergenerational trauma went some way to recognising the roots of his experience and accounting for the particular quality of his relating (the internal working model).

Most of all these explorations began to put him in touch with his most terrifying experience, related to a collapse response (the breakdown that has already happened (Winnicott, 1974)), which we found underlay the vulnerability, humiliation, neediness, and powerlessness that he could not bear (see Chapters Fourteen and Seventeen). It had previously been an important part of his pornographic phantasy that the other person experience these feelings. The more he could come to understand and, in particular, bear the experience himself, the less there was an emotional charge related to the pornography and the more he related differently to women—not so much wanting to be in control and much less fearing (yet unconsciously promoting) their disgust and rejection.

The borderline personality organisation and the freeze response

Anna came into analysis anxious and agoraphobic, feeling unable to cope with the world, feeling desperate, hopeless, and powerless about her position in it. She developed a relationship with a man who initially seemed strong and decisive, yet quickly the shadow side of this showed and he was belittling, hostile, critical, and sometimes abusive towards her. This corresponded with her own early experience of her absent, unemotional, critical mother and her raging, tyrannical father, so that on some level it fitted her expectations and felt normal to her. This also corresponded with her own view of herself. Whilst his hostility, rejection, and abusiveness corresponded with her own undeveloped hostility, rejection, and sadism, he served as the perfect container to carry these qualities (what Fonagy, Gergely, Jurist, and Target (2002) call the "alien self"), disowning (dissociating) them herself, yet keeping her trapped in the relationship with him.

The relationship with this partner allowed her to get in touch with, and develop, her own murderous, rejecting feelings, which had their blueprint in her father's tyrannical, yet impotent, rages (though not impotent in their effect on his children), and her mother's emotional unavailability. Through this development she was then able to extricate herself from the relationship. These developments allowed her to recognise her hostility and sadism towards others too, including towards me whenever she experienced me as emotionally unavailable and not providing the loving care and protection that she had long held out for. Through recognising her fearful, frozen negativity and hopelessness in a non-judgemental way, and slowly recognising her own hostility and rejection towards others, she was able to function in much more effective ways in the fields of both work and friendship. I will describe Anna's profound intrapsychic and interpersonal experiences of collapse and annihilation in the following chapters.

The collapse response and the hysterical personality organisation

Whilst Anna had tried to keep out of the way of her father as much as possible, Nounoushka's tyrannical father intruded into every area of her life from early on: bullying her, putting her down, telling her what to do and what not to do, expecting her to entertain him and sometimes taking some pleasure in her so that she desperately wanted to please him. When she did something wrong however, his anger would frequently turn to violence so that, at times, she feared he would kill her and sometimes felt that he was trying to kill her. He would then tell her that she was making too much of "a few slaps" and expect her to continue as if nothing had happened.

Nounoushka was equally conflicted by her mother who did not stand up to her father and protect her, who was cold and distant, emphasising issues of appearance and behaviour, whilst quietly encouraging Nounoushka's dependence on her when that suited her. One of the worst beatings that she experienced from her father was when, on a family holiday, she went off playing with other children, leaving her mother to feel lonely and isolated.

Nounoushka came into analysis in a desperate state. In the second week of meetings she rang me to tell me she had just taken an overdose; hardly knowing her I rang 999 (I had never done so before nor, so far, since) and, when she came to the next session, she seemed somewhat surprised that I had done so. Her reaction cued me in to the level on which we needed to work, with me needing to find a way of accepting, recognising, and understanding her distress and suicidal impulses yet continuing to think about and explore them with her analytically. My reaction indicates, I think, the concrete level on which she was functioning, by which I mean the power and intensity of her early experiences, held in implicit, procedural memory, which made her act as if these things were absolutely true.

Over time, and with great difficulty, distress, guilt, and shame, she was able to recognise her hurt and woundedness, as well as her furious and murderous feelings towards her parents and towards me when I either did not respond to show that I cared, or I did not respond to prove that I didn't want her dead. So many issues in the relationship with me triggered either feelings of wanting to please me, wanting to be approved of, wanting not to be criticised, wanting not to be irritating, and so on. It was our first job to try to understand what I had done that was triggering her particular reaction and what experience that related to, almost invariably with her parents. We could then look at the way she wished to please me and have me appreciate her—an idealised good parent who would make her feel better; or the way she feared that I would be irritated or murderous towards her—the terrifying bad parent.

The experience of death and the threat of suicide was a constant presence between us, and I came to understand how this represented her experience of collapsing in the face of her threatening, overpowering father, and how this experience was accompanied by an experience of dying and being killed off. We could see, as I will explore further in Chapters Fourteen and Fifteen, that her active wish to kill herself was not only a wish to have a way out of intolerable conflict, despair, and levels of feeling, but also an attempt to take this experience of dying into her sphere of omnipotence (Winnicott, 1953, 1974) (to have it under her own control and to master it), as well as an expression of her murderousness towards herself (an identification with the murderous father), and sometimes towards me but turned back on herself.

This collapse response, with its submission to the other, was elaborated into Nounoushka putting herself into the other person's hands—the personal sacrifice of self—in the hope that the other will take care of "the baby abandoned on the doorstep". In this unconscious bargain, the person is mortified, disbelieving, and furious if and when the other does not fully appreciate this precious gift and take care of their most vulnerable and exposed self. This is characteristic of the hysterical personality organisation (see West, 2007 for an extended clinical example).

The flight response, avoidance, and the schizoid personality organisation

Joe came to analysis as a requirement of his further training, having been working as a counsellor for some time. He had been unhappy and dissatisfied in his marriage, which had broken down a few years before. In analysis he hoped to finally find the kind of treatment and understanding he had not been able to find elsewhere. He felt that he had dedicated himself to his wife and family yet had not been appreciated himself. He reported that his wife had accused him of being critical and had said that she felt she could not please him. In his counselling work he was idealistic and tried to offer his clients the kind of perfect understanding and "meeting" he would have liked to have received himself.

Joe was from a large family, the fifth child of six, and his parents had been busy with family and work life. Joe had learnt to make himself useful at home and thus he got some praise from his parents. He was also keen to avoid two of his older siblings' conflicts and rebelliousness, which got them into constant trouble, although he admired their outspokenness and independence.

Whilst Joe felt he had an ability to care for others, he had become frustrated and eventually disillusioned when his clients did not "improve", and he fell into deep self-doubt about his worth and abilities. In trying so much to look after others, including his children who he cared for part-time, he began to experience burn out and eventually needed to take some time off work. One GP diagnosed chronic fatigue syndrome, although his lack of energy passed relatively quickly.

In exploring his early life in the analysis, we learnt that his mother had been quite profoundly depressed after his birth and that this was perhaps one origin of him becoming a do-it-yourself parent. In the analysis he would jump in with interpretations before I had had a chance to fully formulate my own thoughts, yet he was clearly also dissatisfied with the progress of the analysis and that he didn't feel more different. When I commented on his disappointment and anger with me he denied it and said that it was, of course, his responsibility to change and he couldn't expect more from me. He was clearly anxious to avoid conflict and "took flight" from it with me, although this was also an aspect of his ability to ignore his primitive, core reactions, just as his family had ignored them.

His disappointment, which played such a large part in his life, was related to his wish for a conflict-free, loving, encouraging environment where he would finally be able to be "fully himself". This wish to be able to "be oneself" can play a large part in these dynamics, with the analyst being told that they are either limiting of killing off the patient, or that they are themselves limited, rule-bound and "not enlightened enough to help". As the wish to be able to be oneself is apparently particularly sanctioned by therapy and analysis this pressure can be both confusing and compelling. This plays a large part in how good or bad the analyst is seen to be (the splitting).

On the affectively "positive" side of this split, it is frequently the hope to be able to be one's full, loving self that is behind the patient's love for the analyst; in other words, there is a narcissistic element at the heart of that love. The love can turn very rapidly to denigration and virulent attack when it is frustrated—"hell hath no fury, etc. …". A large part of the work in the analysis was working on his idealisation and recognising his expectations, hopes, and disappointment, and coming to terms with ordinary life where he was an imperfect, sometimes angry, sometimes failing, human being himself. These phenomena are discussed further in Chapters Nine and Eleven on idealisation and the pressures on the analyst.

The obsessional personality organisation and hypervigilance

Daniella came to therapy anxious, phobic, and struggling at work. She felt despairing and hypercritical of herself and her inability to master her anxiety. She had previously been depressed. She recognised that she was always anticipating threat and conflict and that she over-reacted to criticism and the threat of criticism, focusing on those things to the exclusion of good experiences. She felt she ought to be more effective, to know what to do, and to be more in control, and she continually compared herself unfavourably with others.

We recognised that her hypervigilance related to her early life with her father who was extremely ambitious, pushed himself very hard, and had great expectations for his children, although this was usually expressed through being disappointed with them. Her mother was herself anxious and fearful of her husband's criticism and dissatisfaction, and particularly that he would leave her for another woman. Daniella thus found herself having to manage her anxiety and keep it secret from her mother, to whom she felt it would only be a burden.

It was important that we could help Daniella recognise the way in which her anxiety was related to her hypervigilance against further trauma, and explore her unrealistic hope of being in control of her feelings (she had previously had CBT which had been successful only to a limited extent), and her unrealistic expectations on herself. She also had to suffer the disillusionment that merely understanding these things would protect her from anxiety, as well as having to work through her disillusionment with me as someone who might be able to take the bad feelings away and give her control over her psyche. This represented a slow and uncomfortable realisation of what it really means to be human, especially the limitations.

m – extenel beah
me – inner peä'n

A note on self-preoccupation

One of the characteristics that is frequently ascribed to "narcissistic" individuals is their self-preoccupation. This is sometimes described in terms of entitlement, sometimes as an aspect of withdrawal. It was one of the primary characteristics that Freud (1914c) described in his description of narcissism, and he saw it as a withdrawal to a more primitive, autoerotic phase which he called primary narcissism for the infant and secondary narcissism if the adult returns to this state.

My experience has been that the extreme sensitivity of the self and consequent self-preoccupation is precisely due to the wounding to the core self. Like with a physical wound, the pain, sensitivity, and exposure of the wound is ever-present and can frequently dominate consciousness for periods. Ferenczi pointed out exactly this phenomenon to Freud, and Freud gave the example of someone with toothache (1914c, p. 82).

Where there has been such narcissistic wounding it is characteristic that the individual takes everything as if it is referring to themselves— the paranoid aspect (of the paranoid-schizoid position). However, whilst the self-preoccupation is therefore a "sign" of this wounding, it can manifest in different ways: for the individual with a narcissistic personality organisation it is a touchy, aggressive reactiveness; for the individual with a borderline personality organisation it sparks depressive and despairing ruminations about their worthlessness and precarious situation; for the individual with a schizoid personality organisation the self-preoccupation is expressed as a wish to withdraw and avoid others and ruminate on the wounds they have experienced and their disappointments; for the individual with a hysterical personality organisation it is a preoccupation about how they will survive and what the other is thinking about them; for the individual with an obsessional personality organisation it is a preoccupation with what might go wrong, about their anxiety, and about what they need to do to be in control. Thus as Britton says, using Rosenfeld's terms of thick-skinned and thin-skinned narcissism, "inside every thick-skinned patient is a thin-skinned patient trying not to get out, and in every thin-skinned patient is a thick-skinned patient who is usually giving himself a hard time and periodically gives the analyst a hard time" (Britton, 1998, p. 46).

Positive elaborations of the primitive responses

Whilst I have just been describing some of the problematic elaborations of the primitive mammalian defences, it is also important to note that they have positive functions as well. Thus, it is important that we can stand up for ourselves, to "be present" to ourselves and others, to react to intrusions and "fight" against offences. It is clearly possible "not to be narcissistic enough", and to masochistically not react to mistreatment.

Similarly, it is important to be able to put enough distance between ourselves and our emotional reactions at times—the essence of the flight/schizoid response—so that we are able to bear difficulties and persevere in difficult circumstances; this can allow restraint and time for strategic thought.

The freeze response, holding the threat from the aggressor permanently in mind, makes us wary and look deeply at difficulties, limit our expectations, and take responsibility when things go wrong, accepting our role in what happened.

The collapse and submit response allows us to accept defeat, to recognise our limitations, and to turn to others for help. Perhaps it is the essence of a religious attitude where the individual recognises their ultimate powerlessness and turns to a "higher power" for help (see Rosemary Gordon's (1987) paper, "Masochism: The shadow side of the archetypal need to venerate and worship", and Chapter Eighteen on Jung).

The anxious, vigilant response, keeps us alert and makes us take care with what we do, looking out for pitfalls and problems; it clearly has an important role in primitive survival.

Notes

1. I would like to repeat that the aim of outlining these patterns is not to mindlessly classify and pigeonhole individuals, but rather to better understand their motivations, struggles, conflicts, and distress.

The individual is above and beyond all "categories" into which their behaviour may fall and can certainly not be reduced to them. I believe that understanding the underlying early traumatic experience assists in this separation of person from label.

2. Britton writes that "the death wish in hysteria is meant to lead to the consummation of a greatly desired sexual union: it is not intended to separate but to end all separation" (2003, p. 3).

3. This highlights the particular significance of anticipation and expectation that, as I have quoted from Beebe and Lachmann (2002, 2013) and is outlined by many others, is a primary activity for the infant and remains a cornerstone of unconscious functioning.

CHAPTER SIX

Internal working models on different levels and in direct and reversed forms

In her 1999 paper, Jean Knox argues that there is a great deal of overlap between Bowlby's concept of internal working models and Jung's concept of the complex. I suggest that the complex embodies both the trauma-related internal working model derived *from* the trauma as well as the primitive defensive reaction *to* the trauma (the latter was outlined in the last chapter).

Whilst these primitive mammalian defence systems may form the cornerstones of the internal working model, the models are also more nuanced and particular to the individual's early relationships.[1] The internal working model is born out of the child's necessary anticipation and adaptation to those around them, as intricately described by Beebe and Lachmann (2013) (see Chapter Four of this book), who demonstrate how the child's expectation and anticipation forms an integral element of the way they relate. The individual does not react to what the other person has "just done", but to what they expect them to do, thus often playing a significant role in that happening (making it a self-fulfilling prophecy). The development of the internal working model thus allows the individual to predict the behaviour of significant others and to accommodate to them, minimising mismatches and "shocking" surprises, as the core self cannot bear too much difference or intrusion (Ferenczi, 1932a; West, 2004, 2007).

My main aim in this chapter is to describe the way in which the relational patterns embodied in the complex manifest themselves on different levels and in direct and reversed forms (causing internal conflict). It is only when they have been significantly recognised on all the levels I will describe, and in both direct and reversed forms, that the complex loses its disruptive power—it has become integrated into the personality. The crucial therapeutic factor is not recognising that, for example, the patient's unconscious sadism is being projected, but rather it is recognising and working through the whole constellation on all levels, including recognising its traumatic origins. I have found that it is this which allows the therapeutic shift.

In the following sections I will give an example that illustrates the internal working models in practice. I will look at how these are reflected in, and structure, what the patient brings on the objective, subjective, transference, and archetypal levels, and in direct and reversed forms; how they relate to figures that Karpman (1968) described as the "drama triangle" of victim, aggressor, and rescuer, to which Gabbard (1992) added the role of the uninvolved mother (and Davies & Frawley, (1992b, pp. 91–92) have suggested instead "uninvolved parent") who doesn't help or protect. I will also explore how these patterns are reconstructed in the analytic relationship—a co-construction by patient and analyst. This has significant consequences for technique and how the analytic relationship is considered.

Objective, subjective, transference and archetypal levels

In describing his synthetic method, Jung described the ways that a dream could apply on what he called the objective, subjective, archetypal, and transference levels (Jung, 1917/1926/1943). Just as the dream embodies and describes early patterns of relating (West, 2011), so internal working models also apply on these different levels.[2]

The objective level

Anna's foundational experience was of her mother being emotionally unavailable and rejecting, and of her father tyrannically dominating the household. Her internal working models therefore related to being rejected by someone who was emotionally unavailable and of being paralysed by fear of someone tyrannical. In the analysis she was initially broken-down, fearful, and anxious, and felt herself to be powerless. She would frequently recount situations where she had been rejected by others or was too frightened to act. These situations all related to her experience of the external (objective) world, whether that was in the past or present.

It was naturally fundamental that we recognised and explored how these experiences with her mother and father had affected her, and recognised the truly traumatic nature of not being responded to, or being brushed off and rejected whilst watching others being accepted and included, often from a state of intense envy. Additionally it was important that we recognised what it was like to feel paralysed with fear, frozen, silenced, and unable to take any action. In terms of the drama triangle, these examples describe Anna in the "victim" role—the one who is suffering the traumatic experience (although unfortunately the word victim has accrued judgemental undertones).

The subjective level

It was also important that we recognised how, on the subjective level, she was the "victim" of the critical and abandoning parts of herself (as I will describe below, she was also the active aggressor). Thus she ignored and did not respond to her own needs and distress, did not take care of herself, and was ruthlessly bullied and belittled by her "superego", making her believe she was useless and incapable. You could say that this was an internalisation of her parents' attitudes which allowed her to anticipate and pre-empt future rejection or terror, but I have found it helpful to recognise the way the individual is both victim of, for example, bullying attitudes, and the perpetrator of them. This is part of the dissociation that occurs due to trauma, by which I mean, the splitting up of different aspects of the ego resulting in internal conflict.

The transference level

On the transference level, in relation to the analyst, Anna very much primed me to be the good, "rescuer" figure (in the drama triangle), so that it was a significant moment when she began to recognise and let me know that she also found me to be rejecting and unresponsive and that she was afraid of me. I will give a detailed account of these interactions in the next chapter. This rescuer role very much related to her idealised wish for someone to make good the care she had not experienced early on from either her mother or father. We explored this desire in many different ways, helping her to see that much of her anger, envy, and disappointment was in relation to these idealised wishes (see Chapter Nine on idealisation).

The archetypal level

My take on the archetypal level of experience follows from a later quote of Jung's on archetypes, where he wrote:

> These motifs are not *invented* so much as *discovered*; they are typical forms that appear spontaneously all over the world, independently of tradition in myths, fairy-tales, fantasies, dreams, visions, and the delusional systems of the insane. On closer investigation they prove to be typical attitudes, modes of action—thought-processes and impulses which must be regarded as constituting the instinctive behaviour typical of the human species. The term I chose for this, namely "archetype", therefore coincides with the biological concept of the "pattern of behaviour". In no sense is it a question of inherited ideas, but of inherited, instinctive impulses and forms that can be observed in all living creatures. (Jung, 1958, para. 565, original italics)

I think he is exactly describing a form of internal working model here, although in a more generalised form than I would want to describe it, as I would see the archetypal patterns as having "emerged" from actual experience, as described by Knox (2001, 2003a), Saunders and Skar (2001), and Hogenson (2001). These early experiences become foundational to the individual's experience and embodied as the superordinate organising principle of their experience—the trauma-related internal working model as an emergent archetype. Being stored in implicit, procedural memory they have a powerful, deter-mining effect on the individual—talk of conscious intention is way off the mark.

So for Anna, the experience of unresponsiveness and rejection was so early and powerful as to have become foundational for her. She saw it everywhere and in everything. It thus frequently seemed not to relate to particular experiences but to be a universal truth. It is precisely this aspect of early experience that makes it seem absolutely current and about the present, and able to latch on to, and organise, current experience. This is why I think the term archetypal is still useful.

As these patterns are so powerful and, Jung would say, not integrated or humanised, they override what might otherwise be seen as the individual's best interests in ways that seem self-destructive and could be seen as related to a death instinct (Freud, 1937c), although I do not see them in that way (see Chapter Fifteen). I hold that the individual is being true to the original trauma, which needs proper recognition and working through. As there is no coherent narrative to explain and contain them, and as they are held in implicit/procedural memory, the internal working models are enacted rather than thought about. A certain level of re-enactment in the analytic relationship is therefore inevitable (see below).

Reversed mode

The key to understanding the patient's conflicts and difficulties in dealing with their powerful, primitive affects, as well as constructing a coherent identity, is recognising that these internal working models also operate in reversed form, in identification with the aggressor.

Jung understood the "principle of opposites" as central to his understanding of the psyche (Jung, 1955–56, para. 778) and to the development of the individual, although he most frequently discussed this in archetypal rather than personalised form. He recognised the complex as central to bringing the opposites together, particularly as he held that each complex was based upon an archetype.

John Weir Perry (1970) described this opposition in terms of the bipolar nature of the complex, and gives the example of the young man who rails at authority figures at one moment, slipping into the stance of the rebellious son, yet in relation to someone he regards as somewhat less than himself, he becomes a strict disciplinarian (p. 4). (Perry talks in "classical" terms of the mother complex, child complex, and father complex as existing in their own right, and thus he describes the example I have just given as the result of the interaction of two complexes, the father complex and the son complex, whereas I would see the complex as containing the relational dynamic (internal working model) between father and son, or rather, in more generalised form, between someone in authority and someone less powerful).[3]

Whilst a number of people have recognised the reversed form—that the individual will sometimes behave "in identification with the aggressor" (Ferenczi, 1932a,[4] and see also Aron, 2006; Garland, 1998b; and Meares, 1993, 2012), I have found that the concept of the complex is an invaluable container that allows us to recognise all the ways these trauma-related internal working models manifest themselves and the conflicts inherent in them.

It is usually, but not universally, the case that the individual seeking therapy will present the details of their traumatic experience, adopting the role of the done-to "victim". The reversed role emerges from the person's primitive counter-reaction to the traumatic experience, whereby the individual responds in a like-for-like, eye-for-an-eye, "talion" manner (Lambert, 1981). This response often remains unconscious however, as it does not fit with the way the individual sees themselves. Such primitive counter-responses are usually felt to be intrinsically wrong or even anathema, as they express what was unbearably traumatising and thus "bad". As described in the previous chapter, these reactions are usually experienced as something terrible in others, and the individual reacts powerfully against them, being fearful, angry, hurt, and so on.

This is sometimes described as the individual projecting their own unacceptable reactions on to the other, and that may sometimes suffice as shorthand; however it may take some time for the individual to develop and become aware of those reactions in themselves. This will entail having to come to terms with the existence of these reactions and reconciling them with who the person feels themselves to be—someone who can also be, for example, aggressive and wounding. This requires a significant development of the personality.

The exception to this is where the identification with the aggressor is primary, and the vulnerable, victim-like aspects are projected outwards, although the individual may still feel conflicted and bad about their aggression, or at least potentially worried that it will get them into trouble. This is particularly the case for individuals for whom a fight response is primary and who develop a narcissistic personality organisation—see Adam above.[5]

The antagonism towards the victim is sometimes manifested on the subjective level in the individual despising the "weak" part of themselves and/or secretly admiring the hard, apparently invulnerable, aggressor.

Fonagy, Gergely, Jurist, and Target (2002, pp. 11ff.) describe this in terms of the child internalising an "alien self"—the aggressor/abuser aspect of the dynamic—and, in order to feel coherent, the child needs to find someone onto and into whom to eject it, and then to relate to it through projective identification. They thus remain trapped by, and in the thrall of, their bad objects. I see the "internalisation" developing more organically through interactions with the other, as described above (Chapter Four), and by Beebe and Lachmann (2013), and would stress that the experience of the aggressor does become elaborated within the individual's own personality; in other words, it is only alien in so far as the individual has not integrated their own version of the aggressor.

As Liotti (2004a, p. 478) writes, it is precisely because these patterns—victim and aggressor—are so powerful and conflicting that the child is unable to construct a unitary, coherent, and cohesive identity. This is another way of saying that the traumatic complex disrupts the ego complex and compromises the individual's ego-functioning.

It would be simplistic and incorrect to say that the individual ultimately and inevitably comes to behave like the aggressor. Indeed many people expend a great deal of energy ensuring that they do not do so. Simply because the individual has the primitive reaction does not mean that they will act it out in a gross form. I have found however, that in order to no longer be held in thrall by the aggressor or to feel safe from further abuse, the individual may well need to own their own talion response and feel that they can fight fire with fire.

Thus if someone significantly like the abuser approaches them with the intention of hurting, harming, humiliating, or annihilating them, they will be immeasurably helped if they are prepared to fight back in some way or on some level, and to similarly hurt, humiliate, or annihilate (see the example in Chapter Sixteen of someone who was not able to do so, being confined to freeze and collapse responses, and how this made the bad object so much more terrifying). Thus it represents a significant moment when the individual is able to recognise and acknowledge the primitive, talion reaction within themselves that inclines them to act in that way. This takes much of the tension out of the conflict between elements of their identity.

In terms of national politics, countries that have effective armies that can adequately defend their borders do not tend to get invaded, whilst countries without such armies remain vulnerable to invasion. The same applies with individuals. Of course, to simply respond in a like-for-like, talion manner can be most unhelpful. To be able to absorb some suffering is vital for social relations and is the basis of social living, with the role of policing, judgement, and punishment being taken over by a third party.

Even if the individual is going to try to find some more sophisticated and socially adaptive manner of responding—and this applies particularly to the analyst, of course—it is important that they are aware of, and able to accommodate, these primitive reactions. Problems arise when this is not the case and the person's primitive responses leak out, taking them over unawares, so that they suddenly "lose it" and attack the other person, perhaps leaving the individual themselves feeling embarrassed, ashamed, or mortified.

Sometimes analysts have candidly documented such outbursts, for example, Coltart (1986) and Kalsched (2013, pp. 127ff.), and hopefully no harm is done. I would suggest however, that these kinds of primitive responses can be more usefully brought into the analysis much earlier on if the analyst is on the lookout for the patient's talion response to the original trauma and their own talion response to the patient. These can be understood as a welcome, necessary, and helpful development, signalling that the traumatic complex is being fully constellated, rather than an example of the patient's unwanted destructiveness.

In Donald Kalsched's example with his patient Mike, the analyst bawled out his patient when he had committed yet another physical assault and seemed to be not only lacking in guilt but secretly triumphant. I would suggest this occurred because Kalsched does not systematically recognise and address the patient's inevitable embodiment and reversal of their traumatic experience and also, as an analyst, Kalsched apparently adopts a benevolent, almost avuncular role, which could not be maintained (he does not seem to fully appreciate the way the traumas are co-constructed in the analytic relationship, as I will describe in the following chapter).

A masochisto-sadistic response

Additionally, as I have documented previously (West, 2013a) and will describe further below, the individual can act out of their woundedness and attack and punish others who have triggered their wound in some way, justifying their attack by their woundedness. The individual can then become locked into what I have called a masochisto-sadistic pattern where there is an unconscious "charge" in exposing themselves to victimisation and responding in an attacking way themselves. Much bullying behaviour takes this form, with the victim of the bullying often well-aware, and even protective of, the bully's insecurities and vulnerabilities. As van der Kolk (1996a) puts it, "many repeat their family patterns in interpersonal relationships, in which they may alternate between playing the role of victim and that of persecutor, often justifying their behaviour by their feelings of betrayal and helplessness" (p. 196).

On the national level, it is often exactly an identification with such wounding that justifies decades- and sometimes centuries-long wars of attrition, where each new atrocity is justified by the last atrocity that that party incurred, with each party behaving in a masochisto-sadistic manner. The results are almost always barbaric, appalling, and tragic. Perhaps all wars use the justifications of such hurts to blind themselves to the humanity of "the enemy".

I would like to give the final word to an attachment perspective on reversal.

> When infants are separated from their attachment figures, they protest before eventually exhibiting sadness. Eventually they seem to recover and begin to explore their environments with renewed interest; they seem once again to be interested in other people. However, if the attachment figures return, Bowlby (1969/1982) noted that many children respond with coldness and an absence of attachment behaviour, as if they are punishing the attachment figures for abandoning them or are unsure how to organize their conflicting desires to seek comfort and express anger. Bowlby emphasized that this defensive response is best described as "apparent" detachment, because once the children reaccept their attachment figures' care, they are particularly clingy and hypervigilant, not wanting to let the figures out of sight. (Shaver & Fraley, 2008, p. 65)

It is precisely the conflict between the child's attachment needs and their hurt and aggression that is a source of such difficulty for the child's development.

The internal working model in reversed form

To return, finally, to my example. As I described in the last chapter, for Anna, the aggressor roles were initially enacted by her partner and it was only in coming to stand up to him and recognising her talion responses—her wish to kill him off, ignore him, and see him suffer—that she developed this part of herself and was able to extricate herself from the relationship.

It came as a surprise to Anna to slowly recognise how she was the one who was rejecting people's advances when she had previously been so mortified at being excluded. These were all experiences on the objective level. In terms of the drama triangle, this was Anna beginning to take up the aggressor role.

We also recognised that not only did she passively ignore herself, but that she also actively ignored, belittled, and rejected herself (the subjective level), despising her own vulnerability and dependency. This first became obvious in her attitude to the vulnerability of others, but we were able to recognise that she also felt that way about herself.

On the transference level, we recognised the way that she did not respond to me or my interpretations, did not show that she felt I was any good, and was frequently negative towards me and what I would say. She adopted the rejecting mother role, whilst I experienced my wish to relate and be responded to being consistently frustrated and killed off. There were times when I sensed she was getting excited by giving me a good bashing, telling me how useless I was, or saying what she would like to do to me—an identification with father—and I would point this out to her.

I will further discuss the problem of the analyst falling into a passive, masochistic role. In order for this not to happen, however, the analyst has to be able to sufficiently make sense of what is going on to be able to address it. I have happily found that when I am able to do so, and find a way of putting this into words in a constructive manner, the person almost invariably ceases the behaviour. This does not mean that they might not continue their "relational annihilation" of me until such time that we have fully recognised the depth and degree of their own experience; however, the more excited, sadistic aspects of the experience usually abate.

On the archetypal level, we could see how, despite her early experience with her father, she idealised people who were powerful, "invulnerable", aggressive, and belittling of others.

Working in the transference

For me this is also the answer to the long-standing conundrum of how much to address and work in the transference, with some schools focusing more or less exclusively on the transference level. Whilst in one way it is true that the early patterns of behaviour apply on all levels, and thus also apply in the transference, I have found that it is important not to reduce everything to the transference level with "you mean me" interpretations. It is much more effective and helpful to recognise, explore, and work through the patterns as they apply on each of the levels and in direct and reverse forms. This not only makes sense to the patient, and places their experience and behaviour in the context of their objective, historical experience but, as I said earlier, I have found that the traumatic complex retains its hold on the individual until this full exploration has been achieved.

Furthermore, it is important that these different levels and stages emerge in their own time and manner, and that the analyst does not rush into prematurely interpreting the reversed modes until the evidence for them is clear and apparent. In general, these patterns of behaviour are best recognised in retrospect—as with the core of the method outlined here (see Introduction), these things are most helpfully discovered and re-discovered with each person on each occasion.

The reversal in Oedipus—a story of trauma

The Oedipus complex can be seen as just such a reversal following a trauma. In Sophocles' version, Oedipus is abandoned and left to die by his parents and then acts out his reversal in killing his father and, after learning that his mother/wife was also the one who abandoned him, he takes up his sword to kill her (although she has hung herself by the time he arrives). As Steiner (1985, 1990) and Zachrisson (2013) suggest, the myth is not simply concerned with incest and murder, but the drama takes place in relation to Oedipus' attempt to know about himself and his origins and, at the same time, his blatant not knowing of what is apparently obvious. This not knowing and lack of a coherent narrative is characteristic of trauma, as described in Chapter Three.

In not being able to know about himself and integrate the conflict around the reversal within his identity—that he killed the father who tried to kill him—he continues to act out his myth/internal working models and thus becomes incestuously linked with his mother, not having developed the ego-functioning/knowledge that would ensure he remained separate from her. Oedipus taking his mother, Jocasta, as his wife has more to do with taking up a position of power and control rather than love. If we are to take the myth rather more concretely however, it could be argued that the frustration of Oedipus' early attachment needs, due to his early abandonment by his parents, would increase the pressure for an idealised solution, not only to avoid further retraumatisation but also to make good his early deprivation. Taking possession of his mother, the queen, would represent just such a (disastrous) idealised solution, as Oedipus would be taking control of the maternal provision over which he was previously powerless.

Oedipus' story can therefore cogently be seen in terms of trauma rather than, or in addition to, infantile sexuality, although the story itself more supports the trauma theory. Whilst those who have been adopted might readily identify with Oedipus' experience of being abandoned by his parents, this is fortunately not a universal experience for all infants.

I understand the core of the "universal" oedipal phenomenon to relate to the struggle to achieve and accept the limitations of reality-oriented ego-functioning, and to forego the illusory benefits of primary process functioning—looking for the unboundaried, conflict-free, interpenetrating mix-up with the other. This is so much more difficult when ego-functioning has been disrupted through trauma. I will discuss the Oedipus complex and its relationship with ego-functioning, idealisation, and trauma further in Chapters Eight, Nine, Twelve, and Thirteen.

It is my suspicion, as I touched on in Chapter Three, that many practitioners have turned away from properly recognising trauma precisely because they feel they become locked into recognising and reinforcing the patient as passive "victim" of past and current experiences. As the model outlined above makes clear, this need not be the case, and all aspects of the trauma—primitive defensive reactions to the trauma and trauma-related internal working models—need to be recognised on all levels and in direct and reversed forms.

An alternate reaction is for the analyst to get pulled into an identification with the patient, to become heroic, campaigning, or pulled out of analytic mode, not recognising the reversed, "negative" manifestations of the internal working models. I will be discussing these pressures in Chapters Eleven, Twelve, and Thirteen.

Notes

1. Similarly Bowlby recognised that the internal working model provides the nuanced detail for the attachment pattern (Fonagy, 2001, p. 12).
2. Foulkes (1964) also described four levels (of the group)—the current level, the projective level, the transference level, and the primordial level; although he might have divvied up the territories differently there seems to be a great deal of overlap and above all an intuitive sense of the way that certain patterns manifest on different levels. For example, Jung's objective level describes both current and historical actual experience, whilst Foulkes' projective level might describe what Jung called the subjective level (internal characters) in so far as they are projected, and so on.
3. Perry also presaged one aspect of the modern understanding of intersubjectivity, writing that "the way one 'comes on' emotionally tends to determine the nature of the other person's emotional response (sometimes called the self-fulfilling prophecy)" (1970, p. 5).
4. As described in Chapters One and Three, Ferenczi understood the identification with the aggressor as a way of attempting to make the bad object a good object by the individual seeing themselves as bad. In terms of reversal I am meaning simply the identification with the aggressor's way of being/behaving.
5. Although individuals who flee from conflict may also become concerned about the passive aggressive consequences of their flight.

CHAPTER SEVEN

Into the darkest places: microanalysis of the analytic relationship— intersubjectivity, co-construction, and re-enactment

This chapter describes, in detail, the way the patterns of relationship that I have been describing manifest themselves in the analytic relationship—the internal working models on the transference level. As Jung wrote:

> Emotions are contagious because they are deeply rooted in the sympathetic system .... [a]ny process of an emotional kind immediately arouses similar processes in others .... even if the doctor is entirely detached from the emotional contents of the patient, the very fact that the patient has emotions has an effect on him. And it is a great mistake if the doctor thinks he can lift himself out of it. He cannot do more than become conscious of the fact that he is affected. (Jung 1935/1976, paras. 318–319)

Or more succinctly: "The patient, by bringing an activated unconscious content to bear upon the doctor, constellates the corresponding unconscious material in him" (Jung 1946/1954, para. 364).

I have found that in order to work through the traumatic complexes it is necessary to go down to this level of detail in the analytic relationship—a recognition of the nuts and bolts level of relating.

I believe that this is because, as the Boston Change Process Study Group (2007) state, the relational level is foundational. These exchanges have a power and significance way beyond their mundane appearance.

When it comes to the detail of analytic relationship, analyst and patient are on an equal level relationally. Both are open to the responsiveness, silence, withdrawal, looking away, ignoring, warmth, appreciation, negation, and so on, of the other. Whilst the analyst will hopefully be able to contain their reactions to some extent, and call upon their understanding of what is going on, there will still be the same "primitive", by which I mean, basic, human, reactions evoked. In saying this I am giving emphasis to the implicit, non-verbal aspects of relating, in contrast to the verbal, content-driven perspective.[1]

One example of this is where envy is a particular factor for the patient and they ignore the analyst's basic, human, relational needs, imagining them wholly satisfied. This distances the patient and analyst, whilst the analyst is now being slowly, chronically, deprived. At the same time the patient feels all the more isolated as they do not seek to connect up with the "unavailable" and "wholly satisfied" analyst. In the cases I have in mind, the patients' mothers had all been depressed and/or chronically emotionally unavailable—a dynamic that is gradually reconstructed in the analytic relationship.

It is important that the analyst is in touch with their primitive responses as they are key to recognising the early patterns of relating that took place. Racker (1958) points out that if the analyst is not in touch with these kinds of reactions they may fall into passive, masochistic states where the patient's difficulties are not addressed.

Co-construction

In regard to the co-construction of the analytic relationship, Beebe and Lachmann write of infants and their mothers at four months:

> In our dyadic systems view of face-to-face interaction, each person's action is constituted in coordination with that of the partner; each person's behavior is affected both by his own immediately prior behaviour (self-contingency), and by that of the partner (interactive contingency). Both partners are active participants in the co-creation of patterns of relatedness. However, the contributions of the two partners are not necessarily reciprocal. The mother

obviously has a greater range, control, and flexibility of behaviour than the infant. The basic unit of the mother–infant communication system is *action knowledge*, based on predictable patterns of behaviour across time. These predictable patterns of interactions generate expectancies of actions and action sequences. Continuous moment-to-moment variation provides each partner an essential means of sensing the self and the other … what is at stake in the infant's procedural expectancies of self- and interactive contingency is the organization of intimate relating. (2013, p. 139, original italics)

What is true for the infant–mother interaction remains true for the patient-analyst interaction. Regarding "adult treatment dyads" (in other words, patient and analyst), they write: "what we experience as our own behaviour is actually an emergent property of the dyad. To understand ourselves dyadically is to see ourselves as more porous and vulnerable to the state and behaviour of the other than we would often like to think" (ibid., p. 151). Or, discussing malignant regression, Balint puts it this way:

> the form in which the regression is expressed depends only partly on the patient, his personality, and his illness, but partly also on the object; in consequence it must be considered as *one* symptom of the interaction between the patient and his analyst. This interaction has at least three aspects: the way (a) in which regression is recognised by the object, (b) in which it is accepted by the object, and (c) in which it is responded to by the object. (1968, p. 148)

Some form of response by the analyst is required for the particular dynamic to evolve, whether that is "passive consent or active participation", in other words, the analyst's action or inaction plays a key role in the patient's expectations, and the events that unfold are a co-construction by both patient and analyst. I will explore the sometimes extreme pressures experienced by the analyst, and why they may be experienced as extreme, in Chapters Eleven and Twelve.

Reconstruction and re-enactment

I continue to find the way that early experiences and patterns of relating emerge in and structure the analyst–patient relationship truly remarkable. It is as if the past is shining through the present, so that what may appear as the patient's "psychopathology" or an inability to "properly relate", or an attempt to "maintain an infantile perverted state of mind" (Fordham, 1974, p. 198), are in fact invaluable, detailed re-enactments which allow that early experience to be known. Davies describes this co-construction in terms of a "therapeutic enactment", where there is

> a collapsing of past and present; a co-constructed organization of the transference–countertransference matrix that bears such striking similarity to an important moment of the past that patient and analyst together have the unique opportunity to exist in both places at the same time. (Davies, 1997, p. 246)

Such re-enactments are not a licence for "wild analysis" (Casement, 1985, p. 21), where the analyst may justify taking on any role as being "required" to further the patient's therapy. Rather, the analyst has the opportunity to recognise, understand, and contain the role that is being constellated within the containing theoretical frame of the re-creation of the patient's early experience and dynamics, incorporating that understanding into the interpretive dialogue.

In regard to the reliving of early traumatic experience, I have found that this quite frequently includes a re-experiencing of some form of annihilation, dying, or death, often accompanied by a terror of fragmentation or going mad, all of which feels completely impossible, unbearable, and shameful to the patient. Whilst the analyst's understanding of what is going on offers an invaluable containing framework, this experience is nevertheless truly terrifying for the patient, and I have found that extra sessions are sometimes necessary for a time, particularly as the patient's friends and/or family are not able to really understand and bear with what they are going through.

Reconstruction and co-construction—examples

In Chapter Four I gave an example of the relationship with Dorothy where she, at the same time, approached me and turned away. She would tell me her difficulties but not leave enough space for me to respond, or not pick up and explore my comments (partly as, to her, they implied there was something wrong with her, although they were a response to the difficulties she had just been describing), so that I felt I was like the child-Dorothy who was toxic to her extremely anxious mother and was being kept out. Similarly she felt, in not getting the immediate, warm, or enthusiastic responses she hoped for, kept out and not wanted. As I found that what I was saying wasn't being responded to I fell silent, and she experienced me as if I was unavailable and "in my own little world", just as her mother had been. This was therefore a complex set of co-constructed dynamics which reflected her early relational experience in direct and reversed forms.

Into a very dark place

As I have been exploring in the previous chapter, one of Anna's central experiences was of not being responded to by her mother, who was closed down, preoccupied, and unemotional towards her during her childhood. Anna felt kept out, rejected, and, as she got older, she felt that her mother related more warmly towards her siblings. She felt excluded when her mother was interacting with them, and often reacted in various hurt, angry, withdrawing, and defensive ways. This central experience had come to form a core belief about herself—that she was not likeable, let alone loveable, whilst other people were loveable and could be close and intimate.

Despite exploring this in many ways and on many occasions, and despite having had many experiences when she clearly was being valued and responded to, including by me, her central experience and beliefs about herself had not shifted significantly, although she managed to recover from experiences of rejection and exclusion more quickly and she was less distraught when they occurred. In short, however much good experience she had experienced in the relationship with me, we continued descending into dark places. She had begun to be more open about her complaints about me, once comparing me to a dead fish, and describing how she would like to attack me violently, putting an axe through my head, or doing various things that might hurt me and make me react.

Thus, a lot had happened in our relationship up till this point and, I would suggest, to some extent our relationship had developed to the point where the following exchanges could occur. In one session, shortly after I had moved consulting rooms, Anna asked me if I lived in a certain house in the village where I work. Anna very rarely asked direct personal questions. She had asked this question in a kind of offhand way and I recognised it was in a grey area where I might have answered. However, I noted a number of things in my internal reaction to her question: first, that I did not feel inclined to answer, and second, that I might have answered if someone else had asked the question. I felt bad and somewhat conflicted about this, yet I knew enough to respect this reaction and realise it had significance, particularly as I immediately recognised it fitted exactly with her pattern of experience with her family. I also recognised that however many times I had acted to disconfirm that pattern we kept on returning to it.

After some uncomfortable thinking time—I normally respond quite quickly to what people say—I said, recognising something of the import of what I was about to say, and recognising that I was grasping an extremely sensitive nettle, that I wasn't going to answer her question (I will discuss the (hotly disputed) question of disclosure in the following chapter). She seemed immediately shocked, incredulous even, and said so, asking if I was really not going to tell her if that house was where I lived. She then angrily said that I obviously thought she was toxic and that I felt I needed to keep her out; she referred to the fact that in a recent session I had commented on her wish to put an axe through my head as if that meant I thought that she was clearly dangerous and not to be trusted (in fact I had felt heartened that she was in touch with this murderousness in relation to me, which I recognised as progress in working through her traumatic complex). I said something about her experiencing me now as someone who kept her out and excluded her. The session continued in this way with Anna quietly, disbelievingly, angrily, shocked and outraged.

In the following session she said she had thought about not coming back; that she had thought that I might not let her back (a recurring fear); but that (most of all) she had felt suicidal. Whilst feeling suicidal was somewhat unusual for her, she had experienced it on other significant occasions when she had been excluded. She added that she had told a couple of people that she was feeling suicidal but that they hadn't responded well to her, almost dismissing her experience and not being unduly concerned.

I acknowledged all this and commented, recognising the seriousness of what had happened between us, that the worst had happened, that this was the primary traumatic experience with her mother that she feared happening everywhere and had always previously talked about happening with other people, but that now it had happened between us.

There was a lot of further discussion between us about this; however, there was also a simple sense of relief that we could talk about this hitherto almost taboo issue openly between us, that she had survived it, and that we could make sense of it together. I noted in the following weeks that Anna seemed more robust, that she seemed to get on with certain life tasks that she had previously approached very reticently, not only fearing failure and rejection, but believing that she couldn't manage them whilst others could. Perhaps the fear and unbearableness of the experience of rejection and failure, associated as it was to suicidal feelings, had lessened through being lived through with me.

It is, perhaps, important to explore how I had come to respond in that way, and I think that, again, the primitive relational level was key. Anna's primary expectations were that she wasn't likeable and that people wouldn't relate to her, and she related to me largely through bringing and discussing her ongoing difficulties whilst I fell into the role of "picking up the pieces" of her difficult life. This became a rather two-dimensional way of relating, and Anna saw me either (enviously) as comfortably "alright" or as a cold/dead flat fish, whilst in fact my fundamental human needs to be engaged with and related to (other than as a "caregiver") were being frustrated. My analytic presence and interpretations were not wholly unappreciated but they certainly seemed ineffective. On the human level I mostly felt rejected and unimportant (she had been adopting the cold rejecting mother role) and I think I had effectively been killed off. I was not therefore moved to be open and personal with Anna over her question, as all other attempts at warmth, presence, and openness had seemed to sink almost without trace. I was also aware that in not answering I was grasping the nettle that had been just below the surface all along.

Things continued to improve for Anna in her work and relationships, and yet there was still an underlying fragility and experience of bleakness. About six months later, perhaps more in her own time, the full traumatic experienced emerged more completely in the transference between us.

After a lacklustre previous session, where I had offered heartfelt empathic responses in relation to her distress (although little else) and Anna had told me that she found my empathic responses "irritating" (I had effectively been silenced by this comment), she began the session describing how despairing and suicidal she was feeling, and "would people only take her seriously if she did something?!" She was darkly angry with me and said that she didn't think I knew what I was doing, that I wasn't there, that her previous therapist would have made arrangements for her during the break, that she had been feeling dependent on me but was questioning this kind of therapy as it was making her worse. She said it was as if she was reaching out in desperation and getting nothing back. She said she'd like to kill herself in front of her mother and that she wanted to kill me.

When I managed to contain my initial responses (which would have taken issue with what she was saying in various ways), I slowly realised exactly what had been constellated. I suggested that she was reliving with me exactly the experience she'd had with her mother where she was reaching out to someone but was getting nothing back; that she was feeling deeply isolated, alone, helpless, and needy, and that this experience was killing her off. I said that such experiences had been, as a child, annihilating, and that she wanted to turn that around now and wanted to punish her mother and show her what she had done, as well as kill me off.

This was a real "moment of meeting" between us where she had been able to be open and real about core, heartfelt issues, and I had managed to stay with them, be open to them and match them. She was immediately different and it felt as if something important had happened in the room. It felt to me as if I had "got it" and this had somehow contained her and her experience.

Whilst there were a few further, related, follow-on experiences as she worked this dynamic through in other settings, Anna was different after this. She was lighter, clearer, freed up. It was as if we had laid a ghost that had been haunting her. She was able to move on in a different way. I suggest we had significantly detoxified her core relational trauma that had hitherto trapped and limited her and held her in thrall. I will give further examples in Chapters Ten and Fifteen.

Regarding enactment, you could say that I enacted the role of unavailable, unresponsive, annihilating mother with Anna. I would suggest that this re-enactment had developed slowly and organically between us at what was, hopefully, a bearable pace (considering that we were dealing with what felt essentially unbearable), and that the roles were used constructively in order to understand her early experience and ways of relating, and in order to relive and thus work through the traumatic complex.

I am very aware that what happened between us may seem harsh, unhelpful, cruel, or uncaring to some, and also that practitioners in the intersubjectivist/relational school frequently advocate not only disclosure but the positive modelling of acceptance and positive responsiveness see below.[2] I would suggest that my positiveness and acceptance had had only limited effect and that, more to the point, rather than trying to inject even more positivity of a "real relationship" (see the end of this chapter) in a collusion which avoided the trauma, I was, in fact, exactly staying with Anna as she actually was, accompanying her to the darkest places. I would suggest that this is what is required if the patient is to be properly met, "got", or, to use my phrase, accompanied. (To be clear, I should state that I espouse many of the tenets of the relational position myself, and have found many of their contributions invaluable (see Chapter Four)).

Dyadically expanded states of consciousness

Ed Tronick and his colleagues (1998)[3] suggest that humans strongly seek states of emotional connectedness and intersubjectivity, not simply because this motivation is inherent to all humans, but due to the "dyadically expanded states of consciousness" that are achieved when connectedness occurs. The failure to achieve these states is extremely aversive, see for example Tronick's "still-face experiment"[4] (Tronick, Als, Adamson, Wise, & Brazelton, 1978), and has a severely damaging effect on the mental health of the infant. They write:

> The states of consciousness of the infant and of the mother are more inclusive and coherent at the moment when they form a dyadic state (a moment of meeting; see Stern, 1998) because it incorporates elements of the state of consciousness of the other. (Tronick et al., 1998, p. 408)

To put this in other words, the regulation of the self ("inclusive and coherent self-states") goes on significantly through interaction with the other; or again, in slightly different terms, a secure attachment relationship down-regulates states of distress. In describing the effect of chronic denial of these states when a mother is depressed, they describe how,

> [g]iven that the infant's system functions to expand its complexity and coherence, one way open for the infant of the depressed mother to accomplish this expansion is to take on elements of the mother's state of consciousness. These elements will be negative—sad and hostile affect, withdrawal, and disengagement. However, by taking them on the infant and the mother may form a dyadic state of consciousness, but one that is negative at its core. Thus, in the service of becoming more complex and coherent, the infant incorporates depressive elements from the mother's state of consciousness. This dyadic state of consciousness contains painful elements, but its painfulness does not override the need for expansion. (p. 409)

Critically, the individual takes these features into other relationships which often leads to "a debilitating attachment to negative relational experiences" (p. 409). This is another way of describing internal working models or what Lyons-Ruth (1998) calls implicit relational knowing.

I would suggest that the crucial "moments of meeting", as described with Anna, require that the analyst is able to "take on elements of the [patient's] state of consciousness" and that, like the child with the depressed mother, "these elements will be negative". It is the analyst meeting and containing (and not altering or ejecting) these negative states that is key to working through the traumatic complex. In the clinical situations that I am describing in this book, that has entailed being experienced *as* the bad object as a result of the painful and painstaking, organic, co-construction of these experiences by and between both patient and analyst.

Critique of Beebe and Lachmann

In 2013 I attended a conference in Boston[5] where, in the morning Beatrice Beebe gave a wonderful video example of how she had simply "stayed with" a young boy's extreme ambivalence about reaching out to others. In the video you could see that through Beebe's simple mirroring of the little boy's physical reactions and emotional state, he reacted as if he was being "got", and it was lovely to see him come out of his shell.

In the afternoon, however, where the aim was to see how insights from mother–infant interactions could be applied with adult patients, Beebe did not follow the same procedure but rather (to my surprise) attempted to model a very positive responsiveness to a deeply traumatised adult patient, Sandra. Whilst the patient reportedly responded to this (although the treatment was in the early stages), it has been my experience that such methods only go so far and do not address the deepest wounds, as I have been describing here. It is clear that simply staying with adult patients, who have more sophisticated defences, and accompanying them into the darkest places of their trauma, is much more difficult for practitioners.

In the video playback of the session with Sandra, curiously, but significantly, Beatrice Beebe, clearly unintentionally, shook her head from side to side vehemently (once), whilst saying that she "enjoyed working with her and was very happy to continue" (she subsequently documented this in Beebe & Lachmann, 2013, p. 90). No one in the audience brought this to her attention, although some noted it. I would suggest that Beebe's somatic response (and it is precisely this that she was examining (ibid., p. 91)) signifies her unconsciously falling in with the patient's internal working model—namely that she did *not* expect anyone to enjoy working with her. Someone has subsequently clearly pointed this head-shaking out to Beebe and she explains it in the book as "probably a comment on the fact that the sessions would not be frequent" (ibid., p. 79).

This anomaly between work with adults and children is reflected in their book as a whole where they describe important work with children where they stay precisely with what the child brings and report how effective this is; however, when it comes to working with adults they modify their approach so that they are responding more positively or proactively with their patients, for example, Dolores (pp. 83ff.) and Sandra (pp. 88ff.).

This was also true of their previous work where Frank Lachmann described his work with one particular client "Karen" (Beebe & Lachmann, 2002, ch. 3, pp. 45ff.), who used to regularly miss sessions and turn up late. He described how, following a suicide attempt, he telephoned her before each session to remind her of the session, commenting that "whether or not Karen would arrive for her appointments became very anxiety arousing for me" (p. 58), and he continued this practice long after she had begun attending more regularly.

This pattern reflected back to Karen's parents' angry and violent fights, which would wake her at night, with the constant threat of them splitting up (p. 49). She had been so distressed that, at the age of seven, she had made a deal with God that if He would stop her parents fighting she would give up her life. From that time on she was preoccupied with suicide and persistent sleep disturbances.

I would suggest that in avoiding identifying with the experience of Karen as a child, terrified of her parents' abandonment (something "very anxiety arousing"), Lachmann enacted the role of the persistently present parent and did not address Karen's own reversal of this dynamic in her abandonment of him (turning up late or missing sessions), and thus did not address Karen's own abandoning tendencies. I note that the analysis ended with her moving away to another area—an abandonment?

Similarly, in a later case (Beebe & Lachmann, 2013, pp. 80ff.) one patient's underlying early experience of his mother's unresponsiveness was dealt with through Lachmann's positive facial responsiveness. This left me to wonder how deep and lasting the resolution might have been (the patient perennially could not believe that he had achieved what he had), as the core wound was not worked through.

This book is precisely about how difficult it is to stay true to what the patient brings, for both patient and analyst, but also how important that is. If these kinds of early traumatic experiences cannot be properly borne in the analytic relationship I suggest that they cannot be properly worked through. As Casement says, "an analytic 'good object' is not that which is better than the 'bad objects' of the patient's life … it is that which can tolerate being used to represent the worst in the patient's experience" (Casement, 2001, p. 384).

Another example

I have previously described (West, 2013b) how "Sue" was preoccupied with whether I hated her or was fed up with her, as she feared. At first her fears seemed very "alien" and far from the reality of our new relationship, where I was positively engaged with her regarding her life, her difficulties, and her early experiences. However, as time went on we became embroiled in the difficulties of analytic work, including her persistently questioning me about my feelings towards her. Whilst I recognised that this persistent questioning was related to her early experience with her mother, on the primitive relational level it was as if I was not trusted or believed, and as if I was a malevolent presence intent on hurting and rejecting her.

As her fears about me hating her now came to be based on possible implications of what I had said or hadn't said, I fleetingly came to experience moments where, on that primitive level, I did feel hate towards her. I recognised that the early relational trauma she had experienced with her depressed mother, who could not bear her baby's insecure crying and demands on her, had become constellated between us.

This recognition gave me sufficient space around her asking these questions to be able to respond to them differently. Whilst reiterating that I don't talk about my feelings (although recognising that on at least one occasion I had told her I did not hate her), I talked to her as if it was true that I did hate her and talked about it having been unbearable to feel that her mother or I hated her. I said that this had occurred with her mother, or at least we could see why she had felt her mother couldn't bear her at times, being depressed, and that people sometimes did feel hate for each other, and that she sometimes hated people, including me. In this way we were slowly able to explore her feelings and experiences, and talk about and detoxify experiences of having felt hated and not wanted, and having hated, that had previously felt taboo.

In Chapter Eleven I will look at this material in terms of projective identification, role responsiveness, and defences of the self and will explore the pressures on the analyst and the ways and reasons that further enactments can occur, with serious consequences for the analysis.

The real relationship

Strachey (1934) originally coined the phrase "the real relationship", to distinguish what was real from the phantasies that the patient may have about the analyst. This phrase has frequently been used, by both patients and analysts, to refer to the qualities of the analyst as a warm, kindly, and concerned human being, and contrasted with their rational, analytic functioning. Fordham (1974) describes exactly this split, and the patient's quest to obtain the "real person" of the analyst for themselves, or otherwise to believe that the analyst is either denying the patient access to, or is incapable of, such human warmth and kindness. As I will be exploring in Chapter Nine, I suggest that this splitting of the analyst into cognitive and affective elements represents a search for an idealised, conflict-free relationship that bears no risk of retraumatisation (but thus avoids addressing the trauma).

This splitting rests on a misrepresentation, in that the analyst's spontaneous affective-somatic reactions are equally a vital part of their analytic functioning, and that their cognitive responses are equally a part of their human boundariedness, and vital for their engagement with affect. As Damasio (1995, 1999) has pointed out, an individual's rational ego-functioning is build out of and on top of their affective-somatic reactions.

Lyons-Ruth (1998) defines the term real relationship as

> the intersubjective field constituted by the intersection of the patient's and the therapist's implicit relational knowing. This field extends beyond the transference–countertransference domain to include authentic personal engagement and reasonably accurate sensing of each person's current "ways of being with". (p. 33)

As I will be continuing to explore later, the analyst does contribute substantially to the nature of the relationship with their particular, personal, "ways of being with" (Chapter Twelve). Whether or not the analyst considers their cognitive and ego-functions to be intrinsic to who they are, or rather an obstacle to a more human or enlightened way of being (see Chapter Eight), will very much depend on how they have dealt with their own idealisation, and how and whether they have integrated and worked through their own traumatic complexes.

Colman (2003, 2013) has criticised some psychoanalytic models for overemphasising the aspect of phantasy in relationship, specifically in seeing projective identification in those terms, and not sufficiently recognising the real relationship and the role of relationship itself in the analytic process. I think he is absolutely correct in this; however, I would suggest that the primary, overriding value of the analytic relationship is in being able to stay with and bear the patient's experience as it is, allowing the person thereby to connect up with and integrate their complexes with their core self, thereby achieving congruence and an experience of wholeness. As I describe in this book, this involves the whole person of the analyst (cognitive, affective, and somatic), as well as their capacity to allow the patient's most difficult experiences to be made manifest in the analytic relationship.

Notes

1. As Betty Joseph (1985) cogently describes in her paper, "Transference: the total situation", it is vital to recognise the significance of the non-verbal, relational context in which the verbal exchange is taking place.
2. From their, frequently parenthetical, comments it is clear that they struggle precisely in the area with these kinds of patients who "won't get better". I would suggest that this is due to the fact that these negative interactions are installed as part of the individual's core self and core identity.
3. Later known as the Boston Change Process Study Group.
4. When a mother is instructed not to respond to her infant but to keep her face still, "the effect on the infant is dramatic" and "infants almost immediately detect the change and attempt to solicit the mother's attention"; if the attempt fails the infants become extremely distressed and withdraw, lose postural control, and turn to self-comfort (Tronick et al., 1978).
5. *Journal of Analytical Psychology* conference in April 2013 on the theme of "Attachment and Intersubjectivity".

CHAPTER EIGHT

Broad and flexible ego-functioning and the core self—the ego–self axis and ps–dp

I have come to realise, although it may seem rather dry to put it this way, that the key characteristic linking the phenomena related to trauma is the disruption of ego-functioning. This lies behind the trauma itself (and is a definitive element of trauma); the struggle to form a coherent identity; the re-enactment of events that can't be remembered but are held in procedural memory; the subjective experience of disturbance, fragility, regression, and vulnerability; self-denigration and envy; the pressures and distress manifested in the analytic relationship; and the grieving that occurs, in one form or another, if the person is to recover from the trauma and move out of their regressed state and towards a more manageable and fulfilling way of life.

One of the key functions of the ego is to help the individual adapt to their surroundings and protect the core self. The core self cannot bear too much difference, opposition, or unpredictability; it cannot bear the unexpected shock of "things being done to it", of being subjected to someone else, particularly out of the blue. The individual would much prefer to anticipate the worst, even pre-empting and subjecting themselves to the negative experience in advance—whether that is in the form of self-criticism, self-hatred, or self-neglect. This is the individual taking the violation into their "sphere of omnipotence" and "doing it to themself" rather than having it done to them. I understand this as the essence of what Kalsched (1996) describes as the "archetypal defences of the personal spirit", where the traumatised self says "never again!". This is also the origin of the hypervigilance associated with trauma and is a part of the process of internalisation of the aggressor. Thus one of the primary functions of the psyche from early on, as Beebe and Lachmann (2002, 2013) describe so well, is to anticipate and thus attune to the infant's emotional environment.

Where there has been early traumatic experience the ego is likely to respond in various rigid or inflexible ways in order to keep the core self safe. In this chapter I will therefore explore, succinctly, the functioning of the ego, and specifically the ongoing process of development of the ego so that it comes to function in a broad (inclusive) and flexible way. By flexible I mean something like porous, malleable, and open and, specifically, open to the more primitive aspects of the core of the self. A flexible ego is one that is able to malleably integrate these elements and responses with the individual's current way of seeing themselves.

A Jungian view of the ego

The Jungian understanding of the relationship between the ego and the unconscious, or the ego and what Jung called the self, is unique, although it entails a few potential difficulties which I will address in passing.

Whilst the ego is the locus of what Damasio calls the autobiographical self—the self-image and autobiographical memory (the sum of those things with which we identify), as well as reality-orienting functions,[1] and the sense of agency—Jung was clear that our self-image is frequently narrow, sometimes rigid, and often defensive. He was aware, for example, that there are inevitably parts of the self that are either undeveloped, under-developed, or disowned. He called these parts of the self, the shadow, and held that it was an important part of the process of development, which he called individuation, that they be included, owned, and integrated into the ego. This is largely what I am referring to by the "broad" element of broad and flexible ego-functioning (relational psychoanalysts also talk in terms of a multiplicity of self-experiences and self-states (e.g., Seligman, 2003, p. 496)).

The shadow aspects are particularly important in relation to trauma as there is a great struggle to be able to bear the traumatic experiences of, for example, defeat, pain, humiliation, and shame, as well as the aspects of the aggressor—the bully, sadist, or abuser—that have become constellated in the individual *in potentia*. As described in Chapter Five, these are often projected onto someone else, whilst the individual struggles with the attendant affects of rage, hatred, and murderousness towards this aggressor (often in this way developing those traits themselves). It may equally be difficult for someone to own the desire for, or expression of, love, care, and affection, whether they are realistic or idealised, in other words, those elements may reside in their shadow.

It is exactly this resistance to these elements that causes the split in the personality and makes it difficult to form a coherent, cohesive, ego-identity with effective ego-functioning (Liotti, 2004a). The integration of any new element thus entails a greater or lesser alteration in the way we see ourselves "overall"—our broad, inclusive sense of ourselves.

Implicit in this development, and key to it, is the process of being able to disidentify with any particular aspect of oneself; for example, seeing oneself as "wholly good", or "never wrong", or "someone to whom terrible things always happen". This disidentification, as well as being part of the process of altering the way one sees oneself, allows one to be more open to "communications" from the unconscious—what Jung called the self, and what I refer to as the core self. Characteristic of Jung's view of the psyche was that we could put trust in these unconsciously functioning aspects of the personality, the self. He felt they hold a much broader perspective than the ego, are more observant and insightful, and guide the individual and the development of their personality in the process of individuation (see Chapter Eighteen on Jung).

Recognising these unconscious factors in this way requires that we can modify any (unrealistic) attempt to be in total control, and allow ourselves to be guided by this unconscious self. This is the guidance and insight that is available through deeper reflection, dreams, intuition, gut feelings, and even neuroses, illnesses, and other kinds of "symptoms". Analysis also requires a certain level of trust in the process of analysis and the analytic relationship (the analytic third), which includes calling on the analyst's unconscious self, in addition to that of the analysand's. This analytic third is a construct of both analysand and analyst over and above each of them individually (Chapter Twelve).

There is a further aspect of disidentification with the ego which is particularly significant when someone has experienced early relational trauma, or indeed any kind of trauma, which relates to the reliving of the defeat of the ego. As I have already stated, the experience of defeat of the ego—the experience of "collapse & submit"—underlies early relational trauma, even if that response does not become primary and other responses, such as fight or flight, serve to defend against it. Frequently the individual re-experiencing this defeat will experience extreme difficulty, terror, and shame, feeling that they are powerless, that they cannot deal with what is happening, cannot cope, will not survive, and are breaking down, fragmenting, and dying. This is a truly terrifying experience.

It is at this point that the ability to "submit" to things as they are comes in, but this does not necessarily mean giving up, but rather recognising, or re-experiencing, one's limitations, saying "I can do no more than I am" and placing yourself in the hands of a "higher power". This is exactly the higher power that Alcoholics Anonymous recognise as a key moment in someone's struggle with addiction (which has its origins with Jung (Addenbrooke, 2011, pp. 7ff.)), when the individual recognises that their struggle against the addiction through their will-power alone has failed.

What this higher power is, in practice, is open to question, but it may typically be thought of as God, fate, the self (in Jung's sense), the unconscious, or some other way of conceptualising it personal to the individual. It requires faith, and I particularly like Kierkegaard's phrase of a "leap of faith". The ability to allow this shift, this relinquishing of control, is a uniquely significant and usually momentous experience in a person's life; Chapter Eighteen documents these experiences in Jung's own life.

It is frequently a shift that individuals powerfully resist however, terrified that it means that they are failing, doomed, and will die. In fact it allows the individual to be open to the full breadth of capacities beneath and beyond their ken and conscious control. It is the shift to a "new centre of gravity" between the ego and the self, as Jung puts it. I do not see it as a relinquishing of the ego itself, however, but rather as relinquishing the particular, rigid, controlling form of ego-functioning, and shifting to a more flexible form of ego-functioning, as well as encompassing and integrating the early experiences of collapse and annihilation.

The wisdom of unconscious functioning has been thoroughly borne out in recent decades by the findings of neurobiology and neuroscience, which now recognise the wealth of functions, from information processing to integrating memories and reshaping the sense of self, that goes on below the level of consciousness. As Winson writes, "Rather than being a cauldron of untamed passions and destructive wishes, I propose that the unconscious is a cohesive, continually active mental structure that takes account of life's experiences and reacts according to its scheme of interpretation" (1990, p. 96); (and for a view of the neuroscience of the unconscious processes active in dreaming see Wilkinson, 2006, ch. 8; or West, 2011, ch. 12). Antonio Damasio (1995, 1999) has also described how the functions of thinking are built on top of and out of our more fundamental somatic-affective functioning.

However, such "wisdom" from the self is relative and circumscribed and is certainly not absolute. It requires that the ego engages with, understands, and contains these communications from the core self, which are significantly related to internal working models and trauma-related defences particular to the individual. Whilst they may have a sense of power, truth, certainty, and rightness, that is primarily due to their foundational status for that individual.

For example, a patient who believes and behaves implicitly as if they will be seen as special, and as if it is their right to be given access to the analyst's feelings and not to be "kept out" by the analyst's rational, boundaried attempts to explore what is going on (the analyst's ego-functioning), may have been granted exactly such access to one or other parent, in some kind of problematical oedipal constellation. Denying such access requires that the analyst recognise, and appreciate the strength of, such implicit pressures and requires a preparedness to withstand the patient's puzzlement, hurt, and outrage that might well ensue (although the person may also have a sense of relief, though it may not surface until later).

Such implicit beliefs and attitudes then, certainly cannot be followed unquestioningly as a guide to the process of analysis and as a model for how patient and analyst might relate, although they can give a vital indication as to the dynamics that were foundational in the individual's childhood. Similarly the trust that I mentioned does not relate to the essential "goodness" or benevolence of the patient, the analyst, or the process of analysis; it is simply a trust that whatever emerges will be significant. However, whatever that is will need to be worked with discriminatingly.

Implicit in these processes is the primary process functioning of the core self, which seeks out similarities and builds expectations therefrom, including the individual's expectations that others will operate according to these same internal working models. When ego-functioning is disrupted, the pressure on the other to identify and fit in intensifies considerably, as I will explore in detail in Chapter Eleven.

Porges describes how an area located in the temporal lobe of the cortex is responsible for identifying familiar faces and voices, and thus plays a vital role in identifying whether or not they are "safe, danger-ous, or life-threatening" in a process he calls "neuroception" (Porges, 2011, p. 11). He writes:

> If neuroception identifies a person as safe then a neural circuit [known as "the vagal brake"] actively inhibits areas of the brain that organize the defensive strategies of fight, flight or freeze. ... [W]hen situations appear risky, the brain circuits that regulate defensive strategies are activated. Social approaches are met with aggressive behavior or withdrawal. (Porges, 2011, p. 13)

Bowlby called this continual processing of experience "appraisal". When the individual feels under threat they will "prefer" a return to familiarity and the similarity to good experience, although there may also be a certain comfort in the familiarity of bad experiences (see below). Matte Blanco (1975, 1988) called this recognition of the simi-larity between things "symmetry", and understood it as the defining characteristic of unconscious functioning.

When a threat is intense or life-threatening, returning to the safe and familiar will be imperative. This is the imperative of the core self and should not be confused with the dictates of a wise self, although there is implicit wisdom in it. In other words, the analyst's identifica-tion will encourage safety although it should not be seen as a way of life, as certain consequences will ensue (see below). Neville Symington, echoing the mystics and recognising that these experiences arise from beyond the ego, talks in terms of trying to distinguish between the voice of the true god and the false god (2004, ch. 10). This recognition of the limitations of "the voice from/of the unconscious" represents one critique of Jung's concept of the self.

Related to this, as I explored in a paper entitled, "The narrow use of the term ego in analytical psychology: the 'not-I' is also who I am" (West, 2008), is the way that Jung, in his enthusiasm for the wisdom of the self, undervalued the role of the ego and emphasised the passing beyond the ego to the new centre of gravity between consciousness, which he identified with the ego, and the unconscious—calling this new centre the self (Jung, 1929, para. 67). In that paper I suggested that he was not only recommending the disidentification with particular aspects of the personality, which is necessary in order to allow the ego to expand and include new elements, but that he was recommending that that disidentification should in some ways be permanent and, furthermore, that he was giving undue weight to the experience of "no-self", which comes when such disidentifications take place.

I suggest that such experiences relate to the passing disidentifications that occur at times but which, if such experiences are extended beyond their natural scope, represent a suspension of ego-functioning and a move towards core self functioning which can amplify core affects (with no ego-functioning to contain them) and be destabilising and severely problematic for the individual.

When there is a disidentification from the ego there is an unlinking from "the particular" and from everyday reality, and the individual's experience can take on a numinous, impersonal, or transpersonal quality. This is very much the nature of spiritual experience where the individual has transcended the "I" in some form or other. There can then be a numinous identification with the other—whether that is an at-oneness with nature or a sense of union with the other. This is akin to the loss of "I" in the experience of being in love.

If the individual identifies with this core functioning however, they not only become highly sensitised and vulnerable, fearing attack (for which they may employ grandiose, omnipotent-like defences to keep themselves safe), but can also believe themselves to be omniscient in being able to understand the connection between all things. In the power of these extra-ordinary experiences the person can take themselves to be afforded special knowledge and insight with such unshakeable certainty—"the other person just won't be able to see or understand what I can see"—that this experience can become psychotic in nature. Jung frequently warned of the dangers of inflation and identifying with the self (I will explore the nature of spiritual experience further in Chapter Eighteen in relation to Jung himself).

Relationally, someone in this exposed state can "require" the other to identify in order to keep the individual's core self safe. It can also represent a form of intimacy between core selves that those who did not experience it in infancy find compelling. They may then put tremendous pressure on the analyst, as described in Chapter Eleven, not only to maintain this experience but also not to abandon them to an appallingly exposed experience—it is either heaven or hell (Balint, 1968, p. 17).

When individuals are operating primarily on the level of ego-functioning, respecting each other's autonomy and separateness, such intimacy and spontaneous exchanges between the patient's and the analyst's core selves—the Boston Change Process Study Group (1998) call them "moments of meeting"—are inevitably fleeting. I see them as moments of grace, although they can be underpinned by a sense of ongoing connectedness to the other.

The individual's ability to express themselves, to be spontaneous and creative, and to unfold (deintegrate), is the essence of the life force.[2] Mismatches that occur in this process can be experienced as annihilating—the unbearable trampling on new shoots—particularly when ego-functioning has been disrupted. This is the (extremely) sensitive core self that we need to defend at all costs; Donald Kalsched (1996, 2013) calls it "the soul".

However, never to trample on new shoots would require the analyst to accommodate the other to an impossible degree and specifically to incur the annihilation of the analyst's separate individuality. This can lead, in some form or another, to the breakdown of the analytic frame and ultimately of the analysis itself, which must remain essentially a two-person process (see the discussion of new shoots and love in the following chapter). As Balint said in relation to regression and the state of primary love (quoted in Chapter Two), this is a "two-person relationship in which, however, only one of the partners matters" (1968, p. 17).

Relating through ego-functioning inevitably entails limitation and coming to terms with the reality of the other in the analytic situation. This applies equally to the analyst who must recognise their own limited capacity to "make" the patient change/heal. This reality can be temporarily suspended through either the patient's or the analyst's distortion of themselves and the suspension of their own idiom through the identification with the other.

I think these issues/concerns represent a lacuna in Jung's understanding and conceptualisation of the ego–self relationship, and are why he struggled when working with individuals with a borderline psychology, preferring to pass them on to colleagues (Wiener, 2009, p. 16), and why he got into trouble himself with his patient Sabina

Spielrein (Britton, 2003, ch. 2; Gabbard & Lester, 1995, pp. 69ff.; Wiener, 2009, pp. 15ff.).

Rather than sidelining or undervaluing the ego therefore, it is much more constructive if it can be expanded to recognise and embrace the unconscious functioning—"the 'not-I' is also who I am" (West, 2008). I believe the ability to shift between the reality-oriented certainty of the known self and the openness to somatic-affective reactions and communications from the core self is what is meant by a good ego–self relationship (Edinger, 1972; Neumann, 1966), or as I would put it, a good ego-core self relationship. When the individual's ego is functioning broadly and inclusively, it can then be open to the continuous, spontaneous flow from the core self, which will inevitably, at times, introduce new experiences that will challenge the current organisation of the ego (self-knowledge, self-experience, and functioning) and require an expansion as the new experience/knowledge/functioning is accommodated.

Britton's ps–dp and Steiner's psychic retreats

This is akin to (but not identical with) what Britton (1998, ch. 6) has described as the developmental shift from the depressive position to the paranoid-schizoid position and then back to a new organisation in the depressive position: Ps(n) $\rightarrow$ D(n) $\rightarrow$ Ps (n+1) $\rightarrow$ D (n+1). This represents a shift from the known state (the limited ego state in Jung's terms), D(n), to the unknown and uncertainty of the paranoid-schizoid position, Ps (n+1), before a new ego-organisation emerges in a new depressive position, D (n+1).

Britton specifically distinguishes this from regression, which he describes as "a retreat into a pathological organisation that reiterates the past and evades the future" (ibid., p. 72). I would see what Britton refers to as a regressive retreat into a pathological organisation as one of the defensive organisations I have described, consequent upon trauma.

For example, in his original paper outlining such defensive organisations, which he came to call psychic retreats, Steiner (1987) describes a patient who was withdrawn, anxious, and feared being poisoned. In the sessions she would be silent for long periods of time, was sometimes mocking, often smilingly indifferent, often playing with her hair, and occasionally tearful if her analyst let the silence go on too long. Steiner suggests that his patient was in a pathological organisation that interfered with her development.

Reading his paper through the lens of trauma, it becomes clear that his patient was predominantly acting in identification with her depriving and abandoning mother—Steiner tells us that she had been put into a children's home as an infant while the family went on holiday and had refused to recognise her mother when she returned. She then unconsciously re-enacted this in her interactions with her analyst, sometimes acting as the abandoning mother, sometimes capitulated into the abandoned child (if he left her too long in silence), and sometimes entering the hypoactive, closed-down state that had, perhaps, allowed her to get through her mother's absences. I would suggest such re-enactments afforded her analyst an opportunity to understand those dynamics and her traumatic early experiences. I note with interest that the improvements he describes in her state of mind occurred at times when a link was made to her early experiences with her mother, in other words, when her traumas were recognised and acknowledged.

It is clear that those working in a Kleinian frame would not consider ego-functioning as continuous with the depressive position in that the depressive position is understood to be concerned with dependence on, and loss of, the object, whilst the paranoid-schizoid position is concerned with the preoccupation with the survival of the self (Steiner, 1993, pp. 25ff.). I would suggest that the paranoid-schizoid preoccupation with the survival of the self is due to the disruption of ego-functioning.

Regarding the fear of loss of the object, Steiner gives two examples of what he describes as anxieties and defences related to the depressive position (ibid., pp. 36–39). In the first, his patient could not bear not being able to train as a doctor—a situation that clearly derived, as Steiner relays, from the trauma related to his experience of "dying" when he was anaesthetised at age five, followed by his grandmother's death when he was fourteen. In phantasy, being a doctor would enable him to "conquer" death. Steiner's second example was of an extremely anxious, aggressive, and challenging man who brought a dream of a city being destroyed, which he had at the age of fifteen when his parents split up.

In both these examples it is clear that the individuals' ego-functioning had been disrupted by traumatic experience and therefore, for Steiner, the depressive position cannot be seen as co-extensive with the operation of ego-functioning. Perhaps other Kleinian theorists might see this differently.

In summary, if the ego remains flexibly open to the core self, such shifts can occur without long-term suspension of ego-functioning (regression) which will likely entail/require calling up primitive defences in order to protect the core self. For some individuals, their core selves are so well-defended that they do not realise that it is the flow from the core self (within the reality-oriented frame of ego-functioning) and the spontaneous dialogue with the other that is most satisfying; instead they seek tokens and the protective regulation by the object that might allow their self to unfold.

The ego-core self relationship as I have outlined it here is subtly but significantly different from the ego–self relationship as outlined by Kalsched in his book, *Trauma and the Soul* (2013). In taking a more classical Jungian position he discusses the role of the self without exploring the way that the core self (as I have outlined it here) is inherently problematic without the containing function of the ego.

The disruption of ego-functioning

Kernberg understands that pathologies related to the ego are central to borderline functioning, and Mollon (2015) also appreciates the ego's central role for individuals who feel continually in danger of physical and psychological disintegration (discussed further in Chapter Seventeen). One of the functions of ego-functioning is to organise and integrate experience. To quote van der Kolk, McFarlane and Weisaeth again, "in many regards, PTSD should be considered as an information-processing disorder that interferes with the processing and integration of current life experience" (1996, p. x).

According to Lyons-Ruth (2003, 2008) and Lyons-Ruth, Bronfman, and Parsons (1999) this processing, organising, and integrating ability is disrupted by early maternal withdrawal and affective errors in mother–infant relating. Such disruption is also signalled by patterns of discordance and contradiction between mother and infant (the infant is distressed and the mother smiling) and within the infant's own behaviours (smiling and whimpering in the same second) (Beebe & Lachmann, 2013, p. 67). Beebe and Lachmann propose that the infant needs to be protected from the threat of failures of recognition by the parents (pp. 68–69), and they link this to Bromberg's (2011) findings with adults.

Example

I would like to give an example of one person's development in regard to constructively relating to the spontaneity, creativity, and vivacity that comes from contact with the core self, yet also being in touch with the early relational trauma that lay at the heart of her experience, whilst containing this within the bounds of reality-oriented ego-functioning.

Zoë was born into a family in crisis with her parents in the midst of separating. She was the youngest of many children and she experienced much early neglect which resulted in several near-death experiences requiring hospitalisation. Her mother was emotionally absent and, in later years, frequently talked about regretting having had so many children. Zoë never saw her father again after the separation.

Zoë mostly brought herself up, although she was sometimes significantly mothered and cared for by her siblings. However, in the manner of William Golding's (1954) novel *Lord of the Flies*, this was sometimes a cruel democracy where she was teased, humiliated, or told she was a demanding show-off. Yet she was often able to engage her siblings, charmingly, until they had had enough of her and dismissed her or put her down.

At school she rebelled, centred on a heroic, spirited, and occasionally manic, "fight response" towards the rigid and uncaring environment in which she found herself. After lengthy teenage experience with drugs and dangerous relationships, she dedicated herself to someone whom she felt she could nurture and bring on, adopting a care-taking role (Bowlby) and becoming secondary to his "talent". When children came along she dedicated herself to their care, making sure they had a very different experience to her own. With both her partner and her children she had put herself and her core conflicts to one side and dedicated herself to them, offering the care, nurturing, and encouragement that she had not had, as well as providing the containment and stability of reality-oriented ego-functioning for them and, vicariously, for herself.

The relationship with her partner broke down early on however, and she struggled to make a new long-term relationship as prospective partners seemed to be either too unstable and self-centred, or too dull. This was in some ways because, partly through the process of therapy, she had outgrown relationships where she had to put herself to one side and dedicate herself to the other. However, the more "ordinary" potential partners did not reflect her vivacity (which she had previously projected on to others), or she feared she would be too much for them, as she had felt early on for her mother and, at times, her siblings.

In therapy I was immediately struck by her vivacity and directness, as well as her vulnerability. She engaged me in exploring issues around her children and her relationships, and she seemed to feel contained and supported by the analytic relationship. However, when on one occasion she was worrying, in a heartfelt way, that some of her work colleagues might see her as too direct and too much, I asked whether she feared I might find her too much.

This comment shattered a rather idealised split that had been going on where she had taken on trust that, "of course", I would not think that way about her. She was at first mortified and humiliated that she should have been expressing herself in such an open and trusting way, and then furious with me, and with the process of analysis, saying that she clearly wouldn't be able to discuss her difficulties with me any more. She questioned the whole point of "this kind of therapy" and was adamant that anything we might say or explore together wasn't going to make any difference.

She was talking very seriously about terminating the analysis and was talking to me as if I was one of the dull, dead (middle-class) individuals who were cut off from their spontaneity. I pointed out that she was seeing me as a one-dimensional non-person, and I suggested that her fury came from experiences of having had her own spontaneity killed off and belittled in the past. This comment brought us back into dialogue.

So here we had stumbled into her core wound of feeling unwanted, exposed, humiliated, and too much. Another casualty of these exchanges, as we went on to discuss, was the idealised phantasy of me being the loving father who could do no wrong and for whom she could do no wrong. For her, being a disgusting, unwanted piece of shit was a "fact" that was undoubtedly true, and she could not see how it could change (see Chapter One). This led to her feeling hopeless, despairing, and self-attacking.

The challenge for us was to accept, understand, and appreciate her experiences—and particularly her core experiences both of vivacity and spontaneity and feeling she was a piece of shit—whilst grieving for idealised "solutions" (see next chapter), without rejecting the containment and groundedness of ego-centred experience. This represented working though her core traumatic complex due to her early emotional neglect, substantially in our relationship, though recognising it on all levels as I have been describing.

Notes

1. Mollon calls the ego "the organ of adaptation to reality" (2015, p. 107).
2. As attested to by many myths, the life force, or the waters of life can only be sipped from. Those who attempt to imbibe too fully get carried away by what Jung called inflation and an identification with the self. The demarcation between the gods and man must be maintained; witness Prometheus' punishment for stealing fire: being chained to a rock having an eagle peck out his liver—the reputed seat of the soul—each night.

CHAPTER NINE

Idealisation and the longing for paradise—relinquishing the wish for an idealised, conflict-free relationship

Idealisation is an extremely significant phenomenon, particularly when it comes to working through underlying trauma, and it is very important that the analyst can help the patient recognise the origins and functions of the idealisation. It has the potential to ruin the individual's moment-by-moment, current experience as everything that is not ideal is dismissed, including the individual's own self if it isn't what the person feels it should be (leading to self-criticism, self-attack, and envy). It can also derail the analysis if the analyst travels too far in trying to provide the ideal rather than confronting and addressing the reality of the trauma itself. The following quote from Davies and Frawley demonstrates the potential power and depth of idealisation, which applies not only for adult survivors of sexual abuse as they are describing, but wherever there has been trauma:

> It would appear ... to be a universal fantasy among all adult survivors of childhood sexual abuse that once the horrible facts of the abuse become known, the world will be moved to provide a new and idealized, compensatory childhood. ... Often the renunciation of this wish proves to be even more unimaginable for the child than accepting the realities of her abuse. Acknowledging the

impossibility of bringing this fantasy to realization represents a betrayal of her most sacred inner self. (Davies & Frawley, 1992a, p. 25)

Idealisation also plays a key role in the patient and the analyst moving away from the trauma, rather than moving towards it to confront, accept, and work it through. This quote from van der Kolk and d'Andrea flags up some of the important therapeutic issues:

The very act of talking about one's traumatic experiences can make trauma victims feel hyperaroused, afraid and unsafe. These reactions only aggravate post-traumatic helplessness, fear, shame and rage. In order to avoid this, chronically traumatized individuals are prone to seek a supportive therapeutic relationship in which the therapist becomes a refuge from a life of anxiety and ineffectiveness, rather than someone to help them to process the imprints of their traumatic experiences. (van der Kolk & d'Andrea, 2010, p. 65)

In this chapter I hope to demonstrate how idealisation is intimately related to trauma and will discuss how, in a significant way, it emerges from and relates to actual experience related to the core self rather than something that is "merely imagined". It is because these experiences are rooted in actual experience that delusional and paranoid beliefs are so unshakeable, and idealised longings are so tantalising and powerful for the individual.

Myth and primitive functioning

In his book *Longing for Paradise*, Mario Jacoby writes: "The characteristics of humanity in the paradisal state are almost universally enumerated as: immortality; spontaneity; freedom; the possibility of easily ascending to Heaven and meeting with the gods; friendship with the animals and knowledge of their language" (Jacoby, 1980/1985, p. 18).

Rather than seeing these "experiences" as distant possibilities, I believe that they are available to each individual through the functioning of the core self, when ego-functioning is suspended, and if facilitated by a "protective", identifying other. To take each of these characteristics in order.

Regarding *immortality*, it is ego-functioning that brings the experience of time, limitation, and thus mortality. When it is suspended, experiences can feel, terrifyingly or blissfully, that they will go on forever. Freud (1900a) recognised timelessness as one of the characteristics of the unconscious. This can be experienced in particularly intense sessions where the analyst becomes absorbed in (identifies with) the patient and their affects, and time is experienced very differently—as if the session has flown by. In sessions where there is little contact with the core self, the experience is often that the session is dragging on forever.

The other element of immortality, in addition to that of timelessness, is that of invulnerability from death which comes from the sense of omnipotence (and omniscience). This is called up when the core self is under threat and it expands, like some kind of psychic puffer fish, to omnipotently meet every challenge. When ego-functioning is suspended the individual enters a different world, beyond the personal identifications of the ego, and it as if they exist in an eternal realm, without time, body, limitation, or death, and enlivened by the contact with the core self. Omniscience comes from the infinite links that the core self can make between things, so that the essence of everything is known (as described in the last chapter). Man becomes superman, as Nietzsche (1883/1961) said, one of the gods. This is an example of what Jung called inflation.

Spontaneity is a characteristic function of the core self when not under stress, as it always has a ready response to the environment. In analysis this is reflected in free association, although then, hopefully, these responses are filtering "up" to the individual, by which I mean that the individual is centred in ego-functioning. When ego-functioning (which gives a measure of continuity and containment) is disrupted or suspended the individual can feel terrifyingly pulled around in every-which direction, not knowing what they are going to experience next or indeed how they will experience themselves.

A sense of *freedom* occurs through the absence of restraint or limitation by an opposing other. Not constrained by the reality of the other, carried by the other's ego-functioning, nor concerned with the other being different, the individual can feel freed to be "who they really are". In the absence of a stable set of ego-identifications the individual can experience a numinous freeing from limitation and feel *at one with the gods*—at once nothing and everything (in one of his more mystical writings Jung described this as the *Pleroma* (Jung, 2009, pp. 346–347)).

Jung suggests that the experience of the self corresponds with the experience of God (viz. Edinger, 1972).

Similarly in this primordial-numinous place, the individual is in touch with their primitive, animal self, and able to identify fluidly with others, and can thus *"speak the language of animals"*, or trees, rocks, or anything of the natural world (Jung described this as *participation mystique* (West, 2014; Winborn, 2014)).

My point in outlining these experiences is to show that these are not remote possibilities, but very real experiences that can be grasped "if only" the other/the analyst identifies with the individual and provides the protective ego-functioning whilst they experience a timeless, spontaneous, freedom to "finally be themselves". Of course, if and when the analyst lets the patient down they experience a seemingly never-ending, nightmarish hell, rather than the hoped for heaven. This is due to the fact that without a benevolent identifying other, the core self is open to impingement, violation, traumatisation, and retraumatisation.

Back to trauma

Therefore, when ego-functioning is disrupted and the core self is exposed, the individual wishes to maintain the powerful, ideal state that is made available, as well as to protect the core self that is now exposed, ensuring that there will be no further traumatisation. Seeing that the original trauma was, by definition, unbearable for the individual, it is not only natural but good sense that they will seek a world where this will not occur again.

The desire for an ideal typically becomes dissociated from the original traumatic circumstances so that the individual comes to long for this ideal state in its own right, with the traumatic origins and underpinnings of the idealisation becoming lost. In order to return to everyday ego-functioning, with a sense of self-agency, self-determination, and autonomy, the individual will need to be able to mourn the wish for an ideal world or an idealised rescuer who will protect the individual's core self and make good the experiences the individual had or did not have in the past.

Some theorists under-emphasise the continuing role of the ideal in avoiding retraumatisation. Klein, for example, sees idealisation as a primitive defence related to splitting, with the aim of achieving relations with the good object. With her emphasis on the internal world over the external world, she sees the idealisation as keeping the good object separate from the individual's own destructive impulses, which are directed towards the bad object (Hinshelwood, 1989, pp. 318–319).

Freud, on the other hand, recognised the pressures that maintaining the ideal put upon the other, and saw idealisation in terms of narcissism, where "idealisation of the object" is part of an attempt "to recover the supposedly omnipotent state of infantile narcissism" (Laplanche & Pontalis, 1973, p. 202). Freud's concept of primary narcissism would constitute a state where there would be no traumatisation.

Different forms of idealisation

Whilst idealisation is intrinsic to trauma, it takes different forms depending on the types of defence that are primary for the individual, although there are infinite elaborations in that depending on the particular traumas that the individual suffered. Thus someone who experienced impingement and harassment may crave peace and quietude, whilst someone who experienced unrelatedness, absence, and deprivation may crave stimulation.

I should reiterate that such means of defending the core self are necessary, and that we all call upon them to a greater or lesser extent—the core self must be kept safe at all costs (as Winnicott (1960) states, although in his own idiom).[1] Frequently the individual will call upon a number of such defences (Chapter Five), although frequently one in particular will dominate. Each organisation will present different challenges for the analytic pair.

The individual with a narcissistic personality organisation, angrily, "fightingly", blames the other for not living up to their ideal and for causing them distress or "sub-optimal experience" of whatever kind. They make the other feel bad and guilty, and the individual attempts to get the other to fall into line to provide it—this is experienced as being controlling. The analyst can feel very uncomfortable, dreading having to "come up with the answer" or having to come up to scratch (to be ideal), and having to "make the person better" in the way they want. I have invariably found that these individuals experienced similar treatment in their upbringing from a critical and punitive parent, in other words, the behaviour also reflects an internal working model.

The individual with a borderline personality organisation is mortified, petrified (in the sense of frozen to stone), and in thrall of bad experience but, despairingly, cannot give up their relentless hope (Stark, 2006; Potamianou, 1997) that another will provide the consistent, caring, good experience that they never had. On the one hand the analyst is always letting the patient down as they cannot alter the patient's core negative feeling (the analyst can also become frustrated that nothing they do is good enough or at least that it doesn't make a significant difference and will frequently feel that the patient is not appreciating what they are doing). On the other hand the patient's anhedonia (lack of pleasure or positive affect) ties the analyst in to trying to make things better, cementing a firm form of attachment. It is very likely that these accord with the individual's early experience embodied in their internal working models, for example, as I will describe for Michael in the next chapter, he was drawn into the role of caregiver for his depressed and suicidal (anhedonic) mother. Envy, which plays such an agonising part of their experience, is so much more powerful when the individual believes that the envied person is getting their idealised needs met.

The individual with a schizoid personality organisation tries to model good (ideal) behaviour and consideration, giving and fitting in with others and "fleeing" conflict. At the same time they withdraw their core self from relationship, being disappointed in others and the world, idealistically hoping and expecting that others will provide what they have tried, increasingly resentfully, to provide, and becoming increasingly critical of others when they don't reciprocate. As Guntrip puts it, "though [the schizoid individual's] need for a love-object is so great, he can only sustain a relationship at a deep emotional level on the basis of infantile and absolute dependence" (1952/1980, p. 48).

The analyst can try to live up to this ideal, to heroically be the one who is finally good enough, circumventing the depressive feelings of deadness, lack of relationship, and failure. Alternatively the analyst can encourage the schizoid individual to "throw off their chains", exhorting them to achieve the openness and spontaneity of which they "know they are capable", yet with both parties feeling frustrated to the extent that this is not achieved. Frequently the patient had an early experience of a withdrawn, anhedonic parent whom they were unable to make happy, wherein lies the early relational trauma of defeat.

The individual with a hysterical personality organisation, based on the collapse response, has given their heart and soul to the other and put themselves, like the infant abandoned on the doorstep, into the hands of the other, feeling certain that the other will accept this ultimate gift, and mortified and murderous (and this can be turned towards themselves or the other) when the other does not reciprocate this ide-alised self-sacrifice. This would involve taking on the role of protect-ing the patient's core self and making good the massive neglect and/ or abuse that they experienced in infancy. The analyst can find them-selves having to deal with a complex set of responses from the patient, who experiences themselves as having been cruelly betrayed, feeling that the analyst has hurtfully rejected the precious gift of their loving, vulnerable, core self. Typically this individual has experienced parents who were invasive, self-preoccupied, and demanding (see West, 2007 for an extended example).

The individual with an anxious–vigilant personality organisation wants an ideal world where there is no conflict, where nothing can go wrong, where they are in control, and their affective experience is kept within certain narrow limits. The analyst can be drawn into try-ing to bolster this control, lest the patient be exposed to the unbearable experience of being overwhelmed and unable to cope, which they came to analysis specifically to avoid. Typically the individual experienced parents who could not bear too much reality and wanted their own experience maintained within certain narrow limits so that the patient themselves was experienced as disturbing, distressing, or too much.

Love, intimacy, and the oedipal perspective

These states are typically sought through being loved and being in love, as mentioned in previous chapters, where the individual requires a non-oppositional, identificatory state of union with the other. This state can easily be shattered if the other's separateness and hard-edged ego-functioning intrudes, and the much treasured, transcendent states are lost. These states of otherness threaten an experience of annihilation, humiliation, and rejection of the person's most sensitive, vulnerable, core self, often related to an individual's early experience of a collapse response (see Chapter Fourteen). Fordham describes this as the indi-vidual defending against the not-self part of the analyst, that is to say, the part of the analyst that is different from the patient.

The patient hopes that they will finally be able to "be themselves", that is, express this spontaneous core self. As Bollas says: "in adult life, the quest is not to possess the object; rather the object is pursued in order to surrender to it as a medium that alters the self" (1987, p. 14). In other words, the mother is wanted as she will change the self (see the discussion of dyadically expanded states of consciousness in Chapter Seven).

Fordham describes how the patient similarly wants the analyst to "be themselves" (so that the patient can be themselves). If the analyst does not do so, the patient may feel that the analyst needs to cure themselves of their "illness", and feel that they are hiding their self, or hiding behind analytic technique. The disappointing love object can then be mercilessly attacked, not only for frustrating the wished-for and tantalisingly available union, but also for leaving the lover's vulnerable core self mercilessly and heart-breakingly exposed (this is discussed in detail in Chapters Eleven and Twelve).

The oedipal and the ego perspectives

Clearly these situations could be seen in oedipal terms—that the person wants a close, loving, protective, exclusive, and sometimes sexual relationship with the analyst, not disturbed by the imposition of an other. This other could be the father, the mother, the grandparent, or the sibling, or the analyst's self-preoccupation, unavailability, thinking, theory, or containment. As Britton (1998, p. 42) points out, analytic thinking can represent the resented oedipal "third".

Marilyn Lawrence, working with anorexic and bulimic patients, describes a similar aversion to "intrusion" by an other, which she holds comes primarily from an intrusive internal object. She writes: "The more the parental relationship is denied and rejected by the girl, ostensibly because it intrudes upon her exclusive claims to the mother, the more she feels intruded upon" (Lawrence, 2008, p. 90).

I would suggest that, to the extent that the individual turns away from reality towards an ideal world of conflict-free relationship (identification), the more the individual will fear the threat of the intrusive other, which may take the form of the analyst's separateness, interpretation, and ego-functioning.

Significantly, in summing up her book, Lawrence writes: "while the deadly aspects of anorexia and bulimia are sometimes linked with trauma, in other patients they are the outcome of developmental difficulties that appear to have their origins in early infantile relationships in which constitutional factors play a part" (p. 114). I would suggest that the "early infantile relationships" that Lawrence describes correspond to exactly the kind of early relational traumas that I am outlining in this book.

Recognising the presence of this ideal, and its origin as a response to the individual's early relational trauma, allows the analyst and patient to recognise and address the issue, and to go through the inevitably deeply painful and disturbing process of mourning. Ultimately this can represent months or years of depressed or suicidal feelings, which I understand as the individual having to live through the hopelessness, despair, depression, and collapse associated with the original early trauma. The alternative is for the analyst to attempt to avoid opposition, which will ultimately be unsuccessful unless the analysis is to break down, and be accused of betrayal or seduction when the inevitable differences in perspective emerge. See Chapter Twelve for an extended exploration of what the analyst may need to go through in order to allow this process.

My understanding is that the dynamic here is more fundamental, broader, and more inclusive than an oedipal one, and that it involves an idealised regression towards union and primary process functioning in order to avoid retraumatisation.[2] I think this wider frame allows the analyst to recognise more examples of the pattern, as well as to use other terms and metaphors (in addition to the oedipal one) which might more closely relate to the patient's experience.

Whether this wider dynamic is compatible with a traditional Freudian understanding of the Oedipus complex is an interesting point, as my colleague William Meredith-Owen characterises the Oedipus complex as, "the tension between the yearning for wish-fulfilling merger and the acknowledgement of the necessary constraints of reality" (2013b, p. 599), a position wholly consonant with the position I am outlining here. I would understand the "constraints of reality" as being held by ego-functioning, which orients the individual to the situation as-it-is.

Everyday intimacy

Many of the life-enhancing qualities from the core self are available to those who have developed broad and flexible ego-functioning (Chapter Eight), in the form of everyday intimacy. Here individuals can spontaneously respond in a respectful dialogue, bearing to be themselves in the face of a separate other. This will involve conflict, hurt, and getting things wrong at times but, as for the interaction between infant and mother when things are going well, such mismatches can be repaired. It also involves the intimacy of exchange, the closeness of understanding, and the realness of being true to oneself, as well as experiencing the suffering of limitation. This limitation follows from having to accommodate the other person, who is naturally human and not self-sacrificingly ideal.

Example

There was a long period when "Vanessa" slowly and gingerly began disclosing her feelings of love towards me. At first I felt that I would be committing a mortal offence if I questioned the "gift" of this most precious part of herself. It was precisely this pressure that alerted me to the dynamic that was occurring. Whilst I interpreted that Vanessa was seeking the experiences she hadn't had as a child, and suggested that she was wanting to unfold and express her own loving nature, I was also aware that there was another element to the interactions that felt taboo and highly charged, as if I had to take great care not to offend her.

When I began exploring this with her, Vanessa was furious with me, telling me that I could not accept good feelings, and saying that I was trying to kill off anything good or hopeful in her and that I was only interested in bad things. I was very much reminded of the old dictum "Hell hath no fury like a lover scorned", although my intention had been to explore, not to "scorn". However, the relationship was able to survive her fury and we were able to talk about how she had not been able to develop a satisfying, loving relationship, how she feared approaching potential partners, and we went on to explore her internal working model of feeling unappreciated, unwanted, and rejected (the blueprint of which was both her dismissive, self-preoccupied father and her depressed mother).

My questioning had triggered that interpersonal trauma—the slow, chronic annihilation of her unfolding, loving self—and brought the dynamic into stark relief. After this our relationship was able to become more normal, less highly charged; I felt I could speak and behave more freely, and she began to really develop her life, beginning to find release from her attachment to the unavailable bad object. We noted how she frequently reversed this pattern and rejected men if they became interested in her, projecting the feelings of rejection and not being good enough into them or, if they were more desirable, preempting their rejection by assuming they would not be interested.

I have described, above, the numinous feelings of connectedness that can be associated with these feelings of love. If the analyst also holds a belief in the importance of "transcending the ego" and being able to reach such a state of mutual connectedness, perhaps due to their own early experiences of deprivation, then they may well try to maintain states of identification, rather than allowing such states of identification to be eroded by the intrusion of everyday reality, which challenges idealised "solutions". Gabbard and Lester (1995) describe such analysts as "lovesick" although, in broader terms, I would suggest this could be described as the borderline part of the analyst (the part that is not committed to reality-oriented ego-functioning) (Chapter Twelve).

Notes

1. He writes, for example, the false self is "a defence against that which is unthinkable, the exploitation of the True Self, which would result in its annihilation" (Winnicott, 1960, p. 147).
2. Relevant, perhaps, is Sabina Spielrein's view that fusion, rather than sexual pleasure, might be the aim of the sexual act (Kerr, 1993, quoted in Gabbard & Lester, 1995, p. 73), a view that prioritises the dissolution of the ego over sexual pleasure.

CHAPTER TEN

Bringing it all together—an extended clinical example

I would like to present an extended example now and bring together many of the elements from the preceding chapters.

When I first met "Michael" he was extremely depressed and suicidal, deeply nihilistic, hopeless, and despairing, and was in a terrible state of crisis relating to noise from his neighbours. He was experiencing extreme isolation and a deep longing for a partner. He felt that his life in general had been a complete and utter failure. He was also struggling with two life-threatening diseases.

He had been born into extreme emotional and material poverty. His mother had been depressed and suicidal—withdrawn, unmotivated, sometimes lying in bed and hardly able to manage the family, of which he was the middle of three siblings. Her relationship with his father was poor, with his mother sometimes waking the children in the middle of the night to go to relatives when they had had an argument. His father left when Michael was seven years old, tantalisingly saying he'd send for them all when he had made his mark in a new country—something he never did. Meanwhile the children were left at home, sometimes with little or no food to eat, with Michael taking on the role of trying to keep his mother going and the family functioning, all the time fearing that she would gas herself in the oven as a neighbour had done.

Much of the early analysis was spent talking about the appalling bleakness of his life, his conviction that he really should commit suicide, and that life was utterly meaningless and unbearable. A large element of this concerned the absence of a partner, as well as the agony of would-be partners who were tantalising but disinterested and rejecting. Another major source of distress was the noise, stupidity, impingement, and lack of concern of his self-preoccupied, inadequate neighbours. This objective level experience was the nodal point to which we returned, again and again.

We could see how these current preoccupations threaded way back, and mirrored his early experience with his depressed mother, leaving him feeling isolated and being the only one able to cope (yet not really feeling able to do so). The noise, impingement, and disruption he now experienced echoed family life and arguments and, with both parents in their different ways disinterested and abandoning, this mirrored his experience with tantalising would-be partners. He had some CBT to try to address his distress at the noise and impingement, specifically a form of self-hypnosis, which he found helpful.

Michael's negativity and nihilism was predominant. We explored a number of strands within it. First, his own talion-level reversal of his experience, so that he was himself hating, rejecting, and dismissing of the world, life, and people, in the way he had been rejected, dismissed, and hated. His experience of being hated derived from being gay and brought up at a time when that was illegal, a view reinforced by the church, to which he had been powerfully drawn as a child, being overtly homophobic and damning. He thus felt that he, and a core part of him, was not only excluded and ostracised but criminalised and condemned. These experiences underlay his continuing sense of alienation.

Second, was his hatred of this country, which he saw as mean-spirited, cold, badly organised, and brutish in comparison to the country to which his father had gone. We explored how his reaction to this country gave voice both to his reaction to the deprivation he had experienced, as well as his idealisation of the other country, which meant that nothing here was any good. Idealisation played a large part in his attitude to many things in life, including relationships, and he was slowly receptive to my interpretation of his idealisation, particularly when he had himself become disillusioned with his earlier "manic defences", such as extensive holidays or a search for the ideal partner. As time went on, the qualities of his sought-for partner became a lot more realistic, related to simple physical contact, warmth, and comfort.

When I say that we explored these things I do not mean to suggest that he changed his views about them, just that a good deal of the virulence went out of those views. Occasionally I would be drawn into remonstrating about the obvious "factual" distortions in what he'd said, for example, regarding a particularly view about the uselessness of women or an unrealistic idealisation of the other country. Any such remonstrations would make him exasperated, and I quickly recognised that he was primarily expressing the affective response associated with his traumatic childhood experience; for example, trying to make me really appreciate what it might have been like for him as a small boy, at the same time afraid of his mother dying, having his own needs perennially frustrated, yet having to be the one who tried to keep the whole family going, and infuriated at his mother's hopelessness, which "required" his care. I thus came to highly value his views and reactions as giving us direct access and insight into that early traumatic experience.

Regarding his sexual experience, we recognised that sometimes he put himself in situations of extreme vulnerability and danger. As we explored this he recognised that this experience mirrored a half-remembered, terrifying experience of sexual abuse he had as a child, which he was now recreating and re-enacting as an adult. Appreciating and exploring what that experience was like made sense of his behaviour, filled in the gap in his memory to some extent, and enabled him to stop exposing himself to that kind of life-threatening situation.

Whilst these represent his internal working models on the objective and collective/archetypal levels—expecting experiences of this nature everywhere and forming his primary beliefs about the world—they also extended to the way he thought about and treated himself on the subjective level. His early experiences of a lack of attunement or relational repair led to him feeling powerless, bad, unwanted, and unlovable at the core of his being. As Tronick and Gianino (1986) put it, he had developed a negative emotional core.

His attitude to himself had thus been neglectful (although this had improved, perhaps due to previous years of therapy), rejecting, and self-annihilating, exemplified by his powerful wish to kill himself and his conviction that he and life were worthless. As I have discussed in earlier chapters, these self-beliefs, based on foundational early experience, form the core of the individual's identity. They are felt to be true, but unbearable, and if true, to prove that life is unbearable. They are the core of the borderline individual's crisis of identity.

The analyst must thus be able to recognise, respect, and understand this experience, as trying to persuade the patient that they are "not like that really" is both ineffective, misses the point, and risks alienating the patient. Thus, with Michael I largely bore with his experience of himself and his life, only occasionally remonstrating that he and his life did have value really, but, more usefully, trying to explore with him the experiences that had led him to feel that way about himself. One of Michael's previous therapies had failed at this point, as the analyst had not been able to bear (nor presumably understand) the bleakness of his experience and his nihilistic self-view and had tried to "warm him up" by offering physical contact. According to Michael that was the beginning of the end of that relationship as it showed that the analyst had nothing more to offer than that.

Before I explore how things manifested in the analytic relationship between us (the transference level of experience), I would like to briefly describe Michael's extremely lucid and helpful dreams, of which there were literally hundreds, which gave us a very detailed and reliable commentary on what was going on for Michael and in our analytic relationship.

There were a number of themes: journeys describing where he was going and struggles on the way; dreams of having access to food where he had previously been excluded from the feast; of having increasingly effective means of communication—telephones that were with him and functioning rather than broken and lost; the increasing appearance of helpful anima figures who offered food or guidance; a persistent presence of helpful male figures; dreams where he was taking care of a young boy; and a string of increasingly constellated negative anima figures—from a vaporous, terrifying, witch-like presence evolving, through different dreams, into a female Nazi guard; there were also fewer appearances of a malevolent dictator figure who dominated whichever country the dream happened to be set in.

There were also dreams that marked particular turning points, such as a dream where he was able to soar above the trees and land on a platform looking over the forest, which corresponded with a time when he began to be able to free himself from his hitherto constant negative experience and experience moments, and then longer periods, of more positive good experience (this liberation also relates to his very significant spiritual practice which I will discuss below). Dreams of large, awe-inspiring birds that were also dangerous and had to be treated with care; these we understood as symbols of the self. A dream of returning to an old place of study where he was celebrated by those who worked there for his knowledge of "the underworld"—a dream that I felt signalled an inner recognition and appreciation of his remarkable journey through the most dark, difficult, and frequently hellish experiences, aptly described as "the underworld" of myth; and a dream of him being able to speak Chinese and allowing a young Chinese boy to "go first", which seemed to symbolise him having learnt the language of the primitive, childlike parts of himself and beginning to accommodate them rather than try to kill them, and himself, off.

However, when we had finished working on each dream—and there were sometimes two or three per session—he would frequently say, after recognising that the dream had, perhaps, depicted a positive development, "So what? I still feel the same". He called his underlying bad feeling his "base mood". This led him to say that he was going to stop bringing dreams as he felt they just gave him something to do, and interpreting them wasn't making him any better. I agreed and welcomed this as we both recognised that the time taken working on the dreams was preventing us getting to what was perhaps most difficult— exploring his intensely negative and nihilistic feelings in relation to me and the analysis.

Before I describe the detail of our relationship I would just like to chart some of the changes that had taken place in his life. Over the course of three years, and with the help of the CBT for his reactions to noisy neighbours, he stopped engaging in the most dangerous of his sexual activities, he managed his neighbours and his family differently, he spent less time agonisingly chasing impossible partners, he left a very superficial and narcissistic circle and found a more limited but more grounded group of friends, he moved house, and, very significantly, he began working again. He also became more deeply engaged in his (life-long) spiritual practice and moved closer to a deeply motivated spiritual group. His spiritual practice became central to his life and there have been times when he credited it almost wholly for the changes that have taken place. There were a limited number of occasions where he declared that he was, for the first time, feeling okay and different and once or twice, truly happy, although this would quickly erode.

The analytic relationship—the transference level

He now told me more directly that he thought the analysis was a complete waste of time, he didn't know what he was doing here, and, moreover, that he didn't know *what* to do here, he couldn't see how the analysis could work, that he thought life was definitely not worth living and that he might as well kill himself—he spent some time eulogising the euthanasia programmes he had seen on TV.

On one occasion when I was referring to our relationship, probably in the context of him saying he didn't feel connected to anything, he told me that he didn't know what I meant about our relationship, I did not exist for him, I made no difference to him. I remember biting back my response of pointing out to him how much had changed in his life and instead began to explore how he was now in the role of his suicidal mother and I was cast as him, having to painfully engage with her depression and suicidal impulses and recognise his/my sense of impotence to effect any positive change in her/him. I also interpreted that I was not interesting or significant to him, that I "didn't exist", just as he had felt he "didn't exist" for either his mother or father.

Things continued to improve for him to the extent that he began telling me that he was fine but that it was only when he came to analysis that he felt bad, that analysis was stirring up all this stuff, that analysis was the problem and that his friends couldn't see what on earth he was doing by coming. He began to be more openly mocking of the pointlessness of analysis and of life, talking as if this was a completely ridiculous undertaking—I think that previously he had protected me a good deal from this mockery and belittling. I began to experience this as hateful and felt he was being obnoxious; however, I recognised this as a deepening of our relationship and that the relational patterns were becoming more fully constellated between us.

He was very open in his free associations so that, when a particularly difficult challenge emerged, I usually found that he had already provided the clues as to what was going on. For example, when he was mocking on one occasion, I was able to remind him that he had told me that he particularly liked films where naive, optimistic, privileged young people discover, to their horror, that the world is not like they expect and they meet a brutal end. I suggested that this mirrored the way his enthusiasm had been "murdered" by his mother, that he was doing the same to me and wondering how long it would be before I got the message (a masochisto-sadistic dynamic).

This led us to explore the detail of his attachment patterns, and the way that his mother was extremely negative and nihilistic herself. Michael gave many examples of her continual complaints yet, when he suggested doing something constructive about them, she would dismiss his suggestion, rendering him impotent to help. It was clear that this represented a very powerful form of attachment whereby Michael was cast in the role of continually trying to make things better, failing, but required to continually keep trying. This was the role in which I was also cast with Michael.

Herbert Rosenfeld would describe this as destructive narcissism, where, "any wish on the part of the self to experience the need for an object and to depend on it are devalued, attacked, and destroyed *with pleasure*" (1987, p. 22, original italics). However, I would see it as an "effective" mechanism of attachment, based on an insecure–resistant or, in adult terms, dismissive attachment pattern. As Michael recognised this pattern, and his frustration/infuriation and sense of entrapment lessened, I noted that his relationship with his mother improved.

He continued to say that he didn't know what he was doing in analysis and often that he really didn't want to be in the session that day. I pointed out that it was as if I was the needy one making demands on him to come and making him feel bad, just like he must have felt that his mother, who "should" have been looking after him, made demands on him and made him feel worse rather than better. We returned to his excitement about, and attachment to, his negativity and his murdering of enthusiasm, similar to his mother's (an identification with the aggressor) on a number of occasions.

There were occasions when I found myself matching him affectively, in a talion manner, becoming as steely and as uncaring as he was. When on one occasion I didn't offer him a replacement session, he got in touch with his rage and violence in a way that frightened him and left him feeling deeply ashamed and exposed. He experienced enormous pain in his body and his shoulders in particular and, when he described it, it was clear he was describing the hunched-up shoulders and clenched fists of a fight response. Whilst this period was difficult for him, it was also a revelation as he had discovered his ability to positively stand up for himself and fight back, rather than experiencing himself as the powerless victim of the world who could only respond out of bitterness and in a self-destructive way; (earlier in the analysis we had recognised his night-time thrashing leg movements as a manifestation of an unexpressed flight response, an incompleted action tendency, in Levine's terms—see Chapter Seventeen).

We finally came to the dark heart of his trauma, his experience of meaninglessness and pointlessness as well as of isolation and boredom.[1] He had always presented these things as if they were wrong and shouldn't be so (his moral defence—Chapter Eleven), yet he insisted that they were absolutely true, that this was proof that his life was worthless, and that I should certainly be trying to change them but that I would not be able to do so. I understood these as the unbearable truths of his early experience that could not be borne and could not be escaped—the core of the traumatic complex that was initially unthinkable and unbearable, and that the person automatically avoids.

For him there was a paradox, in that exploring his experience of pointlessness felt pointless. These were experiences that he felt were "the way it was", undeniably so. I pointed out that these were valid experiences, that life did feel meaningless if you didn't engage with it, that his early life with his mother had felt appallingly isolated, lacking in warmth, care, and stimulation, and stripped of any meaning due to her depression and lack of engagement. I suggested that this related to experiences where everything had been destroyed and killed off. I did not make these comments "brightly" or cognitively, but from deep within the recognition that life can be like that. Throughout the analysis I have almost always matched his emotional tone as far as was possible and natural.

He was most perturbed that I took this line and asked angrily what good it was. I suggested that these experiences lay at the heart of his being and that he/we had needed to return to them to recognise them, appreciate them, and do them justice. I suggested that in expressing them he was being true to himself and being real with me, and I added that that was the value in our relationship—that he could be himself with me and that that was okay (picking up on the longstanding question of what was the point of our relationship).

There was a further thread to this. In line with his crippling (collapse) reaction to loneliness, boredom, and isolation he had, in fact, been increasingly isolating himself. Finding life outside oppressive, dangerous, hectic, intrusive, and threatening, he longed just to be at home, away from people, to be warm and quiet. Yet at the same time he could not bear the isolation (before, he had often turned to internet sex and pornography to try to fill the void). I suggested that this was exactly his earliest dilemma, that the people to whom he had needed to reach out—mother, father, siblings … and now the internet sex—were toxic, so he withdrew from them, yet he couldn't do without them. He couldn't safely make contact with them so that even when he was with people he felt alone (the child who reaches out towards mother and turns away at the same time—a disorganised attachment pattern).

We have subsequently worked a good deal on the consequences of his earliest experiences of the world being toxic—his schizoid withdrawal—and how he can most usefully reverse that and express, manifest, use, and actualise his self, despite his early experiences of being annihilated. Significantly, however, he has also been able to embrace the wish to isolate himself, as the experience of isolation has become detoxified and thus less conflicted. This has also allowed him to feel that he is no longer so "exposed" to the world—the development, perhaps, of a natural psychic skin (he had first come to be referred through an insightful GP who had picked up on his eczema and referred him on for psychological assessment).

He has also, very significantly, come to accept his life and accept that it is not the way he had been wanting it, relinquishing his fight against it—a fight that had made him feel intensely envious, frustrated, powerless, and ineffective. This has reconciled him to himself and brought him a deep congruence, continuity, and connectedness with his core self, going some long way to resolving the fundamental conflict in relation to his sense of self and identity.

This is the dark and difficult esoteric path through the underworld. It does not garner the individual exoteric success, and can frequently leave the person feeling ashamed and a failure, yet I would suggest that such journeys are no less heroic, rich, dangerous, or illuminating than any mundane exoteric journey. As in Michael's dream, I think the workers at his university were right to celebrate him.

As for the analytic relationship itself, it is not built upon the pleasure principle, it is not about being liked, being nice, kind, or good, for either analyst or patient. It is built on the deeper bedrock of being able to be yourself as you are, being able to be real, and being accepted for that. For both patient and analyst this means staying true to their primitive responses, yet finding a place for those within themselves and finding they are accepted by the other. The challenge to stay real and to face what is most difficult is a gift that the analyst equally receives from the patient and which I received, gratefully, from Michael. Such exchanges engender the deepest respect and appreciation. The connection and bond that develops between analyst and patient is forged through this journeying together through the underworld.

Note

1. Slavin and Klein (2013) see this as the patient's awareness of the "existentially precarious and conflictual context of all attachments", against which the analyst may well defend themselves (p. 169).

CHAPTER ELEVEN

The pressures on the analyst—being human and bearing to be inhuman

Michael Balint describes how,

> [i]f the [patient's] expectations are not or cannot be met, what follows is unending suffering or unending vituperation, or both together. Once this situation has established itself, the analyst will find it very difficult to resist its power, to extricate his patient and himself from it, and still more difficult to terminate the relationship. Often the end amounts to a tragic or heroic finale. (1968, p. 140)

In this chapter I will examine some of the pressures to which the analyst can become subject and explore how these relate to the patient's experience of trauma and early relational trauma. I hope to provide a comprehensible and narrative exploration of these dynamics that can explain why the analyst may come to act in ways that can result in impasses, extreme conflict, the prolonging of the patient's suffering and distress, or engage in enactments that can lead to the breakdown of the analytic relationship. This can occur despite, and frequently because of, the analyst acting with the best of intentions.

Klein, Bion, and Rosenfeld

These pressures are usually understood in terms of Klein's (1946) conceptualisation of projective identification, which she saw as a form of oral-sadistic object relations (an attempt to scoop out and possess the object) or anal-sadistic object relations (an attempt to punish the object and eject unbearable affects). She held these to be related to the splitting that occurs in the paranoid-schizoid position, which also entails an overvaluation of, and dependency on, the object and a consequent "weakening and impoverishment" of the individual's own ego-functioning.[1]

Bion modified this view to suggest that "excessive projective identification" takes place when the infant has been unable to communicate their early, distressing feelings to their caregivers (1959). In line with his theory of thinking, he saw projective identification as essentially a normal part of the process of communication and relating. Specifically, that the infant/patient projects their primitive affects (beta particles) into the parent/analyst in the hope that they can make sense of them, contain them, and, where necessary, act upon them to alleviate the infant's/patient's distress (having understood them with their thinking, alpha-functioning) (1962a, 1962b).

Both the acquisitive and punitive elements of Klein's formulation, and the containing, making-manageable elements in Bion's, can undoubtedly sometimes be observed in the kinds of interactions I am exploring although, as I have said already (Chapter Six), I think these are only elements of a more complex set of interactions (the primitive defences and internal working models on different levels and in direct and reversed forms).

Furthermore, whilst I think the concept of projective identification is an ingenious, generalised formulation, the analyst on the ground will likely be struggling to understand how to engage with what the patient is bringing, and to reconcile that with their empathic experience of the patient's suffering, as well as the (mostly unconscious) dynamics related to concern, helpfulness, and not wanting to be experienced as bad, abandoning, cruel, or inept. It requires a good deal of experience before the concept of projective identification is readily recognisable and useful to the analyst in this context.

Narcissistic omnipotent object relations—Rosenfeld

Herbert Rosenfeld's understanding is more directly rooted in an appreciation of trauma. He describes his work with psychotic patients, whilst recognising that there is a part in borderline and neurotic individuals that functions in a similar way. This includes the analyst, and Rosenfeld stressed that it is important that the analyst is aware of this part of themselves if they are to work safely and effectively in this area and not behave in anti-therapeutic ways (see Chapter Thirteen on the analytic attitude below).

Rosenfeld describes what he called narcissistic omnipotent object relations, where the individual

a. uses "others (objects) as containers into which, feeling all powerful, they project those parts of themselves that are felt to be undesirable or which cause pain and anxiety" and

b. "identifies (by projection or introjection) with the object, to the extent that he feels he is the object or the object is himself. In the case of introjection the object becomes part of the self to such a degree that any separate identity or boundary between self and object is felt not to exist. In the case of projective identification parts of the self become so much part of the object, for example the mother, that the patient has the idea he possesses all the desirable qualities of the object—in fact that he is the object in these respects". (Rosenfeld, 1987, pp. 20–21)

He suggests that these narcissistic omnipotent object relations are partly defensive against the recognition of the separateness of self and object.

It is clear that the core self cannot bear the shock of impingement, rupture, violation, or neglect, which is why so much effort is put into attempting to anticipate the other's reactions (Beebe & Lachmann, 2013). Needing to be protected at all costs from these narcissistic wounds, the core self will call up omnipotent defences in order to do so, whether that is in the form of denial, omnipotence, idealisation, splitting (both of the self, in terms of dissociation, or the other, in terms of good and bad), projection or projective identification, and will react to impingement by the means I have outlined: fight, flight, freeze, or collapse (West, 2013b).

One elaboration of Rosenfeld's theory was a distinction he made between libidinal and destructive narcissism (Rosenfeld, 1971). In libidinal narcissism there is an attempt to control the loving, caring object on whom one is dependent, whilst in destructive narcissism "any wish on the part of the self to experience the need for an object and to depend on it are devalued, attacked, and destroyed *with pleasure*" (Rosenfeld, 1987,

p. 22, original italics). He describes destructive narcissism as having a particular, hidden and hypnotic power, which is a significant factor in the negative therapeutic reaction. He adds that, "such destructive and omnipotent wishes are often difficult to recognize in what a patient does and says because the patient unconsciously experiences them as protective and even benevolent, but very secretly" (p. 22).

As an example of destructive narcissism, Ron Britton (2003, pp. 157ff.) describes Miss L, whose analyst found herself agreeing to all sorts of alterations in the frame, including a reduction in fees and not charging for a missed session. A dream of plotting with her lover-sister-sibling to kill off an old lady, beautifully described the pattern. The way the conscientious analyst found herself fitting in with the patient's dynamic, which reflected the patient's parents' self-preoccupation and their killing off of the other/the patient, demonstrates the depth and power of these patterns, held in implicit/procedural memory. Jean Knox (2009) also writes illuminatingly of the power of these implicit pressures. I gave an example that could be seen in terms of destructive narcissism in Chapter Ten.

Regarding libidinal narcissism, Britton (2003, pp. 161ff.) describes Mrs. D, who fell in love with younger colleagues feeling that they were soulmates who completely understood each other at first, but slowly became preoccupied with how the other viewed her. I explored this theme in Chapter Nine in relation to idealisation.

Sandler—role-responsiveness and identification

Joseph Sandler is critical of the concept of projective identification, particularly in regard to ascribing intention to such interactions. He sees the analyst's natural mirroring responses, which have now been understood to occur through the functioning of mirror neurons as described by Gallese (2001) and Rizzolatti (Rizzolatti & Sinigaglia, 2008), as playing the major role in the analyst's experiences in response to the patient, rather than seeing those as "something that the patient wants to 'put into' the analyst" (a point echoed by Colman (2013)). He also recognised that, "… transference need not be restricted to the illusory apperception of another person …, but can be taken to include the unconscious (and often subtle) attempts to manipulate or to provoke situations with others which are *a concealed repetition of earlier experiences and relationships*" (Sandler, Dare, & Holder, 1973, p. 48, my italics).

He recognised that the process whereby the analyst is influenced by the patient, takes the form of the patient's

> externalisation of the object representation, which has been revised in phantasy to contain the unwanted aspect of the self, on to an external object. This externalisation takes the form of actualisation, a process in which the object is pushed, by a variety of subtle unconscious manoeuvres, both verbal and non-verbal, into playing a particular role for the patient. (Sandler, 1993, p. 1104)

Sandler writes that, rather than call the analyst playing a particular role, "acting out" or "acting in", "I would prefer to see it as what I have called role-responsiveness, which, if it stays within reasonable limits, can be a most useful source of insight into the unconscious wishful phantasy that the patient is trying to gratify" (Sandler, 1993, p. 1105).

Sandler's conceptualisation of role responsiveness coheres with the experience of the patient who is acting from their (unconsciously held) internal working models, which represent powerfully held expectations and beliefs about the world and others. Examples of these are: "No one would really like me/love me/want to relate to me", "People will reject my love and affection", or, perhaps, "People will want me and will let me into their inner self". The patient may well experience considerable frustration, confusion, irritation, and disbelief if the analyst does not both share and act in accordance with the patient's unconscious expectations/internal working models.

Even whilst the analyst engages with the patient from their analytic stance (which may be built on their own internal working models, for example, in the role of a caretaker), the patient's internal working models will have an impact and will begin to be constellated in the analyst on some level or other. The analyst's reactions are "a most useful source of insight" (Sandler (above); Heimann, 1960) that allows them to begin to be aware of and explore the patient's patterns of relating and thus their early experience.

As Racker (1958) points out, the analyst will need to be in touch with their primitive reactions and counter-reactions to the patient, both so that they can properly engage with what the patient brings, and so they do not fall into a passive, masochistic surrender to the patient (which will almost certainly be a repeat of an aspect of the patient's early experience)—see the next chapter for further discussion.

Like Sandler, Robert Caper (1999), describes how, having naturally come to (largely unconsciously) identify with the patient, the analyst must come to disidentify sufficiently to remain separate, to think about and understand what they have learnt about the patient's experience and way of relating, and communicate this to the patient. Jessica Benjamin, as I will explore further below, understands this in terms of the analyst holding the tension between identificatory oneness and the observing function; she calls this "the third in the one"; for example, maintaining an awareness that the patient's distress will pass, alongside the analyst's empathy for the patient (Benjamin, 2004, p. 14).

The analyst communicating their understanding to the patient can hopefully allow the patient to recognise the patterns, to understand what has triggered them, to disidentify with them to some extent, and to thus direct them in a way that is more constructive; although, at base, it is the trauma at the heart of the complex continuing to feel unbearable that fuels the dynamic embodied by the internal working model and that gives it its power, and affects the analyst.

I am particularly interested, however, in why it is so difficult for the analyst to sufficiently disidentify at times, whilst maintaining an empathic understanding, and will suggest that this is due to experiences that are particularly traumatising and "inhuman" that the analyst struggles to allow themselves to experience, acknowledge, and embody (Gabbard, 1997; Knox, 2013). These are frequently not pre-existing feelings for the analyst, but rather experiences that emerge, perhaps for the first time, in relation with the patient.[2] This therefore represents something of a personal journey of discovery and experience for the analyst (Chapter Twelve).

Whilst the foregoing has focused largely on the theory around these experiences I would like to explore the actual experiences as they are met with in the consulting room in more detail and will turn to what Michael Fordham says on the subject, before offering a fuller, narrative picture.

Fordham—defences of the self

Whilst I outlined Michael Fordham's (1974) concept of defences of the self in Chapter Two, I will return to it now to explore how those defences affect the analyst. Fordham, in the most widely read and often quoted paper in the post-Jungian literature, describes the patient's defences of the self—the powerful reactions against what they experience as "not-self" parts of the analyst, in other words, the parts of the analyst that are different from the patient (this is characteristic of the primary process functioning of the core self when it is exposed due to the disruption of ego-functioning).

Fordham describes how the patient reacts against the parts of the analyst that they see as "technical and mechanistic" (which I understand primarily as the analyst's ego-functioning), and attempts to "unmask and obtain" a "good, hidden part" of the analyst for themself. Thus they may treat the analyst's comments and interpretations as cold, unfeeling, and theoretical, or even as attempts by the analyst to defend themself against their own "infantile parts", which the patient holds they are projecting into the patient. They may react "with denigration ending up in load groans, screams or tears whenever the analyst speaks" (Fordham, 1974, p. 193). He describes how the patient becomes extremely distressed and can come to feel that their pain, terror, dread, and confusion is directly caused by what they see as the analyst's "sadism, cruelty and destructiveness".

In my experience the patient can powerfully and viscerally object to any attempt by the analyst to put their understanding (in so far as it offers a different perspective to that of the patient) into words, precisely because they feel that their experience is not being heard, and any words are felt like the analyst "defending themself". Furthermore, the patient naturally objects if they feel they are being packaged, labelled, or reduced to a cognitive construct that will in no way address their powerful affective experiences, which lie at the heart of their sense of themselves.

The analyst needs to have enough trust in the patient, and in the process of analysis, to allow the patient to voice their experience unopposed and concentrate on getting to the truth of the patient's experience, however wrong it may seem. Fordham calls this a psychotic transference precisely because the patient's experiences do not make sense from a rational, that is to say, ego perspective.[3] I will discuss this in the following chapter in terms of the defeat of the analyst's ego, but it is essentially about respecting the (subjective) truth of the patient's experience. Any other perspectives can be worked out later, but until that truth is heard and appreciated little progress can be made.

Fordham describes how the pressure due to the foregoing can produce characteristic effects:

> Feeling frustrated and inadequate in his efforts to help his patient, the analyst can seek to do something that mitigates the situation: he may more or less abandon analysis, submit to the patient's seductions by excessive use of tokens, or allow the patient to take more and more possession of him physically. This can lead to a sexual relation being started. As far as the countertransference comes in here, sexual acts, usually of a polymorphous kind (Meltzer, 1973), may be introduced to frustrate the patient's efforts to induce a regression. The transference contents are, as I have suggested, directed towards inducing helplessness in the analyst and this can change the patient into a threatening, persecuting beast. Such a regression may be stopped by adolescent sexual activity. (Fordham, 1974, pp. 194–195)

One aspect of this, as Fordham describes, is the patient's demand that "you stop being an analyst and become yourself", to which the analyst may sometimes respond by trying to "[be] himself … by making confessions or giving information about himself" (p. 196), something Fordham cautions against. He points out that despite the patient's protestations of harm caused by the analyst,

> the patient does not go away; on the contrary he often contends openly, but more often by implication, that his whole life depends upon the continuation of the analysis and its successful outcome. He so contends, even when he insists, that for a solution to come about the analyst must mature or cure himself first of the illness that he has (in [the] patient's delusion). (Fordham, 1974, p. 196)

Disclosure, and digesting the inhuman

There are some therapists, particularly amongst the relational school, who feel that it is important to answer certain of the patient's questions in order to give the patient a sense of the emotional reality of the relationship, to reassure them of the congruence between what the analyst says and what they are feeling (that may have been so lacking in their early experience), to demonstrate the analyst's capacity to reflect on what they themselves are thinking, including their conflict about making certain interpretations, and to enhance the patient's confidence in their ability to trust their intuitions about the other when they have, perhaps, been deceived, exploited, and come to lose a sense of what is real (Aron, 2006; Beebe & Lachmann, 2002; Benjamin, 2004; Courtois, 2010; Davies, 2004; Davies & Frawley, 1992a; Ogden, Minton, & Pain, 2006).

One clear example of this attitude is in Benjamin's (2004) classic paper "Beyond doer and done to". In the paper Benjamin describes at length how it is important for the analyst not only to recognise the co-constructive, mutually influencing nature of the analytic relationship, but also to see, "both developmentally and clinically, how we actually come to the felt experience of the other as a separate yet connected being with whom we are acting reciprocally" (p. 6). She says that she sees the "engagement in reciprocal recognition of the other as growing naturally out of the experience of being recognized by the other, as a crucial component of attachment responses that require mutual regulation and attunement" (p. 6). One aspect of this is for the analyst to allow themselves to be wrong, to feel guilty and so on, and to communicate that, on occasion, to the patient[4].

Yet in that paper, despite finding herself telling her patient Aliza that, "no matter what she did, she would always have a place in my heart, that she could not break our attachment or destroy my loving feelings" (p. 37), the patient left the analysis (Benjamin says she felt this was "in order to protect our relationship, a third she could not imagine would survive"). Happily she returned, and Benjamin says that she (Benjamin) "was able to reiterate [her] sadness about having been unable to avoid evoking the feeling of being with a dangerous mother who denies what she is doing" (pp. 39–40). It seems that whilst Benjamin was prepared to allow herself to be wrong, she was not, as quoted, prepared to really "stay with" the experience of being experienced as the "dangerous mother who denies what she is doing"—an essential aspect of Aliza's early relational trauma.

I would suggest that it is precisely the perspective of trauma that is missing here, and that through threatening to leave, "recapitulating a long history of breaking attachments" (p. 37), the patient was exposing her analyst to exactly the abandonment that she had experienced. Instead of understanding her patient's experience of "literally dying", and that her analyst "did not care", as a reconstruction of a collapse at her earliest experiences when her mother left her "with strange relatives who barely spoke her language", Benjamin tried to repair the mismatch by her loving, "caring" disclosures. Similarly, her patient's wish to leave, which she "justified" with reference to her analyst having let her down so that "she would never fully regain her trust", could be understood in terms of her patient, Aliza, identifying with the aggressor and becoming the abandoner, rather than the person who was abandoned. Had she interpreted along the lines I suggest, Benjamin might have alerted her patient to the deeper resonances of her experiences, as well as her reversal of the original trauma, thus helping her to bring these conflicting elements together within herself.

Whilst Benjamin's disclosure was apparently ineffective in that Aliza left (although disclosure can have other potential consequences, as I describe below), what is most striking is that, having been to another therapist in the interim and returned to Benjamin, it was precisely the recognition that she was behaving like her mother in being abandoning that had a significant effect. Benjamin comments that on her patient's return[5] she was "able to say what could not be said earlier: how impossibly painful it was for Aliza to feel that she, with her own daughter in the present, in some way replicated her mother's actions" (p. 40); and from there they went on to explore how she had been with Benjamin herself, feeling intensely guilty but relieved. Benjamin comments: "now she had the experience that her love survived the destructiveness of our interaction, my mistakes and limitations" (p. 40).

It is striking from Benjamin's description that the patient recognised her identification with the aggressor immediately and, Benjamin reports, "spoke of how transformed she felt, so much stronger after that session that she often had to marvel at herself and wonder if she were the same person" (p. 40).

The patient's recognition of the way in which they are behaving in identification with the aggressor is a key moment in an analysis that must be approached with care, respect, and a deep sense of import. It is the heart of the conflict that prevents the individual developing a coherent and effective identity, and it carries with it a deep load in relation to unbearable and morally unacceptable behaviour, as I will explore further.

So why did Benjamin feel that she "could not say this before"? Not to address the patient's identification with the aggressor reinforces the idea that that way of behaving is too terrible. Perhaps this *is* the primary reason for her approach, as she describes Aliza's mother as having a "dissociated, disowned, 'violent innocence'" and "responding to any crisis or need with chaos and impermeability", commenting, "it was this mother whom neither of us could tolerate having to be" (p. 37). It is precisely this difficulty bearing, embodying, and addressing the unbearable, "inhuman", traumatising ways of being that are so difficult and so key in an analysis, as I will be exploring further in Chapter Twelve.

Furthermore, Benjamin's analytic stance is to model a different way of responding; as she puts it, "the analytic task … is to help the patient create (or repair) a system of sharing and mutuality" (p. 22). Presumably she feels that what is mutative is to foster the development of this respectful attitude towards the other, and that it was therefore important to promote this kind of exchange with Aliza.

This privileging of the process over the content is characteristic of theorising that does not directly address the particular trauma but focuses instead on the generalised effects, and I think the absence of a fully fledged trauma perspective is telling here. I would suggest that the analytic task in this case, and many others, is precisely to work through what was traumatic and felt "inhuman"—for the mother, following a series of catastrophes, to abandon her child. As Meredith-Owen comments, "the relational eagerness to establish an *endorsing* reverie, may foreclose on a reaching down to engagement with intrinsic ambivalences, often beneath conscious awareness, whose only means of expression may be the negative transference" (2013b, p. 595, original italics).

Furthermore, in relation to their exchanges, just as Aliza had to reassure her mother that she (Aliza) could bear the unbearable, so her analyst's disclosure of her guilt about exposing Aliza to the trauma meant that Aliza, yet again, had to reassure the other—a further level of re-enactment. As with the example of Lachmann in his analysis of Karen (Beebe & Lachmann, 2002, pp. 45ff.), when he continued telephoning his patient to remind her of the session (partly because, he says, he could not bear the anxiety of not doing so), it is clear that both felt unable to really accompany the patient into the darkest of places and trust that they would emerge; furthermore to trust that "the third" that Benjamin describes, would emerge as part of the respectful analytic work between the two. It seems that on this occasion Benjamin was not able to maintain an awareness that her patient's distress would pass, alongside her empathy, thus holding the tension between identificatory oneness and the observing function, what Benjamin calls "the third in the one" (p. 14).

Moreover, regarding the disclosure of the analyst's feelings, as I have commented before (West, 2007, p. 5), it is confusing for the patient if the analyst volunteers or answers "these questions", but not *all* questions. And what if the analyst is experiencing hateful, murderous, or sadistic feelings, or loving and sexual ones (as an aspect of the co-construction)?[6] Whilst the situation with Benjamin's patient is apparently clear, and each situation is unique to the analytic couple, let us suppose for a moment that it was a male therapist saying that his patient "would always have a place in [his] heart, that she could not break our attachment or destroy [his] loving feelings"; how might the patient take such a declaration (see Gabbard and Lester (1995, p. 51) about the disclosure of loving feelings)?[7] And of course on one level it does not make any difference whatsoever whether it is a male or a female therapist, and a female or male patient could have exactly the same reaction to a female therapist; however, there is a collective, stereotypical alert regarding the male seducer that I am tapping into here.

My real point is that the trauma-related internal working models are key, as it will be these that are the template by which such disclosures are understood; for example, whether either the client or the analyst has been impinged upon, violated, or abused or given full, inappropriate access to a parent's emotional life or body. These implicit relational ways of being are exactly the sort that the analyst or patient will "find themselves" falling in with naturally. It is these implicit patterns that need to be addressed and understood as a matter of priority. It is very tempting for the analyst to fall in with what "feels right and natural" for the patient or themselves, particularly if this avoids the inhuman aspects of relationship that are, in fact, all too human.

Being human, being ideal, and being inhuman

To return to Fordham's helpful observation that the patient wants the analyst to be "more themselves" and cure themselves of their own "illness". I think that the "illness" from which the patient feels the analyst is suffering relates to the ideal, whereby the individual "liberates" themselves from their restrictive, limited (and limiting) ego-functioning and follows the lead of their intuitions and inner callings, which are imbued with a powerful veracity and an altered state of consciousness (see Chapter Nine on idealisation). Jung would call this an inflation due to an identification with the (unconscious) self, and flooding by the archetypal layer of the psyche—an experience of "archetypal" affect.

In so far as this state of mind comes to imbue the analytic relationship, the patient and analyst may find themselves experiencing a "special" kind of connectedness and understanding, an ability to know what each other is thinking (see Gabbard and Lester's comments on Jung's relationship with Sabina Spielrein (1995, ch. 5)), a highly charged state of well-being and universal connectedness, that may be felt as a quasi-mystical form of love. Or this state of mind may be more fleetingly glimpsed and, instead, the patient is left vigilantly expecting and fearing the analyst will let them down or betray them in some way, whilst the analyst is left walking on eggshells, feeling that their comments or interpretations will in some way spoil the relationship (Caper, 1995/1999, p. 35).[8]

In order for this state of mind to be sustained in the relationship, the patient requires that the analyst identifies with them, is not discordant, is "good", kindly, all-embracing, all-accepting, and protective (Balint, 1968), and is not challenging or conflictual, does not question the patient's expectations and does not make interpretations from a separate, rational, thinking position.[9] Should the analyst make such interpretations they may be experienced as horrifying, bad, cruel, abusive, and destructive, as Klein describes in terms of splitting and the bad object, or as Fordham describes in terms of defences of the self, and as Balint describes in relation to malignant regression, writing that "if the [patient's] expectations are not or cannot be met, what follows is unending suffering or unending vituperation, or both together" (1968, p. 140).

My sense is that the problem is with interpretation, and certainly interpretation too soon, as how can the analyst think to know or interpret anything about the patient until he has made an earnest journey with the patient to try to discover the root of their struggle? "K" makes exactly this point (Astor, 2007) in a fascinating series of papers exploring his experience of his analysis with Michael Fordham which reached an impasse and was terminated by Fordham. I will be exploring these papers in the next chapter.

The essential point then, is whether the analyst identifies with the patient, adopts a separate position, or is able to find a way to do both.

Benjamin (1988, 1998, 2004) describes how the analyst's identification can be one of "complementary relationship", the relation of twoness, where "there appear to be only two choices: either submission or resistance to the other's demand (Ogden, 1994)". She writes:

> Characteristically, in complementary relations, each partner feels that her perspective on how this is happening is the only right one (Hoffman, 2002)—or at least that the two are irreconcilable, as in "Either I'm crazy or you are." "If what you say is true, I must be very wrong—perhaps shamefully wrong, in the sense that everyone can see what is wrong with me, and I don't know what it is and can't stop it" (see Russell, 1998). (Benjamin, 2004, p. 10)

The relational space has disappeared and the analyst feels pressurised by the patient, whilst the patient feels pressurised and trapped by the analyst.[10] Ron Britton sees this as characteristic of borderline functioning where the countertransference experience is "one of being constrained: either feeling tyrannized by the patient or of having misgivings about being tyrannical" (2003, p. 83).

These pressures relate, I believe, to the traumatic complex. It is imperative for the patient that the trauma is recognised but, in addition, the patient will likely exert intense pressure to avoid the traumatic complex, perhaps with recourse to moving towards idealised ways of being with the other, and to avoid retraumatisation. As I see it, this lies at the heart of the particular kind of splitting that Klein describes that engenders "excessive projective identification" (Bion, 1959)—it is not just about good or bad, but about heaven or hell, life or death, safety or unbearable, retraumatising, life-threatening, torture.

The analyst's act of freedom

Neville Symington, in his classic paper, "The analyst's act of freedom as agent of therapeutic change" (1983), recognises this phenomenon exactly; he calls it the x-phenomenon. I would suggest that the examples that he gives all relate to a particular trauma that his patients wished to avoid, and that the freedom that the analyst experiences occurs when the analyst is able to confront, or even simply think a certain thought in relation to, the trauma; (a thought can be sufficient, says Symington, as he recognises the unconscious nature of the communication between patient and analyst at these times, which goes on "at the primary process level" (p. 291)).

Symington gives three examples: first, "poor Miss M" who he felt "couldn't" pay more. Symington became freed when he challenged the powerless, "poor", victim-like, way she presented herself (her implicit internal working model). Second, an obsessional man who feared that his analyst would think him "pathetic". In suggesting, finally, that he (Symington) was quite free to think that he *was* pathetic, he was demonstrating that the patient's worst fear—his relational trauma—could be borne. Third, a woman who consistently accused him of being dominating, because he was a man and had chauvinistic attitudes, whilst "sadistically", Symington says, dominating him to the extent of physically standing over him and poking him. I would suggest she was demonstrating a masochisto-sadistic reversal of her original, trauma-related internal working model, where her identification with the aggressor is "justified" by the way she experienced her analyst as retraumatising.

The superego, moral outrage, and the moral defence

Symington (1983) holds that the false ideas with which the analyst has unconsciously identified are held by the patient's superego—ideas that the patient has identified with in their parents and their culture. Symington suggests that patient and analyst thus form a corporate entity from which the analyst needs to free himself in the way Symington describes. This "corporate entity" very much echoes Jung's understanding of the collective unconscious, from which the individual needs to distinguish themselves through the process of separation and individuation.

I see the superego somewhat differently; namely, as a function of the core self that not only keeps the individual tuned in to their caregivers and culture, but that also objects, morally, when the individual's core self is traumatised or retraumatised. It is this sense of something being morally wrong when the individual's traumatic complex is being threatened that can exert such a powerful pressure in the analytic relationship.[11]

Being morally wrong is something that human beings tend to find extremely difficult to bear because it threatens the individual with the fundamental, primitive terror of being ostracised from their parents and the community. In the past, when I have been told by patients that I was behaving morally reprehensibly it has had a powerful effect, leaving me confused and feeling extremely bad, to the extent of wanting to avoid its recurrence and protect the patient from whatever it was I had been causing them to experience (see West, 2007 and below).

However, over time I have come to realise that moral outrage is a sign that wounding, and re-wounding, to the individual's core self has occurred. This moral outrage is a feature of the core self and, specifically, its evaluating and valorising function (Solms & Turnbull, 2002, pp. 90–91). In other words, seen constructively, the young child needs to register and react, either against or towards, what feels bad or good and, specifically, to kick up a fuss when they are experiencing extreme threat or danger. If something feels deeply threatening and/or unbearable, in other words, potentially traumatising, it is understandable that the individual signals that this is, for all time perhaps, "wrong" and should not be allowed to occur. Bion also recognised the "moral component … invariant to beta elements … a sense that the link between one object and another … is moral causation" (Bion, 1965, p. 64).

The moral defence

I have described this previously in terms of a moral defence (West, 2007, pp. 207ff.). This is the polar opposite to the kind of moral defence that Fairbairn describes, although, as I discuss below, they are linked precisely by being opposite ways of dealing with the same issue. To give an example: a patient, Shabila, whom I have written about before (West, 2013a), would occasionally become morally outraged at something I had done, and the atmosphere between us would become intense. There were a number of issues that would trigger this reaction in her, one of which was me asking her to wait in the waiting room if she was just a little early for the session. She spoke to me in an appalled, disgusted way, as if I was clearly being inhuman.

Whilst my immediate response was to feel guilt at having caused her such distress, and in identification with her sense that I was wrong, previous experience of being spoken to in this way alerted me that something else was going on. This enabled me to maintain my ground and to put the guilt on hold whilst I tried to think with her about the issue. It would otherwise have been very easy to let the time boundary lapse and let this particular person into the session a couple of minutes early.

I know from previous experiences of allowing such lapses that, whilst the analyst may offer some rationalisation, such as, as Rosenfeld suggests, "it is necessary due to the person's appallingly harsh upbringing and their particular sensitivity", both analyst and (it emerges later) patient have a sense that something is wrong with this arrangement, even whilst it is precisely the kind of "human" response that the patient is demanding.

I have found that the patient is unconsciously disappointed in the analyst; specifically that they have not recognised and directly addressed the real trauma, but have colluded with a belief that it is too bad to face. Such collusions leave the patient essentially at war with the real world for being a place where such woundings occur, and thus confined to pursuing unrealistic, ideal, conflict-free goals.

For Shabila, it turned out that being asked to wait represented two things: first, the waiting before her father came to sexually abuse her—the dread of waiting felt appalling in itself, whilst at least when the abuse was occurring it was "getting it over and done with". Second, the inhuman experience of being left exposed and unprotected by her mother whilst waiting to be abused. This second thread turned out to be particularly significant as, whilst Shabila had been aware of her intensely negative feelings towards her father, her sense of betrayal by her mother, who she came to realise knew of the abuse and did nothing to prevent it, was key. It was vital that she could work on her feelings about her mother's abandonment of her directly, which entailed me resisting trying to "prove" (enacting) that I was a good, caring, responsive, protective mother/analyst different from her own mother. As Gabbard and Lester (1995) put it: "… If the analyst does not allow himself to be experienced as the old object from the past, the patient's efforts to work through experiences from childhood will be compromised" (p. 146).

However, if I had tried to enact the good mother, such enactment can lead to serious difficulties—see the quotes from Fordham above and the lengthy quote from Davies and Frawley at the end of this chapter below; as Gabbard and Lester point out, the trauma cannot be successfully addressed in this way. The analyst's initial response however—the role they feel drawn to enact—in this case the guilty and/or protecting mother, is vitally important in cuing the analyst and patient into the patient's particular, central experience and dynamic.

The past in the present and being real vs. being good

If the analyst takes the patient's protestations to be wholly about the present (not recognising that the somatic-affective element has become dissociated from the original trauma), they will not only be unhelpfully, even dangerously, missing the point, but they will not be able to resolve the traumatic complex. However much the analyst is experienced as "good" or "caring", the patient cannot be sure that they will not change or will not get, for example, fed up and angry "eventually". You cannot disprove a negative—just because air travel is the safest means of transport, it doesn't mean that the next plane on which I travel will not crash. It is addressing the trauma itself that is key, reassuring the patient that "it is not so", or "I am not like that", does not, ultimately, resolve the issue.

As one patient most helpfully and insightfully told me, clearly frustrated when I persisted in being defensive by taking her complaints about me at face value and remonstrating with her view of me: "Listen, these things are ninety per cent about the past, but we won't get to discover that if you keep being so defensive!" The other ten per cent relates to the actual thing that the analyst is doing that is triggering the retraumatisation. The analyst needs to recognise and address that with the patient as soon as possible. With Shabila this was the relatively simple acknowledgement that my asking her to wait was causing her severe distress; but I added, of course, that I thought this could tell us something extremely significant. As Caper puts it: "… if the analyst is to do his job, he must accept the fact that, by withholding immediate solace, he is in a way 'causing' real suffering in the short run for the sake of the greater long-term relief that comes from psychological integration" (1992/1999, p. 26).[12]

Fairbairn's moral defence

A very significant, but very different, though related, moral defence has been described by Donald Fairbairn, which also applies most particularly when there has been powerful early trauma. As Fairbairn described, the child (heartrendingly) takes responsibility for what the parent does to them, believing that they are wrong and that it is their fault. The child does not protest and thus does not alienate themselves from the parent. Thereby the parent, upon whom the child relies, is kept good, and the child can continue to depend upon and be attached to them (I give a detailed example in Chapter Sixteen).

This is the heart of a sado-masochistic dynamic that can often be exploited by the abuser (who might (or might not) have been treated in a similar way themselves), who tells the child that they are bad and wrong and that the child's bad behaviour justifies the parent's treatment, or perhaps even that the child "wants it", as Ferenczi (1932b) describes (see also Knox, 2013).

This kind of moral defence is, on some level, almost universal as children take on responsibility for what they experience, perhaps as a way of taking it into their sphere of omnipotence, and as a means of anticipating future experience. This is key to the process of internalisation. The child needs to learn that "if I do this, that will happen", whether that is a matter of moving their hand so as to pick up a ball, or keeping quiet so that the parent does not get angry (Beebe & Lachmann, 2013).

In saying this I am not wanting to minimise the patient's experience of the analyst's wrongdoing, rather I would hope to understand its origins and to alert the analyst to look for what they are actually doing that may be triggering the original trauma. An alternative, perhaps in counter-response to the accusation that they are doing something so heinous, is to abandon the process of analysis in some way and do something that is "wrong" in a different and perhaps even more terrible sense, as Gabbard and Lester (1995) and Fordham (1974) describe.

I would suggest that these two moral defences represent different ways of dealing with the moral charge associated with the traumatised core self. With the moral defence that I outline, the moral outrage is related to a fight response, characteristic of a narcissistic personality organisation, where the other is held responsible, and angrily blamed, for the retraumatisation. On the other hand, the moral defence that Fairbairn outlines is related to a freeze, collapse, or submit response, associated with a borderline or hysterical personality organisation, where the emphasis is on maintaining the connection with the other.

Conclusion

My primary point is that the pressures on the analyst derive from the pressures to avoid the traumatic complex, whether that is negatively, by not retraumatising the patient, in other words, by not being "bad", or positively, by being an ideal, "good" object different from the original traumatiser. The struggle is for the analyst to find a way to face what originally felt unbearable, wrong, and inhuman. This will be unique to each moment with each analytic pair. It is no easy matter, and requires a developing, creative response calling for faith, boldness, and caution, and drawing on many levels of experience—both rational and affective. It represents an evolution of the relationship itself.

Philip Bromberg puts it very well when he writes:

> the analytic relationship become[s] a place that supports risk and safety simultaneously—a relationship that allows the painful reliving of early trauma, without the reliving being just a blind repetition of the past. It is optimally a relationship that I have described as "safe but not too safe" (Bromberg, 2006, pp. 153–202), by which I mean that the analyst is communicating both his ongoing concern for his patient's affective safety *and* his commitment to the value of the inevitably painful process of reliving. (Bromberg, 2011, pp. 16–17, original italics)

However when the traumas relate to experiences that are felt to be inhuman this can sit very discordantly in a relationship that is fundamentally construed as being human and reparative. If the analyst is prepared to accompany the patient into the darkest places of trauma, and appreciate why this is important, as well as how these dynamics can be properly worked through and understanding the "rules" and logic of that area, then this is the best way of understanding what the patient is trying to communicate. In this way the analyst can address these pressures and work fruitfully, safely, and effectively with these most powerful, agonising, unbearable, and disruptive states of mind.

Davies and Frawley's example

Although they are addressing only some aspects of the phenomena I have been discussing, I would like to end this chapter by quoting Davies and Frawley at some length, describing the analytic deadlocks and disasters that may occur in working with patients who have been sexually abused as children (their paper is required reading for anyone working with trauma). In my experience such dynamics can apply whenever there has been early trauma, although that will manifest differently in the analytic relationship according to the particular early relational traumas. They write:

> The most common deadlock would appear to occur when the therapist assumes the role of omnipotent rescuer and the patient that of the helpless victim.[13] ... Empathic concern for the abused, helpless child is surely the countertransference response most readily and non-conflictually available to the analyst. His grandiose fantasies of rescuing a frightened child represent perhaps the best part of himself or herself. The child, for her part, has found an ally at long last, someone who will listen, care, and respect her particular needs for support, while she recovers and works through memories of her abuse. The analyst will tolerate the patient's regression during this time and provide the necessary ego support to make the working through, mourning process possible. Indeed, some therapeutic modifications may become necessary, for example, double sessions, additional sessions, phone contact between sessions. A safe holding environment must be created to contain the intense affective discharge and ego disorganization that will accompany the traumatic levels of stress reawakened during periods of the treatment.
>
> The therapist's very willingness to accede to the patient's often necessary demands for extra-analytic contacts, however, gives rise to a major therapeutic dilemma. As the analyst struggles to rescue the tortured child from her endless nightmare, he or she may inadvertently interfere with the mourning process—which must go on—by refortifying the child's expectation that complete compensation will be made to her. It is eventually from the analyst, who seems so eager to help, that this compensation will come to be expected. The child, who at first needs certain modifications in analytic technique to begin the recovery and mourning process and to tolerate the regressive disorganisation that ensues, eventually comes to expect and demand these interventions as evidence of the analyst's real concern for her and devotion to her. The treatment parameters thus lose their original ego-supportive function and become symbolic expressions of the analyst's love. They become "the stuff that compensation is made of". An entirely different transference paradigm now exists. The demands that were at first reasonable and uttered with quiet urgency become more strident and entitled. They slowly call for greater sacrifices on the part of

the analyst and become increasingly difficult to keep up with. The relationship has, in essence, become an addiction for the patient, who must receive larger and larger infusions of compensation to be satisfied. As with any addiction, each dose stimulates an inevitable demand for more, and ultimately the demands can simply not be met. One must remember that though the child demands ever-increasing expressions of love as compensation, she has in her dissociated state never experienced anything but abuse, neglect, and betrayal. The analyst must, therefore, fail her. This experience is all she has known.

What has happened? It appears that in attempting to prove himself trustworthy to his ever-doubting patient, by acceding to necessary and sometimes unnecessary demands, the analyst has acted out a masochistic surrender and in so doing has reawakened and called forth the sadistic introject within the patient, that is, that part of the patient who is closely identified with her own abuser. This sadomasochistic re-enactment is even further intensified by the fact that in presenting himself as an omnipotent rescuer, the therapist becomes, in Fairbairn's (1994) terms, an "exciting bad object", one who stimulates and awakens deep-seated desires that cannot at the same time be gratified.

The patient who was sexually abused as a child is vigilantly defended against those who make promises and attempt to resuscitate hope. Promises are broken, and hope leads inevitably to disappointment. Only self-sufficiency and a renunciation of all dependency needs create a margin of safety. To refortify her counterdependent defenses against the "exciting" analyst, the patient calls upon the sadistic introject to launch a full-scale attack upon the therapist's integrity and competence. It becomes the mission of the abuser, within the abused-child persona, to trap the therapist into revealing the emptiness of his promises, thereby rescuing the frightened child from giving hope, in the form of a trusting relationship to the analyst, another chance. Paradoxically, the mechanism of failure begins with the analyst's most ardent wish to help and rescue. It is by dint of his need to be seen as the good and nurturing rescuer, that the analyst assures his position as the exciting, therefore dangerous deceiver who must be destroyed. … the patient clearly perceives the analyst, who has dared come too close, as a dangerous seducer.

The analyst, however, is at a most delicate choice point. To the extent that he backs off, he re-creates the neglect and denial of all the adults who originally failed to rescue the abused child. To the extent that he reassures the patient of his ability to "go all the way," he sets in motion the sadistic introject who will set about the task of proving that the analyst just does not have what it takes and that he in no way means what he says. The analyst's best intentions, experienced as dangerously seductive, must be spoiled. Whether by dint of ineptitude or deceit, the patient views the analyst as unhelpful.

The patient, on the other hand, has gone from the role of helpless victim to that of a demanding, insatiable, and constantly critical abuser. She seduces the analyst into rescue attempts, doomed to fail. The analyst has moved from his cherished role as savior to the increasingly masochistic role of victim who will do, say, give anything to appease the encroaching other. Via projective identification and counteridentification, the patient experiences herself as a victim but is experienced by the analyst as a seductive abuser; the therapist experiences himself as concerned and available, determined to rescue, while to the patient he is cruelly withholding or dangerously seductive. (Davies & Frawley, 1992a, pp. 27–29)

Notes

1. In her paper Klein explicitly disagreed with Fairbairn that "to begin with the bad object is internalised", but holds instead that "anxiety arises from the operation of the death instinct within the organism" (Klein, 1946, p. 4); in other words, in her model, trauma is given a marginal or negligible significance compared to the individual's own destructiveness in the form of the death instinct.
2. The analyst can therefore genuinely say, "That's not me", as they have not hitherto experienced the feeling in that form.
3. Such experience can be readily dismissed as merely paranoid, or as an expression of the paranoid-schizoid position. Analysts tend to have an ambivalent reaction to such paranoid experience, trying to reason the patient out of their paranoid view, or reassure the patient that such things are not true, or dissuade them from "thinking that way". I would suggest that such paranoid reactions tell us most immediately about the patient's traumas; for example, the patient who twists what the

analyst says into an experience of being mocked reveals their powerful, traumatised reaction to being mocked. Paranoid experience gives a clear indication of "where the bodies are buried".

4. Benjamin does state that, "disclosure is not a panacea, that the analyst's acknowledgment of responsibility can take place only by working through deep anguish around feelings of destructiveness and loss" (2004, p. 40). I would suggest that living through the traumatic complex is the main factor, of which recognition of the analyst's and patient's destructiveness (identification with the aggressor) is only one element.

5. As Rosenfeld (1987) comments, our patients generously give us many opportunities to understand what is going on.

6. Davies (2004) gives exactly such an example, which I feel misses the reconstruction of the early traumatic experience of a withholding, unempathic parent, as I will discuss further below.

7. I would suggest that loving feelings are somewhat different precisely in that they relate to primary process, identificatory, core self experiences, which are both extremely powerful and prone to idealisation.

8. Caper writes: "it is just when the analyst is on the verge of making a mutative interpretation that he is beset by the feeling that he is about to do something harmful, something that will jeopardize his 'good' relationship to the patient" (1995/1999, p. 35).

9. One element that is important here is the way the analyst considers their own ego-functioning; whether they see it as intrinsic to their personality, or whether they see themselves as in some way cut-off and, perhaps, wishing to be more open and expressive; in other words, whether they may hold an idealised view of the personality and of relationships and relating (see Chapters Eight, Nine, and Twelve for further exploration).

10. Aron (2006), expanding on Benjamin's (2004) conceptualisation of the doer/done to, complementary dynamic, discusses this in terms of the need to form a "point of thirdness", calling on judicious use of the analyst's self-disclosure. However, I feel that he insufficiently addresses the traumatic aspects that I am describing here.

11. For Melanie Klein too, the superego was not primarily related to the parental figures, although she saw them as due to the individual's own instinctual impulses; for example, she described the superego of a child analysand as "... of a phantastic severity ... this child anticipates, by reason of his own cannibalistic and sadistic impulses, such punishments as castration, being cut into pieces, eaten up, etc., and lives in perpetual dread of them" (Klein, 1927, p. 356).

12. Despite recognising the inevitability of the co-construction of earlier, traumatic experience, Jody Messler Davies (2004), treats her negative,

hateful feelings in response to her patient Karen's uncaring treatment of her as "bad", relating to her own "guilty, shame-riddled self states" (p. 718), and she appears to give herself a hard time because of them as well as disclosing them to her patient. I would question whether these qualities are "bad" in either patient or analyst, but rather see such feelings as natural, primitive responses to traumatic experience. This diminishes the moralising quality in the analytic exchanges and allows the analyst to concentrate on the traumatic experience rather than self-recrimination. Her paper stands as an interesting contrast to my own approach—see Chapters Seven, Twelve, and Fifteen for parallel clinical material.

13. The theme of the attempt to omnipotently cure is also explored by Rosenfeld (1987), Gabbard and Lester (1995), and Caper (1992/1999)—my footnote.

CHAPTER TWELVE

The analyst's journey and the defeat of the analyst's ego—Orpheus and Eurydice and the journey through the underworld*

In this chapter I will look at the inevitable and, in some ways, necessary "defeat" of the analyst's ego when working with people who have experienced early relational trauma. I see this as due both to the fact that the original defeat of the patient's ego, as a result of the trauma, is reenacted with the analyst, and that the primitive, affective-somatic elements split-off from the ego, as a result of the trauma, require the analyst's openness to non-rational forms of functioning in order to be appreciated. If the analyst insists on their rational, ego perspective it is only likely to infuriate, wound, and alienate the patient, and their efforts will ultimately be defeated. If they are not prepared for this, it is likely to cause the analyst intense frustration, to blame the patient, or to terminate the analysis. I will explore the account of the analysis between Michael Fordham and his patient "K", which was terminated by Fordham, to see if light can be shed on the impasse between them.

---

*A section of this chapter was presented at the *Journal of Analytical Psychology* conference, "Reflections on Jungian Clinical Practice: from then till now", in London in March 2015. It has also been published as "Working in the borderland: early relational trauma and Fordham's analysis of 'K'", *Journal of Analytical Psychology, 2016, 61*: 44–62.

I will be comparing the analyst's journey to that of Orpheus, who had to journey to the underworld in order to try to bring back his beloved wife Eurydice, who died after being bitten by a snake when she was being chased by a satyr[1]. Her death, following a sexual "pursuit", may be seen symbolically as representing sexual abuse. Only Orpheus' music got him access to the underworld—the analyst's emotional resonance rather than their verbal reasoning, the right-brain to right-brain communication, as Allan Schore (2003) would put it. When there, he had to petition the god of the underworld, Hades, and his wife, Persephone, for Eurydice's release. They agreed, but only on condition that Orpheus did not look back until he had reached the light. When, fearing he was being tricked, he lost faith and turned to see whether Eurydice was behind him, she was lost forever. I will discuss what I see as the parallels for the analytic journey.

Before that, however, I will look at the kinds of struggles the analyst may experience when working with individuals who have experienced early relational trauma and the experiences they may need to embrace in order to proceed successfully. This section draws on some of the challenges I have experienced thus far in my thirty years working as a psychotherapist and analyst as well as those I have observed supervising others.

Every analysis is a very real journey for both patient and analyst where things are only learnt and seen along the way, and where it only slowly becomes possible to bear, confront, and put certain things into words. I have become increasingly aware of just how much work the analyst has to do, how much they have to process, and, sometimes, how much they have to grow and change. Jung is often quoted in this regard, saying:

> The crucial point is that I confront the patient as one human being to another. Analysis is a dialogue demanding two partners … in any thoroughgoing analysis the whole personality of both patient and doctor is called into play. There are many cases which the doctor cannot cure without committing himself. When important matters are at stake, it makes all the difference whether the doctor sees himself as a part of the drama, or cloaks himself in his authority. In the great crises of life, in the supreme moments when to be or not to be is the question, little tricks of suggestion do not help. Then the doctor's whole being is challenged … The doctor is effective only

when he himself if affected. "Only the wounded physician heals".
But when the doctor wears his personality like a coat of armour, he
has no effect. (Jung, 1963, pp. 153–155)

I will divide my exploration of the analyst's journey into five different
areas:

- being subject to the patient's internal working models without falling
  into masochistic surrender or responding defensively or with blame;
- being and embodying the bad object;
- not having to be the good object, grieving the ideal, and the analyst's
  attitude to trauma;
- the analyst's own primitive defences, personality organisation, and
  internal working models;
- the defeat of the analyst's ego—trusting the patient and the process.

Being subject to the patient's internal working models without falling into masochistic surrender or responding defensively or with blame

In Chapter Seven I described how analyst and patient are on an equal
level relationally (this is not to ignore the inequalities of various kinds,
which are well-known and which I will not list). The analyst is equally
vulnerable to, for example, being ignored, belittled, silenced, bored,
hated, not related to, made to feel stupid, or mocked; or enjoyed,
respected, responded to, engaged with, flattered, built up, liked, or
loved. I would particularly stress the nonverbal and affective elements
in this—the effect that the patient's mood or negativity may have is,
over time, very powerful. Another very powerful effect is when the
analyst senses they will cause intense distress, perhaps through making a particular interpretation or through maintaining a particular
boundary (thus triggering the patient's traumatic complex), as I have
explored in Chapter Eleven (see also Caper, 1995/1999). It is through
these relational means that the patient most directly conveys their
early experience, through the expression of their own internal working
models—their ways of relating to the analyst.

When the analyst experiences being ignored, not related to, blanked
out, or being subject to the patient's nihilism, hopelessness, and dark
moods, it is only too easy for the analyst to feel and communicate in

some way that the patient is "doing it wrong", being destructive or self-destructive, attacking or resisting the analysis, perhaps in order to defeat the analyst (Freud, 1923b), or expressing a defensive psychic retreat (Steiner, 1987, 1993). I would suggest that such interpretations are often born out of the analyst's difficulty to either bear or make sense of the experience, or both. I see the patient as bringing exactly what they need to bring. Quite frequently the patient will be introducing the analyst to experiences or relational forms they have not experienced before, or not in that way—perhaps of sadism or submission or paralysis, and this will represent a particular challenge for the analyst.

Understanding these experiences in the framework of the reconstruction of early relational trauma helps the analyst to make sense of these experiences and thus not act out by, for example, responding defensively or with blame. However, whilst the framework of reconstruction may act as a container for the analyst and patient, I have found that the fundamental task is to be able to bear, live through, understand, and appreciate such experiences (see Chapter Ten for an extended clinical example). It is this that ultimately allows the unbearable fragments of experience to be integrated, and it is precisely these unbearable/traumatic elements of experience that require the analyst to experientially participate in this way. As Stern says, "it is vital for the patient to discover that someone is desirous of knowing what it feels like to be him or her" (1985/1998, p. 32).

This can represent a considerable journey for the analyst—to really stay only with the patient's experience, to trust that the patient can bear for this not to be "made better", to trust that their psyche can contain it, to trust in the analytic process, and that this will work (though there are no guarantees). I see this as akin to the trust that Orpheus needed in order not to look back. Finally, the analyst has to be able to bear the experience themselves and not eject it through premature or critical interpretation; for example, in Chapter Ten I described how Michael repeatedly told me that life was meaningless; it was important that I could bear this and consider his experiences.

Quite frequently such experiences will impact on the analyst's own particular early experiences (see below), not least because to experience some negation of one's self in early life is a near-universal experience. The analyst will need to be able to come to bear such experiences in order to properly address them—the patient usually knows if the analyst is trying to move away from the experience too soon.[2] Rosenfeld described interpreting too soon as one of the anti-therapeutic factors that can lead to impasse (Rosenfeld, 1987, pp. 33ff)—see Chapter Thirteen. An analysis frequently requires such growth and development of the analyst's personality as part of its process and before it can progress.

In relation to this, Bion described one patient's hatred and envy of him that he was able to go through certain experiences without himself breaking down (Bion, 1959, p. 105). There has also been a dispute between Ogden and Caper on how deeply the analyst has to feel something in order for the interpretation to be effective; Caper (1999) writes:

> It has been suggested by some authors—for example, Ogden (1996)—that the analyst must become *quite* identified with the patient's projections and work through this illness laboriously if his understanding of the patient's projections is to be therapeutically effective. I disagree with this position. What is important is only the fact that the analyst has been able to think about the patient's projections, not how much (or little) trouble he has had to go to in doing so. (p. 114, original italics)

I would suggest that certain experiences (what Caper calls projections) will require a good deal of personal work by the analyst in deepening their experience and appreciation of them. Furthermore, that particular dynamics, if they are not readily resolved through being identified and named, will require a greater depth of engagement, experience, and understanding, by both analyst and patient, in order for them to be worked through. This is due, as I understand it, to the depth, importance, power, and centrality of the experience itself. Early relational trauma, deeply embedded in the individual's core identity, frequently requires this depth of work, participation, and experience.

Patterns of blanking and negating, for example, precisely mirror the child's experience of being persistently blanked by a parent, and of experiencing the parent's dark moods, depression, or suicidal feelings. These traumatic experiences amount, subjectively, to being killed off/ annihilated. Over time, the analyst can similarly feel killed off and annihilated, despite being a capable adult (having effective ego-functioning). I recognise that the times when, for example, I would occasionally fall asleep with a patient was an example of me not being able to bear such blanking and represented me protecting myself through sleep.

However, in coming to experientially know something of the patient's experience, it is important that the analyst does not simply put up with the experience, suffer it passively, and fall into a masochistic surrender. This can particularly occur when the patient is outraged and angry at some wounding they have experienced from the analyst and, out of the wound, punish or harangue the analyst in what I have described as a masochisto-sadistic manner (West, 2013a), feeling their anger is entirely justified by their wounded experience.

It is rarely possible to find a helpful response to this experience immediately, and it will very likely take the analyst some time to work out what is going on. If the patient's outrage continues after the analyst has recognised what in their behaviour has triggered the outrage, and explored the traumatic precursors (if the patient is willing to do so), it sometimes becomes clear that there is an emotional charge or excitement involved. This may indicate that the patient has moved from a victim role to some kind of identification with the aggressor, which can then be explored as part of the working through of the traumatic complex and, specifically, of the trauma-related internal working models in both direct and reversed form (Chapter Seven).

One of the important factors for the analyst in moving away from a passive, masochistic position is for the analyst to get in touch with their primitive reaction to what they are experiencing—this may be an experience of irritation, rage, murderousness, sadness, fearfulness, defeat, or collapse. First, getting in touch with this response puts the analyst back in touch with themselves (a disidentification with/from the patient), where they may have become over-identified due to the power of the patient's affect-laden reaction. Second, the kind of reaction the analyst has will cue them in to the reaction the patient might themselves have had to such treatment or, very likely, the kind of incipient reaction they might have had but were not able to safely express; for example, if the analyst feels tearful or angry they might well recognise that it was not possible for the patient to safely express such emotions as a child without further consequences, such as mockery or violence.

Heinrich Racker (1958) writes insightfully about the analyst's tendency to fall into a masochistic surrender and simply suffer these exchanges from the patient. He recommends that the analyst is aware of their response and engages actively with the patient. He writes:

> A change in the analyst's masochistic attitude to the act of analyzing, to the patient, and to the patient's communications can

considerably increase the success of the therapeutic work. Such a change can bring an awakening, a greater readiness for battle and victory, a fuller acceptance of our new parenthood, a closer approach to the patient, a struggle for his love along with greater confidence in it. It can bring willingness to see the positive transference behind the negative, to see the good things together with the bad ones, and the content offered us by the patient together with the resistances. … The struggle with the resistances for the sake of the patient's health thus acquires a certain similitude to the famous wrestling of the Biblical patriarch Jacob with the Angel. This continued undecided the whole night through, but Jacob would not yield and said to the Angel: "I won't let you go unless you bless me". And finally the Angel had no choice but to do so. (pp. 561–562)

Racker is upbeat in his assessment here, and I agree that it is important that the analyst *does* try to challenge the patient's nihilistic points of view; sometimes offering a positive reframing, such as "It wasn't a total disaster, you at least made your point even if they didn't accept it". In my experience however, whilst such reframings might have some effect in demonstrating that the analyst can recognise the patient's achievement, and in keeping sight of the positive aspects without losing them wholly to the negative, such alterations are limited. This is particularly the case if the individual's relational traumas were early and have thus become established at the core of their identity. Such relational exchanges are complex and will need to be explored in various ways and from various perspectives.

Some examples

I described Shabila's response to being asked to wait if she arrived early in the last chapter. My getting in touch with my combative response in relation to her fury with me, which I kept to myself (although my somatic cues could well have signalled something to her), enabled me to hold the space and think further about what was going on.[3]

Dorothy

Dorothy would speak to me in a conversational manner, telling me about her recent experiences in a way that I would find difficult to follow, and I would feel perplexed, unrelated to, somewhat irritated and, over time, isolated, and distressed. Sometimes I would shut down, although usually I would try very hard to fathom what was going on. Eventually I recognised this mirrored the pattern that Dorothy had experienced, with her mother keeping her out, fearing that Dorothy would cause her distress that she could not bear, and retreating to her own dream-like world where she would not be disturbed by others.

Dorothy and I recognised that she would particularly talk to me in this way if I had not, early on in the session, responded to her in the way she hoped (positively and enthusiastically bolstering or praising her) and she was thus keeping me out lest I cause her distress or make her feel criticised by trying to explore what was going on (implying she was wrong in some way). There were parallels in direct and reversed form with her experience with her mother, where she both felt I was the rejecting mother and rejected me, as well as the relational pattern of treating me as if I was the demanding child/analyst who she had to keep at a distance, whilst feeling kept at a distance by me. Ultimately it was important that I could experience the defeat that Dorothy had herself experienced in not being able to get through to her mother—to bear that defeat, and to reflect on that experience with her.

Valerie Sinason (2013) discusses examples by Taylor (1998), Temple (1998), Roth (1994), and Riesenberg-Malcolm (1996) where they talk about experiencing a lack of empathy, irritation, and boredom, or being provoked into a punishing response when listening to a patient describing experiences of difficulty, trauma, or abuse. Sinason understands these situations as due to the child having described an experience of abuse to a parent and having been discredited or not believed, so that they now present their experience in a flat tone, not expecting to be believed and yet thereby also constellating the disbelieving dyad. (Ferenczi (1932b) recognised that the parents' response to the child's disclosure of having been abused was key).

Sinason gives another poignant example of a woman who spoke in a superficial, sing-song, echolalic manner that induced those who heard her to discount her and close off, until it emerged that this apparently superficial response had been her way of distracting her father, asking him if he'd like a cup of tea after he had been beating her mother. Sinason's examples emphasise the patient's experience directly replicating their original response to the trauma, rather than in reversed form.

Frank Lachmann candidly describes his work with "Karen", mentioned already in Chapter Seven, where he recognised that he was not able to bear the anxiety induced in him by his patient missing her sessions, and he took to phoning her before each session to remind her of the session (Beebe & Lachmann, 2002, ch. 3, pp. 45ff.). Discussing this above I suggested that he did not recognise or address the way in which his patient had reversed the pattern and was enacting the role of the much-feared abandoner herself; this may have contributed to the therapy being terminated through the patient moving away (abandoning).

Here, I would like to note that such enactments occur on a fairly regular basis for reasons very much like the one that Lachmann outlines; however, I would suggest that they offer the analyst first-hand experience of, in this case, the overwhelming anxiety/terror for the child of experiencing the original abandonment. The analyst may then be able to use this knowledge in exploring the patient's experience, and in deepening the level of the work. In my experience such appreciation and exploration means that it is possible for the analyst to draw the enactment to a close, with due explanation and discussion with the patient, and thereby deal with the traumatic complex more directly and constructively.

A final note on suicidal feelings. Perhaps one of the most powerful set of experiences that the analyst is likely to meet relate to the patient's suicidal thoughts, impulses, and feelings. These naturally cause concern and alarm, and sometimes therapists attempt to proscribe them, drawing up some kind of contract whereby the patient agrees not to attempt suicide whilst they are in therapy. Yet suicidal ideation in one form or another is almost universal amongst individuals who have experienced profound early relational trauma. I have come to recognise that suicidal thoughts and wishes are not only a frequent reaction to the experience of annihilation, whereby the patient takes their experience of annihilation into their own sphere of omnipotence, but also that they are integral to the experience of collapse and submission (the "death" of the ego), as well as a form of comfort whereby the knowledge that the person could and would kill themselves if they had to has allowed them to continue to bear their terrible experiences. They are also frequently related to significant experience with a caregiver who was suicidal (as described in Chapter Ten for Michael).

Understanding these experiences in relation to their primitive defensive reactions places them in a framework where they can be understood, appreciated, and discussed, as well as seen in a nonpunitive, relational setting, by which I mean, understanding that they are a response to intolerable experience rather than an "attack on the analyst". For example, they may well communicate what it was like for the child to experience the imminent abandonment by their parent through their depressive and suicidal wishes or actions—although this does not mean it was the patient's intention to communicate these things (Colman, 2013). The patient is simply acting from their implicit internal working models.

Being and embodying the bad object

Being wrong and being thought of as bad are two of the most painful experiences for human beings, evoking shame and primitive fears of rejection by the parents or exclusion from the social group. Fitting in with and accommodating to the caregivers are thus hardwired into the brain—it is no surprise that we have dedicated mirror neurones (Gallese, 2001; Rizzolatti & Sinigaglia, 2008) that allow us to identify with and anticipate what our caregivers are wanting and feeling.

Shaming and blaming are thus very powerful forms of punishment and/or control that are wielded against the child, and they frequently form a significant element of early relational trauma. The analyst will also naturally be susceptible to the experience of being wrong or being bad, whether in relation to the patient, their peers, or training body, and it is something that will frequently emerge as part of the reconstruction of the patient's early experience. It is also a feature of the powerful splitting related to avoiding the trauma and the move towards an idealised solution. The analyst thus has to come to terms with being bad in some way. Knox (2013, p. 500) discusses how difficult it is for the analyst to feel as though they actually are the abuser, or to be related to as though they are, and Gabbard (1997) describes how the analyst may try to distance and distinguish themselves from the role of abuser; in the last chapter I gave the example of how neither Benjamin nor her patient could tolerate having to be like the patient's mother (Benjamin, 2004, p. 37).

Being bad

The most common way the analyst deals with the patient experiencing and telling them that they are bad, cruel, uncaring, or unfeeling (or other permutations) is to say that it is "just transference", that they are not bad *really*, or that the analysis allows the patient to work through their bad experiences and bad projections. This is all very well with patients whom the analyst can sense are still in touch with good aspects of the relationship that, perhaps, prevailed at the beginning of the analysis. However, with individuals with a borderline personality organisation this is frequently not the case, for a number of reasons.

First, the patient's negative experience of the analyst may have been prominent or predominant from the beginning of the analysis. Second, the patient is in extreme distress and expresses their conviction that the analyst is being cruel and uncaring with absolute, palpable conviction (see West, 2007) that clearly comes from current experience. Third, any previous good relationship is merely notional (it may still be present "somewhere") and is currently inaccessible as the patient is flooded by the bad, distressing, agonising experience. In the metaphor of Orpheus and Eurydice, the patient has descended into a torturous hell and has little or no hope of rescue.

It is for these reasons that I have always struggled with Michael Fordham's exhortations to the analyst that

> [t]he analytic attitude … needs to be maintained so it is not desirable for the analyst to try "being himself" any more than he is already so doing by making confessions or giving information about himself etc. Nor is it desirable to become excessively passive or guilty at the amount of pain, terror and dread that the patient asserts the analyst is causing. It is important that the analyst should control his guilt about the patient's claim that he causes confusion, is sadistic, cruel and destructive and the like. (1974, pp. 197–198)

I wanted to understand why what I was doing was causing such distress to the patient and, if we were to stay with that, what was the purpose. I suggest that, once again, the perspective of early relational trauma is helpful here.

This perspective allows us to understand that the affective-somatic reaction has become dissociated from the knowledge of the trauma and is being experienced in a very real and powerful way in the present in relation to the analyst. The disruption of the patient's containing ego-functioning means that this primitive, core reaction is extremely powerful and the pressures on the analyst to protect the patient's core self (and their own) are intense (Chapter Eight). This perspective can open up some thinking space for both patient and analyst around their experience. For the patient it can help them to understand why their reaction is so powerful—something which can otherwise be a cause of much disturbance and shame. For the analyst they can begin *not* to take the patient's reaction so personally.

Furthermore, analyst and patient can, in due course, begin to explore what experiences this may be related to, although the immediate task is for the analyst to discern and acknowledge what it is that they are doing that is triggering the patient's reaction. This may be an instance of preoccupation, or a cold tone of voice, or something more obvious, such as cancelling a session or charging for a missed session. I have found it essential that this real-world trigger is identified and owned, including acknowledging the distress it causes. It allows the patient to feel that the analyst is not just bouncing everything back to them, but rather recognises that this is a two-person relationship and that what they do has an effect; in other words, that the analyst has to take responsibility for their actions—see the quotation from Caper (above) about the analyst causing real suffering in the short run for the sake of the greater long-term relief (1999, p. 26).

If the analyst is not blinded by the accusation of being morally wrong (Chapter Eleven), and can continue to think about things under these circumstances (see the example with Shabila above), I think this can reduce the analyst's feelings of guilt and responsibility to manageable proportions. Namely, that they do take responsibility for exposing the patient to something traumatic and hitherto unbearable as part of the process of working through the trauma, with due care and concern for the patient along the way. As Bromberg puts it, "the analyst is communicating both his ongoing concern for his patient's affective safety *and* his commitment to the value of the inevitably painful process of reliving" (Bromberg, 2011, p. 17, original italics). To avoid the trauma altogether could be seen as a dereliction of the analyst's duty of care, as it takes a short-term, "easy" path at the expense of the patient's long-term development and continued suffering.

Finally, and probably most importantly, the analyst has to come to be able to bear and embody the feelings corresponding to the "aggressor" in the original trauma. This is because the more primitive and foundational the experience, the more it has to be actualised and lived through in the analytic relationship. It can take the analyst a good deal of time in order to be able to do this. However, the process of the analysis is precisely one that will slowly engender these feelings and responses in the analyst, and the analyst's challenge is not to deny these experiences their place. It is important that this occurs at the pace that the analytic pair can manage. Supervisors can only point the way in this regard, the analyst will not be able to properly embody the particular bad object "required" by the patient until they are ready.

In becoming able to embody sometimes "inhuman" ways of being—not caring, feeling violent, dismissive, hateful, or sadistic—even if only in passing, may entail a real expansion of the way the analyst sees themselves. They will be changed by the process. Of course, there may be some for whom these ways of being are more readily familiar. For them the journey may be to bring out the loving and vulnerable feelings that currently lie in their shadow—although this is less stereotypically the analyst's type. For me it has meant having to recognise first-hand the ways in which these "inhuman" forms of behaviour are intrinsic and sometimes necessary to human behaviour.

For example, I have come to see sadistic responses as one aspect of the natural, primitive fight response, where the individual deals with their distress by putting it into someone else, thereby moving from a powerless to a powerful position (as described in Chapter Five). It can be a turning point in an analysis when someone is able to achieve this and recognise their wish for revenge on the person or people who wounded them. The wish for revenge and *schadenfreude* are the culturally more acceptable manifestations of this primitive response. Recognising this primitive reaction, for the analyst or the patient, does not, of course, mean that it will become predominant, rather it may hopefully be one of a panoply or reactions available to someone as part of their broad and flexible ego-functioning.

Example

A significant development in my analysis with Nounoushka was in her working through her feelings of betrayal and abandonment by her mother, in addition to her frequent experiences of brutality and violence by her father. Whilst it was her relationship with her father that took up most of our attention early on in the analysis, a dynamic evolved where Nounoushka would flood my answering machine with desperate messages, so many that I did not have time to finish listening to the messages in the break between sessions. Eventually, after a good deal of trying "intermediate solutions", I had to draw a line and insist that she not contact me between sessions, stating that I would not respond to her messages.

She responded immediately to this boundary, ceasing the telephone messages; this settled things between us for a time—perhaps this was due to my expressing an implicit faith in her ability to contain herself, as well as representing a "holding firm" against the invasion by an other—for her it had been her brutalising father. However, the pattern returned sometime later in a darker form. She began leaving messages of more explicitly suicidal intent, talking about her utter hopelessness and that killing herself was both inevitable, the only way out, and that she was about to do so at that moment.

As we explored this further, Nounoushka disclosed that she used to sit on her windowsill at home and tell her mother that she would jump out of the window as she was so unhappy, particularly at times that they had had an argument, but that her mother would not come to check that she was alright. Nounoushka then began leaving me distressed messages rather more out of the blue and, when I did not respond, she would quiz me the next session about whether I had received the message and why I hadn't responded. I struggled a great deal with my response over this and recognised that the dynamic was moving me towards a position where I was the one who seemingly didn't care and abandoned her at her moment of greatest need, with a deep sense of betrayal.

There was one session where it felt she had "done me a favour" by changing the session time and she phoned expressing suicidal impulses afterward. When I did not respond it felt particularly as if I had betrayed her kindness and this led us to exploring the way that she had tried so hard to please her parents and thus felt deeply wounded when her mother remained cold and self-preoccupied, going on holiday for two weeks when she was nine months old, or when her father told her off or beat her for doing things wrong when she had made so much effort to get things right. As we lived through these experiences in our relationship it seemed very much that she was reliving those early experiences, and that I was embodying the cold and abandoning mother and the brutal uncaring father.

The journey to come to embody those figures was slow and agonising (for both of us)—I couldn't do it from a theoretical position but found it was achieved through slowly learning to be it and bear it. In retrospect it felt that, much as we both wanted to avoid it, this was what was required of me in order to allow us both to really know about and work through that early experience. We could see that her later experience of sitting on the windowsill recapitulated her earlier experience as an infant feeling truly powerless and unable to bear being left, and thus being defeated and feeling suicidal.

I similarly learnt to stay with bleak experiences of hopelessness. When I had previously offered positive visions of "light at the end of the tunnel", she would return the next session, equally hopeless. It was as if her early experience of despair was being presented to us time and again until we could finally face it directly, contain it, manage it, and thereby detoxify it. I also explored with her the relational aspect (transference level) of the despair and suicidal feelings, how she was at times in identification with her mother, self-preoccupied and unable to get any comfort from me and wanting to "go away" and abandon me as her mother had (to commit suicide in her terms) and, on the subjective level, that she also wanted to abandon the part of her that wanted to live. In other words, working through the traumatic complexes on different levels and in reversed and direct form.

This involved me having to trust both in the process and in Nounoushka herself—another example of Orpheus having to not look back. I recognised that the times when I would offer reassurance in some form or other were often when I did not trust in her and her ability to know about the good in our relationship. Thankfully, she did not disappear back into hell at those times, although maybe in one sense I did return her to her personal hell for an agonising while longer.

Not having to be the good object, grieving the ideal, and the analyst's attitude to trauma

In relation to omnipotent attempts to rescue and heal the patient, Robert Caper stresses the importance of the analyst being in touch with their own "omnipotently destructive impulses" and suggests that Freud thought that "the analyst's need to cure, which forces him to abandon his realistic analytic modesty, [is] a defense against his own sadistic impulses" (Caper, 1992/1999, p. 23).

I do not see these "omnipotently destructive or sadistic impulses" as necessarily existing fully formed, rather I believe, as I described in the previous section, that through the process of analysis, the analyst slowly gets to know the "inhuman" feelings, impulses, and experiences which are particular to the patient with whom they are working. This represents a vital aspect of the learning, discovery, and development that goes on in and through the process of analysis.

However, I think that difficulties arise not solely through the struggle to avoid embodying the bad object but also through the wish to embody the good object, perhaps in the form of the heroic rescuer; this quote from Davies and Frawley (quoted in full at the end of Chapter Eleven) makes the point well:

> many attempts at analyzing adult survivors of childhood sexual abuse fail because both the therapist and the patient become locked into acting out one particular paradigm to the exclusion of, and as a resistance to, any others. The most common deadlock would appear to occur when the therapist assumes the role of omnipotent rescuer and the patient that of the helpless victim. ... Empathic concern for the abused, helpless child is surely the countertransference response most readily and non-conflictually available to the analyst. His grandiose fantasies of rescuing a frightened child represent perhaps the best part of himself or herself. (Davies & Frawley, 1992a, pp. 26–27)

I will not discuss the fundamental importance of good experience early on in life that is recognised by all theoretical schools, but will rather address the fundamental personal attitudes that may underlie, or certainly powerfully influence, the individual analyst's adherence to certain theoretical positions. These personal attitudes relate, amongst other things, to the analyst's experience in their own analysis/analyses and, I would suggest, the degree to which they have faced and worked through their own traumas, as well as grieved for idealised solutions to those traumas. The analyst's training and beliefs concerning whether a trauma (traumatic sensitivity/traumatic complex) can be worked through or whether it has to be made up for[4] will likely be secondary to their actual experience, but will perhaps be powerful nevertheless. It will be clear by now where I stand on this issue.

I suggest that central to the analyst's position here is the extent to which they have worked through their own wish for an ideal, conflict-free relationship/solution and therefore whether they believe that this is what would be helpful for the patient. One of the reasons that the wish for a conflict-free relationship is so powerful and significant is that it represents the struggle/attempt to be in touch with one's core self. Traumatic experiences lie at the individual's core, and the dissociation from the trauma, and its subsequent avoidance, represents an alienation from one's core self. Therefore it is only safe enough to approach that core if the individual can bear, or has worked through, the trauma (for example, risking being criticised where once this was intolerable due to the early experience of a critical parent), or if there is no risk of retraumatisation—something which almost always requires an idealised solution.

Thus, if the traumatic complex is worked through there is a double benefit in that the individual can accept, and is reunited with, their core self—something which they have been divided against, feeling that they are unacceptable, blaming themselves for being anxious, or wanting to be someone else, or not to exist at all.

However, if the individual requires an idealised solution, it only feels safe enough to be oneself if there is no risk of opposition (and thus potential annihilation). This is often experienced/expressed in terms of the search for a loving relationship where the lover will love and approve the individual's (tentative, sensitive) self and thereby implicitly vouchsafe it.[5] This will, in turn, allow the individual to safely and openly express that self, perhaps loving the lover in return (when this does not occur the individual feels betrayed and their reactions can be intense).[6]

In some cases, one motivation for training or practicing as an analyst is precisely to offer others the kind of care that the individual did not themselves have in childhood, thinking that this is the ultimate solution to the problem of selfhood (they have projected their sensitivities and idealised solutions onto the patient).[7] The analyst is then frequently perplexed when the patient does not respond in the way they believe they themselves would have responded, and they may become resentful and frustrated at providing for the patient what they want themselves, but which may not, in fact, help resolve the patient's difficulties, particularly if it is an idealised solution (see the example of Joe in Chapter Five).

In relation to being the good object, the analyst may be particularly moved by those who are able to express their core selves lovingly and spontaneously, which can be an example of what Gabbard and Lester (1995) describe as the analyst's "lovesickness". The analyst may be adamant that they are acting in order to liberate the patient's self, yet this can get mixed up with more earthly passions, particularly due to the power of affects related to the core self, and lead down the "slippery slope" to sexual relations being started. Fordham (1974) describes this in terms of pressures on the analyst to regress in his paper on defences of the self.

Working through the grieving for an idealised, conflict-free relationship is, I would suggest, not only an issue of central importance and great consequence but also a substantial undertaking, whether that is for the patient or the analyst. In Freudian terms this has much in common with the shift from the pleasure principle to the reality principle, and in Kleinian terms it has many similarities with the struggle to move towards the depressive position (see Chapter Eight). It can frequently entail months or years of depressive and perhaps suicidal ideation—feeling that life is unbearable and not worth living. Hopefully this will have occurred within the containing framework of the individual's analysis/training analysis; however, too often this is not the case.

When the person—analyst or patient—discovers that they can live with things "as they are" and that their core self has not died, but rather that they can engage more naturally, realistically, and fully with life, no longer distracted by the agonising hankering for something that seems forever out of their reach, there can be a substantial sense of peace, rest, and fulfilment, as well as a deepening of the person's experience and sense of self.

The analyst's primitive defences, personality organisation, and internal working models

I do not want to spend a great deal of time on this section as the permutations are endless, except to say that the analyst's own complexes, their particular primitive defences, personality organisation, and internal working models will play a significant part in the nature of the relationship with the patient and how that unfolds. These factors represent the kind of person they are and therefore what they bring to the analytic relationship—the kinds of ways they may relate, their forms of attachment, their openness, warmth, or defensiveness. Of course, essential to this picture is the degree to which the analyst has worked on their complexes and has a degree of working self-knowledge.

One of the reasons that this is important is that it can help the analyst appreciate what may feel natural to them as a way of addressing difficulties, for example, "head on" if they have a more narcissistic personality organisation rooted in a fight response. This style may not, however, be natural for the patient. It thus helps the analyst to appreciate the many possible ways of being. Whilst I am aware of a good deal of subtle and not so subtle prescribing of normative behaviour in psychoanalytic writing, I am also aware that a good deal of this is based on the analyst's own personality and experience (this includes, of course, Freud and Jung (see Chapter Eighteen), and I recognise some of the contributions of my own personality orientation in this book); in other words, it relates to how they deal with difference—including whether they embrace all difference as a matter of principle, which would suggest to me that the analyst may struggle to really accept difference.

Furthermore, it is important that the analyst is able to recognise their own early relational traumas and internal working models in both direct and reversed forms. The reversed forms frequently constitute shadow aspects of the analyst's personality, as they may see themselves as being the one who is, for example, susceptible to being rejected or dismissed without recognising that they are sometimes themselves rejecting or dismissive; they often then justify being dismissive because the patient has in some way dismissed them. These reversed forms are frequently enacted in the analytic relationship.

Related to this, Adrienne Harris (2009) discusses the analyst's contribution to impasse, describing the analyst's recapitulation of caretaking behaviours toward a vulnerable, tragic, or failing parent, sibling, or ancestor figure, in the analytic relationship. If the analyst cannot bear the early loss of, or the shame at the failure to repair, these figures they may continue desperately and omnipotently trying to do so as a form of repetition compulsion.

The defeat of the analyst's ego—trusting the patient and the process

The defeat of the analyst's ego essentially relates to the degree to which the analyst relies on rational means of functioning, whether they need to "know", whether they need to put things into words, whether they can trust in non-rational processes, which are intrinsic to the functioning of the core self (occurring unconsciously), and whether they can bear to have their rational processes frustrated, undermined, and defeated.

In one sense this amounts to whether the analyst can bear being rendered powerless and ineffective, exactly as the patient's own ego-functioning was once overwhelmed and rendered ineffective by the original trauma.[8] This entails being in touch with despair, loss of hope, and failure—whether that is despair about the process of analysis or a personal sense of failure—which are inevitable aspects of the traumatised individual's experience. There will be times when the patient's powerlessness needs to be challenged, but there will also be times when both patient's and analyst's powerlessness needs to be accepted, acknowledged, and verbalised.

This has a number of very practical consequences. The main one is that at the core of the complex lies the unintegrated, affective-somatic aspect of the original trauma. If the analyst insists that the patient "deal with this" through rational means, thinking that they are "doing it on purpose" and that they "could change if they really wanted to", they will soon find that they will become extremely frustrated, and they will likely infuriate, wound, and alienate the patient.

They may very well take the patient's persistently behaving in ways that are not well-adapted as the patient being (wilfully) destructive or self-destructive. This is not to say that the patient may not embrace destructive and self-destructive ways of being at times in order to be more congruent with themselves, and as a way of pre-empting the criticism of those who tell them they are being self-destructive: "If you think I am bad I will *be* bad, if you think I am a failure I will *be* a failure!".

The analyst therefore needs to be able to suspend their ego perspective in order to understand what the patient is communicating. This includes all behaviour that might be thought of as delusional or paranoid. This requires the analyst to trust that there is a kernel of truth in what is going on and that this vital truth needs to be uncovered and appreciated.

Example

As I described in Chapter Ten, Michael would frequently express his conviction that life was meaningless, or his experience of being unbearably isolated, or his fury and disgust at female telephonists who would not have the information he required, who would keep him on hold, who would say they would get someone to ring him back (but didn't), or who would be confused and indecisive. Over time we realised that this attitude towards the telephonists was triggering his rage at his mother who had been depressed and regressed and who had relied on him to run the household. At an even more basic level there was a repeat of his early frustration of his basic attempts at communication with her—not being responded to, her not knowing the answer and being "vacant" or absent, leaving him frustrated, confused, hurt, rejected, and infuriated. If I had in some way covertly lectured him on "the best way of dealing with people", or had in some way addressed his overt misogyny, I would have missed the point, alienated him, and infuriated him further (he knew very well that this way of behaving wasn't helpful).

A shift in attitude

Overall, this encompassing of "bad" roles and experiences represents a shift, explored more in the next chapter, towards an analytic attitude that places greater value on the "reality" of what the patient and analyst experience, rather than on how nice/pleasant/good either party is experienced to be (I gave an example of this at the end of Chapter Ten). Of course, how good or bad the object is experienced is a vital element in the nature of the relationship and the way it unfolds, heading perhaps towards a point where the object is experienced as "good enough" or as both good and bad.

Exploring an impasse—Fordham and "K"

I would now like to look at the extremely rich account of the relationship between Michael Fordham and his patient K, which has been so generously documented in the pages of the *Journal of Analytical Psychology* by K himself in his three papers and responses (2007, 2008, 2014), and by James Astor (2007), with further responses by Richard Carvalho (2007) and Jean Knox (2008). It opens up, in a very clear way, a number of extremely important issues regarding analytic attitude and technique that can lead to tragic consequences for both patient and analyst if they are handled wrongly.

 K was Fordham's patient for ten years and the analysis ended unresolved, terminated by Fordham himself. Astor explains that "[Fordham] felt stuck, he felt the analytic frame was under attack, he perceived the uselessness of his interpretations and eventually he stopped the analysis" (2007, p. 187). One significant event in the analysis had been when K recognised his similar experience to that which Fordham describes in his paper "Defences of the self", and wrote a commentary on it from his perspective as a patient. Fordham was much taken with this commentary and proposed publishing it, with comments by Fordham himself; however, he changed his mind, withdrawing his offer. K found this intensely wounding and "a betrayal".

Following Fordham's death K approached James Astor to see if he could reach some resolution of what had happened in his analysis. He was not strictly looking for another analysis, and early on K laid down his three therapeutic principles: "no interpretation, agreement, encouragement—all of which ... were designed to elicit the ego strengthening [he] so desperately needed" (K, 2008, p. 26). Astor quickly discovered for himself that whatever interpretations he might make were ineffective, and that Fordham had usually already made them before.

K had experienced significant early relational trauma. He was born prematurely and his mother fell chronically ill shortly afterward. K experienced early on her "depressions, withdrawals, fits and diabetic comas, which removed her from him" (Astor, 2007, p. 194). His father never wanted children, "was chiefly interested in himself and brutalized his family, squashing any initiatives they may make" (p. 189); "his scorn and violence were like a dagger to the heart" (p. 195). K says he "experienced [his] father's attacks as murderous in intensity and intention" (K, 2007, p. 226).

In adult life K says he felt "unable to take much pleasure in life, nor [did he] have much confidence or sense of self possession" ... "[he] rarely experienced a feeling of accomplishment ... and in the realm of personal relationship [he was] mostly querulous, uncertain and preoccupied". He comments that what he thought he needed in therapy was "a fairly lengthy process of being bolstered up" (2008, p. 21). He experienced a deep ongoing pain, which Fordham was not able to alleviate in the analysis. As K and Fordham saw it, "good and bad were fused together in him, except the bad overwhelmed the good" (Astor, 2007, p. 192). K attributes his negativity in part to his "limited capacity to see favourable changes whereas his capacity to see deterioration was highly developed". Astor understood this as arising from the fact that K's "need to destroy was stronger than his own means of self-protection and that this arose out of intense pain" (2007, p. 198).

In what follows I will concentrate on the issues around the impasse between Fordham and K, omitting much else that was clearly significant in the analysis. K evidently experienced both Fordham and the analytic method as killing him off at times, as he had experienced with his father (something which Fordham interpreted to him (Astor, 2007, p. 192)); as K put it, "even the lightest interpretation may inadvertently be taking away a whole world" (K, 2008, p. 25). He experienced interpretations as annihilating and the analytic method, in so far as it called on interpretation, as retraumatising (Knox, 2008)—it was striking on a core wound, the early relational trauma.

Particular examples of this were when Fordham responded "curtly" to K's suggestion about exploring the paternal transference more and, of course, most significantly, when changing his mind about publishing K's commentary on "Defences of the self". Furthermore, Astor tells us that, "by speaking analytically Fordham sounded to K as if he was not empathizing with K's pain, and so did not really care" (Astor, 2007, p. 192), although Astor assures us that Fordham felt deeply about what was happening (p. 193).

K longed to be heard, to be received, not to be "translated by interpretation"; he longed "to be welcomed" (2008, p. 20), to know "that Fordham was affected by [his] state" (Astor, 2007, p. 192) and, obviously, not to feel annihilated by the analysis. If we look at this through the perspective of K's traumatic early experience, there are a number of facets that overlap. There is the theme of being unable to affect or get through to the other person (his mother), of not being heard because the other is too self-preoccupied (his father and mother, though in different ways), of not being welcomed (not experiencing a positive response from either mother or father), and of being directly killed off (primarily by his father's scorn and brutality, but also by his mother's absence).

The unfolding of the infant's nascent core self, the process that Fordham called deintegration (1969), is vital but fragile, and when the reaching out is not received, or is rejected, it is experienced as annihilating. Some narcissistic wounding of this kind is inevitable, but when the mismatches between infant and caregiver are not repaired, the individual develops a negative emotional core (Tronick & Gianino, 1986). What I have just been describing in terms of K's early experience certainly would have led to these negative experiences and ways of being becoming embedded at the core of his identity, and have left him hypervigilant for further rejections, as he reports. This is characteristic of a borderline personality organisation, a term which K embraced (K, 2008, p. 25).

When K makes an impassioned and well-argued plea, both to Fordham in the analysis and later on in his published papers, that the analyst needs to be more human, to show what they are feeling, and to show *that* they are feeling, he is asking no more and no less than that his core self be allowed to safely unfold without further experiences of opposition and annihilation (that is, retraumatisation). K says clearly that he wanted to know that Fordham was a feeling person, that he was affected by K's situation, and that K could get through to him.

Why might K have thought this was not the case? In my experience of such situations, by the time the patient is feeling this way the analyst has already done something to trigger the patient's core trauma, which thus evokes a more or less overt primitive defensive reaction of some kind from the patient. The analyst's core defensive reactions are then automatically, unconsciously, triggered and they will, at the very least, be guarded, which the patient may very well interpret as the analyst being uncaring, cut off, or theoretical. The deeper dynamic has already begun to be constellated.

Perhaps Fordham could have said something along the lines of what Jessica Benjamin said to her patient, as discussed in the last chapter, namely that, "no matter what she did, she would always have a place in my heart, that she could not break our attachment or destroy my loving feelings" (Benjamin, 2004, p. 37). However, I note that after a year of meeting with James Astor, when K had established that he was warm, responsive, and empathic, K announced that he wanted to stop the therapy and also to leave his wife (Astor, 2007, p. 193). Similarly Benjamin's patient, after Benjamin had said what I just quoted, left the analysis and found another therapist for a while. Why might this be?

I would suggest that it was an expression of the internal working model in reversed form, so that when the threat of being rejected and kept out by a sadistic, self-preoccupied father or a cold, depressed mother had passed, K shifted to the other side of the dynamic and enacted the rejecting, heartless role himself; as his wife commented, "only ever interested in himself" (ibid., p. 193).

The deeper dynamic between Fordham and K

In response to feeling annihilated by Fordham, K responded, in talion fashion, by annihilating Fordham—undermining his effectiveness, and no longer listening to his interpretations; as Astor puts it, "resistance, rage and rejection, followed by K feeling awful about himself" (ibid., p. 192). K gives one example of responding extremely irritatingly to Fordham's interpretation of a dream and pressing Fordham to say why he persisted in interpreting dreams, until Fordham responded with "good-humoured exasperation" but with "his patience quite worn out", that he did so "because he liked them!" (K, 2007, p. 221). This is an example of what I mean by the analyst and patient being on equal terms relationally, although I believe such exchanges go on much more subtly from the beginning of any analysis.

Fordham and K were both aware that K experienced Fordham like his father at times; that at times K treated Fordham like his father had treated him; and that K's attitude to himself, belittling and punitive, was like an internalisation of the father; or as I would put this, the internal working model in direct and reversed mode on the transference and subjective levels. According to Astor, Fordham and K agreed that, "it was therapeutically inefficient to interpret out of a transference that K's internal father was a denigrating, self-interested person lacking in feeling for his son, since it brought little relief or change to K in the long term" (Astor, 2007, p. 194).

Yet I would suggest that understanding the interaction in terms of trauma and the natural and necessary responses to it, takes away some of the guilt about what Astor terms K's "need to destroy" which might be thought of as "merely" destructive or self-destructive. Appreciating the unbearable experience of being annihilated, ignored, and not heard, helps us understand the natural talion reversal of being murderous and annihilating in turn. I see K's apparently self-destructive behaviour not as maintaining an infantile perverted state of mind, as Fordham (1974) describes,[9] but as K necessarily staying true to, and recapitulating, his early experience of relational trauma in the analysis where it might then be recognised, known, appreciated, and integrated. This perspective can then begin to alleviate the implicit moralising element of the patient being "bad" and doing "the wrong thing".

Similarly K saw Fordham as bad, theory-ridden, rigid, and inhuman at times. His papers contain a powerful sense of taboo against the analyst being anything like his rejecting, annihilating, self-preoccupied father or his unresponsive, unhearing mother. This is the moral outrage characteristic of the self's response to the threat of retraumatisation: "This is wrong and should not happen!" (West, 2007, and Chapter Eleven of this book).

So when K writes, "I don't see any way for it but that the analyst acknowledges the destructive aspect of the method being used ..." (K, 2008, p. 24), I would agree, as I think it is very important that the analyst and patient identify what it is that is triggering the patient's distress. I would then explore with K the way that he experienced Fordham (or a subsequent analyst) and his interpretations as annihilating in so far as they triggered his early relational traumas in a significant way. I would acknowledge that these traumas had been triggered, and that the traumatic situation had become co-constructed in the analytic relationship with due (deep, genuine) appreciation of what it is like to be taken back to something that has hitherto been unbearable. This is a way of addressing the conflict described by Jean Knox as follows:

> The key issue for all models of psychotherapy seems to be to define the conditions under which a purely interpretative approach is likely to hinder the patient's individuation process because it demands more self-awareness than the analysand can bear and, on the other hand, the conditions under which well-meaning attempts to adopt a relational approach based on attunement may lead to the kind of disastrous boundary violations which Gabbard has so vividly described. (Knox, 2008, p. 35)

It is clear that in their relationship the traumatic dynamic had become constellated both ways, with K feeling killed off by Fordham and, at the same time, K killing Fordham off. K had taken the dynamic into his sphere of omnipotence. By the time of writing his second paper K had become aware of this, and writes, movingly and insightfully:

> I suddenly found memories of my father's vituperous cruelty floating into my mind ... I asked: why so cruel? where from? Then I suddenly realized that despite many years of trying I was asking because I was still struggling to come to terms with the same trait in myself and that it was there that so much of my trouble was coming from. (K, 2008, p. 28)

What went wrong?

It seems to me that Fordham and K were both potentially very close to working through the traumatic complex—it was fully constellated in the analysis. Fordham wrote that he "cannot convince [himself] that a bad start in life will account for the syndrome", although he does recognise that "early disasters … can be most relevant" (1974, p. 197). However, I believe that the perspective of early relational trauma, as described in this book, can help the analyst make sense of what is going on and contain and make best use of the primitive reactions that are evoked in themselves, and interpret to the patient in a benign manner.

Astor suggests that, in ending the analysis with K, Fordham might have been acting on a sadistic response that had become constellated in him. I would expect at some point exactly to experience a parallel sadistic response from K to the one his father expressed, and to experience that towards K. I hope I would be able to recognise this as an opportunity to work on the detail of his early experiences.

Further to my comments about the taboo and the moral defence earlier, I note that neither Fordham nor Astor seems to have effectively addressed K's idealisation. Astor, for example, writes that "[t]his mismatch between Fordham's absence of responses in the paternal transference and K's need for a loving interested father contributed to the impasse" (2007, p. 195). Astor then goes on to wonder if this impasse and absence of response was due to a lacuna in Fordham's ability to address issues in regard to his own father.[10]

Astor writes as if the need for a loving, interested father might be met in analysis, rather than that its traumatic absence might inevitably be constellated and then, hopefully, recognised and worked through (thus representing a loving, interested father in a deeper form); as Casement puts it, "an analytic good object … is that which can tolerate being used to represent the worst in the patient's experience" (Casement, 2001, p. 384).

Astor tells us that Fordham distrusted K's predominant view of his father as "a denigrating and ruthlessly critical person", due to his "transference experience of K" (2007, p. 194)—presumably his experience of K being denigrating and ruthlessly critical himself. Yet the perspective of trauma allows us to understand how experiences that are bearable to the well-functioning adult ego are unbearable and annihilating to the child.[11] Astor tells us (if I understand him correctly) that Fordham was wary of identifying with the patient and the patient's "delusion" (p. 198), and presumably this is related to his understanding of defences of the self as an aspect of a psychotic transference.

I would suggest that K's experiences of his father, which Fordham seems to have considered to some degree delusional, were veridical to the traumatised infant/child, but unmodified; or, put another way, they are the dissociated, affective-somatic elements of the trauma. If Fordham had been able to put aside his rational, reality-oriented, ego-perspective for a while, he might have been able to recognise that the apparent "molehill" that K was describing, was the terrifying "mountain" of his father's belittling criticism that had once crushed him as a child.

As K himself wrote in his original commentary on "Defences of the self", "… at this juncture the analyst avowedly does not yet understand why the patient behaves as he does" (in Astor, 2007, p. 188). I would understand K's ongoing pain, which Fordham was not able to shift, as the infant's plaintive call that leads analyst and patient to the core experiences of trauma, and that continues until it is met and understood. In K's case, I suspect that this pain relates to the appalling isolation that comes when the people on whom you depend and to whom you want to reach out, feel too toxic to do so safely (this represents a disorganised attachment pattern) (again, see Michael, Chapter Ten).

In addition, if Fordham had addressed K's internal working model in both direct and reversed form—K feeling killed off and killing Fordham off—I suggest he would have accounted for the conflicting mixture of woundedness and attack (the masochisto-sadistic dynamic) that is so perplexing for the analyst.

To conclude—I suggest that the perspective of early relational trauma, its relation to an idealised solution, its reconstruction, co-construction, and re-enactment within the analysis in direct and reversed forms, and the defeat of the analyst's ego, can throw light on the impasse that occurred in K's analysis with Fordham.

In order to accept the defeat of their ego, the analyst needs to trust in both the process and the patient's psyche, just as, in order to emerge from Hades, Orpheus had to trust that Eurydice was behind him, and not to look back. This is necessary if the analyst is to help the patient emerge from the living hell of their early traumatic experience, which has become encrusted at the individual's core.[12] These considerations are central to the analyst's analytic attitude, which I discuss in the next chapter.

Notes

1. In some versions it is a shepherd, Aristaeus, who was overwhelmed by her beauty, made advances to her, and pursued her when she ran away; in another version Aristaeus is an Athenian merchant.

2. I am reminded of the story of the mother who took her son to the guru to ask him to tell her son to give up eating sweets. The guru asked them to come back the following week, whereupon he told the boy to give up sweets. The mother asked him why he hadn't told the boy to do that the previous week, to which he replied that he had himself been eating too many sweets then.

3. As I described in West, 2013a, "I was able to point out to her that perhaps she was not the weak and powerless person (victim) that she felt herself to be, but rather that she had not only some powerful self-protective responses, but also active wishes to hurt and harm me" (p. 88). With the moral charge contained between us we could then reflect together on what that had been like, and I could appreciate more of her appallingly traumatic experience of waiting for her father under those circumstances.

4. Perhaps in a parallel way to the two primary ways of comforting an infant: soothing-by-mirroring (empathic staying with) or disruption-soothing (distracting the child with some intense alternate emotion, e.g., throwing up in the air, or "look at the birdie!") (Fonagy, Gergely, Jurist, & Target, 2002, p. 174).

5. Or to withdraw and be alone, undisturbed by others, although this does not have the same result, as the individual's need for relationship is not satisfied, even though it may be specifically disavowed and disowned—"I don't need/want anyone".

6. There is a balance of attachment needs and the needs for self-expression and self-actualisation here, although the latter almost all require relationship. In Bowlby's terms, the needs for self-expression and self-actualisation might represent expressions of other behavioural systems, for example, the exploratory, sociable, or caregiving systems. I will touch on the importance of self-expression and self-actualisation further in the final chapter.

7. Perhaps an influential example of this is Heinz Kohut, whose case studies of Mr. Z were in fact significantly based on his own material (Cocks, 2002; Strozier, 2001).

8. Olinick offers a traditional approach to this phenomenon, understanding it in terms of a negative therapeutic reaction, where "a depressive, sadomasochistic rage, which is projected and induced in the [analyst], in a desperate effort at defence against the expectation of inner loss and helpless regression" (1964, p. 546).

9. Although Fordham did recognise that the patient was attempting to "bring (these states of mind) into relation with another person" (Astor, 2004, p. 492).

10. Astor reports that Fordham was conflicted in relation to his own father who had had a breakdown after Fordham's mother died suddenly

when Fordham was fourteen years old. His father became depressed and there was "an ambiguity over his death, which was on a railway crossing" (Astor, 2007, p. 200). In regard to idealised solutions Astor reminds us that Fordham "fell violently in love with a younger woman" when his wife was very ill and completely dependent on him (ibid., p. 199); this might suggest that Fordham had not worked through some of his own idealised solutions to early relational deprivations.

11. Astor puts this as follows: "A veridical perception is one which has integrated both confusing, illusory perceptions and inferences to arrive at a true/veridical depth perception" (2007, p. 194).

12. In one version of the myth, when Orpheus failed to bring back Eurydice he was ripped apart by Dionysius' followers, the Maenads—let us not visit that fate on Fordham.

CHAPTER THIRTEEN

Trauma and the analytic attitude

The patient brings exactly what they need to

The analytic attitude that I will be advocating in this chapter is based upon an attempt to stay with, accept, contain, explore, understand, and communicate exactly what the patient brings, thereby allowing these expressions and dynamics to be integrated into the patient's broader personality, just as the dynamic is integrated into the analytic relationship. From the very beginning of the analysis, the patient demonstrates what their traumas are to the analyst, both explicitly and implicitly, and, almost always, wants to enlist the analyst in avoiding those traumatic areas—the complex—but usually also in resolving them. From the very first session the analyst is therefore presented with various options, and the patient will be watching the analyst's reactions intently—is the analyst going to move towards the traumas or move away from them? How is the analyst going to (help me) resolve them?

Normative therapies

The "aphorism" with which I have headed the chapter captures most of what I want to say about the analytic attitude. It also addresses the curious phenomenon, often met with in case presentations and papers, whereby the analyst implies or behaves, implicitly or explicitly, as if the patient should be doing something different, or should not be behaving the way that they are. I suggest that such attitudes may indicate that the analyst is struggling with their primitive reactions emerging in relation to the patient. Whilst this is a natural interim position while the analyst is coming to terms with the relational dynamic, I suggest that it is unhelpful if it becomes hardened into a prolonged attitude. Sometimes, again, this attitude is predicated on a belief as to the particular nature of healthy functioning.

This attitude of acceptance of what the patient brings does not, however, entail a passive, masochistic acquiescence to whatever the patient does and however they want to behave towards the analyst. The analyst will need to actively explore and address the dynamic, and perhaps even set limits on what is accepted in order to maintain their personal boundaries at times, for example, in relation to the patient leaving the room at the end of the session or flooding the analyst with communications between sessions. These are all invaluable sources of information about the patient's experiences, and hopefully they can be contained through being discussed; however, sometimes this may not be enough and the analyst may need to actively maintain or enforce a boundary, as Kernberg comments (1975, p. 85; and see West, 2007, pp. 25ff. for an example).

This analytic attitude offers, I believe, the best opportunity for the patient's behavioural patterns to be known and addressed, and for the traumatic complex to be worked through and integrated—an analytic understanding born out of relational knowing. This may well require some (considerable) internal work and journeying on behalf of the analyst, as described in the last chapter.

Properly recognising the role of trauma, and of the reconstruction and co-construction of that trauma in the analytic relationship, for me, makes sense of the analytic attitude by putting it in context. I think it can otherwise sometimes seem arcane, arbitrary, or cruel. The analyst is always trying to make a clear space to come to know, and to realistically address, the early relational traumas and dynamics associated with them. It also makes sense of the pressures on the analyst, which might otherwise seem senseless, pathological, or destructive on the part of the patient—they are part of the reconstruction (see Chapter Eleven).

The understanding that what is constellated in the analytic relationship is a reconstruction of the original trauma is, for me, a matter of rediscovery, not a matter of theory. As such it remains a hypothesis and, as with any hypothesis, it is continually being retested. Any "negative result" will call the hypothesis into question and will require its modification and development.

To recognise that the analytic relationship is thus a co-construction by patient and analyst of significant dynamics in the patient's (primarily) and analyst's (secondarily) early relationships offers a very particular perspective on the analytic process. Davies describes this in terms of a "therapeutic enactment", where there is

> a collapsing of past and present; a co-constructed organization of the transference–countertransference matrix that bears such striking similarity to an important moment of the past that patient and analyst together have the unique opportunity to exist in both places at the same time. (Davies, 1997, p. 246)

Winnicott (1974), Davies and Frawley (1992a), Bouchard, Normandin, and Séguin (1995), Lindy (1996), Davies (1997), Gabbard and Lester (1995), Gabbard (1997), Frawley-O'Dea (1998), and Courtois (2010) stress the inevitability and opportunity for insight that can come from such therapeutic enactments. The patient needs to be able to externalise and constellate the traumatising-abusive figures from their past in order to be able to do work with them, and a great deal of the unconscious, co-constructed dynamics are bent towards ensuring that this occurs.[1] As Davies and Frawley put it:

> included in our conceptualization of the transformational aspects of the treatment are the patient's experience of the analyst's availability and constancy, the analyst's willingness to participate in the shifting transference–countertransference reenactments, and, finally, his or her capacity to maintain appropriate boundaries and set necessary limits. (1992a, pp. 30–31)

Trauma and traditional approaches

Whether or not putting trauma central to an understanding of the practice of analysis represents a radical alteration in perspective is an interesting and perplexing question. Freud's relatively early paper, "Remembering, repeating and working-through" (1914g), recognised that the patient's early relational conflicts are re-enacted and worked through in the transference–countertransference/analytic relationship. And yet he saw many of those conflicts as relating to internal conflicts relating to infantile sexuality or oedipal issues, so that real-world trauma was less emphasised—see Chapter Three for a discussion of this issue. Melanie Klein and her followers put even more emphasis on the individual's own inner conflicts—envy, destructiveness, and the death instinct, as well as the functioning of projective identification and paranoid-schizoid mechanisms.

Yet, reading some of the middle-school Freudian analysts' accounts of their analytic practice it is clear that they are very much working in the spirit of trauma. First, there is Winnicott's classic "draft" paper, "Fear of Breakdown", where he writes, "[t]he only way to 'remember' [the traumatic experience of breakdown] is for the patient to experience this past thing for the first time in the present, that is to say, in the transference. This past and future thing then becomes a matter of the here and now" (1974, p. 105).

In her paper "Slouching towards Bethlehem", Nina Coltart (1986) poetically describes how the analyst's attitude facilitates the birth of the "beast" that is slouching towards Bethlehem. This beast clearly represents the patient's early object relations, those "beyond words" (p. 194), becoming constellated in the analytic process.

In her example, however, she describes how, when she had become thoroughly identified with her patient's "primary hatred of a genuinely powerful mother" (p. 195), she then enacted this role, "and suddenly became furious and bawled him out for his prolonged lethal attack on [her] and on the analysis" (p. 194). I would hope that this dynamic— the powerful, demanding, narcissistic mother in direct and reversed forms—could be recognised and in some way addressed without the analyst acting out the role in this way; although this may sometimes happen. Coltart describes how her enactment "changed the course of the analysis" (p. 195), implying that this was in a favourable way. I would suggest, however, that she had hitherto had the opportunity to "analyse", that is to say, stay with, experience and interpret, the complex dynamic that was going on with her patient. Sometimes the analyst's enactments do not lead to such apparently favourable outcomes.

On the other hand Enid Balint's paper, "One analyst's technique" (Balint, 1991), gracefully describes the process of the analyst having to wait, to not be intrusive, to not "withdraw, find good solutions, comfort, or try to relieve anxiety", and that patient and analyst have to "endure not being able to be helped or to give help, to rescue or be rescued" (p. 122). In this way the heart of the issue can emerge, and she describes the experience of a patient who was "wet" and abandoned by mother, who repeated the same pattern upon her analyst and how this was triggered by the analyst's unexpected cancellation of a session (p. 124). Balint comments that the process "depends on the shared ability [of patient and analyst] to endure the unendurable" (p. 123). Her example is also clearly dealing with preverbal experiences, held in implicit memory.

Similarly Betty Joseph's paper, "Transference: the total situation" (Joseph, 1985), extends the analyst's appreciation of what is being constellated in the analytic relationship to include implicit patterns of relating that have much greater significance and hold precedence over conscious ways of relating and verbal dialogues that may be constitute only the surface layer of the analytic dialogue.

Yet, as with Joseph's paper "Addiction to near-death" (Joseph, 1982), which will be discussed in Chapter Fifteen, trauma is not understood as having a one-to-one correspondence with what happens in the analytic relationship, largely due to the fact that the patient's internal elaborations of the traumatic complex, which are understood as the patient's own destructiveness, are seen as primary. Whereas my understanding is that the ego-destructiveness—the patient's non-reality oriented and apparently self-destructive ways of behaving—are due to the patient's attempt to (finally) have the trauma recognised, understood, and borne.

Both Coltart's and Balint's papers emphasise the need to wait and that "[t]he seductive impulse to use the power of one's thinking and theorizing to take possession of the patient too soon can be great, but will … be of little ultimate value to him" (Coltart, 1986, p. 191). This clearly builds upon Bion's recommendations regarding analytic attitude, namely that the analyst should proceed without memory, desire, and understanding. Bion writes that "[t]he analyst must focus his attention on O, the unknown and unknowable. The success of psycho-analysis depends on the maintenance of a psycho-analytic point of view; the point of view is the psycho-analytic vertex; the psycho-analytic vertex is O" (Bion, 1970, p. 27).

Whilst it may not have been what Bion himself meant, this attitude is clearly consonant with being open primarily to the underlying, non-verbal, affective-somatic experience of the patient and their implicit ways of relating, and that knowledge about it is secondary. Patient and analyst can have intellectual knowledge about the patient's difficulties but what is most effective is when both patient and analyst "learn from experience" (Bion, 1962a). Knowledge and understanding can get in the way, and Michael Fordham described how it was important to "not know beforehand", and said that he consigned his analytic knowledge to an imaginary mental filing cabinet (Fordham, 1993).[2] In the last chapter I described this as one element of the defeat of the analyst's ego.

Similarly, as Bion suggests, the "desire" for the patient to, for example, change or "get better", can impede the recognition of the dynamic that is actually occurring, which may be, for example, an enactment of the patient not being able to affect their caregivers' states of mind or to "make them better". "Memories" and expectations can similarly clutter up the analytic space and impede the recognition of what is going on at that moment, for example, a distressing re-enactment of the parent forgetting the patient may be occluded by the analyst's struggle not to forget. The lived recognition of the pattern, and the exploration of the continuing significance of the dynamic—perhaps the patient forgets others and is preoccupied about being forgotten—is what is most important. The analyst being able to bear being forgotten and to bear being the forgetter, in the spirit of discovery, may be part of the analyst's journey in this.

This implicitly recognises the unconscious "thinking" and processing that goes on in both patient and analyst, which is the cornerstone of Jung's appreciation of the unconscious functioning of the self, in contrast to the relatively more limited understanding of the ego. Bion's work has been extended by Meltzer (1984) in his appreciation that "dreaming is thinking" and in Ogden's understanding of "waking-dreaming", "talking-as-dreaming", and of the way we "dream ourselves into being" (Ogden, 2009, chs. 1 & 2).

From a different vertex, some analysts' work appears to be primarily informed by what the patient is not doing; for example, Money-Kyrle writes:

> all adult thinking, all later acts of recognition, are hampered by the
> difficulties which beset the first ones, ... [namely] ... the recognition

of the breast as a supremely good object, the recognition of the parents' intercourse as a supremely creative act, and the recognition of the inevitability of time and ultimately death. (1971, p. 443)

Steiner (1996) gives the example of a patient who apparently pre-emptively "interpreted" the building work that was going on outside the consulting room, and that was bogged down so the workers could not proceed with the foundations, linking that with the analysis being bogged down (p. 1080)—the interpretation he anticipated his analyst would make. Steiner interpreted that the patient envied and hated the foundations of their work, Steiner's capacity to symbolise. He comments that following his interpretation, "the patient made transient contact with a part of his personality that he usually disowned" (Steiner, 1996, p. 1081); and further that in standing up for analysis in the face of his patient's attacks on it, he was showing a more creative aspect of his parents' relationship, and he references Money-Kyrle's recognition of the value of parental intercourse. This is in line with Steiner's understanding of psychic retreats, which he sees as defensive organisations of the personality that are resistant to change.

As I have already described (Chapter Eight), I see what Steiner calls psychic retreats as overt recreations, offering the opportunity for recognition of early relational traumas, rather than disguised, pathological ways of being. In the case he describes, and of course this is entirely speculative, the patient's behaviour might have reflected the expectations on him as a child to in some way "behave properly", which represented an envious, hateful dismissal of the child's own personality and creativity. If this is correct, Steiner in turn re-enacts this himself, dismissing the patient's communications as attacks, just as the patient dismisses Steiner's own creativity (see the discussion of Fordham's analysis of his patient K in the last chapter). I note that elsewhere in his paper he describes a patient's experience of the analyst, the mother who betrayed him, and the father to whom the patient is forced to submit as "clearly ... distortions" (p. 1080).

Curiously in that paper Steiner (1996) does try to introduce the perspective of trauma, through the back door as it were, but as a reason that individuals cling to these psychic retreats/defensive patterns due to a feeling of "resentment that is focused on traumatic experiences in which the patient has felt injured or wronged". He continues, "if the patient is unable to redress the wrong through the exacting of revenge, the injury smoulders on as a grievance sometimes being held on to and nursed, and even providing a source of strength and purpose" (p. 1078). He cites an early version of Feldman's paper on grievance, which he went on to publish in 2008, where Feldman (2008) holds, referencing Money-Kyrle, that the original trauma is the oedipal wound.[3] That the patient is not able to behave in a way that is consistent with the most favourable form of psychic functioning is, of course, why they are in analysis. Their approach to trauma is significantly different to the one outlined here.

Rosenfeld's anti-therapeutic factors

In discussing clinical technique it is striking that Rosenfeld first mentions how readily patients seek to openly communicate their predicament to the analyst, proffering the analyst numerous attempts to understand (1987, p. 32). He also says that the "analyst depends to a crucial extent on the functioning of his personality as an important instrument" (p. 33).

I would like to briefly outline the anti-therapeutic factors that Rosenfeld cites as leading to clinical impasses. He singles out three particular difficulties. First, the analyst's tendency to adopt particular directive roles (p. 34). He recommends against taking either a "surgical approach" or too "motherly" a role, citing Pearl King saying that she is "committed to take on whatever role my patient may unconsciously assign to me" (King, 1962, p. 225). He specifically cautions against the analyst's "narcissistic desire to do well". Mentioning traumatised patients in particular, he says that their attempts to "share [their] terrifying experiences" with the analyst by very forceful projections may "appear to be attacks on the analyst and his work". He writes that, if the analyst

> does not err on the side of providing corrective experience, a second anti-therapeutic response to which the analyst can so easily resort is to interpret the projections as sadistic attacks on his noble efforts to help. In this case the patient also feels rejected and withdraws. (p. 36)

Second, is the analyst giving vague interpretations that do not accurately address the patient's anxieties or that are badly timed, for example, following too long a silence or interpreting too quickly, so that the patient feels the analyst finds their problems unacceptable and that the analyst is trying to eject them. He suggests that a predominant anxiety is often the fear that the patient will drive the analyst mad or that the analyst will drive the patient mad.

Third, is the analyst giving interpretations that are rigid and, when the patient objects in some way, the analyst is not able to modify their interpretation to address the patient's perspective, but rather keeps on inflexibly pursuing a particular line of interpretation. Related to this he also mentions how the analyst may collude with one aspect of the patient's personality in order to keep other unwelcome problems out of the analysis.

These points resonate with Jean Knox's cautioning against the analyst adopting too rigid an analytic attitude, particularly when an abusive dynamic is being constellated in the analytic relationship; she writes that "there is a real danger that when therapists respond to the sense of being seen as an abuser by an increasingly determined adherence to analytic technique, this may actually become an unconscious identification with, and enactment of the projection of, the abuser" (Knox, 2013, p. 502).

These points relate to the analyst's ability not to see things wholly from an ego perspective (by which I mean, what is most "constructive and reality-oriented"), but rather to address what the patient is actually bringing instead of in some way communicating that they "should" be bringing something else. This is essentially about adopting an attitude where one is learning from what the patient brings in each particular session. This may involve the analyst rediscovering a new theory for each session for each patient (Fordham, 1993), or an attitude of discovery/rediscovery of analysis itself (Ogden, 2009).

Analytic attitude and borderline psychology

The attitude of acceptance that I am advocating is especially pertinent to working with individuals with a borderline psychology, as they readily feel criticised and misunderstood and have an acute eye on whether the analyst is seeing things from their perspective; in other words, whether or not the analyst is identified with them. This is in part because they are frequently harshly critical of themselves and cannot properly understand why it is that they do what they do, and why they cannot do what they would like to be doing (frequently that is to fit in with and function "like everyone else"). This is an aspect of self-criticism/superego functioning derived from the universal, primitive functioning that monitors where we are in relation to others—so necessary to help us adapt to our caregivers, family group, and society. The more that ego-functioning is disrupted, the more that the individual's core self is exposed, the greater will be their underlying need to mirror others or be mirrored by them.

I also think, however, that individuals with a borderline personality organisation *are* frequently misunderstood and blamed for being self-destructive and so on. This book is, of course, an attempt to better understand their situation.

Ron Britton understands this need for understanding and agreement in terms of the patient's fear of "malignant misunderstanding". He holds that those with "borderline disorder", who he terms thin-skinned narcissists, keep their primary object as good (maintaining empathic understanding) through splitting. This engenders a third object, the father/analyst, who breaks up the relationship with the good object, who is feared to be the source of malignant misunderstanding. This is experienced as an attack, which threatens not only the loss of the good object but the patient's integrity itself and an ensuing collapse into states of chaos and terror. This chaos he links with Bion's (1959, p. 107) understanding of the ego-destructive superego (Britton, 1998, pp. 54–57). Britton writes: "the need for agreement is inversely proportional to the expectation of understanding" (p. 57). He understands this dynamic, then, very much in terms of the "Oedipus situation".

Whilst he acknowledges the contribution of trauma for these individuals, referencing Rosenfeld, he concludes that there is also an innate factor for some individuals, "a kind of *psychic atopia*, a hypersensitivity to psychic difference, an allergy to the products of other minds" (p. 58, original italics). This is also one of the phenomena he understands in terms of narcissism as "a *force* or *innate tendency* within the personality that opposes relationships outside the self" (Britton, 2004, p. 478, original italics). This "allergy to the products of other minds" very much echoes Fordham's (1974) understanding of defences of the self. Britton describes this as like the sensitivity of the body's immune system and that "[w]here this sensitivity is considerable what is required in the way of understanding is perfect understanding. Less than *perfect understanding* might therefore be perceived as *misunderstanding*" (Britton, 1998, p. 58, original italics).

I understand that this sensitivity to sameness and difference is true for all individuals and that it normally functions unconsciously as a part of our processing of experience (Chapter Eight; Matte Blanco, 1975, 1988; West, 2004, 2007), but that it is brought forcefully to the surface by the disruption of ego-functioning due to trauma. As described in this book, ego-functioning cannot be repaired until the trauma is worked through, which requires that the trauma is recognised and understood. One could say that the individual staying true to the trauma rather than "getting better" (the negative therapeutic reaction), represents an attack on ego-functioning in order that the trauma does not get unsuccessfully glossed over. However, it is probably more correct to say that ego-functioning cannot be repaired until the uncontained traumatic affective-somatic element is contained through lived understanding.

In regard to separation, Steiner describes how, for the patient to emerge from their psychic retreat in order to face psychic reality, requires the "relinquishment of the object and an experience of separateness from it, [where] … the reality of dependence on the object has to be acknowledged and then the reality of the loss of the object has to be faced in order for mourning to be worked through, and both are often vehemently resisted" (1996, p. 1076). I see the mourning as, in large part, the individual being able to relinquish and mourn for the ideal, non-traumatising childhood being instituted in the present. Separation also requires working through the profound experience of the collapse and submit response, which thus constitutes a repair of their ego-functioning (see Chapters Fourteen and Fifteen).

Britton describes how the agreement that is required by the patient can be achieved through the patient either "slavishly submitting or tyrannically controlling", where

> the analyst will follow [the patient] dutifully putting into words [the patient's] subjective experience while feeling constrained from making any other comments, or [the patient] will feel impelled to sacrifice her own subjective experience and incorporate instead [her analyst's] descriptions of the patient. (1998, p. 57)

I see this differently. I do not see the analyst as simply slavishly following the patient, but rather that the patient's description of their current-day experience opens an invaluable window into their early experience, which requires a great deal of work by the analyst to understand what is going on. This includes identifying what is being triggered in and by the real-world situation, understanding how that relates to historic experience (the objective level), how it is being constellated in the analytic relationship (the transference level) as well as internally (the subjective level) (see the example of Michael in Chapter Ten). Furthermore, this specifically includes the reversal of these patterns on all these levels, in other words, the actions in identification with the aggressor.

The individuals whom I have known who have been furious if I deviated from their perspective have all had a dominating, narcissistic parent, usually the father, who forcefully demanded compliance. I understand their "tyranny" to reflect a re-enactment of this early dynamic, with the patient sometimes being tyrannical and sometimes feeling tyrannised by me.

Example

To take further my understanding of how trauma relates to the oedipal configuration, Dorothy had a number of explicitly oedipal-themed dreams, where she couldn't get into the bedroom where she could see that I was naked inside; or dreams where she had been invited into my (grand) house but the visit was spoilt because she was not part of my family. She frequently complained of her intense experience of isolation, of other people being unavailable, of them not wanting her, and of falling apart when something went wrong so that she was unsupported in dealing with it. At these times, feeling unconnected to others, she lost any sense of personal continuity. She believed that the only solution would be for someone to be constantly present and available, ideally a partner but also a dedicated friend, and that she was excruciatingly, envy-inducingly, excluded from this possibility.

The traumatic roots of these idealised, oedipal configurations were only too easy to see in her perennial experience of exclusion by both her mother, due to her mother's extreme anxiety and nervous withdrawal, and her father, who was also a frightening, angry, depressed, and dissatisfied presence. We had frequently discussed things in these oedipal terms, which was of some help in addressing her idealisation. In Chapter Four I described how Dorothy would at the same time reach out for help, telling me of her distress, yet turn away, announcing that she shouldn't be feeling like this and that she should terminate the analysis. On one level, her attitude towards me represented a sullen punishment and rejection of me for not being this ideal.

Alarmingly, she found herself getting worse rather than better—by which I mean sometimes experiencing intense distress, hopelessness, and feelings of disintegration—despite the fact that she was functioning so much better in all other areas of her life. It was only when we finally appreciated that her deep, intense experiences of fragmentation, terror, neediness, shame, and humiliation, which mirrored her first breakdown many years before, represented a detailed reliving, in the analysis, of the collapse (response) she had experienced due to her mother's consistent, tantalising unavailability, that these experiences were contained and her oedipal configuration was worked through. This included recognising the reconstruction in the analytic relationship.

The analytic attitude and trauma theory

In trauma circles the analytic attitude is contentious, and is frequently seen as inhuman, deeply distressing, anti-relational and traumatising. As Rosenfeld and Knox (explored above) suggest, the surgical, blank-screen approach can easily retraumatise the patient, particularly if the patient has a history of being met by blankness, or it can leave the patient feeling unheard, unseen, and unresponded to.

In parallel with the Boston Change Process Study Group's (2007, p. 144) understanding, I hold that the interactions between the patient and others, and thus naturally also between patient and analyst, are foundational. It is on these kinds of relational interchanges, both transferential and extra-transferential, that I find myself naturally focusing as the most significant elements of the analysis.

I am very much aware, therefore, that the analyst's way of being with the patient—when, how, and in what way they respond, what silences they leave, their tone of voice and so on—is absolutely key to the analytic process. Furthermore, that in being relational, the analytic relationship is the essential site for the reconstruction and re-enactment of early relational patterns. The relationship will inevitably trigger and give access to the original traumas. It is therefore of the utmost importance that the analyst is alert to what their way of being with the patient is triggering at any particular moment, and that they explore that as a matter of priority.

For some of these reasons I therefore understand the analytic process primarily as a dialogue where, by and large, I respond to what the patient has said in a turn-taking way (Knox, 2010). I do not think it is necessary that I speak only when I have a fully formulated "interpretation" to make, as I understand that a lot of work, by both patient and analyst, goes into making any interpretation, and that any interpretation is merely one communication along a long, dialogic path. This may very well include the analyst sharing their uncertainties about what they are saying, and volunteering that what they are about to say is provisional, waiting on the response of the patient. I therefore see interpretations, too, as co-constructions by both patient and analyst, that are constantly open to revision and development. This is simply a matter of being realistic about the contributions of both parties to any understanding.

The analyst's perspective, however, born of their countertransference experience, must not be dismissed. Both parties' experiences need to be respected and need to be included in the final picture; this is not least because interpretations are most frequently about relational dynamics. In saying this I am thinking of situations when the patient might tell the analyst that they are being cruel, wrong, distant, or defended (Fordham, 1974). Whilst every situation is unique, I have found on a number of occasions that under these circumstances the analyst is "simply" (although it is not simple at all) maintaining their ego-based position with its implicit separateness. Any distress that this involves for the patient needs to be closely explored.

I do not, therefore, think it is helpful for the analyst to initiate contra-experiential, upbeat, affectively "positive" ways of relating and responding in the relationship, either as a corrective emotional experience or for any other reason. This is largely because, from personal experience, it does not work and usually constitutes an unsuccessful collusion in avoiding exactly the trauma that needs addressing, as Winnicott (1974) describes. The analyst is letting the patient down, even if the patient might be temporarily relieved by the positivity, and might be able to challenge their deeply held belief that, for instance, "no one would want to have anything to do with me".

At some point the patient will need to return to the trauma of people "not wanting to have anything to do with me", to work it through. As Winnicott says, "there is no end … unless the thing feared has been experienced" (1974, p. 105). It is only too easy for the patient to feel that the analyst cannot really bear to confront the depth of the despair that they experience over this issue and thus to feel confirmed that "no one would want anything to do with me as I *really* am", and thus feel alienated from themselves through what feels like an unbearable truth. Individuals with a borderline psychology are less able to gloss over the real trauma anyway, as it is so powerful and disruptive of ego-functioning. To quote Bromberg again: "… the analytic relationship … allows the painful reliving of early trauma, without the reliving being just a blind repetition of the past" (Bromberg, 2011, pp. 16–17).

Despite Beebe and Lachmann's brilliant observations and analysis of parent–infant interactions, they provide examples, in both their books, of situations where they have tried to introduce upbeat, positively toned interactions that I would respectfully suggest will ultimately be limited in their effectiveness (as already discussed in Chapters Seven and Eleven).

What I believe is corrective and new, as many have said before (e.g., Casement, 2001), is for the patient to be known, accepted, and "accompanied", and for their early relational traumas to be experientially known about (perhaps for the first time) and appreciated.

van der Kolk, McFarlane, and van der Hart (1996, p. 417) raise the question of whether psychodynamic or psychoanalytic psychotherapy is suitable for this client group partly due to the complexity, power, and difficulty associated with the transference–countertransference dynamics, as well as the power of the individual's overwhelming affects that can make exploratory and verbal therapies difficult. Ogden, Minton, and Pain (2006), from their sensorimotor perspective, write as follows:

> PTSD patients experience their traumatic memories as timeless, intrusive, sensory fragments that often cannot be expressed as a narrative, whereas people who have suffered a trauma but do not suffer from PTSD usually recall traumatic memories as an integrated whole that can easily be expressed as a narrative. This observation calls into question the benefit of purely verbal therapies as modalities for processing information that is experienced primarily at a sensory level and suggests the need to explore body-centred methods. (p. 156)

I hope I have addressed the question of analytic attitudes being "purely verbal", stressing the degree to which the verbal element emerges out of lived, affective experience. The patient becoming retraumatised, flooded, and overwhelmed by unbearable affect, is a very real concern when working with these individuals however, as is the need to be constantly alert to the somatic and affective elements of their experience. Schmahl, Lanius, Pain, and Vermetten (2010) conclude that psychodynamic psychotherapy is the most useful treatment for patients with complex PTSD, but with the proviso that it must be modified in order to include a range of sensorimotor techniques that enable affect regulation, build self-awareness, and facilitate mentalization; Knox (2013) discusses these issues further and offers just such a modified model (see also Chapter Seventeen of this book for further exploration).

Those working explicitly with trauma and dissociation often call on Janet's three-stage therapeutic process of first, stabilisation of the patient, second, exploration of the traumatic memories, and third, relapse prevention, integration of the personality and rehabilitation (e.g., van der Hart, Nijenhuis, & Steele, 2006). For the individuals I am describing in this book the traumas, being early relational traumas, are frequently thoroughly integrated into their personality, although I would see this as also being true for people who are diagnosed as having complex PTSD. Furthermore, as van der Kolk, McFarlane, and van der Hart (1996, pp. 417–418) point out, many people present themselves for analytic therapies unaware of the nature of their traumas, but simply hoping for assistance for their distress. It is inevitable that this will be true of a significant number of individuals in any analyst's practice and that the knowledge of their experiences will only emerge as part of the process of analysis.

I have found that respectful engagement with what the patient is bringing, whether that is their powerful impulses to commit suicide or powerful reactions to what the analyst is or is not doing, can almost always be contained by intense listening (in the spirit of trying to learn from and understand the patient's experience), staying with, accompanying, and finally putting the experiences into words. Whilst the analyst's experience will not, by any means, be identical with the patient's, I have almost always found that if the analyst acts with integrity, calmness, respect, and seriousness, their accompanying the patient is "good enough"; although one caveat is that patients in newly established analyses tend to find it more difficult to traverse these "darkest places" compared to those in more well established ones.

Regarding the analytic attitude being inhuman and a retraumatising way of relating: in placing trauma at the heart of the work, I am clearly signally some kind of a shift from traditional, historic ways of psychoanalytic and Jungian analytic practice, not least in focusing on the moment-by-moment intersubjective/relational aspect of the analysis. I would want to be all the time alert to the ways in which the analyst's pauses, responses, silences, tones of voice, affect, mood, or lack of a response, may be affecting the patient. I recognise that this is exactly the stuff of early relational trauma and I would want to actively explore these experiences with the patient, acknowledging what is being triggered, as well as the patient's somatic-affective responses. This is the way that I understand that the narrative of the early relational experience is reconstructed from previously unrecognised, implicit ways of being.

In conclusion, I would suggest that an analytic approach, as embodied in the analytic attitude I have outlined here, is necessary in order to properly and fully address, contain, and understand the complex, powerful, and kaleidoscopic pressures, dynamics, and transferences related to early relational trauma and thus allow the analysis to be undertaken safely and successfully. This frequently entails accompanying the patient into some of the darkest places. I would contend that some other models encourage the therapist to unhelpfully enact certain roles, for example, as rescuer or saviour, that might hinder the full working through of the patient's traumatic experiences in so far as they have become incorporated and elaborated into their wider personality. These enactments may at worst lead to the breakdown of the analysis,[4] as outlined in previous chapters.

As I described with Michael in Chapter Ten, the analytic relationship is built upon both analyst and patient being able to remain true to their separate selves and their primitive responses. It is a relationship that is built on this "realness", and as such it engenders the deepest respect of, and appreciation for, the other.

Notes

1. Grotstein (2005, p. 1060) describes this as "projective transidentification" where the patient's sensorimotor activities have a "hypnotic-like power" to induce, evoke, or prompt a response on the part of the analyst, who is "inherently equipped (programmed) to empathize with it", through means of mental, physical, and verbal, "prompting, gesturing, priming, 'nudging', prosody, and other similar modes". Although see also Sandler's alternate understanding of role responsiveness discussed in this book.

2. However, it is not about the *suppression* of memory, desire, and understanding, rather it is the non-identification with it. Fordham gives an example (1993, p. 131) of a desire, a memory, and knowledge arising spontaneously in him, which he seems to repress, concluding that, had he made an interpretation from it, it would have got in the way of what developed (he cites the interpretation—that his patient was feeling trusting and loving towards him due to the successful previous session—which does indeed seem "clunky"). He does not, however, say what emerged. I would suggest that the fact that he felt desire that the patient's unusual warmth towards him continue was itself significant, and probably extremely pertinent, but we cannot now know what that was.

3. Young and Gibb (1998), following Steiner, understand grievance as, "a defence against psychic pain, against feelings of vulnerability and helplessness, and against feelings of guilt for destructiveness done in phantasy or reality towards others" (p. 94). Whilst some elements of their understanding are undoubtedly correct, I note that none of the patients they describe working with in the light of this understanding took up their offer of further therapy, sometimes terminating after the first consultation—"the operation was successful but the patient died".

4. Courtois (2010, pp. 460–461) describes the significantly larger proportion of those working with individuals who have been sexually abused who tragically re-enact a latter-day version of the original abuse.

CHAPTER FOURTEEN

When the earth swallows you up—shame, regression, and the collapse response

T he following four chapters all address different aspects of the freeze, collapse, and submit responses. The first chapter focuses on shame, the second on suicidality and the spectre of death, the third on dissociation and dissociative identity disorder, and the fourth on the body, somatisation, and working analytically with the body. The following quote from Ogden, Minton, and Pain sets the scene:

> A loss of an internal locus of control is common for clients who have relied upon any of the immobilizing defences: freezing, submission, or submissive behaviors. Traumatized people often "cannot return to the previous personality type but assume submissive, slave like personalities, and their ability for assertive behaviour becomes impaired to one degree or another" (Krystal, 1988, p. 157). Failing to understand that this loss is a common result of a bottom-up immobilizing defensive response, they then may feel ashamed and inadequate and berate themselves afterward for their lack of assertiveness. (2006, p. 105)

Shame is not like other affects. It is a global affect that colours the individual's core sense of self, so that the person does not just feel that they

223

have done something bad or wrong, but rather that they *are* bad or wrong. In parallel to Tronick and Gianino's (1986) understanding of the development of a negative emotional core consequent upon mismatches that aren't repaired, Sullivan recognised that painful anxiety-provoking aspects of early relations with significant others are unavoidably structured into the self, creating a sense of "bad-me" in the infant through the empathy with the mother's anxiety (Greenberg & Mitchell, 1983, p. 103; quoted in Knox, 2013).

Shame is the visceral essence of feeling bad about yourself. It is therefore a powerful factor in preventing the individual from reaching out to others (deintegration), and is thus central in states of insecure attachment, powerlessness, and blighted self-agency. Mollon writes that the birth of shame lies in "not being able to evoke an empathic response in the other" (Mollon, 2002, p. 26; quoted in Knox, 2013, p. 499). Shame is a key factor in the individual getting stuck in states of regression.

The person wants the earth to swallow them up, to crawl into a hole and die and, as I will explore, when this is intense, they feel the earth *has* swallowed them up and that they have "died" as they have "frozen", are unable to function, and have lost touch with (dissociated from) their everyday sense of self (ego), being taken over by shame. Shame is associated with the profound threat reaction of freezing and collapse, associated with the activation of the unmyelinated dorsal polyvagal nerve (Porges, 2011; Schore, 2003), where the individual dissociates from their normal sense of self just prior to death (in the same way that the gazelle collapses just before the lion strikes).

Intrinsic to this collapse response there is an experience of dying to one's everyday sense of oneself (ego), and related to that is an experience of annihilation, death and dying, as well as suicidal impulses, thoughts, and wishes. Shame is thus the affective aspect related to the somatic impulse towards self-annihilation and self-destruction (whereby the individual takes the annihilatory experience associated with the collapse response into their sphere of omnipotence, pre-empting and adapting to the annihilatory environment—see particularly Chapters Fifteen and Sixteen).

Shame is apparently a sophisticated social emotion whereby the individual regulates themselves to society and learns to fit in, yet it has extremely primitive roots in that the experience of social exclusion and social shaming is extreme. Panksepp writes that while shame is a "cognitive-type emotion", it is also liked to more primitive affective substrates (Panksepp, 1998, p. 301). Jacoby (1996) cites Aristotle and suggests that there are two forms of shame, one form serving social adaptation, the other personal integrity. He gives the following example:

> I may be too ashamed to express my dissenting opinion in a group for fear of being laughed at, rejected, or not taken seriously. But as soon as I arrive home, I am ready to "kill myself" for shame for having been such a coward, so incapable of standing up for myself. I lose self-respect because I did not stand up for what is true for me—indeed, I may have even denied it.[1] (p. 22)

Jacoby further suggests there are different manifestations of shame: in an inferiority complex; embarrassment and shame when unacceptable or repressed feelings leak out (individuals often use alcohol or drugs to self-medicate the shame and to overcome the inhibition of the freeze response[2]); humiliation and masochism (Jacoby, 1996, ch. 5).

Judith Herman (2011, p. 159) holds that shame is intrinsic to the development of traumatic disorders and is intimately related to trauma, dissociation, and disorganised attachment, which Liotti (2004a) regards as inextricably interlinked (or three strands of a single braid, as he puts it rather more poetically). Herman writes:

> The subjective experience of shame is of an initial shock and flooding with painful emotion. Shame is a relatively wordless state, in which speech and thought are inhibited. It is an acutely self-conscious state; the person feels small, ridiculous, and exposed. … In shame, the self is passive … it is an acutely painful disorganizing emotion … [s]hame engenders a desire to hide, escape, or to lash out at the person in whose eyes one feels ashamed. (2011, pp. 160 & 162)

Shame may come about through active shaming due to bullying, humiliating and sadistic belittling of the child, or through passive shaming through non-responsiveness and neglect so that the child comes to feel that their relational needs are shameful (the example quoted in Chapter Four of the boy whose mother shouted at him when he inadvertently made physical contact is a good example (BCPSG, 2007)). Bromberg (2011, p. 43) describes how this kind of negation of the self is experienced as annihilatory and leads to dissociation of the self.

Shame may also come about through violation and abuse, where something has been done to the child that they were powerless to prevent and as a result they feel ashamed of themselves and of the body that experienced it. Fonagy, Target, Gergely, Allen and Bateman (2003) describe the abused child's shame as "an intense and destructive sense of self-disgust, verging on self-hatred" (p. 445).

Lewis (1990) describes "feeling traps" where the individual feels ashamed of feeling ashamed or enraged and ashamed of feeling enraged. These are intense states of shame that spiral in intensity making the agonising experience of shame ever more intolerable; Herman describes this as shame "feeding upon itself" (2011, p. 163).

Example

Sarah, who had been feeling more human, natural, effective, and generally "better" recently, came to the session feeling "as bad as ever … worse than ever". She was tearful and despairing and had felt deeply depressed the day before. We could easily trace the trigger for this to her doctor changing her medication and her crippling indecision about whether this was the right thing. She said she didn't know what to do and that she felt helpless, had turned to her husband for support and reassurance, and didn't know if she would be able to go to work.

I recognised that she was experiencing a powerful freeze/collapse response, where her thinking capacities had become impaired, where she felt exposed, alarmed, and ashamed at not being able to function properly, and terrified that this would continue. Her alarm had quickly escalated into panic and her depression had been triggered through feeling there was something terribly wrong with her and that she could not do anything to get out of it. A perennial fear of hers was that people would notice (the muscles governing facial/social responses "freeze" in response to such threats (Porges, 2011)) and the intense shame that is experienced is unbearably painful.

At those times when the individual feels collapsed, helpless, and bad, they naturally turn to others in a dependent/needy way to be reassured that they are alright, which then intensifies their feeling of badness for being needy and neither self-confident nor independent. On this occasion Sarah's feeling was reinforced by my impending break, which had perhaps played a part in her increased sense of vulnerability.

I realised that I had not hitherto appreciated the depth, power, and significance of her primitive freeze and collapse responses and how they underlay her feeling that there was something fundamentally wrong with her. I could see how these responses might have been due to the fundamental insecurity that had pervaded the family home, manifested in her father's disgruntlement, anger, and blaming—of which she had been the focus on a number of key occasions—and her mother's persistent anxiety and dependence on her daughter, Sarah.

I discussed these things with Sarah, explaining that she was experiencing a profound, deeply disturbing, and distressing reaction to threat—a collapse response—amplified by her own panicked reaction to her thinking capacities becoming inhibited. As Herman writes, understanding that shame is normal allows patients to emerge from the "feeling trap" (2011, p. 165). We linked this experience to her experiences during childhood. Her comment, early on in the analysis, of having been "like a rabbit caught in the headlights" as a child, took on a new depth and significance.

The experience of publicly freezing, significantly sometimes called "dying" (on stage, for example), is deeply humiliating and the threat of it recurring can be terrifying. Sometimes the threat means that the individual wants to hide away and not be seen (van der Kolk links being ashamed with the flight response apparently for this reason (2014, p. xi)). Prolonged early experiences of not being responded to can lead to the child collapsing, submitting, feeling powerless, giving up hope, and feeling ashamed. Such experiences often lie behind shyness and the difficulty in "being yourself". These are things we pick up on the social level about people pretty much immediately, reinforcing the shame and making the individual want to hide away.

Understanding these most primitive, disturbing reactions, which are out of the everyday realm of experience, entails some psycho-education in the same way that the analyst might name and normalise what someone is feeling who has been hitherto cut off from their emotions. The subsequent, more challenging task is in bearing with the patient whilst they live these feelings through and, particularly, as they live them through in relation to the analyst. Thus, with Sarah we had to go on to live through experiences where she felt I expected her now to be alright and to know what to do, just as her father had expected of her. We also had to work through her conflict about being dependent on me as her mother had been on her, feeling that it was at the same time wrong, natural, expected, and inevitable; there was an allied fear that I would get fed up with her, just as she feared others would.

Stuck in regression

I have found that these issues of shame, related to experiences of the freeze and collapse responses, lie at the heart of states of regression. The individual feels both powerless and stuck, exposed and vulnerable, often needy and dependent, as well as bad and wrong, and ashamed of feeling this way. They don't feel they can be themselves, and reaching out to others evokes shame and the threat of rejection and humiliation. They therefore become frozen and stuck, cut off from a sense of self-agency that could allow them to function more effectively. Sometimes they might have a sense of negative self-agency, feeling that everything they do will go wrong—preemptively protecting against rejection and often, unconsciously, inducing it.

Example

In Chapter Four I discussed Dorothy's conflict about making contact with others who might be rejecting or hurtful, reaching out and turning away at the same time (her disorganised attachment pattern), and in the last chapter (Thirteen) I briefly described her deep, intense experiences of fragmentation, terror, neediness, and shame/humiliation, which mirrored her first breakdown many years before. These were triggered in the present by current-day rejections, domestic disasters that emphasised her aloneness, and by having set a date to end the analysis.

It was these fears and experiences, which were increasingly contained within the analysis (friends might well not have known what she was experiencing), that lay behind her continuing to feel bad and concerned about herself, feeling that she was indelibly wrong, and fearing that she could never function as she hoped (would always be in some way "regressed"). Whilst we had done much work on recognising the way she reacted to other people's moods and comments as if they were all her fault, rather than recognising that they were frequently these individuals' issues, it was only by living through these fragmentation and collapse experiences, and getting to know and to some extent master them, that they became less feared and she was more quickly able to recover from them when and if they were triggered. Feeling bad, wrong, and ashamed is an agonising experience that takes a great deal of working on to understand and address. As I described in Chapter Twelve, this working through with Dorothy entailed that I also felt defeated at times—an experience that can engender shame in the analyst as well, due to the fact that they have not been able to "evoke an empathic response in the other" (Mollon, 2002, p. 26, quoted above).

Having become aware to this phenomenon I have found that these experiences of collapse invariably lie at the heart of profound regressions or, to put that in different terms, such experiences of collapse lie at the heart of prolonged disruptions to ego-functioning and the exposure of the core self that is characteristic of borderline phenomena. Frequently individuals defend against such experiences through the narcissistic/fight responses or schizoid/flight/avoid/denial responses but, as described for Adam in Chapter Five, over time these defences tend to erode to reveal these deeper terrors.

Winnicott and the fear of breakdown

Winnicott gathers these phenomena together under the term "breakdown", an "unthinkable state of affairs" where there is "the breakdown of the establishment of the unit self" (Winnicott, 1974, p. 103). He describes the "primitive agonies" associated with this state as a return to an unintegrated state, falling forever, failure to remain embodied (depersonalisation), a loss of the sense of being real, and a loss of the capacity to relate to objects (p. 104). He also links the experience of emptiness and non-existence, and the fear of death, to this "syndrome".

Winnicott locates these experiences in the past, "a breakdown that has already been experienced" (p. 104). Whilst I am certain this is true, and that such collapse responses did occur in the past (and have left their deep marks in various ways), I am very much aware that they can recur and be triggered afresh in the present. This event that is not known and not remembered, "a fact that is carried around hidden away in the unconscious" (p. 104), is characteristic of trauma, as I have been describing (Chapter Three), and is the affective-somatic element that latches on to current experience, pressing for recognition and integration.

I mostly agree with Winnicott when he says, echoing Ferenczi, that "the only way to 'remember' in this case is for the patient to experience this past thing for the first time in the present, that is to say, in the transference" (p. 105). Living the experience through in the transference is one element of working through the traumatic complex, getting to know it, understand it, bear it, and no longer live in terror of it; however, I think it is important to recognise how the experience manifests on all levels. In Chapter Seventeen I will look at Phil Mollon's (2015) conceptualisation of the "disintegrating self", which is also very much related to Winnicott's understanding of breakdown.

In the following chapter I will present an example of someone who incorporated the collapse response centrally into her personality—elaborated into a hysterical personality organisation—and particularly explore her experience of death and suicide. I will be comparing and contrasting my approach to that of Betty Joseph's, as outlined in her paper, "Addiction to near-death".

In Chapter Sixteen I will explore dissociation and dissociative identity disorder, which I understand as also linked to inescapable trauma that leads to the collapse response, and, further, to a dissociation from the everyday ego and the formation of a fragmented personality.

Notes

1. He cites St. Peter's denial of Christ on the night before his crucifixion.
2. Schore (2003, p. 160) proposes that shame is mediated by the parasympathetic nervous system and serves as a sudden "brake" on excited arousal states.

CHAPTER FIFTEEN

In thrall to the spectre of death— suicidality, submission, and collapse

In this chapter I will be exploring the elaboration of the collapse and submit response and the way that the individual becomes in thrall to the experience of death and dying that accompanies it. As the individual takes the experience of death and dying into their sphere of omnipotence, they become closely engaged with the experience of death and suicide—Rothschild (2000, pp. 96–97) gives a good, brief, example. I will explore how the individual becomes in thrall to the experience of death, which they cannot bear, yet from which they find it extremely difficult to escape. Understanding the experience in terms of a primitive collapse response makes it more comprehensible, more "acceptable", more bearable, and facilitates the working through of the traumatic complex. It facilitates a shift from the individual feeling that they *are* bad, mad, or wrong, to understanding why they feel that way, and moving towards a broader, more benevolent, more compassionate, and more realistic sense of themselves.

In submitting, the individual hands themselves over to the other, originally as a capitulation, as a surrender to their fate, unable to struggle any further against the other's overwhelming power or position (like the antelope and the lion). This pattern can sometimes become incorporated and elaborated in the personality into a submission in the hope for protection and care. However, in making this self-sacrifice the person becomes appallingly exposed and, in particular, in disavowing their own ego-functioning—which reinforces the exposure—they are unable to extricate themselves and they become powerless and trapped. With the danger of abandonment, which feels unbearable and annihilating, the individual can come to live in thrall to this spectre of death.[1]

I understand this as the primitive collapse and submit response being elaborated into a hysterical personality organisation where, as Bollas (2000, p. 12) says, the individual "suspends the self's idiom" (see Chapter Five in this book). Another key characteristic of this configuration, as I have outlined in the previous chapter, is that of shame, humiliation, and a feeling of being intensely and inalienably bad or wrong, although this can be reclaimed (temporarily) as long as the other is accepting and positive, as Balint describes in relation to malignant regressions.

In the Kleinian literature this may be understood in terms of Meltzer's concepts of adhesive identification and the claustrum, Joseph's understanding of an addiction to near-death, or what Steiner describes as defensive organisations and psychic retreats. Britton also writes illuminatingly about hysterical personality organisations, proposing that, "the death wish in hysteria is meant to lead to the consummation of a greatly desired sexual union: *it is not intended to separate but to end all separation*" (2003, p. 28, original italics).

Betty Joseph and the addiction to near-death

In her classic paper, Betty Joseph (1982) describes a clinical picture where,

> in their external lives these patients get more and more absorbed into hopelessness and involved in activities that seem destined to destroy them physically as well as mentally .... in all these patients the place where the pull towards near-death is most obvious is in the transference .... they may speak in a way which seems calculated to communicate or create despair and a sense of hopelessness in themselves and in the analyst, although apparently wanting understanding. It is not just that they make progress, forget it, lose it or take no responsibility for it. ... The pull towards despair and death in such patients is not ... a longing for peace and freedom from

effort …. There is a felt need to know and to have the satisfaction of seeing oneself being destroyed.

She continues:

> So I am stressing here that a powerful masochism is at work and these patients will try to create despair in the analyst and then get him to collude with the despair or become actively involved by being harsh, critical or in some way or another verbally sadistic to the patient. If they succeed in getting themselves hurt or in creating despair, they triumph, since the analyst has lost his analytic balance or his capacity to understand and help and then both patient and analyst go down into failure. At the same time the analyst will sense that there is real misery and anxiety around and this will have to be sorted out and differentiated from the masochistic use and exploitation of misery. (Joseph, 1982, p. 449)

I would suggest that the patient is here constellating a re-enactment of exactly the kind of critical, dismissive, and sadistic experiences that constitute their early relational trauma, although this tends to lead to a masochisto-sadistic response where the bad object is attacked in a way that often approaches an identification with the aggressor (Chapters Five and Six). Towards the end of the paper Joseph writes:

> None of the patients whom I have in mind as particularly belonging to this addictive group, have really very seriously bad childhood histories, though psychologically in a sense they almost certainly have—as, for example, a lack of warm contact and real understanding, and sometimes a very violent parent.

The prolonged lack of "warm contact and real understanding", and a "very violent parent" are exactly the kind of early relational traumas that I am describing, which have significant, severe effects on the individual. She continues:

> Yet in the transference one gets the feeling of being driven up to the edge of things … and both patient and analyst feel tortured. I get the impression from the difficulty these patients experience in waiting and being aware of gaps and aware of even the simplest

type of guilt that such potentially depressive experiences have been felt by them in infancy as terrible pain that goes over into torment, and that they have tried to obviate this by taking over the torment, the inflicting of mental pain on to themselves and building it into a world of perverse excitement, and this necessarily militates against any real progress towards the depressive position.

It is very hard for our patients to find it possible to abandon such terrible delights for the uncertain pleasures of real relationships. (ibid., pp. 455–456)

I understand these phenomena differently, in terms of a re-enactment of experiences related to the collapse response and, as Joseph does suggest, of the individual taking the trauma into their sphere of omnipotence (an identification with the aggressor on the subjective level). I will discuss her views and other Kleinian contributions below.

In contrast to Joseph, to quote Ogden, Minton, and Pain again:

A loss of an internal locus of control is common for clients who have relied upon any of the immobilizing defences: freezing, submission, or submissive behaviors. Traumatized people often "cannot return to the previous personality type but assume submissive, slave like personalities, and their ability for assertive behaviour becomes impaired to one degree or another" (Krystal, 1988, p. 157). Failing to understand that this loss is a common result of a bottom-up immobilizing defensive response, they then may feel ashamed and inadequate and berate themselves afterward for their lack of assertiveness. (2006, p. 105)

I will now give an example that clearly overlaps with Joseph's clinical outline, recognises many of the phenomena she describes, yet frames these phenomena in terms of early relational trauma, linking it to the transference in a detailed rather than a generalised way.

Clinical example

I gave a brief description of Nounoushka in Chapter Five in relation to the hysterical personality organisation, and in Chapter Twelve I discussed how we came to co-construct her experiences of being abandoned at times of her greatest distress. I would like to go into more detail here and draw out her deep sense of being trapped and in thrall to the spectre of death in order to give a fuller picture, and to contrast it to Kleinian approaches. In particular, I will be putting her traumatic experience as central to our work, although I do recognise that in "Transference: the total situation", Joseph (1985) recognises the significance of implicit patterns of relating (internal working models)—although she puts it in different terms—and their significance for the analytic relationship and the outcome of the analysis.

I have described above how Nounoushka's tyrannical, bullying father intruded into every area of her life, trying to control everything that she did and punishing her verbally, and frequently with physical violence, if she did not comply. Similarly her anxious, distant mother used Nounoushka to bolster her own sense of self and to counter her insecurity, whilst not standing up for Nounoushka in the face of her husband's near obsessional control of their daughter.

Nounoushka was desperate to try to please both her "dismissive" (in terms of attachment styles), controlling father, who was himself highly anxious and hypochondriacal, and her needy, insecure mother. Nounoushka's submission was therefore both required as a matter of self-preservation with her violent father, who would brook no opposition—he might literally have killed her on a number of occasions, even if "accidentally"—and in the hope of pleasing her anxious and unavailable mother. For Nounoushka there was a massive split between her fear of her hateful, abusive father (or anything she experienced like him), her unavailable, unresponsive mother (and anything she experienced like her), and a longed-for, idealised, loving, rescuer figure, as she had hoped her mother or I might be.

In the analysis we painstakingly addressed her experience of her father's controlling, bullying, raging, and violence and, slowly, and with great shame and difficulty, began to recognise her own rages and violence, both towards her parents, towards herself, towards people on the street, and towards me.

Similarly, we painstakingly looked at her experience with her mother's wish for her to be sweet and nice, a part of what Nounoushka called the "sugar world"—she and her mother would occasionally eat sweets together as a treat when her mother had allowed her to bunk off school and be with her. With similar difficulty we recognised the way that she hoped I would be an ideal rescuer, someone who would always be pleased with her and whom she could never alienate.

Inevitably she was frequently anxious that I would get fed up with her, think she was a burden, or be critical and rejecting towards her in any way. She was vigilant (in a paranoid way) for the slightest hint of rejection or displeasure in me. Whilst early in the analysis we had been able to explore this fairly easily, as the relationship deepened these exchanges took on more power and import. In an intermediate phase of the analysis I had sometimes offered some reassurance easily and lightly; however, I duly noted that it made little long-term difference and the search for reassurance began to take on more terrifying proportions. Sometimes I found myself unable to resist giving it, even though I was by then clear it was ineffective as, in subsequent sessions, Nounoushka would return equally strongly to her preoccupation with whether I was critical or fed up with her. Joseph understands this partly in terms of the patient's attempt to get the analyst to be critical, which I would see as the patient trying to constellate and re-enact the early traumatic situation.

After a time I became more able to name her underlying fears straight out, for example, that she was at that moment fearing that I'd be disgusted with her and would reject her, rather than hedging around with confusing dialogues about whether I was saying, meaning, feeling, or thinking whatever it was she feared. In being able to face, name, and discuss the traumas and link them to her early experiences rather than seeking to avoid them, they became more manageable.

These traumas were frequently triggered in and by the relationship with me, and it was vital that we could identify what I had done or said, or not done and not said, that was evoking these responses in her. In this way we began to work through her traumatic complex, although I will return to the question of reassurance further below.

Another significant vector, that Joseph describes well in her "Addiction to near-death" paper, was Nounoushka's self-attack, her identification with the aggressor on the subjective level, so that she could frequently recognise the way she was "torturing herself" with fears of what I might be feeling towards her. At times she described powerful impulses to physically attack, hurt, and destroy/kill herself, which is presumably what Freud (1937c) would describe as a manifestation of the death instinct and which Joseph describes in terms of the patient's wish/satisfaction in seeing themselves destroyed. This is very much the issue of being in thrall to the spectre of death that I am describing.

I understand it in terms of Nounoushka's frequent experiences where her father bullied and dominated her, insisting on her submission to him in a way that clearly amounted to a repeated experience of annihilation. I would suggest that she had to accommodate to this experience and thus instituted her own primitive, unconscious, self-annihilatory reactions (the basis of her hysteric personality organisation perhaps).

This also became manifest in a terror that she would not be able to breathe or swallow, or that she would vomit. We linked this in part to her terrified, freeze reaction, which constricted her breathing; to her grandmother forbidding her to cry when her parents went away so that her feelings became terrifyingly bottled up in her throat; and to her father's hostility and disgust if she ever vomited.

All these reactions were then underpinned by shame, and a terror of manifesting/expressing herself lest she meet with opposition. This rendered her continually vulnerable and dependent on the vagaries of the other, just like the collapsed antelope is wholly exposed to what the lion may do. This collapsed position thus generates a need/neediness and a total dependency on what the other is thinking or feeling. Some of the attacking and punishing of the self is also an attack on these needy parts of the self that expose the individual to danger. As in Stockholm syndrome the collapse thus binds the individual more powerfully to the other.

This also relates to what Britton (quoted above) says about the death-wish not being intended to separate but to end all separation, so that the individual can no longer be attacked by a separate other. Under the conditions of her early life it made good sense, if she could not be "perfectly good" and beyond criticism, and if the other (and that now included me) was not perfectly ("ideally") trustworthy, to "suspend her own idiom", remove herself from the possibility of opposition and "kill herself off" rather than face being assailed further. With her intense shame militating against her "standing up" and "being herself" she was therefore trapped in this oppressed, powerless position, highly sensitised to what I may think or feel towards her. These are clearly characteristics of what Kleinians would call the paranoid-schizoid position.

Similarly, in reversed mode, I could sometimes feel oppressed and trapped by the concern about triggering her suicidal impulses. For example, she might become anxious towards the end of a session and, when there was no time to explore her question in any other way, she might ask whether I found her a burden. I was faced with offering reassurance, or recognising the truth of what she was requiring us to live through (that such exchanges were, on the superficial level, "a burden"),[2] or saying that I was not going to answer her question and explore it the next session—at which she might return to knock on my door a few minutes later to tell me that she would certainly not survive.

We went through all of these permutations at times, with Nounoushka getting more experience of being able to manage her experiences of hurt, collapse, outrage, murderousness, confusion, and suicidal impulses, and me getting more experience in bearing feelings of anxiety, concern, fear, responsibility, badness, and anger; additionally I became better able to bear being seen as cold, heartless, uncaring, and, sometimes, murderous (in this I am drastically condensing many months of analytic work, mostly at four times per week). This dynamic was therefore fully constellated on the transference level (this entrapment and thrall was very much what Meltzer (1990) would call an example of a claustrum).

I had to recognise that my responses or lack of responses absolutely triggered the retraumatisations, but I came to trust that these were all developments in the analytic relationship that were arising at a time when the relationship could now contain them. Over time, we each had to develop both the range of experiences we could bear, and understand the context and dynamics of those affective and somatic experiences. I see this as the essential process of the analysis, which itself represented the development of the relationship, the development of each of us individually, and the progress of the analysis. Understanding the process in the terms I have described served as an important container for this experience.

In her paper Joseph describes clinical material very similar to that which I am describing here. Her conclusion and summary of her paper is as follows:

> This paper describes a very malignant type of self-destructiveness seen in a small group of patients. It is active in the way that they run their lives and it emerges in a deadly way in the transference. This type of self-destructiveness is, I suggest, in the nature of an addiction of a particular sado-masochistic type, which these patients feel unable to resist. It seems to be like a constant pull towards despair and near-death, so that the patient is fascinated and unconsciously

excited by the whole process. Examples are given to show how such addictions dominate the way in which the patient communicates with the analyst and internally, with himself, and thus how they affect his thinking processes. It is clearly extremely difficult for such patients to move towards more real and object-related enjoyments, which would mean giving up the all-consuming addictive gratifications. (1982, p. 456)

I see it as an addiction only in the sense of a repetition compulsion that continually re-presented the original traumatic dynamics for us to work through. Every expression of Nounoushka's wish to kill herself contained a three-pronged question/relational dilemma: "Do you care enough to rescue me, are you so heartless as to let me die, or are you so murderous that you want me dead?" In other words, which side of the (three-way) split are you on: rescuer, passive bystander, or abuser (Gabbard, 1992, 1997; Karpman, 1968)? I recognised that remaining in the passive, victim position also legitimised her counter-response of hatred or punishment of me—the masochisto-sadistic dynamic (West, 2013a).

Relinquishing the ideal was a significant aspect of our work. As Davies and Frawley put it, "[a]cknowledging the impossibility of bringing this fantasy [of a new and idealized, compensatory childhood] to realization represents a betrayal of [the patient's] most sacred inner self" (1992a, p. 25). A significant amount of her depression, despair, and hopelessness was related to this, often focused on her wish for a "cure". Exploring the wish for this cure felt taboo for quite some time, but we were eventually able to see how it also contained a wish for an ideal world where there would be no opposition, as well as for "rescue", obviating the need for her to face the shame and difficulty of manifesting herself. Manifesting herself/incarnating is, of course, the only way of building self-agency—an essential and central aspect of ego-functioning (Knox, 2010).

We often talked about defeat and being defeated, and I often felt defeated myself (Chapter Twelve), by which I mean that any ego-oriented activity to "make things better" was defeated and I could only, exactly, bear with and accompany her in her experience, and that was frequently in feeling powerless and without hope.

Ultimately it turned out that we had to both recognise and live through all aspects of her disintegrative, collapsing/submitting experiences and all of the particularly traumatising experiences with her parents, which were unconsciously, exactingly reconstructed in the analytic relationship. Nounoushka recognised that reassurance did not work in "protecting" her from these experiences, which included: the experience of death, dying, and suicide; the intense feelings of shame and humiliation that left her unable to bear being seen or looked at; and, underlying it all, an intense feeling of being wrong and bad and being thought to be bad, wrong, hated and not cared about by the other—a reconstruction of her father's blaming, dismissal, and his telling her she was a disaster and a catastrophe who would come to nothing.

It was only in being able to live with such experiences and know about them (rather than allergically avoid them), and recognise their nature as a natural response to what she had experienced, rather than feel that there was something inalienably wrong with her, that she could move through, detoxify, and integrate these foundational experiences (the traumatic complex). In terms of the journey through the underworld, at crucial times she no longer experienced me as Orpheus, accompanying and leading her back to life, but rather as the torturing, sadistic, uncaring Hades himself.

As time went on Nounoushka was able to understand that I could, at the same time, mirror and embody, for example, the despair that she was feeling about her situation, and feel hopeful that our relationship was able to contain and thus work through that despair; in other words, she began to appreciate the way the analytic process worked.

I have found on a number of occasions that when the patient's experiences of annihilation, breakdown, and fragmentation have been early, prolonged, intense, and thus foundational, they have needed to be reconstructed and lived through in this way. Such highly toxic/ poisonous experiences need precisely to be lived through and contained by and within the analytic relationship in order for them to be detoxified.

This process of jointly living through the powerlessness, defeat, collapse, and death related to the collapse response exemplifies the process that Jung (1946/54) described in "The psychology of the transference" in relation to the alchemical treatise *The Rosarium Philosophorum*. There he describes how the analytic couple go through various stages from an initial stage of confusion and darkness (*nigredo*), followed by a mixing of the individual personalities in joint experience (*solutio* and *coniunctio*), followed by the experience of death (*putrefacto*), stages of abstraction (ascent of the soul), purification (*albedo* and *ablutio*), and incarnation (*rubedo*—reddening), before a release from the traumatic complex and the "rebirth" in a new form (Fabricius, 1976; Jung, 1946/54).[3]

There was one further, key element related to her desperate search for reassurance that was required for her to be released from the traumatic complex. Her father's reactions to her in particular, had had a profound impact and she was (understandably) hypervigilant to what the other was thinking and feeling towards her. In her "exposed" place, related to the collapse response, she reached out all the more powerfully for reassurance from the other. This way of being was reinforced (and presumably to some extent instituted) by her father's near-obsession with what Nounoushka was thinking and feeling towards him, to which he, in turn, had had powerful responses.

Ultimately she came to recognise that this "dependency", as she put it, on what the other person was thinking and feeling towards her was a dead end that itself had to be relinquished. This required that the traumatic complex's power had lessened so that she was no longer held in its thrall, but also that she recognised that my reassurance was not the solution. This is the situation of the child who has become "clingy" through traumatising interactions with the parent(s) and desperately seeks for this to be "undone" by good experience.

Whilst, at the right time, the "gleam in the mother's eye" helps the child construct a positive, viable sense of themselves, as Kohut (1971) and Winnicott assert, the child needs to be able to move on to going about their own business, released from an absolute dependence on the mother's approval (and hopefully secure in the mother's good-enough feelings, as well as able to deal with her ambivalent feelings). In the end this leads to recognising that the mother is a separate individual in her own right whose feelings towards the person as an adult have only a limited effect.[4] For me this demonstrates the limitation of any relational approach that aims to counter the patient's negative self-feeling primarily through the analyst's positive disposition.

These experiences in the analysis allowed Nounoushka to move towards reclaiming her own life—giving up and working through an addiction to alcohol, and repairing and re-instituting her ego-functioning through coming to know about and understand her early experience and her responses to those experiences. Thus she was able to move towards being as-she-is in the non-ideal world as-it-is. This represented a significant exploration of, and journey through, her personal underworld-hell.

I would suggest that, whilst Joseph superficially recognises the "psychologically ... bad childhood histories", she emphasises the way that the traumatic experiences have been elaborated on the subjective level, which she sees as self-destructiveness and addiction to near-death. I think she does not do justice to the objective levels of experience (the original traumas), nor relate the detailed, complex, reconstructions, and co-constructions on the transference level to particular, traumatic, early experiences.

Notes

1. Rosemary Gordon (1987) explores whether masochism is the shadow side of the archetypal need to venerate and worship, the latter being some of the positive forms related to submission (see Chapter Five).
2. Any passing "irritation" was outweighed by the more profound sense of connection and the importance and significance of the "journey" we were undertaking—moving beyond what was good or bad, pleasant or unpleasant, to what was real and realistic, in both her and me. This is not to say that the irritations were not sometimes to the fore; however, I understood such experiences both in terms of what was being reconstructed and also as indicating that we were more profoundly living through the relational trauma.
3. This process mirrors the intrapsychic union with the dissociated complex and the processes required for its detoxification and integration, resulting in the emergence of a more whole individual. However, this process takes place largely within an interpersonal relationship.
4. Fonagy's understanding of mentalization suggests that if the parent had treated the child in this way from the beginning—as a separate and respected individual in their own right—such traumatising interactions would not have occurred in the first place (Fonagy, Gergely, Jurist, & Target, 2002).

CHAPTER SIXTEEN

Dissociation and dissociative identity disorder

In this chapter I will explore dissociative identity disorder (DID), which used to be known as multiple personality disorder, which is one of the psyche's responses to profound, prolonged, and inescapable early trauma, usually involving one or both parents. When those to whom the child would naturally turn for protection are the source of greatest danger, violation, and abuse the psyche instigates profound structural defences.

This chapter presents only a basic outline of dissociative identity disorder; however, I hope it may serve as an introduction for those who may not be familiar with this important type of personality organisation. For a more in-depth understanding I would refer you to excellent books by Valerie Sinason (2002), Phil Mollon (1996), Elizabeth Howell (2011), Richard Kluft (2013), or the definitive book by Onno van der Hart, Ellert Nijenhuis, and Kathy Steel (2006), *The Haunted Self: Structural Dissociation and the Treatment of Chronic Traumatization*, as well as the International Society for the Study of Trauma and Dissociation's "Guidelines for treating dissociative identity disorder in adults" (2011).[1]

Pierre Janet understood dissociation as the characteristic, underlying mechanism of hysteria, a term that covered dissociative, somatising, conversion, borderline personality, and post-traumatic stress disorders (van der Hart & Friedman, 1989). As van der Kolk describes, referring to Janet, trauma disrupts

> the proper information processing and storage of information in narrative (explicit) memory …. The traumatized individual is left in a state of "speechless terror" in which words fail to describe what has happened. … Janet proposed that traumatic memories are split off (dissociated) from consciousness, and instead are stored as sensory perceptions, obsessional ruminations, or behavioral reenactments. (van der Kolk, 1996b, p. 286)

Schmahl, Lanius, Pain, and Vermetten (2010) link dissociation with the primitive mammalian collapse response as expanded upon in this book. The core of the self cannot bear too much intrusion or impingement and, when the individual cannot escape from the threat, collapse and dissociation occurs. As Ferenczi wrote in his clinical diary:

> What is "trauma"? "Concussion," reaction to an "unbearable" external or internal stimulus in an autoplastic manner (modifying the self) instead of an alloplastic manner (modifying the stimulus). A neoformation of the self is impossible without the previous destruction, either partial or total, or dissolution of the former self. A new ego cannot be formed directly from the previous ego, but from *fragments*, more or less elementary products of its disintegration. (Splitting, atomization.) The relative strength of the "unbearable" excitation determines the degree and depth of the ego's disintegration. (Ferenczi, 1985, p. 181, quoted in Peláez, 2009, pp. 1229–1230, original italics)

These split-off fragments of experience disturb consciousness, as described by Jung, through the action of the complex (the dissociated affective-somatic elements of traumatic experience) on the ego-complex. When the child cannot escape the threat, the ego-complex itself may split, forming discrete, autonomous, reality-orienting, ego fragments called "apparently normal parts of the personality" (ANPs), which allow the person to continue to orient and adapt themselves to their situation and the world. Additionally, the somatic-affective fragments of traumatic experience also continue a discrete, autonomous existence, often based around fight, flight, freeze, or collapse responses; these are known as "emotional parts of the personality" (EPs).[2]

In this way, the child growing up in an abusive environment finds a way of turning a blind eye to the abuse that is going on, so that the abuse is experienced by another part of themselves, whilst at the same time the ANPs allow the person to survive, adapt, cope, and manage their situation. Schmahl, Lanius, Pain, and Vermetten (2010) describe some of the constructive and beneficial consequences of dissociation, writing:

> chronic early life dissociation can also serve as a developmental protective and resilience factor (Loewenstein & Putnam, 2004; Vermetten, Dorahy, & Spiegel, 2007), which allows for as normal development as possible of cognitive function (capacity for abstract and complex thought), some capacity for attachment to others (despite attachment schemas that may be disrupted), a sense of humor and artistic and creative abilities, among others. (p. 182)

When there is one predominant ANP and one EP, that is, one predominant way of relating and one split-off emotional complex, this is known as primary structural dissociation. This is what is understood to occur when there are "simple" types of acute distress disorder, PTSD, or dissociative disorder. Schmahl, Lanius, Pain, and Vermetten (2010) suggest that hyperarousal predominates in these states.

When there is one predominant ANP and more than one EP, in other words, more than one complex emotional reaction, this is known as secondary structural dissociation. This is understood to occur when the trauma has been longer lasting and more complex, and is understood to cover diagnostic categories such as complex PTSD, trauma-related borderline personality disorder, disorders of extreme stress not otherwise specified (DESNOS), and dissociative disorder not otherwise specified (DDNOS). Schmahl, Lanius, Pain, and Vermetten (2010) suggest that hypoarousal predominates in these states.

When there are more than one ANP (way of relating to the world) and more than one EP (discrete sets of emotional reactions) and these are more elaborated and autonomous (including the use of different names and physical features), this is known as tertiary structural dissociation or dissociative identity disorder (DID) (van der Hart, Nijenhuis, & Steele, 2006, p. 8).

The child who goes on to develop dissociative identity disorder has had to develop several ways of coping with their situation; that is, they had to develop various apparently normal parts (of their personality), which may be characterised by such qualities as "ignoring difficulties and carrying on regardless", "challenging and argumentative", "hopeless and submissive", "caregiving and protective", "outgoing and cheerful", "inquisitive and exploring", "sexual and attracting", and so on.

These characteristics, as with any personality organisation, may be elaborated and personalised forms of fight, flight, freeze, or collapse responses, or based on Bowlby's attachment, caregiving, social, exploration, and sexual systems, or Panksepp's SEEKING, RAGE, FEAR, PANIC, LUST, CARE, and PLAY systems. As there are multiple personalities each will often tend to be more singular in their presentation, and their roots in these primitive defensive responses or behavioural systems may be seen more clearly.

However, each set of apparently normal personalities will be unique to the person and the particular set of difficulties they had to meet. These parts of the personality "protect" the self (the collective system of ANPs and EPs) and allow the person to carry on, cope, and survive, thus they are often called "protector" parts. It has been a part of their role to maintain the dissociation, keeping awareness of the traumas from affecting the person's ability to cope with life. In the long run it is usually the breakdown of these coping systems that brings the person to seek help.

Similarly, depending even more on the particular nature of the abusive situations, there will be emotional parts (of the personality), EPs, who will be the ones who experienced the abuse(s) (usually structured around a collapse or submit response), centred around experiences of betrayal, sexual abuse, physical abuse, humiliation, and other forms of emotional abuse. In addition there are parts who embody and personify the various responses to the abuses—whether that is an angry, fight response, vulnerability, despair, shame, woundedness, revenge, or suicide. Additionally, there are those parts that identify with the aggressor, sometimes knows as "perpetrator" parts or introjects (Boon, Steele, & van der Hart, 2011; Howell, 2011; Vogt, 2012). There will also be parts that carry the wish to attach, relate, and make contact with others, and it is very important that these parts too are recognised and engaged with, although it is frequently the case that these parts are treated with suspicion or dislike by the others for being naive or for exposing the person to danger by approaching others at all (van der Hart, 2013).

Working with patients with dissociative identity disorder

I have learnt a very great deal about trauma, and how to work with the trauma that each individual has experienced, through working with people with DID, and I am very grateful for the experience and for the patience and understanding that I have been shown by my patients. That work has informed a good deal of what I have written in this book although some further comments can be made about working with someone with DID.

The majority of people with DID do not manifest the overt, rapid changes between ANPs and EPs, where the person might embody a vulnerable child part at one moment, an angry raging part at another, and a "reasonable" ANP part a moment later (Kluft suggests that only six per cent of people with DID present in this way (ISSTD, 2011, p. 118)). Such presentations have become quite well-known through books, TV programmes, such as "The United States of Tara", and films such as *Sybil*. Such shifts do happen, of course, when the person is under pressure or a particularly powerful event makes the shift manifest. In the majority of people the ANP protector parts usually manage the person's life so that the emergence of the EPs occurs only under certain circumstances, perhaps when the person feels safe enough or, again, when they have had an experience significantly similar to the original traumas (they have been triggered).

It is quite often the case that someone presenting for therapy might not be aware of having dissociative identity disorder, or even of having parts, but may well be struggling with the distressing effects of the condition, for example, problems with memory, sudden changes in perception, cognitive functioning, powerful/overwhelming emotional experiences and "state attacks" (which occur when a traumatic experience is triggered for one of the EPs and the person is wholly taken over by their reaction to the trauma, with the present experienced in the same way as the past). The person is often deeply ashamed of these experiences, as not to know your own mind, what you think or believe, or what is/was reality, makes life extremely precarious. In addition, there is the intense shame about "not being like other people". The person may very well try to disguise such "shameful" reactions, which may also mean that it takes longer to understand what is going on, particularly if the analyst has not had previous experience with someone with DID.

In the analysis, the central attitude is to enquire and explore which parts (both ANPs and EPs) are to the fore and most involved in what is going on at any particular moment. The analyst's primary task is then to come to know, understand, and in some way engage with those parts, and to understand their role in the present and thus their origins in the past. A part that has been abused (an EP) has taken on the massive burden of suffering the abuse for the person as a whole, and will be continually vigilant for the same kind of abuse happening again. Thus anything in the person's life, and particularly in the therapy, that is associated with the abuse, however obliquely, will trigger that part. It is through this part voicing his/her concerns, if he/she can bear to do so, that his/her experiences and continuing sensitivities can come to be known.

"Typically" the other parts of the personality, as was the case with the original trauma, will not want to know about that part or his/her experiences, and may well be very hostile, belittling, and rejecting of this part, often mirroring aspects of the original abuse that that part experienced. The analyst's role is to engage with all these reactions and thus to piece together, with the patient, the way that each part has responded to their experiences and what that part's role was, and remains, within the personality system.

Through the analyst and patient accepting each part's reaction and nature, the part will feel known and hopefully understood and accepted. As many of these exchanges take place over time, "co-consciousness" emerges, so that more parts of the person may be present whilst any particular part is expressing itself. This can allow a greater sense of continuity, as the switching between parts can be extremely distressing, as the person doesn't know what their primary experiences of themselves is going to be from moment to moment.

Over time, the person can come to trust in the operation of the personality system as a whole and, all together, bear the experiences, memories, and continuing sensitivities in a way that was not possible earlier in life—once again making the unbearable bearable. In the larger picture, the analyst and patient are working towards integration, which means helping all the ANPs to accept and work with the EPs, recognising their enormous value in continuing to look out for dangers, as well as their enormous sacrifices and burdens in the past, which can now, hopefully, be shared. Thus, vulnerable parts can gain by connection to protective parts, which can be managed by ANPs.

Onno van der Hart (2013) sees the ultimate goal as the dissolution of the parts into the whole, and I defer to his greater knowledge and experience here; however, the limits of my experience are such that I only know about the parts working more harmoniously together as a collective and in that process sometimes losing their discreteness. Perhaps these are very similar things; however, I am sensitive to anything that may be experienced as "annihilating" to the parts, of which they will inevitably have had appallingly painful previous experience. It is important that such "goals" are discussed and decided upon with the person as, for some, this form of integration (dissolution of the parts) is not wanted.

As I mentioned above, the analytic relationship will inevitably trigger many of the original traumas as it involves matters of trust and safety as well as, more basically, the challenge of being in the same room with another person and communicating with them. It is vital that the analyst is alert for the parts' reactions and, most importantly, and as with the patients described previously, appreciates that these reactions are an aspect of the re-experiencing and re-enactment of the original traumas. Thus, the analyst will need to be able to recognise what it is that they are doing that is triggering one (or more) of the parts, and understand that primarily as a means of understanding the person's traumatic experiences and their varied reactions to the traumas. The analyst may need to make clear that it was not their intention to cause the distress, whilst recognising that that distress is an inevitable part of real-life experience, which is yet invaluable in allowing patient and analyst to know about and work through their early experience.

For these reasons, as well as the shame associated with "being like this", the patient will do a great deal of, often unconscious, testing of the analyst to assess if they are able to work in the way that is needed with the parts, as well as to gauge their response to the fierce, protector parts. The analyst must learn to respect these protector parts and the role they play in helping the patient manage.

To reiterate, people with DID may present like anyone else, functioning through their apparently normal parts for a long time before the analyst becomes aware of the presence of the emotional parts. A history of severe trauma should alert the analyst to the possibility of a dissociative identity disorder, and experience of working with someone with DID will make the signs clearer; for example, suddenly becoming completely flooded by an intense response and it being as if that is "the whole picture", or feeling completely alienated from vulnerable experiences that have been explored before and which now feel unreal or, more mundanely, being unable to remember or relate to what took place in the previous session.

Practitioners with a great deal of experience of working with people with DID will often, from early on, engage directly with EPs as well as ANPs, and these practitioners recommend a three-phase form of treatment that has its origins with Janet. In my, more limited, experience I have worked with exactly what the person brings, engaging with and getting to know the different ANPs and making contact with the EPs as that has been allowed by the ANP protectors—see my discussion of respecting the individual's autonomy in the next chapter.

There is a steep learning curve for the analyst when they first begin working with someone with DID, the main thing being to recognise that you are working with a collective of parts and that you really cannot and must not (if you do not want to cause great distress and ultimately alienate your patient to the degree that they may leave) treat the person as if they are in control of the EPs or know about the EPs' early experiences "really".

It is equally unhelpful to make interpretations along the lines of "you are trying to …" as it will inevitably be one of the parts that is, for example, getting angry, denying the need for therapy, or feeling suicidal. Talking to the patient as if they are a coherent "you", who is in charge of what they are feeling and expressing, is both misguided and deeply shaming. Shame is an incredibly important factor for the patient with DID, and the person, and certain parts in particular, are likely to feel a great deal of shame about being seen or known (see Chapter Fourteen).

The analyst needs to understand that the ANPs and EPs really are autonomous. It is thus important that the analyst adopts a collaborative attitude rather than assuming that they "know" what is going on and interpreting from a position of "certainty". This is particularly because you are working with a group rather than a singular personality, and a subtle switch may have taken place so that, until it is confirmed, you can never assume that you know which ANP or EP is to the fore.

As I said earlier, the main task of the analysis is to get to know the parts and their motivations and functions and how they relate to the collective personality as a whole. With each new experience, piece of knowledge, and interaction with the analyst, the client is a small step nearer to integration. The therapeutic process is a series of a great many such steps.

Example: a darker, more dangerous kind of bad object

I would like to give an example that demonstrates how the bad object can be so terrifying.

L and I had been working together for some time and had developed an understanding of her ANPs and EPs, how they had come about, and their particular role in protecting L and enabling her to continue to function.

In one session she mentioned, almost in passing, that the terrifying state attack (see below), which had been a lifelong, frequent experience by one of the small emotional parts, seemed to have reduced dramatically since it had been worked with in a different way in one of the sessions just after an attack—I had suggested visualising something in a particular way, which, despite her initial scepticism, seemed to have worked. She saw me looking hesitant and asked me if I remembered the state. I said, hesitantly, that I did but not particularly clearly although, as I was thinking, more of the details came back to me and then I "connected up" to the memory.

L then fell silent for quite some time and was tearful. After a while I asked if she was having difficulty in speaking and communicating what she was thinking about this. (In the silence I wondered, amongst other things, if she was struggling with a positive feeling towards me, as she had credited me with having said something that had addressed the fearful state of mind, and feeling positive towards me was very difficult and dangerous for her as it exposed her more to being hurt. I was wrong in this intuition).

In the following session she explained, with some difficulty, that the small emotional part she had been talking about had been hurt that I had forgotten something that had been so terrifyingly awful to her (she added that the adult parts recognised that I had just been taking some time to remember), and that two other parts had been involved, one feeling that I had been rejecting and dismissive, and the other feeling bad and ashamed for having said anything in the first place. I acknowledged this, saying it made sense, but I found myself unable to say much more in relation to this as I felt frozen, as if I had done something wrong and that she was angry with me. Somehow I felt like a rabbit in the headlights, unable to respond. After a while of silence, with me struggling with my perplexing mutism—my primitive response—she left the session early.

In the following sessions we were able to begin to really look together at what had gone on. She explained that she had left early because she felt I was just leaving her in a terrible state, in a punishing, possibly sadistic way, which had been how she had felt at the beginning of the therapy: that I was being like her sadistic father who took pleasure in her discomfort.

I explained that, in fact, I had found myself unable to say anything, and that I had had a primitive response, as if I was frozen to the spot. I said this reminded me of how I imagined she might have felt with her father. This seemed to relieve some of the tension/fear that I had been sadistically punishing her and it became easier to discuss things.

I said I had felt that she was angry with me, that I had done something wrong. She said she had not felt any anger and reminded me of what we had been talking about recently, that she had (in some ways "remarkably") never felt any anger towards her parents, but had always felt that they hadn't done anything wrong and that they were alright. (This is the moral defence that Fairbairn describes, where the child feels that they are wrong and this keeps the parents good and thus available to be related to). She said she knew this was magical thinking.

We went over the scenario again and I insisted that I had done something wrong when I had taken time to remember what the little part had experienced. She said, again, that no I hadn't done anything wrong, rather I had become "bad", and bad meant not that she felt angry towards me, but rather that I was bad and would be angry and hateful and would attack her. We went through this once again and, finally, I got it.

I suggested that she was stuck in the primitive collapse response (the activation of the dorsal vagal nerve (Porges, 2011)—although I didn't say that) and could not fight back, but rather could only collapse and disappear. She said yes, her father had been able to "kill her without even touching her" (annihilate her through his attitude, feelings, look, and so on). She described how she would be desperate to find anything good in him, just so that she could latch onto that and make him not be the terrifying bad–angry–sadistic person who could kill off her completely powerless self at will.

This felt like a revelation to me, as I could better understand how this kind of "bad father" would be truly terrifying, and that the child who has such collapse responses would be completely petrified and completely powerless. With the more sophisticated fight or flight responses being unavailable to her she was trapped in a terrifying situation where her father had to be kept good by internal, magical means. She does actually have a number of emotional parts that are capable of anger (although never towards her parents), but they are kept safely locked away.

We went on to explore how the dying-and-collapsing is related to dissociation from her body and dissociation from the parts that do the experiencing (an essential element of the dissociative identity disorder). I could understand more clearly the terrors she had experienced in relation to me, and how these primitive collapse responses, due to her parents' overpowering treatment and inescapable domination of her, meant that she would have experienced them as overwhelmingly terrifying, possibly to the point of bringing her dissociative identity organisation into being.

Notes

1. For a very accessible book that opens up many different perspectives I particularly recommend: *A Shining Affliction: A Story of Harm and Healing in Psychotherapy* (Rogers 1995).
2. The terms ANP and EP were introduced by the psychiatrist Charles Myers in 1916, but the terms alters, parts, and sub-personalities are also sometimes used.

CHAPTER SEVENTEEN

The body remembers—working analytically with the body

This book has placed the earliest patterns of relating, and the most primitive, affective-somatic experiences and reactions, as central to an understanding of the functioning of the psyche. It has charted how these form the foundation stones of the personality, and become incorporated and elaborated into our more conscious, "sophisticated" personality. The work of many trauma therapists—van der Kolk, Herman, Levine, Rothschild, Siegel, Ogden, Minton, Pain, van der Hart, Nijenehuis and Steele—and neuroscientists—LeDoux, Damasio, Panksepp, and Schore—and others, have made clear how these primitive experiences are still calling the shots. In my work I have found it necessary, in order to properly address the most distressing and difficult states of mind, to work with these primary experiences, to recognise the early relational traumas, and explore the detail of the interactions between the patient and analyst, as I have described.

As I have been writing this book however, I have been conscious of the ambivalent attitude towards analytic psychotherapy of two of the main authorities on trauma work whom I have quoted extensively in this book—Bessel van der Kolk and the sensorimotor approach of Pat Ogden, Kekuni Minton, and Clare Pain. This includes both implicit and explicit communications as far as Bessel van der Kolk is concerned as, having attended a conference in Boston in 2013 where he spoke eloquently about trauma, I noted that he had few good words to say about analytic psychotherapy as a form of treatment.

This conflict comes to a head in this chapter where I will talk about working analytically with the body, which some might find an oxymoron, although others will not; and, to reiterate, my shorthand definition for analysis is that it is a process where the analyst attempts to stay as close to what the patient brings as possible, accompanying them on their journey. Rothschild is integrative in her approach, writing:

> Bridging the gap between the verbal psychotherapies and the body-psychotherapies means taking the best resources from both, rather than choosing one over the other. Integrated trauma therapy must consider, consist of, and utilize tools for identifying, understanding, and treating trauma's effects on both mind a body. Language is necessary for both. The somatic disturbances of trauma require language to make sense of them, comprehend their meaning, extract their message, and resolve their impact. When healing trauma, it is crucial to give attention to both body and mind; you can't have one without the other. (2000, pp. xiii–xiv)

I hope I have thus far demonstrated the clinical significance, in fact the centrality, of the uncontained, affective-somatic remnants of early relational traumas and trauma-related internal working models, specifically, how the analysis is frequently precisely organised around following these as they unfold. They are understood to be the primary "source", and this places trauma as central to the analytic process in a way that I believe is already significantly different to traditional analytic approaches. Furthermore, the traditional analytic trope of the patient's intentionality is also challenged by recognising that these relational patterns are held in implicit/procedural memory and are thus not under the patient's conscious control and are primarily enacted, something which has in the past been frowned upon, as if the patient (or analyst for that matter) was doing something wrong; this is happily more rarely the case nowadays.

The verbalisation of the understanding of what is going on—the interpretation—is thus the end product of quite a long process, and often takes the form of a simple commentary based on how the analyst understands what is emerging. This commentary is not apart from the process itself, but rather the way that the dialogue proceeds, the tone of voice in which the analyst conveys what they have to say, how they position themselves in relation to the patient's experience and so on, is an essential part of the analytic process.

In my work I am therefore attuned to the patient's somatic and affective cues, not only for what they tell us (patient and analyst) cognitively about the patient's experience, but also what that affective-somatic experience is like for the patient; specifically how unbearable or distressing it may be, and my role in making it so. The caveat here is that when working with trauma you are always working with things that are experienced as unbearable. I therefore keep a cautious eye on how I approach what I know feels impossible for the patient, and try to keep a balance between risk and safety, as Bromberg (2011, p. 16) describes.

The key question, and the dividing line between approaches, is, when something is extremely distressing for the patient, when some key aspect of the individual's trauma has been triggered, should the analyst step in in some way to actively regulate the patient's distress? By this I mean, to in some way ground the patient or help them to feel safe, perhaps encouraging them to feel their body on the seat and their feet on the floor, and to note and track the distress in their body, and follow it as it decreases? Or, to take it a step further, to take more charge of addressing the traumatic experience as a whole by, for example, following Janet's three-stage model of treatment—first making sure the individual is secure and functioning well-enough, deliberately not addressing any traumatic area until they are ready ... and so on?

And a second element that straddles the dividing line between approaches is whether or not to try to maintain a positively toned role in the therapy, essentially remaining the good, helpful object—whilst appreciating that someone who has been traumatised is particularly exposed and raw in the way I have been describing throughout, and will require particular sensitivity from the analyst regarding this.

My developing understanding is that it is the analyst's attitude and the analytic relationship itself that is the primary way in which the patient's experience and distress is met and regulated. Recognising the person's experience, staying with them while they struggle with it and verbalise what they can, being affected by this experience and recognising those effects, making sense of it with them where possible, and putting that sense into words where necessary, is the core of the interactive regulation that goes on between infant and parent as well as between adults (Beebe & Lachmann, 2002, 2013; Bion, 1962a). I have found that this attitude is almost always sufficient within the analytic session itself. As Michael (Chapter Ten) told me once, the analytic thinking and interpretation was essential in helping him to see what was going on.

I have come to recognise however, as I work more deeply with peoples' affective-somatic fragments of experience and states of mind, that when they are re-experiencing and reliving their early traumas, for example, experiencing states of annihilation, they invariably reach the limits of what they find bearable. This is particularly the case between sessions, perhaps reinforced by the fact that they have come to find that their interaction with the analyst has down-regulated their distress and thus the separation from the analyst at the end of the sessions is experienced as a more frightening and disturbing loss. I have thus found that some people need a means of self-regulation/settling their current state. Of course, many people have developed or discovered their own means of achieving this, whether in the form of a relaxation technique, meditation, going out for a walk, and so on.

However, I have found it helpful, when someone asks for help with these experiences, to tell them about a technique for grounding themselves, as I will describe later in this chapter.[1] To repeat, this is a technique that I let them know about that people can use to ground themselves. Within the session itself I almost invariably stay with what the patient is communicating, implicitly communicating that both they and I can bear, stay with, and make sense of their experience.

Other than to let them know of this technique I have not found it helpful to take charge of or direct the regulation of the patient's experience for a number of reasons. The primary one is the paramount importance of the patient's autonomy, which I see as in some way sacrosanct. This is particularly so with patients who have been traumatically controlled, violated, or abused, or told what or what not to do and how to behave, which is so characteristic of early relational trauma.

Related to this is that it is precisely this autonomy, and an implicit trust in the patient's psyche, that determines when a particular dynamic or issue is constellated. If the therapist takes control of what is addressed and when, a fundamental position of respect for the patient's psyche and timing is lost, although granted that the therapist can attempt to back off if they discover they have gone in too soon (and as my term "gone in" implies, this approach can easily be experienced as invasive).

A secondary consideration, also of vital importance, is that in adopting a "helpful" role, the analyst may be setting up an expectation that they are taking up an idealised, saviour/rescuer role, and that they will continue to do so; this is doomed, ultimately, to fail (see Chapters Nine and Eleven). Additionally, they may be rejecting the more difficult roles of the bad object, uninvolved caregiver, and so on, which are so much a part of the natural dynamics of traumatic experiences, as I have been describing. To perennially adopt such positively toned roles gives the message either that the traumatic experience itself is truly unbearable, or that the bad object, of which the individual will have a version themselves *in potentia* as part of their talion response, is unacceptable.

This is not to say, of course, that there may not be periods in the analysis, often quite lengthy ones, where a positively toned experience with the analyst predominates—a positive transference–countertransference— where the analyst is experienced as being helpful, kind, considerate, thoughtful, caring, and so on. Related to this is that it can be important to recognise any early correspondences of helpful, stabilising figures from childhood—aunts, uncles, or grandparents perhaps—although the relationship between patient and analyst is also establishing a new dynamic in its own right.

However, in trying to extend this period unnaturally, I have found that the analyst significantly obstructs the emergence of the person's particular trauma-related internal working models, and thus an understanding of their early experience and the working through of the traumatic complex. I have found that a new phase in the analysis is signalled when the analyst begins to note feelings of, for example, irritation or heavy-heartedness, where they previously felt more in tune with the patient. Thus the analyst needs not to clutter up the analytic space by trying to be, for example, helpful, when the patient is trying to work on the analyst being unhelpful.

Or again, the patient can become drawn into having to reassure the therapist that they are good and effective in a similar way to which they had to reassure a parent, who had in some way catastrophically let them down—that they were good/likeable/loveable and that they hadn't done anything wrong. Jean Knox (2007) documents a good example of this in her paper, "The fear of love: the denial of self in relationship", where she describes an individual's struggle with parents who could not tolerate emotional separation as they wanted to maintain a perfect, loving contingency with their son (see also Benjamin, 2004, and my comments on that paper in Chapter Eleven).

Or, another re-enactment, I have found that patients who have been forced to submit at the hands of narcissistic and controlling parents may particularly submit themselves to the analyst's control, or feel subject to the analyst's control in a way that very quickly comes to mirror the original dynamic in some way (see Rachel in West, 2007). Or again, perhaps the analyst is expected to "make the patient better", just as the patient, as a child, was expected to "make the parent better" (see Michael in Chapter Ten).

I have heard trauma therapists privately expressing their frustration that certain patients are not responding to their treatment protocols, whether those are CBT or EMDR related, without realising that the frustration and the implicit sense of criticism and failure is precisely what is being constellated and needs addressing. And I have now lost count of the number of people who I have seen following extensive treatment with CBT that was successful on one level but that did not fundamentally address the person's difficulties and, specifically, their early relational traumas.

Finally, there is the issue of the type of patients one sees and their expectations. Being registered as a Jungian analyst and psychotherapist I primarily see people who have struggled with the kind of early relational trauma I have been describing. For these people their traumas are embedded in their personality, which generally functions adequately, sometimes more, sometimes less effectively. There could be people who might present for therapy in such a distressed and dysregulated state that I might well suggest they try another form of therapy, at least initially. Analytic psychotherapy does require that the person is able to manage their life to some extent—to have some relatively effective ego-functioning.

Certainly, for individuals who have experienced a single incident trauma later in life, whether that is a motor accident, a sexual assault, or an experience of war, particularly if their early life experience was not significantly traumatic, trauma therapy, CBT, Brainspotting, or EMDR are the treatments of choice and I would not take someone on for therapy under those circumstances.

Some theoretical precursors

The study of psychosomatic phenomena has a long history in psychoanalysis, beginning with Freud himself and continued more recently by Joyce McDougal. McDougal (1989) calls on the work of Freud, Klein, Winnicott, and Bion to explore "the unconscious significance of psychosomatic manifestations and to examine the extent to which these are linked to the vicissitudes involved in becoming a person and to failures of the internalisation processes by which individual identity is constructed" (p. 48). Whilst her study is very much within the psychoanalytic tradition, relating these manifestations largely back to Freudian drive theory, she is also interested in the archaic form of symbolism in which emotional messages bypass the usual cognitive and language structures and are expressed directly by the body. These are themes that have been expanded upon in this book already.

Orbach (2004, 2009), coming from a relational perspective, takes the argument further and, echoing Winnicott's dictum that "there is no such thing as a baby", argues that there is no such thing as a body, there is only a body in relationship with another body—that "our personal body unfolds and develops its individuality in the context of its relationship to and with an other and other bodies" (Orbach, 2004, p. 23). Her view emphasises the role of the embodied therapist in allowing the body of the patient to come into being and into relationship.

This is not Orbach's core point, but my own somatic reactions in the session are often key in orienting me to what is going on for the patient and between us; and when someone is describing some kind of bodily pain or distress I usually find my own body resonating with some version of what they are describing, enabling me to more closely feel along with their experience.

Coming from the other direction, there is a growing and illuminating appreciation from practitioners in the medical field of the psychic and traumatic factors that underlie so many of the apparently unexplained medical symptoms and illnesses; see for example, Sarno (1991, 1998, 2006), Clarke (2007), Anderson (2007), Anderson and Sherman (2013), and Oldfield (2014). There is such a coherent picture emerging now that Luyten, van Houdenhove, Lemma, Target, and Fonagy (2012) hold that it is not correct to say that these symptoms are "unexplained", and term them "functional somatic disorders".

Dr. David Clarke (2007), working as a medical practitioner, discovered, by listening carefully to his patients' stories of nausea, vomiting, dizziness, headaches, fatigue, difficulties in swallowing or breathing, coughs, gastro-intestinal symptoms, bladder problems, back pain, pain in the feet and ankles, itching, and many other symptoms, that these were frequently caused by relational trauma (he calls it stress) in childhood. The examples he gives of such stresses are of being hit or beaten, repeatedly shamed or mocked, being made to feel that nothing you do is good enough, being sexually abused, neglected, witnessing violence, parental use of drugs or alcohol, being given inappropriate responsibility, and a chronic fear of danger (pp. 34–35). He also recognises that intense current stress, a traumatic event leading to PTSD, depression, and anxiety, can also lead to the kinds of significant physical symptoms that I have listed above. He understands these as the body's reaction to intense and chronic stress.[2]

Phil Mollon (2015) addresses what he calls somato-psychic disorders, emphasising the primacy of physical conditions that affect the mind, in contrast to the theoretical overvaluing of the dynamics of the psyche alone (p. 1 & ch. 11). In his book he is describing many clinical situations parallel to those I am describing here, although there are many others that are significantly different. His central thesis is that the individual is "living in a constant struggle with the threat of falling apart, of disintegrating, both physically and psychologically" (p. 239). Similarly to this book, Mollon also emphasises the importance of the ego ("the organ of adaptation to reality" (p. 107)) and the prominence of primary process functioning.

Mollon understands the underlying cause of these disintegrative experiences to be struggles with an autistic spectrum temperament and attention deficit hyperactivity disorder (ADHD), suggesting that ADHD may be "a hidden core within borderline personality disorder and mood instability" (p. 17). In contrast to Mollon I understand this experience of disintegration and the fear of falling apart, in the cases I have described, as due to experiences of profound threat and the consequent collapse response. He specifically disagrees with this conceptualisation in terms of primitive mechanisms of defence (pp. 5–7), although it seems that he is, like me, most concerned not to ascribe intention to the patient who is struggling with uncontained affect and a lack of sense of agency (pp. 61–62). In classifying ADHD, it sounds as if he is ably describing the hyperactivity (ADHD) and sometimes hypoactivity (attention deficit disorder, ADD), and hypervigilance related to trauma; however, I have no argument with his contention that there is a neurobiological basis to these problems, particularly the autistic spectrum traits.

Despite the differences, our approaches have much in common, particularly some aspects of his psychotherapeutic technique, although I am critical of the Kohutian approach as I believe it militates against the most difficult trauma-related dynamics being constellated and worked through.

The body in analysis

To turn, finally, to addressing somatic issues more directly. The soma is, of course, continuous with the psyche. Antonio Damasio (1995, 1999) points out that our somatic responses are very much part of our affective responses, so that part of the experience of feeling nervous is the somatic element in the stomach, or that feeling fear is something that is experienced throughout the body. Thus I tune in to and listen out for somatic cues as part of the person's whole reaction.

I quite frequently find myself pointing out that an experience of, for example, nausea that the person is experiencing may be an aspect of their anxiety. This occasionally comes as a surprise for some people as they have not linked their somatic responses to what they feel. This is sometimes a sign, however, that the person's body is "keeping the score", to use van der Kolk's phrase, and that they could not previously make the link because they could not allow themselves to be aware of what they felt, for example, towards a relative who was abusing them. The only symptom was that they found themselves feeling curiously sick when that person was around.

This symptom might then have been addressed, less or more effectively, in other ways, through medical means or investigations. This might, secondarily, allow the person to get some of the benign looking after they had not been getting at home, or it might have opened them up to further intrusions and violations that are medically sanctioned yet tragically "wrong"; both alternatives might be true to some extent.

There are certain somatic reactions that do tend to fall into particular patterns however. It had been an eruption of Michael's eczema that had brought him to seek out analysis (via an insightful GP and then psychiatrist) when I first met him. Later in the analysis, as described in

Chapter Ten, Michael began experiencing intense feelings of pain in his shoulders and arms, as well as his torso. When I asked him to embody them for me, he hunched up into a clear, boxer's fight position. This was at a time when he was just getting in touch with intense, murderous rage and violence that had previously been locked up, with Michael feeling himself to be powerless in the world. This growing awareness of his locked-in fight response, an "incomplete action tendency" as Levine describes, coincided with one phase of him shifting out of his paralysed, passive, negative, borderline personality organisation.

Previously, when Michael had been particularly distressed at intrusive noise from neighbours, he would find his legs endlessly, distressingly, flailing at night, like someone trying to run away, in a clear, incompleted flight response. Addressing this intrusion through CBT and self-hypnosis was effective and helpful, although our understanding of it also formed part of our work.

John experienced a bodily symptom that puzzled us for some time. His hands became weak and extremely painful so that he was hardly able to write at times. He had many investigations that were inconclusive. When I asked what his hands might be voicing, what they might be trying to say to us, he talked of their weakness and fear, and we made links to not being able to cope in the world, not being able to work, of becoming dependent but with no one to look after him. This mirrored his experience with his mother who had been profoundly depressed throughout his early years.

Whilst the pain and strength in his hands did, very slowly, improve, through little decisive action on our part—listening to them in the way I have described made little appreciable difference—it was only when he began to get in touch with his agonised, humiliated, collapse response, triggered at not being able to get through to his mother, that the symptom that his hands had been carrying made sense. By this time the pain and paralysis in his hands had mostly disappeared (although it would sometimes flare up when the collapse response was triggered in some form). It was as if they were holding the pain until he and I could emotionally get in touch with (rather than just intellectually know about) his experience of collapse, and the agonising pain, humiliation, and terror with which it was associated.

Difficulties in breathing are frequently associated with the freeze response, where the person (or animal) stills their breathing so that they are not heard and may pass for dead. Porges describes how such stilling may sometimes be life-threatening; indeed, his theory grew out of exploring the "vagal paradox", whereby the slowing of the heart rate, which he had been seeing as protective, could, at other times, deprive the infant's brain of oxygen in a way that could be fatal (Porges, 2011, pp. 4ff.). Breathing anomalies can therefore indicate experiences of fear or terror, of the individual having had to hold themselves still for significant periods in order to try to stay safe—L, described in the last chapter, experienced this.

There may also be particular sensations of pressure on the person's chest or legs that are fragmentary traces of having been held down and rendered powerless. It is again important to explore whether the specific sensation or breathing difficulty may have been triggered by something particular that the analyst had done or said, which can give another source of insight into the original experience.

Overall, in my experience, once progress has been made understanding the upper-level, more (apparently) rational conflicts, the individual tends to experience the more primitive, raw, somatic symptoms that may well underpin them. Individuals find experiencing versions of the collapse response particularly alarming and distressing, feeling that this is indisputable evidence that there is something wrong with them, that they are incurable, and that they are getting worse. Whereas, in contrast, I understand that we are finally reaching the primitive, affective-somatic roots of the person's experience, without which the traumatic complex cannot be fully worked through.

There are often experiences of anxiety, disgust, or self-loathing in relation to certain parts of the body or certain bodily functions, for example, a fear of being sick. Exploration has come to reveal that the body has been holding experiences of intrusion or violation, or sometimes reflects a parent's particular disgust of the child's bodily needs or bodily functions—perhaps the parent found the child's physical needs or their wish for physical affection repulsive.

In regard to blushing, which is the characteristic response related to shame (as Darwin noted (1872, p. 160)), sometimes this has a particular significance and terror as a parent may have taken a sadistic delight in teasing, taunting, and humiliating the child, of which blushing would have been a sign that they had succeeded in "getting through". Blushing is thus frequently experienced as being particularly mortifying.

I have also known the experience of hypochondria, a feeling that there is something medically wrong and/or that the person is dying, to be related to early collapse responses, where the feeling of dying is the only (somatic) remnant of that experience. These experiences of dying, as I have described in previous chapters, may be intricately re-experienced and relived in the process of analysis.

Yoga, meditation, and body-based therapies

Almost all the patients that I have been discussing here have spontaneously (and usually before coming to see me), taken up yoga, meditation, exercise, or, mindfulness practices, and found them very helpful. I thoroughly support these practices and recognise that they provide an invaluable means of getting some distance and perspective on obsessive mental preoccupation related to the traumatic complex. These practices loosen the identification with the cognitive, "fixed ideas" related to the trauma, opening the individual up to their unconscious functioning. In addition they help to establish a safe, relaxed, grounded, somatic experience in distinction from the distressed, hyper- and hypo-aroused bodily states associated with trauma. van der Kolk (2014) writes of this grounding, pointing out that it can help establish "islands of safety" within the body.

> This means helping patients identify parts of the body, postures, or movements where they can ground themselves whenever they feel stuck, terrified, or enraged. These parts usually lie outside the reach of the vagus nerve, which carries messages of panic to the chest, abdomen and throat … (2014, p. 245)

Rothschild (2000) discusses these in terms of "oases", where the individual can have a break from traumatic experience (she mentions anything from gardening and dog walking to computer games); "anchors", where there is a particular good relationship or good experience to return to; or a "safe place", a safe physical location to which the individual can return in imagination (pp. 92ff.). In addition to mindfulness and yoga, van der Kolk singles out EMDR, communal rhythms and theatre, internal family systems therapy, and Pesso's model of restructuring inner maps for particular mention in regard to recovering from trauma (2014, chs. 13–20).

The grounding technique that I tell people about is taken from Frances Sommer Anderson and Eric Sherman (2007, 2013), who worked with Dr. Sarno. She describes it by the acronym EGO, where the individual *exhales* slowly and allows their body to initiate inhaling; *grounds* themself where they are sitting, receiving the support of the chair and the floor beneath their feet; and *orients* themselves to their environment by looking around and about them. This decreases activation of the sympathetic nervous system and helps the individual to come out of their hyperaroused state.

I should also add that each person I have described above had had very significant spiritual experience and often a long-standing spiritual practice. Like Kalsched (2013), I have found this almost universal amongst people who have experienced trauma and early relational trauma in particular due, as I would put it, to a significant defeat of their ego. This leads me to further explore the very important question of the role of spiritual experience, which I will do in the next chapter through exploring Jung's early relational trauma, the "defeat" of his ego, and his spiritual experience.

Jungian body–soul work

Whilst I have quoted Ogden, Minton, and Pain's work on sensorimotor therapy at some length, there is also a rich vein of Jungian body therapy, based on the work of Marion Woodman who developed what she called BodySoul Rhythms. Marian Dunlea, Wendy Bratherton[3] and others, have taken Marion Woodman's work forward and explore psyche and soma together in their BodySoul and BodyDreaming programmes. This involves listening to the somatic unconscious and paying attention to unfolding dreams. In this way, guided by the self, space is provided for the unconscious to emerge through movement, voice, painting, and clay work. This enables the freeing up of the complexes held within the body. Their work also draws on Levine's somatic experiencing, attachment theory, and the emerging research from the field of neuroscience, some of which I have outlined already. Through personal experience of their therapies I can vouch for their effectiveness.

Notes

1. My early experience of this was mixed and, on the few occasions that I tried this, I felt that my patients experienced me as being patronising, showing a lack of trust in them or the analytic process,

and acting in a way that was uncharacteristic of our relationship. I have subsequently learnt to wait until they ask for such guidance.

2. It is, perhaps, important to say that these symptoms are not imagined but are as real as any other symptom caused by an organic agent.

3. See mariandunlea.com & wendybratherton.com for more details.

CHAPTER EIGHTEEN

Jung's early relational trauma and spiritual experience

In this chapter I will explore Jung's personality and theories in the light of his early relational trauma, and will discuss the defeat of the ego, and spiritual experience further. As Jung put it, "… the experience of the self is always a defeat for the ego" (1955–56, para. 778), a quotation that I see as central to his personal experience and theorising, as I will explore in detail below. Regarding his personal history, Jung wrote: "my life is the story of the self realisation of the unconscious" (1963, p. 17); I will understand "the unconscious" in rather more personal terms than Jung himself would have done.

Jung was generous in his autobiography, *Memories, Dreams, Reflections* (Jung, 1963), and much has already been written about him that I do not want to repeat here, Winnicott (1964), Atwood and Stolorow (1977), Feldman (1992), Satinover (1985), Shamdasani (1995), Meredith-Owen (2011, 2013a, 2015), and Kalsched (2013) being notable examples. We have also had access, since 2009, to Jung's *Red Book*, which documents his confrontation with the unconscious following his break from Freud and allows us a better understanding of his deepest, most profound and personal experiences and explorations.

Central to Jung's experience is the question of his exposure to, and experience and use of, what I understand as his non-ego experiences, which Jung understood as archetypal experiences of the collective unconscious and experiences of the self. These have generally been pathologised in various ways, notably by Winnicott (1964), and Atwood and Stolorow (1977), whilst some others have questioned Winnicott's diagnosis of childhood schizophrenia, suggesting that he had a "psychotic structure" instead (Satinover, 1985). Meredith-Owen suggests that Winnicott undervalued the constructive and containing aspects of Jung's experience of the self (Meredith-Owen, 2011), although few commentators have embraced Jung's transpersonal experience as fully as Kalsched (2013, ch. 8).

I understand Jung's journey as a creative response to the early experiences of the defeat of his ego and associated experiences of annihilation due to his early relational trauma. I use the term "defeat" because it both echoes Jung's own use ("… the experience of the self is always a defeat for the ego") and mirrors the subjective and clinical experience, although that can also include experiences of death and dying. I believe that Jung reconstructed and re-enacted many of these experiences in adulthood, but was not wholly successful in working through his traumatic complexes. However, as is classically the case where there has been early relational trauma, the outworkings of his traumas were dissociated from his early experience, and were lived through in their own right. This is characteristic of borderline psychology.

Whilst some individuals with such a personality organisation are preoccupied with powerful states of alienation, hatred, murderousness, and invasion, which disrupt their adaptive, reality-orientating, ego-functioning (as I have been documenting in this book), Jung was similarly preoccupied, in a way that also sometimes alienated him from those around him, but largely with the powerful, overwhelming, "archetypal" states of mind that were brought to the surface (Jung, 1911–12, para. 631), replaying the early defeat of his ego, as I will explore.

Biography

The bare bones of Jung's early life are as follows—and I would refer you to Jung's rich and lucid autobiography itself if you have not recently read it, as well as Deirdre Bair's (2003) excellent and thoroughly researched biography. His earliest memories were largely impersonal. They were of awakening in a pram to the "glorious beauty of the day with an indescribable sense of well-being, with the sun glittering through the leaves and blossoms of the bushes"; of spooning up warm milk with bits of bread in it in his high-chair; of being shown the Alps, red in the evening sun, by an aunt; of sorrow at not being able to go to the nearby mountains with other children; of taking pleasure in the water of the lake; of almost slipping through the railings into the nearby Rhine Falls; and fascination with the drowned body of a boy who had been pulled from the Falls, which had been laid in the wash-house (Jung, 1963, pp. 21–22).

Despite having been the first of four children to survive—a brother, Paul, born two years before Jung, had lived only five days—his mother was soon "indifferent" towards the young Carl and "lethargic" and, after their move to a new house when he was six months old, she was "profoundly depressed", with the maid taking care of him "for weeks on end while his mother shut herself in her bedroom" (Bair, 2003, pp. 19ff.). His parents were at first apathetic towards each other but later the relationship deteriorated, where "conversations, such as they were, usually consisted of [his father's] invective and [his mother's] muffled response, followed by long periods of her silence".

Jung remembered his father, a pastor, singing to him at night whilst he was suffering from eczema. This was at a time when there were "dim intimations of trouble" in his parents' marriage and his mother spent "several long stays in a rest home near Basel", whilst his father told his parishioners she "required hospitalization for a vague physical ailment" (ibid., p. 21). Jung wrote:

> presumably her illness had something to do with the difficulty in the marriage … [f]rom then on I always felt mistrustful when the word "love" was spoken[1] … the feeling I associated with "woman" was for a long time that of innate unreliability. "Father" on the other hand, meant reliability and—powerlessness. (Jung, 1963, p. 23)

He remembered being looked after by an aunt, and a maid who had black hair and an olive complexion—he said that this type of girl later became associated with his anima.

The difficulties between his parents continued for some time, with his father sleeping in the same room as the young Carl for three years. At the age of seven Carl was having choking fits, of which he comments, "the atmosphere in the house was beginning to be unbearable" (ibid., p. 34). Again it was his father who comforted him.

He experienced "vague fears at night" and was preoccupied by death in the form of drowned bodies from the Rhine Falls, graves, and the funeral services, presided over by his father, where "[b]lack, solemn men in long frock coats with unusually tall hats and shiny black boots would bring a black box" (p. 24). He came to believe that Lord Jesus "took" people to him, putting them into a hole in the ground (partly due to a prayer he recited every night).[2] One day, on seeing a Jesuit, dressed in black, coming down the road towards him he ran, terrified, to hide under a beam in the darkest corner of the attic.

Around this time he had the earliest dream he could remember. It was of a dark, rectangular, grave-like, stone-lined hole in the ground containing a large phallus, twelve to fifteen feet high and one and a half to two feet thick, with an aura of brightness above it. He was terrified it might crawl off its throne towards him, at which point he heard his mother's voice above him calling out, "Yes, just look at him. That is the man-eater!" He understood his mother's comment to refer to either Lord Jesus or the phallus (the two had become linked in his mind) being the "man-eater" that took little children under the ground (pp. 26–27). For years he could never succeed in overcoming his secret distrust of Jesus (p. 29).

He built towers with bricks, which he then "rapturously destroyed by an 'earthquake'" (p. 33); he had a sacred fire that only he could tend; sometimes he would sit on a particular stone wondering, "Am I the one who is sitting on the stone or I am the stone on which *he* is sitting?" (p. 35) (what he identified as himself was clearly mobile—later on he identified with eighteenth-century figures). He writes that, in his tenth year, "my disunion with myself and uncertainty in the world at large led me to an action which at the time was quite incomprehensible to me": he carved a little manikin with frock coat, top hat, and shiny black boots (much like the figures of whom he had been afraid), and placed it in a pencil-case along with a smooth, oblong blackish stone from the Rhine, which he had painted with watercolours to look as though it were divided into an upper and a lower half. He hid this on one of the beams under the roof where he knew no one would find it; he writes, "I felt safe and the tormenting sense of being at odds with myself was gone" (pp. 36–37). He concludes that "the possession of a secret had a very powerful formative influence on my character; I consider it the essential feature of my boyhood" (p. 37); (he had symbolically made his core self safe, incorporating the terrifying aggressors).

At the age of twelve he was physically timid and, when one day he was pushed over by a schoolmate and hit his head, he realised he could use it as an excuse to get out of school. Thereafter he had fainting spells whenever he had to return to school and was kept off for well over a year, with the doctors struggling to diagnose what was wrong. He used the time away from school to "plunge into the world of the mysterious", but reports that he did not feel happier for it, and had "the obscure feeling that I was fleeing from myself" (p. 47). One day he overheard his father expressing his concern that his son wouldn't be able to earn his own living. He was shocked and set about studying, ignoring the fainting attacks that came until, after a short time, they disappeared completely.

In contrast, as he grew older and grew in physique, he reports that he could at times be "inclined to violent rages" and once successfully fought off seven boys so that no one dared to attack him again (p. 61). Several years later still, his confidence had grown further, something he relates to his study of Schopenhauer and Kant; of this he wrote, "whereas formerly I had been shy, timid, mistrustful, pallid, thin and apparently unstable in health, I now began to display a tremendous appetite on all fronts, I knew what I wanted and I went after it" (p. 89).

Regarding his school years he describes his "unstable self-assurance" whereby at times he recognised his inflatedness, feeling important and dignified, but at other times he felt his inferiority and smallness; sometimes he wished to sink "fathoms deep into the ground" (p. 42). This split developed into what he came to call his Number One and Number Two personalities. Number One was an everyday person who was, "the son of my parents, went to school, was less intelligent, hard-working, decent and clean than other boys". Whilst Number Two was "grown up—old, in fact—sceptical, mistrustful, remote from the world of men, but close to nature, the earth, the sun, the moon, all living creatures, and above all close to the night, to dreams, and to whatever 'God' worked directly in him" (pp. 61–62).

Winnicott describes this as Jung's "split personality", suggesting that Jung had recovered from "childhood schizophrenia". Jung himself comments on the split saying that, "this has nothing to do with a 'split' or dissociation in the ordinary medical sense. On the contrary it is played out in every individual" (p. 62). He took it to be the split between the ego and the self.

From an early age Jung recognised that he was different from his schoolfellows. Throughout his teenage years, the experiences of what he came to call "God's world" alienated him from other children, and Jung had to learn to keep them to himself (the boys in his class had given him the nickname "Father Abraham"). This emphasises his experience not only of "almost unendurable loneliness" but also that, as he put it when writing his autobiography at the age of eighty-three, "the pattern of my relationship to the world was already prefigured: today as then I am a solitary, because I know things and must hint at things which other people do not know, and usually do not even want to know" (p. 58).

He describes two other significant psychological experiences in his teenage years. First, on walking to school one day at the age of fourteen, it felt as if he emerged from a dense cloud, and he felt:

> [N]ow I am *myself*! It was as if a wall of mist were at my back, and that behind that wall there was not yet an "I". But at this moment *I came upon myself*. Previously I had existed too, but everything had happened to me. Now I happened to myself. Now I knew: I am myself now, now I exist. (p. 49, original italics)

I think this is a relatively common experience of teenage years—the first experience of reflexive self-consciousness, where the person becomes properly conscious of themselves for the first time. I remember the experience of emerging from just such a mist myself.

The second is more complex. On this occasion he was walking through Basel and experienced a great terror of a thought that he could not bear to let himself think. This terror continued for an agonising three days until, eventually, he allowed the thought to come. It was of an enormous turd coming from God sitting on his throne and falling upon Basel Cathedral, shattering it and breaking the walls of the cathedral asunder (p. 56). Once he had submitted to the thought, and survived it, he felt enormous relief. This was one of the many experiences that Jung had that he felt were a direct experience of God and His grace.

On one level this is the not-uncommon experience of the discovery of the autonomy of the unconscious—the discovery that "I" (the ego) do not create my thoughts, but that they come as if from outside. Examples where this autonomy is most clear: among writers, artists, and in creative activity, where the individual relies on inspiration and the flow of words and ideas that "come" to them; in a darker frame, this is the experience of the individual who experiences intrusive, obsessional thoughts; or again, in a religious frame, where the individual has to find some way of coming to terms with the "morally reprehensible" thoughts that come into their mind. This is sometimes elegantly dealt with by seeing thoughts, and particularly "bad" thoughts, as being like birds flying across one's mind, but the individual's "moral" struggle is not to let them roost. Jung's struggle was to allow himself the freedom to have "good" and "bad" thoughts.

Of course, where the individual has experienced early relational trauma, these thoughts will likely reflect impulses of a terrifying, sexualised, envious, punishing, or murderous nature, either towards the self or others (or both), which will inevitably "roost", almost always making the person feel bad about themselves. Much work on the person's traumatic complexes may be necessary in order to allow the thoughts to be accepted, accommodated, and understood, in other words, integrated. It could be, therefore, that the thought of God's turd shattering the cathedral echoes Jung's unconscious identification with an omnipotent, annihilating, phallus-turd-"man-eater"-God who destroys fragile man-made structures (egos, houses, cathedrals, and so on), see Meredith-Owen (2013a) and below.

Whilst, in general, thoughts can come to be owned and integrated into the personality, their source to some extent always remains outside of the ego, in the primitive regions of the psyche/brain. In other words, one cannot control what one thinks and feels, although, of course, one can always attempt to repress unacceptable thoughts and feelings—and Jung's experience with the turd and the cathedral is exactly an example of a failed attempt at repression. Or, again, the individual can come to acknowledge the source of the unacceptable thoughts and feelings, for example, of anger, hatred, or envy, as within themselves, and develop some kind of attitude towards them, owning them and steering them in a constructive direction when they arise.

It is significant that as a child Jung took the source of these thoughts and impulses to be God, and in so doing he recognised God to be both loving and terrible (Jung, 1963, pp. 63ff.). Of course, his understanding of God changed over the years from his first experiences in childhood, developing into his mature understanding of "the self". Whilst he remained agnostic over the experience of an objective God, he had many, many experiences of what people over the millennia have called

God, so that he said, famously, that he "did not *believe* in God, he *knew*". Perhaps this harked back to differences between Jung and his father, a pastor, over the question of "faith" (which his father recommended), in contrast to "knowledge" through direct experience (on which Jung called) (ibid., pp. 73 & 92). I will come back to speculate on how it was that Jung took these experiences to be of God and the significance of that further on.

Jung and his early relational trauma

What I have to say about Jung must, of course, remain speculative, but I hope to apply some of the understandings outlined hitherto, and identify some of the patterns that were formative in Jung's life that may help us understand the future course of his life, his struggles, his psychic experiences, and his theorising.

What stands out concerning Jung's early life is his early relationship with his mother and his dream of the phallus, in the context of his warm and loving relationship with his father. In my clinical experience, individuals who have been unable to get through to their primary caregiver—the mother (usually)—experience a profound experience of defeat, accompanied by experiences of powerless and annihilation (Chapters Thirteen to Seventeen). I have suggested this is related to the collapse/submit response.

For Jung there was clearly "sufficient" care in his childhood—from his father, his aunt, the maid, and his material circumstances—for him to have the good experiences he describes, for example, the "indescribable well-being"; however, the primary defeat still leaves its profound mark. I would suggest that this is reflected in the dream of the "castrated" phallus (as Feldman, 1992, puts it), reflecting an experience of being rendered powerless. Whilst this amounts to an annihilation (the phallus is dead/buried), reflecting the beliefs of the Egyptians (Jung says the tomb was Egyptian in appearance), there is "life after death" and the phallus is very much alive, in fact now of monumental proportions—twelve to fifteen feet high and one and a half to two feet thick.

Powerlessness, destruction, and the defeat of the ego

I will return to the dream in a moment; however, I would like to note the other experiences of terror, death, and destruction in his early life. There were the early terrors of being killed by Jesuits, of being taken by Jesus, and his fascination with the drowned boy from the falls. There is also the building of towers and towns, which he "rapturously destroyed" as if by an earthquake. In all of these situations the young Carl was significantly powerless against overwhelming forces outside his control, as symbolised so perfectly by an earthquake. I would suggest that this reflects the collapse of his sense of agency and his experience of powerlessness to get through to his mother, so that one is vulnerable and acted upon from outside (notably he attributes being powerless to his father in his autobiography).

Winnicott (1964) and others (Feldman, 1992; Meredith-Owen, 2011, 2013a) suggest that this destructiveness (simply) represents a projection of Jung's own aggression. I do not agree and would suggest that this is the kind of misrepresentation that can lead to an impasse in working with individuals with a borderline personality structure. I suggest, instead, as I am describing throughout regarding borderline functioning, that Jung was being true to, and recreating and re-enacting, his early experience of the defeat of his ego—the experience of being annihilated (this does not mean that he did not also have an aggressive counter-reaction to that annihilation—see below). As I will go on to explore, I would suggest that he was able to master and make some good use of the experiences that followed from the defeat, although he was not able to integrate them fully into an expanded sense of self, centred in his ego.

Life after death—rebirth and transformation

To return to the phallus[3] dream. The phallus, having been cut off and buried, has been transformed—grown in power and to enormous proportions. Jung wrote extensively about rebirth, and the transformation that follows death and rebirth—it would be fair to say it was one of his preoccupations. For example, in the book that signalled his break from Freud, *Symbols of Transformation*, published in 1911–12, there is a long and detailed chapter (Chapter 5) about rebirth in many different cultures and traditions that comes about through separation from the mother, something which requires the son to "bear the fear of death" (para. 415). Furthermore, as discussed Chapter Fifteen, in one of his most original papers Jung (1946/54) documents the death, rebirth, and transformation of both patient and analyst within the analytic relationship, with reference to a sixteenth-century alchemical treatise, *The Rosarium Philosophorum*.

I would suggest that Jung is describing exactly the defeat of the ego, and the alteration and expansion of consciousness that comes as a result. A key question is whether the individual is able to bear, contain, and integrate the experiences that follow this "death" of the old ego structure without falling into chronic inflation or psychosis, and return to a new, expanded ego structure. I will argue that in Jung's case he did not return to a life centred in the ego and that he, to some extent, permanently sidelined the ego and the personal sphere. As he approvingly quotes one of the alchemists writing about the philosopher's stone and the aim of the process of alchemy, "it is my own transformation, not a personal transformation but the transformation of what is mortal in me into what is immortal. It shakes off the mortal husk that I am and awakens to a life of its own" (Jung, 1940/1950, para. 238).

"The experience of the self is always a defeat for the ego"

So, with the phallus killed off and buried it is transformed and has an "aura of brightness above it". von Franz (1975) suggests that, for the Romans, the phallus symbolised "a man's sacred genius, the source of his physical and mental creative powers".[4] With the defeated ego also symbolised, as I will explore below, by a decapitation (viz. castration), Jung's everyday, "overground", personality Number One was displaced, and the power of the "underground", primitive functions of the unconscious personality (Number Two) came to the fore. Or, as Meredith-Owen paraphrases Feldman (1992, p. 266), this was "Jung's first experience of the profound potential of his own mind" (Meredith-Owen, 2013a, p. 15).

These primitive functions of the psyche are elements of the unconscious, core self, which are always working away in the background, processing our experience. Jung writes of them: "it is as if the 'eyes of the background' do the seeing in an impersonal act of perception" (Jung, 1963, p. 68) (note the phallus in the dream also has a seeing "eye"). This is what Jung understood as the self.

As Meredith-Owen points out, in the dream the phallus is ensconced in a clear representation of the vagina. Whilst he suggests this echoes the primal scene, I would suggest it is in a permanent state of depersonalised, creative generation ... or destruction (it is the "man-eater" ... and

I am sure I don't need to rehearse the links between sex and death here).[5] Without containment by the ego the individual is exposed to overwhelmingly powerful forces—Jung called them archetypal. In the dream he is terrified that this man-eating phallus will crawl off its throne towards him. Such primitive, powerful affect can overwhelm and "kill off" the individual's everyday sense of self—the ego—and Jung documents the struggle he had to maintain his sanity (Jung, 2009, pp. 238ff.). It can also transport the individual, as Jung writes:

> A person sinks into his childhood memories and vanishes from the existing world. He finds himself apparently in deepest darkness, but then has unexpected visions of a world beyond. The "mystery" he beholds represents the stock of primordial images which everybody brings with him as his human birthright, the sum total of inborn forms peculiar to the instincts. I have called this "potential" psyche the collective unconscious. If this layer is activated by the regressive libido there is a possibility of life being renewed, and also of it being destroyed. Regression carried to its logical conclusion means a linking back with the world of natural instincts, which in its formal or ideal aspect is a kind of *prima materia*. If this *prima materia* can be assimilated by the conscious mind it will bring about a reactivation and reorganization of its contents. But if the conscious mind proves incapable of assimilating the new contents pouring in from the unconscious, then a dangerous situation arises in which they keep their original, chaotic, and archaic form and consequently disrupt the unity of consciousness. (Jung, 1911–12, para. 631)

I have worked with many individuals who, whilst exploring their early traumas, experience this disruption of their consciousness by the powerful affects, sensations, or intrusive memories, and are convinced that they are dying and/or going mad (Anna and Nounoushka in this book). They have been profoundly relieved to learn that these experiences can be understood in more prosaic terms related to trauma.

As Jung writes, about his confrontation with the unconscious (after his break from Freud), "I hit upon this stream of lava, and the heat of its fires reshaped my life. That was the primal stuff which compelled me to work on it ..." (Jung, 1963, p. 225). It was a lifetime's work to make constructive use of this upwelling affect and not get too carried away by states of inflation (to which he sometimes succumbed) or psychosis (lava is deadly if you get too close to it), as well as to recognise the constructive functioning of the self (which I call the core self).

I understand the archetypal/collective aspect of what Jung called the self to be precisely due to the sameness-recognising aspect of the core self, which recognises our community and connection with others,[6] "collective" patterns, and abstracts from the particular to the general (symbolisation). Matte Blanco (1977, 1985) described this as symmetry (see Carvalho (2013) for a discussion of this in a Jungian context, or West (2007), or Chapter Eight in this book on the ego–self relationship). This experience also entails the suspension of the personal level held by the ego (see the quote above about "shaking off the mortal husk").

A slight deviation for Winnicott's claim about destructiveness

So is this the source of what Winnicott calls Jung's destructiveness, which Winnicott held he was projecting onto God, for example, in Jung's feared, waking fantasy of the turd falling on Basel cathedral? I think the reason that Winnicott's suggestion strikes a wrong chord is that there is a great deal of difference between the self-assertive, anger and aggression that is related to a fight response and the more profound, primal, collapse response that is associated with annihilation, destruction, disintegration, and catastrophe, against which the individual is (almost) powerless. The term aggression hardly fits the latter.

I think there are times when individuals do experience a primitive fight response, perhaps as a primitive talion reversal of the early trauma that they experienced. However there have been many other times when I have made this interpretation to people—that they are afraid of being attacked/killed/criticised by others because they are projecting their own anger/murderousness/criticism into them—and whilst they can usually "get it" as an intellectual possibility it doesn't really make a difference to them. In these cases I usually find that the person's deepest reaction was a freeze or collapse response, as with Jung, and that the "truth" of what they are experiencing reflects something deeper and more annihilatory, in the way I have been describing for Jung.

The reversal of Jung's annihilatory experience is perhaps represented by his phantasy/vision of a monstrous flood covering all the low-lying lands between the Alps and the North Sea. When it came to Switzerland the mountains grew higher and higher to protect the country. There were "mighty yellow waves, the floating rubble of civilisation, the drowned bodies of uncounted thousands" and the whole sea turned to blood. On the personal level one could argue that this represents Jung's annihilation of everything alien to him (not-self), including the whole of Freudian psychoanalysis, triggered by his break from and critique of Freud. It could also be seen, on the subjective level, as a vision of the internal flood that he was about to experience (see below).

Individuals often find this profound, annihilatory experience deeply disturbing to the point of feeling they are going mad, and Jung was relieved when he was able to think that his was a premonitionary vision of the First World War rather than a product of his own phantasy (Jung, 1963, p. 200); this was not the first time he resorted to a useful "denial", as I will describe.

This is not to say that it does not represent a massive development (one that Jung did not fully achieve) when the individual has sufficiently worked through the experience of their annihilatory experiences, to have a human-level, aggressive, fight response towards their traumatising objects, as I described in Chapter Ten for Michael. I would suggest that it is precisely this move from a more profoundly traumatised collapse/submit response to be able to mobilise an aggressive, fight response towards the threatening object, that amounts to the struggle for the individual to "use the object" as is described in Winnicott's (1969) classic paper. However to insist on the "projection of your own aggression" interpretation to people who have had experiences such as Jung's, represents a distortion that is only likely to deepen an impasse (see also K's situation described in Chapter Twelve).

It is the experience of being affected so powerfully, as I suggest Jung was, that causes the individual to erect their profound narcissistic defences and to attempt to anticipate and pre-empt what will happen.[7] It is for this reason that "incarnation"—allowing the core self to be affected, and living from the core self—is such a threat to those who have experienced trauma. This is very much true of Jung and perhaps accounts for Winnicott's suggestion that he had not achieved an indwelling "unit status"[8] (see my discussion below of Jung's *Answer to Job* where Christ represents just such an incarnation of God).

Submission

To return to Jung, the question remains of how he managed to negotiate the threat of these potentially overwhelming "unconscious contents". I suggest that it was due to his submission to them, and to the constructive way he was able to position himself in relation to them, engaging with them emotionally and intellectually. I will discuss his submission first before looking at his schizoid defences, followed by an example of his creative/intellectual adaptation as described in the *Red Book*.

I suggest that Jung was able to accept the power of these forces, framing them as outside of himself, and making a positive submission towards them in accordance with the "submit" element of the collapse/ submit response. Being brought up in a religious household—his father being a pastor—offered him a framework in which he could understand his experiences as from, and in relation to, God.[9] As Jung wrote in *Memories, Dreams, Reflections*, "one must be utterly abandoned to God; nothing matters but fulfilling His will" (p. 57).

This voluntary giving up of the identification with the ego and the submission to something other—call it God, the universal mind, or the unconscious self—is central to all direct spiritual experience. Jung was able to make this leap.[10] This is an example of a constructive "use" of the collapse response, which can underlie veneration (Gordon, 1987) and spiritual experience (see Chapters Five and Fifteen). In a fascinating book Tsultrim Allione (2008) describes the ancient Buddhist practice of Chöd, where the individual learns to "feed" the "demons" of which they are terrified, rather than avoiding them—an example of the kind of submission and self-sacrifice I am discussing.

Jung was careful to give responsibility and power for what he experienced to God. When an individual identifies with and takes ownership of such experience for themselves they experience states of inflation; if these identifications become fixed this can develop into psychosis.

I suspect that Jung's submission was also facilitated by the good experience he had had with his father, who was there to respond to him after the "defeat" with his mother—it allowed him to trust that if he "let go" he might be "caught" (though not, of course, without due risk and terror). I suggested in Chapter Five that the lack of such good experience keeps the individual locked in a state of hostile terror towards the uncaring, abandoning world in the form of a borderline personality organisation, whereas those who have had some measure of good experience with a primary caregiver, or at least their availability, even if it was in order to support the caregiver, are more likely to present themselves submissively in a hysteric or a schizoid personality organisation (for the schizoid personality this is more a question of compliance whereas for the hysteric personality it is more a fully fledged self-sacrifice).

It is striking that Jung seems to have taken his father's care for granted (as children often do perhaps), in some ways undervaluing him, and similarly repeated that attitude in relation to Freud, apparently readily falling into the role of "Crown Prince". This has usually been understood in terms of Freud wanting to avoid psychoanalysis being seen as a Jewish domain, but I suspect that Jung's early experience (internal working model) of being the cherished crown prince to his father may have played a part on the personal/relational level in him fitting naturally into that role with Freud. Little wonder perhaps that Freud was so wounded at Jung's "betrayal", fainting on a couple of occasions.

For Jung's part he seems not to have felt understood, not allowed to be himself, and restricted by the petty, narrow, "border guard" Freud, as well as his narrowly religious father, something he rebelled against on all occasions. Clinically, the person who submits to the other person's care and patronage can quickly come to feel taken over, and that the other person is not "getting it right" for them (Jung, 1963, p. 187); in other words, the person discovers that the other is a separate individual who is not doing what the subject wants.

Jung seemingly felt that he surpassed both his father and Freud due to his deeper personal experience holding sway over their belief in a creed, whether that was Christianity for his father, or the central significance of infantile sexuality for Freud.[11] This attitude is intensely alienating to those who do not subscribe to the individual's overt or covert sense of superiority. Jung's inflation in this regard served to deny his attachment to both men and may account for some of the depth of his reaction when his connection to Freud was broken; by which I mean that he was not in touch with the importance of such attachment until it was lost, which made his experience of annihilation more profound.

Schizoid defences and the flight response

I suggest that we need one further element to understand Jung's personality structure and functioning, namely his schizoid defences. The individual for whom the collapse response is primary, as it was for Jung for a while (another example being his fainting reactions in relation to going to school), is left open, exposed, vulnerable, powerless, and passive. It was overhearing his father expressing his concern about his son's ability to earn a living in the future that jolted Jung out of this state and into his other "main" form of defence—his intellectual/schizoid defence.

As Bollas states, the schizoid individual's primary attachment is to their mind, and as Winnicott (1964, p. 453) put it, Jung "went down under and found subjective life". The mind and subjective life are more reliable alternatives to the unreliable parent. Here is a means by which the individual can withdraw in order to limit the impingement on the exposed and traumatised core self. Jung learnt from early on to withdraw from his school fellows to protect himself from their comments and lack of "understanding" for this odd, young Carl, seeing himself as "a solitary"—something that became a lifelong position. I suggest that this is reflected in the figure of the lone crusader, parading unseen through the midday streets of Basel, which was the other half of the dream that relates to his break from the "peevish border guard" Freud (Jung, 1963, pp. 186–190). Jung surely identified with this crusader figure and his quest for the "great secret" that lay behind the Grail stories, which was, "in the deepest sense, my own world, which had scarcely nothing to do with Freud's". He describes this part of the dream with the crusader as "numinous in the extreme" (p. 189).

This reliable mind represented the cornerstone of his intellectual curiosity and prowess, which could come in at times of distress. Jung gave one example of when he was furious at being falsely accused of cheating and describes how "there was a sudden silence, as though a soundproof door had been closed on a noisy room … a mood of cool curiosity came over me" (p. 84). I would suggest these defences are symbolised by the "mountains" that rose up to protect Switzerland from the flood of Jung's vision/phantasy, and the cliffs, upon which the city that housed the tree of life stood in his "Liverpool" dream, as I will shortly explore.

These dual defences—collapse/submit (giving access to the primitive "source") and schizoid/flight—perhaps represent the primitive basis for his number two and number one personalities. This curious, reliable mind was also invaluable in making sense of his confrontation with the unconscious, as I will now describe.

The Red Book—Elijah, Salome and the snake

The "Liber Primus" in the *Red Book* documents Jung's experiences immediately following his break from Freud in 1913. Jung experienced a deep sense of disorientation and had a powerful feeling that "there was something dead present, but it was also still alive" (Jung, 1963, p. 196). This was followed by a dream of sarcophagi (the Egyptian tomb again) where various dead figures, from a nineteenth-century man to a twelfth-century crusader, came alive (p. 197). His disorientation remained and he finally, "consciously submitted [himself] to the impulses of the unconscious" (p. 197). He then allowed himself to return to his childhood play of village building, which was followed by the phantasies/visions of the flood, described above, to which Jung was now to become subject on the internal level.

On 12 December 1913 he was sitting at his desk and he let himself "drop into the depths", whereupon he had a phantasy of a blond-haired corpse floating by, a black scarab, and the red, newborn sun—he understood these as "a hero and solar myth, a drama of death and renewal".[12] This was followed by a dream of Jung and an unknown, brown-skinned man, "a savage", shooting the heroic Siegfried. In the dream Jung was anxious to avoid blame and was relieved when "a tremendous downfall of rain" wiped out all traces of the dead (p. 204).

Jung was clear that this dream represented the heroic idealism of the ego, with which the individual tries to impose their will, having to be abandoned, "for there are higher things than the ego's will, and to these one must bow" (p. 205). Understanding the dream on the personal/objective level Siegfried may easily slip into Sigmund (Freud), and Jung could be seen to be anxious to avoid blame for the oedipal murder of his adoptive father. As I will explore further, in prioritising the collective/archetypal level over the personal level this was never worked through.

The fantasies then continued, significantly, with Jung encountering Elijah, Salome, and a black snake, then a figure he called Philemon who became his primary guide and taught him many things (pp. 203–210). The figure of Salome, who is at first blind, is particularly significant as Salome inveigled her father, Herod, into cutting off John the Baptist's head (the decapitation of the ego[13]); Jung writes, "a thinker should fear Salome, since she wants his head, especially if he is a holy man" (Jung, 2009, p. 248).

In the *Red Book*, in the section entitled "Resolution" (ibid., pp. 251ff.), which is the conclusion of the first part of the book ("Liber Primus"), Jung finds Christ in his last hours on the cross. A black snake is at the foot of the cross and it wraps itself around Jung, "squeezing [his] body in its terrible coils" in a position that parallel's Christ's crucifixion, until blood "streams down [his] body". This blood—Jung's suffering and sacrifice (?)—cures Salome of her blindness. Jung then "kneel[s] at the feet of the prophet [Elijah], whose form shines like a flame", and the prophet tells him that his "work is fulfilled here" (ibid., p. 252).

I suggest that here, at the heart of Jung's most profound personal experiences, the themes of the phallus dream are repeated, with Jung surrounded by the symbols of death and rebirth, the defeat of the ego (killing Siegfried, and the presence of the blind Salome), and his sub-mission to both more primitive (the snake) and more spiritual (Elijah) forces. Whilst there is an identification with Christ (an inflation), he is also at pains to resist the inflation as, in the next section, while Elijah transforms into a huge flame of white light, Jung "hurries out into the night, like one who has no part in the glory of the mystery" (p. 252). This sequence also shows the potentially creative and healing aspect of this contact with primal forces (Salome's sight is restored), symbolising perhaps that the sacrifice of the ego (Jung's "crucifixion") is now not being done blindly.[14]

Internal working models

Whilst I have largely explored Jung's early life in terms of his primitive defensive reactions to his mother's unavailability, we can also look at how it was structured by his internal working models (another aspect of the traumatic complex). So, just as Jung's mother was deep and other-worldly and was at times withdrawn and rejecting of the young Carl and his father, so this "way of being with others" (Stern) seems to have characterised Jung's peer relationships throughout his life, whether that was with his schoolmates, in his marriage (of which more below), or in his professional life—withdrawing to a "Jungian" enclave.

Reading the opening chapters of his autobiography, I was struck a number of times by how warmly he speaks of his father, describing him on one occasion as "my dear and generous father, who in so many matters left me to myself and had never tyrannized over me" (1963, p. 73). I wonder if this internal working model is reflected in his manner with patients, treating them as individuals in their own right, worthy of respect and being taken seriously, with their concerns having meaning that he was happy to discuss and explore with them.

I note too, the patient to whom he was happy to sing a lullaby, which had such a powerful effect on her (Dunne, 2000, p. 94); this reminds me of his father singing to him at night when he had eczema, or holding him while he had a choking fit. I have already discussed, above, how his relationship with his father may have set a template for his relationship with Freud; I will explore his relationship with his wife below.

The dream of the tree of life in Liverpool

Many of these themes are present in the dream Jung had in 1927 of the tree of life in Liverpool, which also, I suggest, gives us an insight into what Jung was not able to integrate and work through.

In the dream he was in Liverpool, a "dirty, sooty city", it was "night, and winter, and dark, and raining". He was with a number of Swiss companions and they climbed from the harbour up "the alley of the dead" to the clifftop city on the plateau (reminding him of Basel). On the plateau was a dimly lit, broad square, with the various quarters of the city arranged radially around the square. "In the centre was a round pool, and in the middle of it a small island. While everything round about was obscured by rain, fog, smoke and dimly lit darkness, the little island blazed with sunlight. On it stood a single tree, a magnolia, in a shower of reddish blossoms. It was as though the tree stood in the sunlight and was at the same time the source of light". His companions commented on the abominable weather and did not see the tree. They expressed surprise that another Swiss had chosen to settle there, whilst Jung thought that he knew very well why he had done so (Jung, 1963, p. 223).

Jung suggests that, "the liver, according to an old view, is the seat of life—that which 'makes to live' … [and was] why [he] was able to live at all" at a time when everything was "extremely unpleasant, black and opaque" (p. 224). However, I would also point out that the liver is the organ that processes the blood from the stomach, breaking down, balancing, and creating nutrients for the body to use, whilst getting rid of harmful substances—a pretty good symbol for the process of digesting and integrating experience. I would suggest then that, whilst the dream may offer us some universal insights into the role of the self, it also offers us a good portrayal of Jung's struggles and state of mind. So, whilst Jung writes, "I saw that here the goal had been revealed. One could not go beyond the centre. The centre is the goal, and everything is directed towards that centre. Through this dream I understood that the self is the principle and archetype of orientation and meaning" (ibid., p. 224), I would suggest that it tells us more.

Jung had been able to access the "real city" of his core self, which is perched on its rocky, schizoid defences. He has done this by ascending via the "alley of the dead"—the death of the ego—to discover the tree of life—the self. He had chosen to settle near to this source, like the Swiss in the dream, whilst his companions, with their man-in-the-street (ego) perspective, only saw the abominable weather; and Jung tells us that his life was bleak at this time.

It is not clear what he was referring to when he writes that everything was "extremely unpleasant" at that time; however, the dream describes it, symbolically, as being dirty, sooty, night, winter, dark, and raining, with everything around obscured by rain, fog, smoke, and dim light. These are surely depressive feelings, but to what might they refer? I would suggest that on one level they refer to his early experiences of cold/winter (emotional coldness), smoke (breathing difficulties), rain (tears), fog (confusion), and the generally dirty, sooty/shitty feelings relating to the separation from his mother.

I suggest that in the everyday world (the objective level), Jung struggled with re-experiencing, and being "subject" to powerlessness, unwantedness, and abandonment—the direct experience of the trauma—but instead stayed in an identification with the aggressor (the reversed form), being the one who left his wife Emma feeling unwanted.[15] It was Emma who had to experience the feelings of loss and rejection, whilst he flew close to the wind (and beyond) with Sabina Spielrein (Bair, 2003, ch. 11), flirted with other women, taking Toni Wolf as his long-standing companion (ibid., ch. 14) (mirroring the mother and maid split), or withdrew to his lakeside retreat; Emma threatened to divorce him three times.

And yet, unless you really face the traumatic experiences and work them through, the interim solutions are not satisfactory and the original situations keep re-presenting themselves. For example, we know that Jung considered "letting himself drown" one day, while swimming in the lake, when he felt overwhelmed by his inability to ensure that both his wife and Toni Wolff felt equally respected (ibid., p. 266); similarly

Toni Wolff was herself replaced by Marie Louise von Franz (Bair, 2003, pp. 368ff.). Perhaps the only compensation was to withdraw to live nearby to the tree of life, yet the dream points out its situation on a rocky, smoky, cold, rainy, clifftop plateau, drawing attention to the costs of such a choice, with a split between what his Swiss, man-in-the-street companions could see and what Jung could see.

Or, from another perspective, Jung's early deprivation was expressed, as is typically the case, in idealisation and the search for idealised, numinous states of loving at-one-ment, or in affairs. Writing to Freud, Jung said that he had great difficulty in getting his wife, whom he was analysing, to accept his "polygamous components": "Analysis of one's spouse is one of the more difficult things unless mutual freedom is assured. The prerequisite for a good marriage, it seems to me, is the license to be unfaithful" (Freud & Jung, 1974, p. 289).

Keeping it transpersonal

It is clear that Jung's experiences after his break from Freud were not solely about that break, but were also about reworking old, early, traumatic experiences (the "return from the dead"), as well as the "solutions" that they proffered—the power from the severed phallus, the upwelling of lava from the core of the personality, and immersion in the sameness-recognising (symmetrising) functioning of the unconscious/ core self that gives the individual's experience a numinous, impersonal, transpersonal, collective quality (as if their experience applies to all mankind rather than just the individual themselves—see Chapter Eight).

Jung had outlined the different levels on which symbols can apply— the objective, subjective, transference, and archetypal levels—yet when it came to his own dreams and life experience he preferenced the subjective and collective/archetypal levels over the personal and transference levels. The shadow side to this attitude is that when you move away from the ego you move away from the personal level where these issues also need to be worked through; as a result the individual can get stuck on the transpersonal level.

Yet it is clear that this was a very conscious choice for Jung, who thought he had the solution to Freud's reducing everything to the infantile level. Writing in the chapter "The Sacrifice" (Jung, 1911/12), which he said he knew would "cost him his friendship with Freud"

(Jung, 1963, p. 191) (and before his personal experiences documented in the *Red Book*), Jung directly challenges the significance of, and regression to, infantile experience, suggesting instead that the ego needs to be sacrificed in order to free the individual from the mother. He wrote:

> Christ's teaching means ruthlessly separating a man from his family … namely that of freeing man from his family fixations, from his weakness and uncontrolled infantile feelings. For if he allows his libido to get stuck in a childish milieu, *and does not free it for higher purposes*, he falls under the spell of unconscious compulsion. Wherever he may be, the unconscious will then recreate the infantile milieu by projecting his complexes, thus reproducing all over again, and in defiance of his vital interests, the same dependence and lack of freedom which formerly characterized his relations with his parents. His destiny no longer lies in his own hands … (Jung, 1911/12, para. 644, my italics)

I would suggest that as Jung did not also work through these complexes on the personal, ego level, he exactly reproduced the infantile milieu himself and was indeed subject to it, whilst taking himself to be free.

In summary

Working through a traumatic complex involves embracing both sides of the traumatic experience—the internal working models in direct and reversed forms—a coming to terms with the traumatic experience itself (being subject to it in direct form) and the way the individual may be re-enacting the trauma on others (reversed form). This means achieving some kind of acceptance of the reality of the experiences, against the great pressures and defences to move away from them into an idealised,[16] other world (the luminous tree in the clifftop city). Early traumatic experiences were originally unbearable and, in so far as they haven't been worked on, they remain so. The process requires working on what feels impossible.

It was on the subjective/archetypal level that Jung elaborately re-experienced the defeat of his ego as described in *Memories, Dreams, Reflections* and, in detail, in the *Red Book*. As I have partially described already, starting his journey being despised and rejected (Jung, 2009, p. 229), reaching out to his soul, and finding it in a barren, "desert" state

(p. 235), he prepares for sacrifice and to follow "the spirit of the depths" (p. 234), killing off the hero (the Siegfried dream), sacrificing thought and control, foregoing vanity and cleverness, and trusting to follow the soul even if it leads him through madness (p. 238). Following this sacrifice, his path reveals certain wisdom to him through the appearance of and engagement with Elijah, Salome, the snake, and numerous other figures.

Although, whilst not without great difficulty and courage, Jung did bear this sacrifice of the ego, this is different from when such a defeat is inflicted upon you on the objective/personal level—having to deal with the depressive feelings relating to not getting an ideal, conflict-free relationship and having to experience frustration and deprivation, things that are inevitably a part of any relationship.

As a result of not working through his difficulties on the personal level, including with Freud, Jung lived a significantly solitary existence, continuing not to feel understood or accepted by the generality, and struggling to form close friendships. For this he turned to his long-standing rationalisations that this was his path and that people couldn't or wouldn't understand him; although, of course, this expectation would have fitted in with his early experience of not being heard by his mother as she shut herself in her room for weeks on end. Perhaps having experienced this long-term exclusion on the professional front it was too tempting to be offered the opportunity to be an insider for a time, and thus he accepted a post as president of a professional society from the German (Nazi) regime.

It could be argued that Jung being unable to bear and struggle with these issues on the everyday level led to many of the accusations that have been levelled against him (his shadow): that of being a womaniser, a mystic, being obscure, trying to form a religion with him as cult-leader, being anti-Semitic and a Nazi sympathiser (Bair, 2003, pp. ix–x).

Characteristically Jung does describe exactly the kind of struggle that I envisage, but it is between Job and God in Jung's (1952) essay "Answer to Job".[17] In it, Jung declares that whilst Job recognises his inferior position in relation to God, God is forced to recognise Job's integrity, and that this initiates a process of transformation in God that eventually leads to His incarnation as Jesus. God as Jesus, of course, experienced exactly the *human* incarnation, including suffering, rejection, and eventual crucifixion, that I am questioning whether Jung was able to achieve. As I have mentioned, this difficulty in incarnation on the human/personal level may be what Winnicott means by Jung not having achieved an indwelling "unit self".

In Jung's "defence", I would suggest that he was "simply" reconstructing and re-enacting his early patterns of experience, which are what feel most real and most true to the individual. To work through the unbearable early traumas without an analyst (capable of understanding) would have been a real feat, especially when he could transpose the battles on to the subjective and archetypal levels. That he did not achieve this on the objective, everyday, ego-level is a loss however—to him personally (if I can be allowed to wish that for someone else and their family) and to some aspects of Jungian theory.

However, as many people have frequently observed, both he and Freud were pioneers and it would be wholly unrealistic to expect them to have successfully explored their whole territory, and each other's, thoroughly. That they were not able to achieve more mutual understanding, accommodation, and theoretical reconciliation is a great shame as their theories, one centring on the ego, the other on the unconscious/self, clearly have the potential to enrich each another.

My main criticism of Jung's theorising is that he did not realise that the necessary disidentification from the ego, made so natural for him by his own ego's early defeat, is only an interim stage in the process of the individual coming to broaden the way they see themselves in an expanded but personal form of ego. This would include recognising their non-ego experience, continuing to be open to it, and being flexible enough to integrate it. This is what I have described as broad and flexible ego-functioning (West, 2007, 2008, and Chapter Eight in this book). There is nothing intrinsically narrow or problematic about the ego, neither is there anything unimpeachably sacrosanct or correct about the wisdom of the unconscious—both need to be seen in the light of the other.[18]

A good deal of the sense of rightness associated with the core/archetypal level comes when current experience mirrors early experience. Hence, for Jung the defeat of his ego seemed, on the deepest level, "right", whilst for others, being unloved may seem "right" (as well as terribly wrong). In addition, the powerful and potentially overwhelming nature of non-ego experience—the experience from the perspective of the core self—is compelling (Chapter Eight). Thus the ego lends sobriety and "depressing" reality-orientedness, whilst the unconscious/self lends intoxication, inflation, insight, and inspiration. The personality is in dynamic process and both poles will come into play. In other words, things emerge from the unconscious, brimming with power, novelty, joy, and excitement, or sometimes, terror, anxiety, horror, and dread, that, over time, will need to be incorporated into the way we see ourselves and behave.

Emergent archetypes and reductionism

I hope it will be clear from what I am saying that this is not an attempt to "reduce" Jung's experience to early relational trauma,[19] but rather to show the way that early relational trauma deeply structures our psyche and therefore our life experience—it is the stuff of which we are made. Working through the traumatic complexes allows the individual to disidentify from the traumatic experiences and thus experience themselves more broadly and inclusively, to engage with the world in more varied forms (vulnerable, creative, aggressive etc., etc.), and in a more reality-oriented way.

I would also suggest that the internal working models I have described represent the earliest patterns of behaviour that constitute archetypal patterning as described by Jung. As I explored in Chapter Six, this is an understanding of archetypes as emergent, emerging from the individual's particular experience, that may be similar for many individuals though not necessarily universal (Hogenson, 2001; Knox, 2001, 2003a; Saunders & Skar 2001). In other words, not everyone shares Jung's early experience but many have experienced something significantly similar.

Jung's early experience elucidates the archetypal patterning of death (of the ego) and rebirth particularly clearly. When he describes "his myth" he was thereby describing the patterns of being that felt natural and right to him—a recapitulation of his childhood experiences: "[his] life [as] the story of the self realisation of the unconscious" (Jung, 1963, p.17)—an unconscious structured by these internal working models.

Notes

1. Bair reports that on the way to stay with his aunt his father repeatedly told him that his mother "love[d] him" and would return soon (Bair, 2003, p. 21).
2. "Spread out thy wings, Lord Jesus mild / And take to thee thy chick, thy child / If Satan would devour it / No harm shall overpower it / So let the angels sing!" (Jung, 1963 p. 24).

3. The term phallus has an extra level of symbolic meaning, relating for example to potency and creativity, from/to the word penis.
4. Quoted in Feldman (1992, p. 266).
5. Curiously, Jung (1911–12, para. 619) himself argues that a parallel symbol symbolises the individual staying in the mother's womb. Whilst he takes himself to be arguing for the sacrificial death of the ego and leaving mother, contra Freud, I wonder if he does not achieve that himself.
6. Jung called this *participation mystique* (see West, 2014).
7. I would also suggest that Winnicott's understanding of the individual "taking an experience into their sphere of omnipotence" (1953, 1974) is essentially the process of adaptation and accommodation to outer experience that is part of the individual's attempt to anticipate future experience and master their compulsively repeated trauma, as explored in Chapter Four.
8. Fascinatingly, Sedgwick (2008) and Meredith-Owen (2011, 2015) explore Winnicott's own three-part dream, dreamt whilst working on his review of *Memories, Dreams, Reflections*, of the absolute destruction of the world and of all people, followed by absolute destruction where he (Winnicott) was the destructive agent, then of waking up (in the dream) and knowing that he had dreamt the other two parts. This is itself a perfect dream example of annihilation through a collapse response that is then dreamt in reversed mode, followed by awareness (integration/mastery) of both polarities of the experience. This is not the place to embark on an exploration of Winnicott's psychology(!), although Sedgwick and Meredith-Owen have both made illuminating comments on the links between the two men, including recognising Winnicott's ongoing psychological struggles and his fantasy that his head needed to be split open and something removed—the dissociative split not reached in either of his analyses—that it took working on his review of *Memories, Dreams, Reflections* to reach.
9. Religions frequently perform this invaluable function in helping an individual organise and make sense of such supra-ego experiences.
10. An early experience of trauma, where the individual is left working on the experience of the core self/non-ego experience is almost a characteristic of the early lives of saints. St. Thérèse of Lisieux, for example, was separated from her mother soon after her birth until she was fifteen months old. She went on to develop what she called "the little way", recognising her smallness and limitations; in this she attempted in all ways to "strip herself of self" (Thérèse of Lisieux, 1972).
11. It may well be that his father's speaking from a position of faith rather than direct spiritual experience was one of the reasons that Jung associated him with "powerlessness", as he did not share in the power

afforded by the numinous mysteries and experiences of the core self, which Jung had experienced, as I have been discussing and as demonstrated by the phallus dream.

12. The account of these experiences were written out in the *Black Book* and later copied into the *Red Book* in an intense period between 12 November 1913 and 19 April 1914.

13. This fantasy echoed the headless figure that emerged from his mother's bedroom door at the height of his disturbance in relation to her (when he had the coughing fits). He described a "faintly luminous, indefinite figure whose head detached itself from the neck and floated along in front of it, in the air, like a little moon. Immediately another head was produced and again detached itself" (Jung, 1963, p. 33).

14. A not dissimilar transformation goes on in relation to the thrice-repeated vision of the flood whereby, at the end of the third "dream", a leaf-bearing tree (which Jung links to the tree of life) has leaves that have been transformed by the effects of the frost into sweet grapes full of healing juices, which he plucked and gave to the crowd (Jung, 1963, pp. 199–200). The freezing (which controlled the flood), like the constriction of Jung by the snake, has wrought a healing transformation.

15. In the word association tests he undertook with Binswanger his complexes around money, power, ambition, sex, and divorce came out clearly (Bair, 2003, ch. 8)—he was someone who wanted to call the shots.

16. My understanding of idealised experience is that it is not "imaginary" but requires very particular, "ideal" circumstances under which it can be achieved—see Chapter Nine.

17. Job's life is an excellent description of the schizoid individual's journey from unreal "goodness", to grounded, fruitful, reality (see Newton (1993), West (2007, ch. 10)).

18. Kalsched (2013, ch. 8) puts forward a lucid description of a traditional view of the relationship between ego and self, different to the one I am describing here, closer to Jung's own understanding.

19. Jung wrote, for instance (arguing against Freud), "There is absolutely no point in everlastingly reducing all the finest strivings of the soul back to the womb. It is a gross technical blunder because, instead of promoting, it destroys psychological understanding" ... "the real issue is the moral achievement of the whole personality" (Jung 1921/1928, paras. 279 & 281).

CHAPTER NINETEEN

Summary and conclusion—emerging from trauma and returning to everyday life

D o we need to go into the darkest places? I know of no one who hasn't challenged this at some point in the analysis, including me as the analyst. When I am in the role of analyst (rather than that of patient), I travel hopefully—"perhaps it won't be necessary this time …"—yet I have found time and again that the person's psyche is intent on taking us there and I have come to appreciate the wisdom in that. As Jung writes:

> a complex can be really overcome only if it is lived out to the full. In other words, if we are to develop further, we have to draw to us and drink down to the very dregs what, because of our complexes, we have held at a distance. (Jung, 1938/1954, pp. 96–99)

This point is reinforced by Winnicott who writes: "… there is no end unless the bottom of the trough has been reached, unless *the thing feared has been experienced*" (1974, p. 105, original italics).

Vitally, when patient and analyst live through the later version of the original relational trauma, something is freed up and the analysis moves on. I have known many people who have had an apparently successful analysis, but their core relational traumas have been inadequately addressed and they have come to haunt the individual, in one form or another, later on. I have conducted such analyses myself and realise that I have sadly let those patients down. Developing the individual's ego-functioning is a necessary part of working things through, but it is not sufficient.

Working through the traumatic complex

The experience and consequences of early relational trauma are power-fully amplified due to the fact that in (understandably) avoiding the truly unbearable experience of the trauma that is at the core of their being, the individual is also alienated from the core of their self. Trauma becomes soul-murder (Shengold, 1975; Wirtz, 2014). To the extent that the individual cannot bear to be themselves and has to avoid everyday life in order to prevent being retraumatised, they are alienated from real life as-it-is. Or, to make a parallel point, the disruption of their ego-functioning due to the trauma has meant that they are not only ill-equipped to face reality, but that they have also lost a rooted sense of themselves from which to do so. The quotes from Jung and Winnicott above thus hold deep truths.

The traumatic experience is able to be borne, and the traumatic com-plex worked through, by analyst and patient addressing the trauma, the primitive defences against it, and the trauma-related internal work-ing models on all levels and in direct and reversed forms, including the way they have become embodied in both the patient, the analyst, and the analytic relationship. This amounts to a significant develop-ment and broadening of both individuals' identities, as they come to be able to recognise, bear, and integrate feelings of loss, abuse, shame, fragmentation, failure, death, and despair (to name just a few of the likely experiences and affects).

This is the integration of the different affects and experiences that Jung spoke of when he wrote the following, challenging Freud's meth-ods: "the essential factor is the dissociation of the psyche and not the existence of a highly charged affect and, consequently, the main thera-peutic problem is not abreaction, but how to integrate the dissociation" (Jung, 1921/1928, para 266).

In fact, I think Jung and Freud were both right, and that the highly charged affect is a significant factor, as expressed in the power of the affects that disrupt the individual somatically, emotionally, and cognitively, as well as the moral charge and woundedness that binds the individual to the traumatic experience.

As these different elements are integrated and the affective charge lessens, the individual can begin to be released from the wheel of torture that was the trauma, to disidentify from the trauma, and to identify more broadly with other aspects of their identity. As their ego-functioning develops they are able to focus on "more important things" in their lives and get over new woundings more easily due to a different focus. Most importantly their sense of self-agency develops. A benevolent cycle can then hopefully take hold, with the individual developing their sense of effectiveness and becoming more able to recover from the inevitable setbacks that will still occur.

In integrating their early traumatic experiences these individuals have had to come to terms with the fact that they have been indelibly affected and altered by them, and they have had to find a place for these experiences, and their reactions to them, within themselves. However, they are no longer conflicted and alienated from themselves, they have an integrity and a depth of experience, character, and perspective that is uncommon and, quite frankly, impressive.

The analyst's task in orienting the individual towards facing their traumatic experiences and accompanying them on their journey, and by their involvement themselves *becoming* part of that journey, is invaluable. As Anne Alvarez writes of her work with children, "when a child sees that someone other than himself *gets it*, as it were, I think we do witness the 'dyadically expanded states of consciousness' which Tronick describes (Tronick et al., 1998)" (Alvarez, 2010, p. 871); or, to paraphrase Daniel Stern (1985/1998, p. 32), to know that someone is intent on knowing you as you really are offers the most profound experience of being understood and accepted. For their part, the analyst, in being challenged to face, embody, and use the most primitive aspects of their personality and, indeed, to engage their whole self, is also enlivened, enriched, and encouraged to be real. I know of no greater experience that one person can have with another.

REFERENCES

Addenbrooke, M. (2011). *Survivors of Addiction: Narratives of Recovery.* Hove: Routledge.

Ainsworth, M., Blehar, M., Waters, E., & Wall, S. (1978). *Patterns of Attachment: A Psychological Study of the Strange Situation.* Hillsdale, NJ: Erlbaum.

Allione, T. (2009). *Feeding Your Demons: Ancient Wisdom for Resolving Inner Conflict.* London: Hay House.

Alvarez, A. (2010). Levels of analytic work and levels of pathology: The work of calibration. *The International Journal of Psychoanalysis, 91*: 859–878.

American Psychiatric Association (1980). *Diagnostic and Statistical Manual of Mental Disorders* (3rd ed.). Washington, DC: Author.

Anderson, F. S. (2007). *Bodies in Treatment: The Unspoken Dimension.* New York: The Analytic Press.

Anderson, F. S., & Sherman, E. (2013). *Pathways to Pain Relief.* CreateSpace Independent Publishing Platform.

Aron, L. (2006). Analytic impasse and the third. *International Journal of Psychoanalysis, 87*: 349–368.

Astor, J. (2002). Analytical psychology and its relation to psychoanalysis. *Journal of Analytical Psychology, 47*: 599–612.

Astor, J. (2004). Response to Dr. Britton's paper. *Journal of Analytical Psychology, 49*: 491–493.

Astor, J. (2007). Fordham, feeling, and countertransference: Reflections on defences of the self. *Journal of Analytical Psychology*, 52: 185–205.

Atwood, G., & Stolorow, R. (1977). Metapsychology, reification and the representational world of C. G. Jung. *International Review of Psychoanalysis*, 4: 197–213.

Bair, D. (2003). *Jung: A Biography*. Boston, MA: Little, Brown.

Balint, E. (1991). One analyst's technique. In: *Before I was I: Psychoanalysis and the Imagination* (pp. 120–129). London: Free Association, 1993.

Balint, M. (1968). *The Basic Fault*. London: Tavistock.

Beebe, B., & Lachmann, F. (2002). *Infant Research and Adult Treatment: Co-constructing Interactions*. Hillsdale, NJ: Analytic Press.

Beebe, B., & Lachmann, F. (2013). *The Origins of Attachment: Infant Research and Adult Treatment*. Abingdon: Taylor & Francis.

Benjamin, J. (1988). *The Bonds of Love: Psychoanalysis, Feminism, and the Problem of Domination*. New York: Pantheon.

Benjamin, J. (1998). *Shadow of the Other: Intersubjectivity and Gender in Psychoanalysis*. New York & London: Routledge.

Benjamin, J. (2004). Beyond doer and done to: An intersubjective view of thirdness. *Psychoanalytic Quarterly*, 73: 5–46.

Bion, W. R. (1959). Attacks on linking. *International Journal of Psychoanalysis*, 40: 308–315. Reprinted In: *Second Thoughts* (pp. 93–109). New York: Jason Aronson, 1967.

Bion, W. R. (1962a). *Learning from Experience*. London: Heinemann.

Bion, W. R. (1962b). The psycho-analytic study of thinking. *International Journal of Psychoanalysis*, 43: 306–310.

Bion, W. R. (1965). *Transformations: Change from Learning to Growth*. London: Tavistock.

Bion, W. R. (1970). *Attention and Interpretation*. Oxford: Routledge.

Bion, W. R. (1992). *Cogitations*. London: Karnac.

Bohleber, W. (2007). Remembrance, trauma and collective memory. *International Journal of Psychoanalysis*, 88: 329–352.

Bohleber, W. (2010). *Destructiveness, Intersubjectivity and Trauma: The Identity Crisis of Modern Psychoanalysis*. London: Karnac.

Bollas, C. (1987). *The Shadow of the Object: Psychoanalysis of the Unthought Known*. New York: Columbia University Press.

Bollas, C. (2000). *Hysteria*. Abingdon: Taylor & Francis.

Boon, S., Steele, K., & van der Hart, O. (2011). *Coping with Trauma-Related Dissociation: Skills Training for Patients and Therapists*. New York: Norton.

Boston Change Process Study Group (BCPSG) [Stern, D. N., Sander, L. W., Nahum, J. P., Harrison, A. M., Lyons-Ruth, K., Morgan, A.

C., Bruschweilerstern, N., & Tronick, E. Z.] (1998). Non-interpretive mechanisms in psychoanalytic therapy: the "something more" than interpretation. *International Journal of Psychoanalysis, 79*: 903–921. Reprinted In: Boston Change Process Study Group. *Change in Psychotherapy: A Unifying Paradigm.* New York: Norton, 2010.

Boston Change Process Study Group (BCPSG) (2007). The foundational level of psychodynamic meaning: implicit process in relation to conflict, defense, and the dynamic unconscious. *International Journal of Psychoanalysis, 88*: 843–860. Reprinted in: Boston Change Process Study Group. *Change in Psychotherapy: A Unifying Paradigm.* New York: Norton, 2010.

Bouchard, M., Normandin, L., & Séguin, M. (1995). Countertransference as instrument and obstacle: a comprehensive and descriptive framework. *Psychoanalytic Quarterly, 64*: 717–745.

Bowlby, J. (1969). *Attachment and Loss, Volume 1: Attachment.* Harmondsworth: Penguin Books.

Bremner, J. D. (1999). Acute and chronic responses to psychological trauma: Where do we go from here? *American Journal of Psychiatry, 156*: 349–351.

Bretherton, I. (1991). Pouring new wine into old bottles: the social self as internal working model. In: M. R. Gunnar & L. A. Sroufe (Eds.), *Self Processes and Development: Minesota Symposia on Child Psychology*, vol. 23 (pp. 1–41). Hillsdale, NJ: Erlbaum.

Brett, E. A. (1996). The classification of posttraumatic stress disorder. In: A. C. McFarlane, L. Weisaeth & B. A. Van der Kolk (Eds.), *Traumatic Stress: The Effects of Overwhelming Experience on Mind, Body, and Society* (pp. 117–128). New York: Guilford Press.

Breuer, J., & Freud, S. (1893). On the psychical mechanism of hysterical phenomena. *Studies on Hysteria, S. E., 2*: 1–17. London: Hogarth.

Britton, R. (1989). The missing link: parental sexuality in the Oedipus complex. In: R. Britton, M. Feldman, & E. O'Shaughnessy (Eds.), *The Oedipus Complex Today: Clinical Implications.* London: Karnac.

Britton, R. (1998). Subjectivity, objectivity and triangular space. In: *Belief and Imagination: Explorations in Psychoanalysis* (pp. 41–58). Hove: Routledge.

Britton, R. (2003). *Sex, Death, and the Superego: Experiences in Psychoanalysis.* London: Karnac.

Britton, R. (2004). Narcissistic disorders in clinical practice. *Journal of Analytical Psychology, 49*: 477–490.

Bromberg, P. (2011). *The Shadow of the Tsunami: and the Growth of the Relational Mind.* New York: Routledge.

Bucci, W. (1993). The development of emotional meaning in free association. In: J. Gedo & A. Wilson (Eds.), *Hierarchical Conceptions in Psychoanalysis* (pp. 3–47). New York: Guilford Press.

Bucci, W. (2011). The interplay of subsymbolic and symbolic processes in psychoanalytic treatment: it takes two to tango—but who knows the steps, who's the leader? The choreography of the psychoanalytic interchange. *Psychoanalytic Dialogues, 21*: 45–54.

Bureau, J.-F., Martin, J., & Lyons-Ruth, K. (2010). Attachment dysregulation as hidden trauma in infancy: early stress, maternal buffering and psychiatric morbidity in young adulthood. In: R. Lanius, E. Vermetten & C. Pain (Eds.), *The Impact of Early Life Trauma on Health and Disease: The Hidden Epidemic* (pp. 48–56). Cambridge: Cambridge University Press.

Caper, R. (1992/1999). Does psychoanalysis heal? A contribution to the theory of psychoanalytic technique. *International Journal of Psychoanalysis, 73*: 283–292. Reprinted and revised in: R. Caper, *A Mind of One's Own: A Psychoanalytic View of Self and Object* (pp. 19–31). Abingdon: Taylor & Francis, 1999.

Caper, R. (1995/1999). On the difficulty of making a mutative interpretation. *International Journal of Psychoanalysis, 76*: 91–101. Reprinted and revised in: R., Caper, *A Mind of One's Own: A Psychoanalytic View of Self and Object* (pp. 32–44). Abingdon: Taylor & Francis, 1999.

Caper, R. (1999). *A Mind of One's Own: A Psychoanalytic View of Self and Object.* Abingdon: Taylor & Francis.

Carter, L. (2011). A Jungian contribution to a dynamic systems understanding of disorganized attachment. *Journal of Analytical Psychology, 56*: 334–340.

Carvalho, R. (2007). Response to Astor's Paper. *Journal of Analytical Psychology, 52*: 233–235.

Carvalho, R. (2013). A vindication of Jung's unconscious and its archetypal expression: Jung, Bion, and Matte Blanco. In: A. Cavalli, L. Hawkins & M. Stevns (Eds.), *Transformation: Jung's Legacy and Clinical Work Today* (pp. 31–58). London: Karnac.

Casement, P. J. (1985). *On Learning from the Patient.* Hove: Routledge.

Casement, P. J. (2001). Commentaries. *Journal of the American Psychoanalytic Association, 49*: 381–386.

Cassidy, J. (2008). The nature of the child's ties. In: J. Cassidy & P. R. Shaver (Eds.), *Handbook of Attachment: Theory, Research, and Clinical Applications* (pp. 3–22). New York: Guilford Press.

Cassidy, J., & Mohr, J. J. (2001). Unsolvable fear, trauma and psychopathology: theory, research and clinical considerations related to disorganized attachment across the life cycle. *Clinical Psychology: Science and Practice, 8*: 275–298.

Cicchetti, D., Rogosch, F. A., & Toth, S. L. (2000). The efficacy of toddler-parent psychotherapy for fostering cognitive development in offspring of depressed mothers. *Journal of Abnormal Child Psychology, 28*: 135–148.

Cicchetti, D., & Walker, E. F. (2001). Editorial: Stress and development: Biological and psychological consequences. *Development and Psychopathology, 13*: 413–418.

Clarke, D. D. (2007). *They Can't Find Anything Wrong!: 7 Keys to Understanding, Treating, and Healing Stress Illness*. Boulder, CO: Sentient Publications.

Cocks, G. (2002). Heinz Kohut: The making of a psychoanalyst. *Journal of the American Psychoanalytic Association, 50*: 1385–1390.

Colman, W. (2003). Interpretation and relationship: ends or means? In: R. Withers (Ed.), *Controversies in Analytical Psychology* (pp. 352–365). Hove: Brunner-Routledge.

Colman, W. (2013). Bringing it all back home: how I became a relational analyst. *Journal of Analytical Psychology, 58*: 470–490.

Coltart, N. (1986). Slouching towards Bethlehem ... or thinking the unthinkable in psychoanalysis. In: G. Kohon (Ed.), *The British School of Psychoanalysis: The Independent Tradition* (pp. 185–199). New Haven, CT: Yale University Press. Also in: Coltart, N., *Slouching Towards Bethlehem ... and Further Psychoanalytic Explorations* (pp. 1–14). London: Free Association, 1993.

Courtois, C. (2010). *Healing the Incest Wound: Adult Survivors in Therapy* (2nd ed). New York: Norton.

Crandell, L. E., & Hobson, R. P. (1999). Individual differences in young children's IQ: A social-developmental perspective. *Journal of Child Psychology and Psychiatry, 40*: 455–464.

Damasio, A. (1995). *Descartes' Error: Emotion, Reason, and the Human Brain*. New York: Avon Books.

Damasio, A. (1999). *The Feeling of What Happens: Body, Emotion and the Making of Consciousness*. London: Vintage.

Darwin, C. (1872). *The Expression of Emotions in Man and Animals*. London: John Murray.

Davies, J. M. (1997). Dissociation, therapeutic enactment, and transference–countertransference processes: A discussion of papers on childhood sexual abuse by S. Grand and J. Sarnat. *Gender and Psychoanalysis, 2*: 241–257.

Davies, J. M. (2004). Whose bad objects are we anyway? *Psychoanalytic Dialogues, 14*: 711–732.

Davies, J. M., & Frawley, M. G. (1992a). Dissociative processes and transference-countertransference paradigms in the psychoanalytically oriented treatment of adult survivors of childhood sexual abuse. *Psychoanalytic Dialogues, 2*: 5–36.

Davies, J. M., & Frawley, M. G. (1992b). Reply to Gabbard, Shengold and Grotstein. *Psychoanalytic Dialogues, 2*: 77–96.

Davies, J. M., & Frawley, M. G. (1994). *Treating the Adult Survivor of Childhood Sexual Abuse: A Psychoanalytic Perspective*. London: Harper Collins.

Dunne, C. (2000). *Jung, Wounded Healer of the Soul*. London: Continuum.

Edinger, E. (1972). *Ego and Archetype: Individuation and the Religious Function of the Psyche*. Boston, MA: Shambhala.

Ellenberger, H. F. (1970). *The History of the Unconscious: The History and Evolution of Dynamic Psychiatry*. New York: Basic.

Fabricius, J. (1976). *Alchemy: The Mediaeval Alchemists and their Royal Art*. London: Aquarian Press.

Feldman, B. (1992). Jung's infancy and childhood and its influence upon the development of analytical psychology. *Journal of Analytical Psychology, 37*: 255–274.

Feldman, M. (2008). Grievance: The underlying oedipal configuration. *International Journal of Psychoanalysis, 89*: 743–758.

Ferenczi, S. (1932a). Confusion of tongues between adults and the child. In: M. Balint (Ed.), E. Mosbacher and others (Trans), *Final Contributions to the Problems and Methods of Psycho-analysis* (pp. 156–167). London: Hogarth, 1955.

Ferenczi, S. (1932b). On shock. In: M. Balint (Ed.), E. Mosbacher and others (Trans), *Final Contributions to the Problems and Methods of Psycho-analysis* (pp. 253–254). London: Hogarth, 1955.

Ferenczi, S. (1985). *The Clinical Diary of Sándor Ferenczi*, J. Dupont (Ed.), M. Balint & N. Zarday Jackson (Trans). Cambridge, MA: Harvard University Press, 1988.

Fonagy, P. (1991). Thinking about thinking: some clinical and theoretical considerations in the treatment of a borderline patient. *International Journal of Psychoanalysis, 72*: 639–656.

Fonagy, P. (2001). *Attachment Theory and Psychoanalysis*. New York: Other Press.

Fonagy, P., Gergely, G., Jurist, E., & Target, M. (2002). *Affect Regulation, Mentalization and the Development of the Self*. London: Karnac.

Fonagy, P., Gergely, G., & Target, M. (2008). Psychoanalytic constructs and attachment theory and research. In: J. Cassidy & P. R. Shaver (Eds.), *Handbook of Attachment: Theory, Research, and Clinical Applications* (pp. 783–810). New York: Guilford, 2010.

Fonagy, P., Steele, H., Moran, G., Steele, M., & Higgit, A. (1991). The capacity for understanding mental states: the reflective self in parent and child and its significance for security of attachment. *Infant Mental Health Journal, 13*: 200–217.

Fonagy, P., Steele, H., & Steele, M. (1991). Maternal representations of attachment during pregnancy predict the organization of infant–mother attachment at one year of age. *Child Development, 62*: 891–905.

Fonagy, P., Target, M., Gergely, G., Allen, J. G., & Bateman, A. W. (2003). The developmental roots of borderline personality disorder in early attachment relationships. *Psychoanalytic Inquiry, 23*: 412–459.

Fordham, M. (1969). *Children as Individuals*. London: Hodder & Stoughton.

Fordham, M. (1974). Defences of the self. *Journal of Analytical Psychology, 19*: 192–199. Reprinted in: Fordham, M., *Analyst–Patient Interaction:*

Collected Papers on Technique, S. Shamdasani (Ed.) (pp. 138–145). London: Routledge, 1996.

Fordham, M. (1993). On not knowing beforehand. *Journal of Analytical Psychology, 38*: 127–136.

Foulkes, S. H. (1964). *Therapeutic Group Analysis*. London: Allen & Unwin.

Frawley-O'Dea, M. G. (1998). What's an analyst to do: shibboleths and "actual acts" in the treatment setting. *Contemporary Psychoanalysis, 34*: 615–633.

Freud, S. (1894a). The neuro-psychoses of defence. *S. E., 3*: 41–61. London: Hogarth.

Freud, S. (1895c [1894]). Obsessions and phobias. *S. E., 3*: 69–82. London: Hogarth.

Freud, S. (1897b). *Abstracts of the Scientific Writings of Dr. Sigmund Freud (1877–1897). S. E., 3*: 223–257. London: Hogarth.

Freud, S. (1900a). *The Interpretation of Dreams. S. E., 4*. London: Hogarth.

Freud, S. (1914c). On narcissism: an introduction. *S. E., 14*: 67–102. London: Hogarth.

Freud, S. (1914g). Remembering, repeating and working-through (further recommendations on the technique of psycho-analysis II). *S. E., 12*: 145–156. London: Hogarth.

Freud, S. (1916–17). *Introductory Lectures on Psycho-Analysis. S. E., 15*: 1–240.

Freud, S. (1923b). *The Ego and the Id. S. E., 14*: 1–66. London: Hogarth.

Freud, S. (1924c). The economic problem of masochism. *S. E., 14*: 155–170. London: Hogarth.

Freud, S. (1926d). *Inhibitions, Symptoms and Anxiety. S. E., 20*: 75–176. London: Hogarth.

Freud, S. (1937c). Analysis terminable and interminable. *S. E., 23*: 209–254. London: Hogarth.

Freud, S., & Jung, C. G. (1974). *The Freud/Jung Letters*, W. McGuire (Ed.). Princeton, NJ: Princeton University Press.

Gabbard, G. O. (1992). Commentary on "Dissociative processes and transference-countertransference paradigms" by Jody Messler Davies and Mary Gale Frawley. *Psychoanalytic Dialogues, 2*: 37–47.

Gabbard, G. O. (1997). Challenges in the analysis of adult patients with histories of childhood sexual abuse. *Canadian Journal of Psychoanalysis, 5*: 1–25.

Gabbard, G. O., & Lester, E. (1995). *Boundaries and Boundary Violations in Psychoanalysis*. Arlington, VA: American Psychiatric Publishing.

Gallese, V. (2001). The "shared manifold" hypothesis. *Journal of Consciousness Studies, 8*: 33–50.

Garland, C. (1998a). *Understanding Trauma: A Psychoanalytical Approach*. London: Karnac.

Garland, C. (1998b). Thinking about trauma. In: C. Garland (Ed), *Understanding Trauma: A Psychoanalytical Approach* (pp. 9–32). London: Karnac.

George, C., Kaplan, N., & Main, M. (1985). *Adult Attachment Interview protocol*. Unpublished manuscript, University of California at Berkeley.

Golding, W. (1954). *Lord of the Flies*. London: Faber & Faber.

Gordon, R. (1987). Masochism: the shadow side of the archetypal need to venerate and worship. *Journal of Analytical Psychology, 32*: 227–240.

Greenberg, J. R., & Mitchell, S. (1983). *Object Relations in Psychoanalytic Theory*. Cambridge, MA: Harvard University Press.

Grotstein, J. S. (2005). "Projective transidentification": An extension of the concept of projective identification. *International Journal of Psychoanalysis, 86*: 1051–1069.

Gunderson, J. G., & Singer, M. T. (1975). Defining borderline patients: an overview. *American Journal of Psychiatry, 132*: 1–10. Reprinted in: M. H. Stone (Ed.), *Essential Papers on Borderline Disorders* (pp. 453–474). New York: New York University Press, 1986.

Guntrip, H. (1952/1980). *Schizoid Phenomena, Object-relations and the Self*. London: Hogarth.

Hanly, C. (1986). The assault on truth: Freud's suppression of the seduction theory. *International Journal of Psychoanalysis, 67*: 517–519.

Harris, A. (2009). You must remember this. *Psychoanalytic Dialogues, 19*: 2–21.

Heimann, P. (1960). Counter-transference. *British Journal of Medical Psychology, 33*: 9–15.

Herman, J. L. (1981). *Father–Daughter Incest*. Cambridge, MA: Harvard University Press.

Herman, J. L. (1992). *Trauma and Recovery: The Aftermath of Violence—from Domestic Abuse to Political Terror*. New York: Basic.

Herman, J. L. (2011). Shattered shame states and their repair. In: J. Yellin & K. White (Eds.), *Shattered States: Disorganised Attachment and its Repair* (pp. 157–170). London: Karnac.

Herman, J. L., Perry, J. C., & van der Kolk, B. A. (1989). Childhood trauma in borderline personality disorder. *American Journal of Psychiatry, 146*: 490–495.

Herman, J. L., & Schatzow, E. (1987). Recovery and verification of memories of childhood sexual trauma. *Psychoanalytic Psychology, 4*: 1–14.

Hesse, E. (1996). Discourse, memory, and the Adult Attachment Interview: a note with emphasis on the emerging cannot classify category. *Infant Mental Health Journal, 17*: 4–11.

Hinshelwood, R. D. (1989). *A Dictionary of Kleinian Thought*. London: Free Association.

Hoffman, I. (2002). Forging difference out of similarity. Paper presented at the Stephen Mitchell Memorial Conference of the International Association for Relational Psychoanalysis and Psychotherapy. New York, 19 January.

Hogenson, G. (2001). The Baldwin effect: a neglected influence on C. G. Jung's evolutionary thinking. *Journal of Analytical Psychology, 46*: 591–612.

Howell, E. F. (2011). *Understanding and Treating Dissociative Identity Disorder: A Relational Approach*. New York: Routledge.

International Society for the Study of Trauma and Dissociation. (2011). [Chu, J. A., Dell, P. F., Van der Hart, O., Cardeña, E., Barach, P. M., Somer, E., Loewenstein, R. J., Brand, B., Golston, J. C., Courtois, C. A., Bowman, E. S., Classen, C., Dorahy, M., Sar, V., Gelinas, D. J., Fine, C. G., Paulsen, S., Kluft, R. P., Dalenberg, C. J., Jacobson-Levy, M., Nijenhuis, E. R. S., Boon, S., Chefetz, R.A., Middleton, W., Ross, C. A., Howell, E., Goodwin, G., Coons, P. M., Frankel, A. S., Steele, K., Gold, S. N., Gast, U., Young, L. M., & Twombly, J.]. Guidelines for treating dissociative identity disorder in adults, third revision. *Journal of Trauma & Dissociation, 12*: 115–187. Available as a download from: http://www.isst-d.org/default.asp?contentID=49.

Jacoby, M. (1980/1985). [1985: English translation]. *Longing for Paradise: Psychological Perspectives on an Archetype*. Boston, MA: Sigo Press.

Jacoby, M. (1996). *Shame and the Origins of Self-esteem: A Jungian Approach*. Abingdon: Taylor & Francis.

Janet, P. (1893a). *L'état Mental des Hystériques: Les Stigmates Mentaux*. Paris: Rueff & Cie.

Janet, P. (1893b). *Contribution à L'étude des Accidents Mentaux chez les Hystériques*. Paris: Rueff & Cie.

Janet, P. (1893c). L'Amnésie continue. *Revue Generale des Sciences, 4*: 167–179.

Janet, P. (1894). *Létat Mental des Hystériques: Les Accidents Mentaux*. Paris: Rueff & Cie.

Janet, P. (1904). L'Amnésie et la dissociation des souvenirs par l'émotion. *Journal de Psychologie, 1*: 417–453.

Joseph, B. (1982). Addiction to near-death. *International Journal of Psychoanalysis, 63*: 449–456.

Joseph, B. (1985). Transference: the total situation. *International Journal of Psychoanalysis, 66*: 447–454.

Jung, C. (1911–12). *Symbols of Transformation. C.W. 5*. London: Routledge & Kegan Paul.

Jung, C. G. (1917/1926/1943). On the psychology of the unconscious. In: *Two Essays on Analytical Psychology, C.W. 7*. London: Routledge & Kegan Paul.

Jung, C. G. (1921/1928). The therapeutic value of abreaction. In: *The Practice of Psychotherapy, C.W. 16*. London: Routledge & Kegan Paul.

Jung, C. G. (1929). Commentary on *The Secret of the Golden Flower. C.W. 13*. London: Routledge & Kegan Paul.

Jung, C. G. (1934). A review of the complex theory. In: *The Structure and Dynamics of the Psyche, C.W. 8*. London: Routledge & Kegan Paul.

Jung, C. G. (1935/1976). The Tavistock lectures. In: *The Symbolic Life, C.W. 18.* London: Routledge & Kegan Paul.

Jung, C. G. (1938/1954). Psychological aspects of the mother archetype. In: *The Archetypes and the Collective Unconscious, C.W. 9i.* London: Routledge & Kegan Paul.

Jung, C. G. (1940/1950). Concerning rebirth. In: *The Archetypes and the Collective Unconscious, C.W. 9i.* London: Routledge & Kegan Paul.

Jung, C. G. (1946/54). The psychology of the transference. *C.W. 16.* London: Routledge & Kegan Paul.

Jung, C. G. (1952). Answer to Job. In: *Psychology and Religion: West and East, C.W. 11.* London: Routledge & Kegan Paul.

Jung, C. G. (1955–56). *Mysterium Coniunctionis, C.W. 14.* London: Routledge & Kegan Paul.

Jung, C. G. (1958). Schizophrenia. In: *The Psychogenesis of Mental Disease, C.W. 3: 256–271.* London: Routledge & Kegan Paul.

Jung, C. G. (1963). *Memories, Dreams, Reflections,* A. Jaffé (Ed.). New York: Random House.

Jung, C. G. (2009). *The Red Book.* New York: The Philemon Foundation & W. W. Norton & Co.

"K". (2007). "What Works?" Response to the paper by James Astor. *Journal of Analytical Psychology, 52*: 207–231.

"K". (2008). Report from borderland: an addendum to "What Works?". *Journal of Analytical Psychology, 53*: 19–30.

"K". (2014). On the analysand's need to know the real person of the analyst. *Journal of Analytical Psychology, 59*: 333–345.

Kalsched, D. (1996). *The Inner World of Trauma: Archetypal Defences of the Personal Spirit.* Abingdon: Taylor & Francis.

Kalsched, D. (2013). *Trauma and the Soul: A Psycho-Spiritual Approach to Human Development and its Interruption.* Abingdon: Taylor & Francis.

Kardiner, A. (1941). *The Traumatic Neuroses of War.* Washington, DC: National Research Council.

Karpman, S. (1968). Fairytales and script drama analysis. *Transactional Analysis Bulletin, 7*: 39–43.

Kernberg, O. (1975). *Borderline Conditions and Pathological Narcissism.* New York: Aronson.

Kerr, J. (1993). *A Most Dangerous Method: The Story of Jung, Freud, and Sabina Spielrein.* New York: Knopf.

King, P. (1962). The curative factors in psycho-analysis—contributions to discussion. *International Journal of Psychoanalysis, 43*: 225–227.

Klein, M. (1927). Symposium on child-analysis. *International Journal of Psychoanalysis, 8*: 339–370.

Klein, M. (1946). Notes on some schizoid mechanisms. In: *Envy and Gratitude: and Other Works, 1946–1963* (pp. 1–24). London: Virago.

Kluft, R. P. (2013). *Shelter from the Storm: Processing the Traumatic Memories of DID/DDNOS Patients with the Fractionated Abreaction Technique*. North Charleston, SC: CreateSpace Independent Publishing Platform.

Knox, J. (1999). The relevance of attachment theory to a contemporary Jungian view of the internal world. *Journal of Analytical Psychology, 44*: 511–530.

Knox, J. (2001). Memories, fantasies, archetypes: an exploration of some connections between cognitive science and analytical psychology. *Journal of Analytical Psychology, 46*: 613–636.

Knox, J. (2003a). *Archetype, Attachment, Analysis: Jungian Psychology and the Emergent Mind*. Hove: Brunner-Routledge.

Knox, J. (2003b). Trauma and defences. *Journal of Analytical Psychology, 48*: 207–233.

Knox, J. (2007). The fear of love: the denial of self in relationship. *Journal of Analytical Psychology, 52*: 543–563.

Knox, J. (2008). Response to "Report from borderland". *Journal of Analytical Psychology, 53*: 31–36.

Knox, J. (2009). When words do not mean what they say. Self-agency and the coercive use of Language. *Journal of Analytical Psychology, 54*: 25–41.

Knox, J. (2010). *Self-agency in Psychotherapy: Attachment, Autonomy, and Intimacy*. New York: Norton.

Knox, J. (2013). "Feeling for" and "feeling with": developmental and neuroscientific perspectives on intersubjectivity and empathy. *Journal of Analytical Psychology, 58*: 491–509.

Kohut, H. (1971). *The Analysis of the Self*. New York: International Universities Press.

Koos, O., & Gergely, G. (2001). A contingency-based approach to the aetiology of "disorganized" attachment: the "flickering switch" hypothesis. *Bulletin of the Menninger Clinic, 65*: 397–410.

Kreisman, J. J. & Straus, H. (1989/2011). *I Hate You—Don't Leave Me: Understanding the Borderline Personality*. New York: Penguin Putnam.

Krystal, H. (1978). Trauma and affects. *Psychoanalytic Study of the Child, 33*: 81–116.

Krystal, H. (1988). *Integration and Self-Healing: Affect, Trauma, and Alexithymia*. Hillsdale, NJ: Analytic Press.

Lambert, K. (1981). *Analysis, Repair, and Individuation*. London: Karnac.

Lanius, R., Vermetten, E., Loewenstein, R., Brand, B., Schmahl, C., Bremner, J., & Spiegel, D. (2010). Emotion modulation in PTSD: Clinical and neurobiological evidence for a dissociative subtype. *American Journal of Psychiatry, 167*: 640–647.

Lanius, R., Vermetten, E., & Pain, C. (2010). *The Impact of Early Life Trauma on Health and Disease: The Hidden Epidemic*. Cambridge: Cambridge University Press.

Laplanche, J., & Pontalis, J.-B. (1973). *The Language of Psychoanalysis*. London: Hogarth.

Lawrence, M. (2008). *The Anorexic Mind*. London: Karnac.

LeDoux, J. (1996). *The Emotional Brain: The Mysterious Underpinnings of Emotional Life*. New York: Simon & Schuster.

Levine, P. (1997). *Waking the Tiger: Healing Trauma: The Innate Capacity to Transform Overwhelming Experiences*. Berkeley, CA: North Atlantic Books.

Levine, P. (2005). *Healing Trauma: A Pioneering Program for Restoring the Wisdom of Your Body*. Louisville, CO: Sounds True.

Lewis, H. B. (1990). Shame, repression, field dependence, and psychopathology. In: J. L. Singer (Ed.), *Repression and Dissociation: Implications for Personality Theory, Psychopathology and Health* (pp. 233–257). Chicago, IL: University of Chicago Press.

Lichtenberg, J. (1989). *Psychoanalysis and Motivation*. Hillsdale, NJ: Analytic Press.

Lindy, J. D. (1996). Psychoanalytic psychotherapy of posttraumatic stress disorder: the nature of the therapeutic relationship. In: B. van der Kolk, A., McFarlane, & L. Weisaeth (Eds.), *Traumatic Stress: The effects of overwhelming experience on mind, body and society* (pp. 525–536). New York: Guildford Press.

Liotti, G. (1992). Disorganized/disoriented attachment in the etiology of the dissociative disorders. *Dissociation, 5*: 196–204.

Liotti, G. (1995). Disorganized/disoriented attachment in the psychotherapy of the dissociative disorders. In: S. Goldberg, R. Muir & J. Kerr (Eds.), *Attachment Theory: Social, Developmental and Clinical Perspectives* (pp. 343–363). Hillsdale, NJ: Analytic Press.

Liotti, G. (1999). Understanding the dissociative processes: the contribution of attachment theory. *Psychoanalytic Inquiry, 19*: 757–783.

Liotti, G. (2004a). Trauma, dissociation, and disorganized attachment: three strands of a single braid. *Psychotherapy: Theory, Research, Practice, Training; 41*: 472–486.

Liotti, G. (2004b). The inner schema of borderline states and its correction during psychotherapy: a cognitive-evolutionary approach. In: P. Gilbert (Ed.), *Evolutionary Theory and Cognitive Psychotherapy* (pp. 137–160). New York: Springer.

Liotti, G. (2007). Disorganized attachment and the therapeutic relationship with people in shattered states. In: J. Yellin & K. White (Eds.), *Shattered States: Disorganised Attachment and Its Repair* (pp. 127–156). London: Karnac, 2012.

Loewenstein, R. J., & Putnam, F. W. (2004). The dissociative disorders. In: B. J. Sadock & V. A. Sadock (Eds.), *Comprehensive textbook of psychiatry* (9th ed.) (pp. 1844–1901). Baltimore, MD: Williams & Wilkins.

Luyten, P., van Houdenhove, B., Lemma, A., Target, M., & Fonagy, P. (2012). A mentalization-based approach to the understanding and treatment of functional somatic disorders. *Psychoanalytic Psychotherapy, 26*: 121–140.

Lyons-Ruth, K. (1998). Implicit relational knowing: its role in development and psychoanalytic treatment. *Infant Mental Health Journal, 19*: 282–289. Reprinted in: Boston Change Process Study Group (BCPSG). *Change in Psychotherapy: A Unifying Paradigm* (pp. 30–53). New York: Norton, 2010.

Lyons-Ruth, K. (1999). The two-person unconscious: intersubjective dialogue, enactive relational representation, and the emergence of new forms of relational organization. *Psychoanalytic Inquiry, 19*: 576–617.

Lyons-Ruth, K. (2003). Dissociation and the parent-infant dialogue: a longitudinal perspective from attachment research. *Journal of the American Psychoanalytic Association, 5*: 883–911.

Lyons-Ruth, K. (2008). Contributions of the mother–infant relationship to dissociative, borderline, and conduct symptoms in young adulthood. *Infant Mental Health Journal, 29*: 203–218.

Lyons-Ruth, K., Bronfman, E., & Parsons, E. (1999). Maternal frightened, frightening, or atypical behavior and disorganized infant attachment patterns. *Monographs of the Society for Research in Child Development, 64*: 67–96.

Lyons-Ruth, K., Dutra, L., Schuder, M., & Bianchi, I. (2006). From infant attachment disorganisation to adult dissociation: relational adaptations or traumatic experiences? *Psychiatric Clinics of North America, 29*: 63–86.

Lyons-Ruth, K., Yellin, C., Melnick, S., & Atwood, G. (2003). Childhood experiences of trauma and loss have different relations to maternal unresolved and hostile-helpless states of mind on the AAI. *Attachment and Human Development, 5*: 330–352.

Lyons-Ruth, K., Yellin, C., Melnick, S., & Atwood, G. (2005). Expanding the concept of unresolved mental states: hostile/helpless states of mind on the Adult Attachment Interview are associated with disrupted mother–infant communication and infant disorganization. *Development and Psychopathology, 17*: 1–23.

MacLean, P. D. (1990). *The Triune Brain in Evolution*. New York: Plenum Press.

Main, M., & Hess, E. (1990). Parents' unresolved traumatic experiences are related to infant disorganized attachment status: is frightened and/or frightening parental behaviour the linking mechanism? In: M. T. Greenberg, D. Cicchetti & E. M. Cummings (Eds.), *Attachment in the Preschool Years* (pp. 161–182). Chicago, IL: Chicago University Press.

Main, M., Kaplan, N., & Cassidy, J. (1985). Security in infancy, childhood, and adulthood: A move to the level of representation. In: I. Bretherton & E. Waters (Eds.), *Growing points of attachment theory and research (Mono-*

graphs of the Society for Research in Child Development) (pp. 66–104). Chicago, IL: Chicago University Press.

Main, M., & Morgan, H. (1996). Disorganization and disorientation in infant strange situation behaviour: phenotypic resemblance to dissociative states? In: L. Michelson & W. Ray (Eds.), *Handbook of Dissociation* (pp. 107–137). New York: Plenum Press.

Main, M., & Solomon, J. (1990). Procedures for identifying infants as disorganised/disoriented during the Ainsworth Strange Situation. In: M. T. Greenberg, D. Cicchetti & E. M. Cummings (Eds.), *Attachment in the preschool years: Theory, Research, and Intervention* (pp. 95–124). Chicago, IL: Chicago University Press.

Masson, J. M. (1984). *The Assault on Truth: Freud's Suppression of the Seduction Theory.* New York: Farrar, Straus & Giroux.

Matte Blanco, I. (1975). *The Unconscious as Infinite Sets.* London: Karnac.

Matte Blanco, I. (1988). *Thinking, Feeling and Being.* London: Routledge.

McDougall, J. (1989). *Theatres of the Body: Psychoanalytic Approach to Psychosomatic Illness.* London: Free Association.

Meares, R. (1993). Reversals: on certain pathologies of identification. In: E. Goldberg (Ed.), *Progress in Self Psychology, Vol. 9* (pp. 231–246). Hillsdale, NJ: Analytic Press.

Meares, R. (2012). *A Dissociation Model of Borderline Personality Disorder.* New York: Norton.

Meredith-Owen, W. (2011). Winnicott on Jung; destruction, creativity and the unrepressed unconscious. *Journal of Analytical Psychology, 56*: 56–75.

Meredith-Owen, W. (2013a). On revisiting the opening chapters of *Memories, Dreams, Reflections.* In: Cavalli, A., Hawkins, L., & Stevns, M. (Eds.), *Transformation: Jung's Legacy and Clinical Work Today.* (pp. 3–30). London: Karnac, 2013.

Meredith-Owen, W. (2013b). Are waves of relational assumptions eroding traditional analysis? *Journal of Analytical Psychology 38*: 593–614.

Meredith-Owen, W. (2015). Winnicott's invitation to "further games of Jung-analysis". *Journal of Analytical Psychology, 60*: 12–31.

Meltzer, D. (1968). *The Psycho-Analytic Process.* Perthshire: Clunie Press.

Meltzer, D. (1973). *Sexual States of Mind.* Perthshire: Clunie Press.

Meltzer, D. (1984). *Dream Life: A Re-examination of the Psychoanalytic Theory and Technique.* London: Karnac.

Meltzer, D. (1990). *The Claustrum: An Investigation of Claustrophobic Phenomena.* London: Karnac.

Miller, A. (1981). *Prisoners of Childhood: The Drama of the Gifted Child and the Search for the True Self.* New York: Basic.

Miller, A. (1984). *Thou Shalt Not Be Aware: Society's Betrayal of the Child.* New York: Farrar, Straus & Giroux.

Mollon, P. (1996). *Multiple Selves, Multiple Voices: Working with Trauma, Violation, and Dissociation*. New York: Wiley.

Mollon, P. (2002). *Shame and Jealousy: The Hidden Turmoils*. London: Karnac.

Mollon, P. (2015). *The Disintegrating Self: Psychotherapy of Adult ADHD, Autistic Spectrum, and Somato-Psychic Disorders*. London: Karnac.

Money-Kyrle, R. (1971). The aim of psychoanalysis. *International Journal of Psychoanalysis, 52*: 103–106.

Neumann, E. (1966). Narcissism, normal self-formation and the primary relationship to the mother. *Spring, 66*: 81–106.

Newton, K. (1993). The weapon and the wound: the archetypal dimensions in "Answer to Job". *Journal of Analytical Psychology, 38*: 375–397.

Nietzsche, F. (1883/1961). *Thus Spoke Zarathustra: A Book for All and None*. Harmondsworth: Penguin.

Ogden, T. (1994). *Subjects of Analysis*. Northvale, NJ: Aronson.

Ogden, T. (1996). The perverse subject of analysis. *Journal of the American Psychoanalytic Association, 44*: 1121–1146.

Ogden, T. (2009). *Rediscovering Psychoanalysis: Thinking and Dreaming, Learning and Forgetting*. Hove: Routledge.

Ogden, P., Minton, K., & Pain, C. (2006). *Trauma and the Body: A Sensorimotor Approach to Psychotherapy*. New York: Norton.

Oldfield, G. (2014). *Chronic Pain: Your Key to Recovery*. Bloomington, In: AuthorHouse.

Olinick, S. L. (1964). The negative therapeutic reaction. *International Journal of Psychoanalysis, 45*: 540–548.

Orbach, S. (2004). The body in clinical practice, part one: there's no such thing as a body. In: K. White (Ed.), *Touch: Attachment and the Body* (pp. 17–34). London: Karnac.

Orbach, S. (2009). *Bodies*. London: Profile Books.

Ornstein, A. (1983). Fantasy or reality? The unsettled question in pathogenesis and reconstruction in psychoanalysis. In: A. Goldberg (Ed.), *The Future of Psychoanalysis* (pp. 381–396). New York: International University Press.

Panksepp, J. (1998). *Affective Neuroscience: The Foundations of Human and Animal Emotions*. New York: Oxford University Press.

Peláez, M. G. (2009). Trauma theory in Sándor Ferenczi's writings of 1931 and 1932. *International Journal of Psychoanalysis, 90*: 1217–1233.

Perlow, M. (1995). *Understanding Mental Objects*. London: Routledge.

Perry, J. W. (1970). Emotions and object relations. *Journal of Analytical Psychology, 15*: 1–12.

Person, E. S., & Klar, H. (1994). Establishing trauma: the difficulty distinguishing between memories and fantasies. *Journal American Psychoanalytic Association, 42*: 1055–1081.

Porges, S. (1995). Orienting in a defensive world: mammalian modifications of our evolutionary heritage. *Psychophysiology, 32*: 301–318.

Porges, S. (2004). Neuroception: a subconscious system for detecting threats and safety. *Zero to Three. Bulletin of the National Center for Clinical Infant Programs, 24*: 19–24.

Porges, S. (2005). The role of social engagement in attachment and bonding: a phylogenetic perspective. In: C. S. Carter, L, Ahnert, K. E. Grossman, S. B. Hardy, M. E. Lamb, S. W. Porges & N. Sachser (Eds.), *Attachment and Bonding: A New Synthesis* (pp. 33–54). Cambridge, MA: The MIT Press.

Porges, S. W. (2011). *The Polyvagal Theory: Neurophysiological Foundations of Emotions, Attachment, Communication, and Self-regulation*. New York: Norton.

Porges, W., Doussard-Roosevelt, J. & Maiti, A. K. (1994). Vagal tone and the physiological regulation of emotion. *Monographs of the Society for Research in Child Development, 59*: 167–186.

Post, R., Weiss, S., Smith, M., Li, H., & McCann, U. (1997). Kindling versus quenching: Implications for the evolution and treatment of posttraumatic stress disorder. In: R. Yehuda & A. C. McFarlane (Eds.), *Psychobiology of posttraumatic stress disorder* (pp. 285–295). New York: New York Academy of Sciences.

Potamianou, A. (1997). *Hope: A Shield in the Economy of Borderline States*. London: Routledge.

Quinodoz, J.-M. (2005). *Reading Freud: A Chronological Exploration of Freud's Writings*. Hove: Brunner-Routledge.

Racker, H. (1958). Psychoanalytic technique and the analyst's unconscious masochism. *Psychoanalytic Quarterly, 27*: 555–562.

Richman, A. (2013). The nature of trauma and dissociation. *Online module for Confer Conference, "On the nature of trauma and dissociation"*. http://www.confer.uk.com/module-trauma.html.

Riesenberg-Malcolm, R. (1996). "How can we know the dancer from the dance?": hyperbole in hysteria. *International Journal of Psychoanalysis, 77*: 679–688.

Rizzolatti, G., & Sinigaglia, C. (2008). *Mirrors in the Brain: How our Minds Share Actions, Emotions*. Oxford: Oxford University Press.

Robertson, J., & Bowlby, J. (1952). Responses of young children to separation from their mothers. *Courrier du Centre International de L'Enfance, 2*: 131–142.

Rogers, A. G. (1995). *A Shining Affliction: A Story of Harm and Healing in Psychotherapy*. London: Penguin.

Rosenfeld, H. (1971). A clinical approach to the psychoanalytic theory of the life and death instincts: an investigation into the aggressive aspects of narcissism. *International Journal of Psychoanalysis, 52*: 169–178.

Rosenfeld, H. (1987). *Impasse and Interpretation: Therapeutic and Anti-therapeutic Factors in the Psychoanalytic Treatment of Psychotic, Borderline and Neurotic Patients*. London: Routledge.

Roth, P. (1994). Being true to a false object: a view of identification. *Psychoanalytic Inquiry, 14*: 393–405.

Rothschild, B. (2000). *The Body Remembers: The Psychophysiology of Trauma and Trauma Treatment*. New York: Norton.

Russell, P. (1998). Crises of emotional growth (a.k.a. theory of the crunch). Paper presented at the Paul Russell Conference, Boston, MA.

Sandler, J. (1993). On communication from patient to analyst: not everything is projective identification. *International Journal of Psychoanalysis, 74*: 1097–1107.

Sandler, J., Dare, C., & Holder, A. (1973). *The Patient and the Analyst: The Basics of the Psychoanalytic Process*. London: Allen & Unwin.

Sarno, J. E. (1991). *Healing Back Pain: The Mind-Body Connection*. New York: Grand Central Publishing.

Sarno, J. E. (1998). *The Mindbody Prescription: Healing the Body, Healing the Pain*. New York: Warner Books.

Sarno, J. E. (2006). *The Divided Mind: The Epidemic of Mindbody Disorders*. New York: Harper Paperbacks.

Satinover, J. (1985). At the mercy of another: abandonment and restitution in psychosis and psychotic character. *Chiron: A Review of Jungian Analysis, 1985*: 47–86.

Saunders, P., & Skar, P. (2001). Archetypes, complexes and self-organisation. *Journal of Analytical Psychology, 46*: 305–324.

Schmahl, C., Lanius, R. A., Pain, C, & Vermetten, E. (2010). Biological framework for traumatic dissociation related to early life trauma. In: R. Lanius, E. Vermetten & C. Pain (Eds.), *The Impact of Early Life Trauma on Health and Disease: the Hidden Epidemic* (pp. 178–188). Cambridge: Cambridge University Press, 2010.

Schmideberg, M. (1959). The borderline patient. *American Handbook of Psychiatry, vol 1*, S. Arieti (Ed.). New York: Basic.

Schore, A. (2003). *Affect Regulation and the Repair of the Self*. New York: Norton.

Schuengel, L., Van Ijzendoorn, M., & Bakermans-Kranenburg, M. (1999). Frightened maternal behaviour linking unresolved loss and disorganized infant attachment. *Journal of Consulting and Clinical Psychology, 67*: 54–63.

Sedgwick, D. (2008). Winnicott's dream: some reflections on D. W. Winnicott and C. G. Jung. *Journal of Analytical Psychology, 53*: 543–560.

Seligman, S. (2003). The developmental perspective in relational psychoanalysis. *Contemporary Psychoanalysis, 39*: 477–508.

Shamdasani, S. (1995). Memories, dreams, omissions. *Spring Journal, 57*: 115–137.

Shaver, P. R., & Fraley, R. C. (2008). Attachment, loss, and grief: Bowlby's views and current controversies. In: J. Cassidy & P. R. Shaver (Eds.), *Handbook of Attachment: Theory, Research and Clinical Applications* (pp. 48–77). New York: The Guildford Press.

Shengold, L. (1975). Soul murder. *International Journal of Psychoanalytic Psychotherapy, 3*: 366–373.

Shengold, L. (1979). Child abuse and deprivation: soul murder. *Journal of the American Psychoanalytic Association, 27*: 533–559.

Shengold, L. (1989). *Soul Murder*. New Haven, CT: Yale University Press.

Shengold, L. (1992). Child abuse and treatment examined. *Bulletin of the Anna Freud Centre, 15*: 189–204.

Siegel, D. (1999). *The Developing Mind*. New York: Guildford Press.

Sinason, V. (2002). *Attachment, Trauma and Multiplicity: Working with Dissociative Identity Disorder*, V. Sinason (Ed.). New York: Brunner-Routledge.

Sinason, V. (2013). Psychoanalytic approaches to the treatment of trauma. *Confer module "The nature of trauma and dissociation"*. http://www.confer.uk.com/module-trauma.html.

Slade, A. (2008). The implication of attachment theory and research for adult psychotherapy: research and clinical perspectives. In: J. Cassidy & P. Shaver (Eds.), *Handbook of Attachment: Theory, Research and Clinical Applications* (pp. 762–782). New York: The Guildford Press.

Slavin, M., & Klein, E. J. (2013). Probing to know and be known: existential and evolutionary perspectives on the "disorganized" patient's relationship with the analyst. In: Beebe, B. & Lachmann, F., *The Origins of Attachment: Infant Research and Adult Treatment*. Abingdon: Taylor & Francis.

Solms, M., & Turnbull, O. (2002). *The Brain and the Inner World: An Introduction to the Neuroscience of Subjective Experience*. New York: Other Press.

Stark, M. (2006). Transformation of relentless hope: a relational approach to sadomasochism. http://www.lifespanlearn.org/documents/STARK-tranform.pdf .

Steiner, J. (1985). Turning a blind eye: the cover up for Oedipus. *International Review of Psychoanalysis, 12*: 161–72.

Steiner, J. (1987). The interplay between pathological organizations and the paranoid-schizoid and depressive positions. *International Journal of Psychoanalysis, 68*: 69–80.

Steiner, J. (1989). The psychoanalytic contribution of Herbert Rosenfeld. *International Journal of Psychoanalysis, 70*: 611–616.

Steiner, J. (1990). The retreat from truth to omnipotence in Sophocles' *Oedipus at Colonus*. *International Review of Psychoanalysis, 17*: 227–237.

Steiner, J. (1993). *Psychic Retreats: Pathological Organisations in Psychotic, Neurotic and Borderline Patients*. London: Routledge.

Steiner, J. (1996). The aim of psychoanalysis in theory and in practice. *International Journal of Psychoanalysis, 77*: 1073–1083.

Stern, A. (1938). Psychoanalytic investigation of and therapy in the borderline group of neuroses. *Psychoanalytic Quarterly, 7*: 467–489.

Stern, D. N. (1985/1998). *The Interpersonal World of the Infant: a View from Psychoanalysis and Developmental Psychology*. London: Karnac.

Strachey, J. (1934). The nature of the therapeutic action of psychoanalysis. *International Journal of Psychoanalysis, 15*: 127–159.

Strozier, C. B. (2001). *Heinz Kohut: The Making of a Psychoanalyst*. New York: Farrar, Straus & Giroux.

Symington, N. (1983). The analyst's act of freedom as agent of therapeutic change. *International Review of Psychoanalysis, 10*: 283–291.

Symington, N. (2004). The true god and the false god. In: *The Blind Man Sees: Freud's Awakening and Other Essays* (pp. 112–123). London: Karnac.

Taylor, D. (1998). The psychodynamic assessment of post-traumatic states. In: C. Garland (Ed.), *Understanding Trauma: A Psychoanalytical Approach* (pp. 47–62). London: Karnac.

Temple, N. (1998). Developmental injury—its effect on the inner world. In: C. Garland (Ed.), *Understanding Trauma: A Psychoanalytical Approach* (pp. 155–166). London: Karnac.

Therese of Lisieux, St. (1972). *Story of a Soul: The autobiography of St. Therese of Lisieux*. Washington: Institute of Carmelite Studies.

Tronick, E. Z., Als, H., Adamson, L., Wise, S., & Brazelton, T. B. (1978). The infant's response to entrapment between contradictory messages in face-to-face interaction. *Journal of the American Academy of Child and Adolescent Psychiatry, 17*: 1–13. Reprinted in: Tronick, E. Z., *The Neurobehavioural and Social-Emotional Development of Infants and Children* (pp. 262–273). New York: Norton, 2007.

Tronick, E. Z., Bruschweiler-Stern N., Harrison A. M., Lyons-Ruth, K., Morgan A. C., Nahum J. P., Sander, L., & Stern, N. D. (1998). Dyadically expanded states of consciousness and the process of therapeutic change. *Infant Mental Health Journal, 19*: 290–299. Reprinted in: Tronick, E. Z., *The Neurobehavioural and Social-Emotional Development of Infants and Children* (pp. 402–411). New York: Norton, 2007.

Tronick, E. Z., & Gianino, A. (1986). Interactive mismatch and repair: challenges to the coping infant. *Zero to Three, Bulletin of the National Center for Clinical Infant Programs, 5*: 1–6. Reprinted in: Tronick, E. Z., *The Neurobehavioural and Social-Emotional Development of Infants and Children* (pp. 155–163). New York: Norton, 2007.

van der Hart, O. (2013). Study day on dissociative identity disorder at The Bowlby Centre, London, 30 November 2013.

van der Hart, O., & Friedman, B. (1989). A reader's guide to Pierre Janet: a neglected intellectual heritage. *Dissociation, 2:* 3–16.

van der Hart, O., Nijenhuis, E., & Steele, K. (2006). *The Haunted Self: Structural Dissociation and the Treatment of Chronic Traumatization.* New York: Norton.

van der Kolk, B. (1996a). The complexity of adaptation to trauma: self-regulation, stimulus discrimination, and characterological development. In: A. C. McFarlane, L. Weisaeth & B. van der Kolk (Eds.), *Traumatic Stress: The Effects of Overwhelming Experience on Mind, Body, and Society.* (pp. 182–213). New York: Guilford Press.

van der Kolk, B. (1996b). Trauma and memory. In: A. C. McFarlane, L. Weisaeth & B. Van der Kolk (Eds.), *Traumatic Stress: The Effects of Overwhelming Experience on Mind, Body, and Society* (pp. 279–302). New York: Guilford Press, 1996.

van der Kolk, B. (2005). Developmental trauma disorder: toward a rational diagnosis for children with complex trauma histories. *Psychiatric Annals, 35:* 401–408.

van der Kolk, B. (2014). *The Body Keeps the Score: Mind, Brain and Body in the Transformation of Trauma.* Harmondsworth: Penguin.

van der Kolk, B., & d'Andrea, W. (2010). Towards a developmental trauma disorder diagnosis for childhood interpersonal trauma. In: R. Lanius, E. Vermetten & C. Pain (Eds.), *The Impact of Early Life Trauma on Health and Disease: The Hidden Epidemic* (pp. 57–68). Cambridge: Cambridge University Press.

van der Kolk, B., Greenberg, M., Boyd, H., & Krystal, J. (1985). Inescapable shock, neurotransmitters, and addiction to trauma: toward a psychobiology of post-traumatic stress. *Biological Psychiatry, 20:* 314–325.

van der Kolk, B., & McFarlane, A. C. (1996). The black hole of trauma. In: B. van der Kolk, A. McFarlane & L. Weisaeth (Eds.), *Traumatic Stress: The Effects of Overwhelming Experience on Mind, Body, and Society* (pp. 3–23). New York: Guilford Press.

van der Kolk, B., McFarlane, A., & van der Hart, O. (1996). A general approach to the treatment of posttraumatic stress disorder. In: B. van der Kolk, A. McFarlane & L. Weisaeth (Eds.), *Traumatic Stress: The Effects of Overwhelming Experience on Mind, Body and Society* (pp. 417–440). New York: Guildford Press.

van der Kolk, B., McFarlane, A. & Weisaeth, L. (1996). *Traumatic Stress: The Effects of Overwhelming Experience on Mind, Body, and Society,* B. van der Kolk, A. C. McFarlane & L. Weisaeth, (Eds.). New York: Guilford Press.

van der Kolk, B., Weisaeth, L, & van der Hart, O. (1996). History of trauma in psychiatry. In: B. van der Kolk, A. C. McFarlane & L. Weisaeth (Eds.), *Traumatic Stress: The Effects of Overwhelming Experience on Mind, Body, and Society* (pp. 47–76). New York: Guilford Press.

Vermetten, E., Dorahy, M. J., & Spiegel, D. (Eds.) (2007). *Traumatic Dissociation Neurobiology and Treatment*. Washington, DC: American Psychiatric Press.

Vogt, R. (2012). *Perpetrator Introjects, Psychotherapeutic Diagnostics and Treatment Models*. Kroning: Asanger Verlag.

von Franz, M-L. (1975). *C. G. Jung: His Myth in Our Time*. Boston: Little, Brown.

Weiss, J. (1993). *How Psychotherapy Works*. New York: Guildford Press.

West, M. (2004). Identity, narcissism and the emotional core. *Journal of Analytical Psychology, 49*: 521–552.

West, M. (2007). *Feeling, Being and the Sense of Self: A New Perspective on Identity, Affect and Narcissistic Disorders*. London: Karnac.

West, M. (2008). The narrow use of the term ego in analytical psychology: the "not-I" is also who I am. *Journal of Analytical Psychology, 53*: 367–388.

West, M. (2010). Envy and difference. *Journal of Analytical Psychology, 55*: 459–484.

West, M. (2011). *Understanding Dreams in Clinical Practice*. London: Karnac.

West, M. (2013a). Trauma and the transference-countertransference: working with the bad object and the wounded self. *Journal of Analytical Psychology, 58*: 73–98.

West, M. (2013b). Defences of the core self: borderline functioning, trauma, and complex. In: A. Cavalli, L. Hawkins & M. Stevns (Eds.), *Transformation: Jung's Legacy and Clinical Work Today* (pp. 131–154). London: Karnac, 2013.

West, M. (2014). Trauma, *participation mystique*, projective identification and analytic attitude. In: M. Winborn, (Ed.) *Shared Realities: Participation Mystique and Beyond* (pp. 51–69). Cheyenne, WY: Fisher King Press.

West, M. (2016). Working in the borderland: early relational trauma and Fordham's analysis of "K". *Journal of Analytical Psychology, 61*: 44–62.

Wiener, J. (2009). *The Therapeutic Relationship: Transference, Countertransference, and the Making of Meaning*. College Station, TX: Texas A & M University Press.

Wilkinson, M. (2006). *Coming into Mind: The Mind-Brain Relationship: A Jungian Clinical Perspective*. New York: Taylor & Francis.

Wilkinson, M. (2010). *Changing Minds in Therapy: Emotion, Attachment, Trauma, and Neurobiology*. New York: Norton.

Winborn, M. (2014). An overview of *participation mystique*. In: M. Winborn, (Ed.). *Shared Realities: Participation Mystique and Beyond*. Cheyenne, WY: Fisher King Press.

Winnicott, D. W. (1953). Transitional objects and transitional phenomena—a study of the first not-me possession. *International Journal of Psychoanalysis*, *34*: 89–97.

Winnicott, D. W. (1960). Ego distortion in terms of true and false self. In: Winnicott, D. W., *The Maturational Processes and the Facilitating Environment: Studies in the Theory of Emotional Development.* (pp. 140–152). London: Hogarth, 1965.

Winnicott, D. W. (1964). *Memories, Dreams, Reflections*: by C. G. Jung. *International Journal of Psychoanalysis*, *45*: 450–455.

Winnicott, D. W. (1967). The location of cultural experience. *International Journal of Psychoanalysis*, *48*: 368–372.

Winnicott, D. W. (1969). The use of an object. *International Journal of Psychoanalysis*, *50*: 711–716.

Winnicott, D. W. (1974). Fear of breakdown. *International Review of Psychoanalysis*, *1*: 103–107.

Winson, J. (1990). The meaning of dreams. *Scientific American*, November: 86–96.

Wirtz, U. (2014). *Trauma and Beyond: The Mystery of Transformation.* New Orleans, LA: Spring Journal.

Young, L., & Gibb, E. (1998). Trauma and grievance. In: C. Garland (Ed), *Understanding Trauma: A Psychoanalytical Approach* (pp. 81–95). London: Karnac.

Zachrisson, A. (2013). Oedipus the king: quest for self-knowledge—denial of reality. Sophocles' vision of man and psychoanalytic concept formation. *International Journal of Psychoanalysis*, *94*: 313–331.

INDEX